The Muslims of medieval Italy

The New Edinburgh Islamic Surveys
Series Editor: Carole Hillenbrand

TITLES AVAILABLE OR FORTHCOMING

Contemporary Issues in Islam Asma Asfaruddin
The New Islamic Dynasties Clifford Edmund Bosworth
Media Arabic (2nd Edition) Julia Ashtiany Bray
An Introduction to the Hadith John Burton
A History of Islamic Law Noel Coulson
Medieval Islamic Political Thought Patricia Crone
A Short History of the Ismailis Farhad Daftary
Islam: An Historical Introduction (2nd Edition) Gerhard Endress
A History of Christian–Muslim Relations Hugh Goddard
Medieval Islamic Science Robert Hall
Shi'ism (2nd Edition) Heinz Halm
Islamic Science and Engineering Donald Hill
Muslim Spain Reconsidered Richard Hitchcock
Islamic Law: From Historical Foundations to Contemporary Practice Mawil Izzi Dien
Sufism: The Formative Period Ahmet T. Karamustafa
Islamic Aesthetics Oliver Leaman
Persian Historiography Julie Scott Meisami
Pilgrims and Pilgrimage Josef Meri
The Muslims of Medieval Italy Alex Metcalfe
The Archaeology of the Islamic World Marcus Milwright
Twelver Shi'ism: Unity and Diversity in the Life of Islam Andrew Newman
Muslims in Western Europe (3rd Edition) Jørgen Nielsen
Medieval Islamic Medicine Peter E. Pormann and Emilie Savage-Smith
Islamic Names Annemarie Schimmel
The Genesis of Literature in Islam Gregor Schoeler
Modern Arabic Literature Paul Starkey
Islamic Medicine Manfred Ullman
Islam and Economics Ibrahim Warde
A History of Islamic Spain W. Montgomery Watt and Pierre Cachia
Introduction to the Qur'an W. Montgomery Watt
Islamic Creeds W. Montgomery Watt
Islamic Philosophy and Theology W. Montgomery Watt
Islamic Political Thought W. Montgomery Watt
The Influence of Islam on Medieval Europe W. Montgomery Watt

The Muslims of medieval Italy

ALEX METCALFE

EDINBURGH UNIVERSITY PRESS

Edinburgh University Press Ltd
22 George Square, Edinburgh
www.euppublishing.com

Typeset in Goudy by
Koinonia, Manchester, and
printed and bound in Great Britain by
CPI Antony Rowe, Chippenham and Eastbourne

A CIP Record for this book is available from the British Library

ISBN 978 0 7486 2007 4 (hardback)
ISBN 978 0 7486 2008 1 (paperback)

Published with the support of the Edinburgh University
Scholarly Publishing Initiatives Fund

Contents

Acknowledgements

The valuable comments of readers, who were able to share their informed opinions on certain chapters, were much appreciated, in particular the thoughts of Michael Brett and Graham Loud. I am also very grateful to the Series Editor, Carole Hillenbrand, for affording me the opportunity to write this book in the first instance. In addition, I would like to express my thanks to the Arts and Humanities Research Council (UK) for their generous funding of research leave during 2006/7, which gave me the time to write a shorter book than the one I had originally drafted. Finally, I would like to note the input of Lyn Flight and Alison Grant for their expert copy-editing skills and suggested amendments.

Notes and abbreviations

Alexander of Telese *Alexandri Telesini Abbatis, Ystoria Rogerii Regis Sicilie Calabrie Atque Apulie*, Ludovica de Nava (ed.), FSI, no. 112, Rome, 1991.

Amari-Nallino, *SMS*² M. Amari, *Storia dei Musulmani di Sicilia*, 2nd rev. edn, C. A. Nallino (ed.), 3 vols, Catania, 1933–9.

Amatus *The History of the Normans by Amatus of Montecassino*, trans. by Prescott N. Dunbar, rev. with introduction and notes by Graham A. Loud, Woodbridge, 2004.

Annales Siculi Appended to Malaterra (see below), pp. 109–20.

*BAS*² Ar. *Biblioteca arabo-sicula, ossia raccolta di testi arabici che toccano la geografia, la storia, le biografie e la bibliografie della Sicilia*, 2nd rev. edn, M. Amari and U. Rizzitano, 2 vols, Palermo, 1987–8.

*BAS*² It. *Biblioteca arabo-sicula, ossia raccolta di testi arabici che toccano la geografia, la storia, le biografie e la bibliografie della Sicilia. Raccolti e tradotti in italiano*, M. Amari (ed.), 2 vols and appendix, Turin and Rome, 1880–9. 2nd rev. edn, U. Rizzitano, A. Borruso, M. Cassarino, and A. De Simone (eds), 2 vols and appendix, Palermo, 1982.

Book of Curiosities Emilie Savage-Smith and Yossef Rapoport (eds), *The Book of Curiosities: A critical edition*. World-Wide-Web publication at: www.bodley.ox.ac.uk/bookofcuriosities (March 2007).

BSOAS *Bulletin of the School of Oriental and African Studies* (University of London).

Cusa, *Diplomi* *I diplomi greci ed arabi di Sicilia*, S. Cusa (ed.), Palermo, 1868–82. Reprinted Cologne and Vienna, 1982.

*EI*² *The Encyclopaedia of Islam*, H. A. R. Gibb *et al.* (eds), 2nd edn, 11 vols and supplement, London, 1960–.

Falcandus Eng. *The History of the Tyrants of Sicily by 'Hugo Falcandus' 1154–69*, trans. and annotated G. A. Loud and T. E. J. Wiedemann, Manchester, 1998.

Falcandus Epistola *La Historia o Liber de Regno Siciliae e la Epistola ad Petrum Panormitane Ecclesie Thesaurarium di Ugo Falcando*, a cura di G.

B. Siragusa, Roma, 1904, pp. 169–86.

Falcandus Lat. *La Historia o Liber de Regno Siciliae e la Epistola ad Petrum Panormitane Ecclesie Thesaurarium di Ugo Falcando*, a cura di G. B. Siragusa, Roma, 1904.

Falcandus, *Letter to Peter* *The History of the Tyrants of Sicily by 'Hugo Falcandus' 1154–69*, trans. and annotated G. A. Loud and T. E. J. Wiedemann, Manchester, 1998, pp. 252–63.

FSI Fonti per la Storia d'Italia (Istituto storico italiano per il medioevo, Rome)

Ibn al-Athīr, Eng *The Chronicle of Ibn al-Athīr for The Crusading Period from* al-Kāmil fī'l-ta'rīkh, *Part 1. The Years 491–541/1097–1146: The Coming of the Franks and the Muslim Response*, trans. by D.S. Richards (Aldershot, 2006) and *The Chronicle of Ibn al-Athīr for The Crusading Period from* al-Kāmil fī'l-ta'rīkh, *Part 2. The Years 541–589/1146–1193: The Age of Nur al-Din and Saladin*, trans. by D. S. Richards (Aldershot, 2007).

Ibn Ḥawqal *Opus Geographicum (Ṣūrat al-Arḍ)*, ed. J. H. Kramers, 2 vols, (Leiden, 1938–9).

Malaterra *De Rebus gestis Rogerii Calabriae et Siciliae Comitis et Roberti Guiscardi Duci fratris eius*, Ernesto Pontieri (ed.), RIS, 2nd series, vol. 2, Bologna, 1927–8.

MEFRM *Mélanges de l'École française de Rome: Moyen Âge.*

MGH *Monumenta Germania Historica (SS = Scriptores; SRG = Scriptores Rerum Germanicarum* etc.). Available online at: www.dmgh.de.

Peter of Eboli *Liber ad honorem Augusti sive de rebus Siculis*, Codex 120 II der Burgerbibliothek, Bern, 1994.

QFIAB *Quellen und Forschungen aus italienischen Archiven und Bibliotheken.*

Richard of San Germano Ryccardi di Sancto Germano Notarii Chronicon, C. A. Garufi (ed.), (*Rerum Italicarum Scriptores*, 2nd edn, Bologna, 1938).

RIS *Rerum Italicarum Scriptores*, L. A. Muratori (ed.), 2nd series, Bologna.

Roger II diplomata *Rogerii II Regis Diplomata Latina (Codex Diplomaticus Regni Siciliae*, 1st series), C.-R. Brühl (ed.), Cologne and Vienna, 1987

Roger's Assizes *The Assizes of King Roger*, Eng. trans. Graham A. Loud, online at: www.leeds.ac.uk/history/weblearning/MedievalHistoryText-Centre/medievalTexts.htm, last accessed on 13 June 2008.

Genealogical tables, maps and figures

Genealogical tables

Maps

Figures

Genealogical tables

1 Rulers of Sicily, Bari and Ifrīqiya during the Aghlabid period

AH/AD	*Amīrs* and *wālīs* of Sicily and Bari[1]	*Amīrs* of Ifrīqiya
184/800		Ibrāhīm I b. al-Aghlab b. Sālim al-Tamīmī
197/812		'Abd Allāh I b. Ibrāhīm, Abū l-'Abbās
201/817		Ziyādat Allāh I b. Ibrāhīm, Abū Muḥammad
212/827	(1) Asad b. al-Furāt	
213/828	(2) Muḥammad b. Abī l-Jawārī[2]	
214/829	(3) Zuhayr b. Ghawth(?)[3]	
	(4) Aṣbagh b. Wakīl (al-Hawwārī), Farghalūsh[4]	
	(5) 'Uthmān Ibn Qurhub[5]	
217/832	(6) Muḥammad b. 'Abd Allāh b. al-Aghlab, Abū Fihr[6]	
220/835	(7) Ibrāhīm b. 'Abd Allāh, Abū l-Aghlab[7]	
223/838		Al-Aghlab b. Ibrāhīm, Abū 'Iqāl
226/841		Muḥammad I b. al-Aghlab, Abū l-'Abbās
	Khalfūn (*amīr* of Bari, 847–52)	
236/851	(8) Al-'Abbās b. al-Faḍl b. Ya'qūb b. Fazāra[8]	
	Mufarraj (*amīr* of Bari, 853–6)	
	Sawdān (*amīr* of Bari, 857–71)	
247/861	(9) Aḥmad b. Ya'qūb (b. Fazāra?)[9]	
	(10)'Abd Allāh b. al-'Abbās b. al-Faḍl (b. Fazāra)[10]	
248/862	(11) Khafāja b. Sufyān[11]	
249/863		Ziyādat Allāh II b. Muḥammad
250/863		Muḥammad II b. Aḥmad, Abū l-Gharānīq
255/869	(12) Muḥammad b. Khafāja (b. Sufyān)[12]	
257/871	(13) Aḥmad b. Ya'qūb b. al-Muḍā b. Salma[13]	
	(14) Muḥammad b. Abī l-Ḥusayn[14]	

AH/AD	*Amīrs* and *wālīs* of Sicily and Bari[1]	*Amīrs* of Ifrīqiya
	(15) Al-Ḥusayn b. Aḥmad b. Ya'qūb (b. al-Muḍā b. Salma)[15]	
	(16) Rabaḥ b. Ya'qūb b. Fazāra[16]	
	(17) Abū l-'Abbās b. Ya'qūb b. 'Abd Allāh[17]	
	(18) Al-Ḥusayn b. Rabāḥ (b. Ya'qūb b. Fazāra)[18]	
259/872	(19) 'Abd Allāh b. Muḥammad b. Ibrāhīm b. al-Aghlab b. Sālim[19]	
261/874	(20) Aḥmad b. Ya'qūb b. 'Umar b. 'Abd Allāh b. Ibrāhīm b. al-Aghlab Abū Mālik, al-Ḥabashī[20]	
261/875		Ibrāhīm II b. Aḥmad, Abū Isḥāq
264/878	(21) Ja'far b. Muḥammad[21]	
	(22) Al-Aghlab b. Muḥammad b. al-Aghlab, Khurj al Ru'ūna[22]	
	(23) Al-Ḥusayn b. Rabāḥ (b. Ya'qūb b. Fazāra)[23]	
267/881	(24) Al-Ḥasan b. al-'Abbās[24]	
268/882	(25) Muḥammad b. al-Faḍl[25]	
271/885	(26) Al-Ḥusayn b. Aḥmad[26]	
	(27) Sawāda b. Muḥammad b. Khafāja (b. Sufyān al-Tamīmī)[27]	
273/887	(28) Abū l-'Abbās b.'Alī[28]	
276/890	(29) Sawāda b. Muḥammad b. Khafāja (b. Sufyān al-Tamīmī) (as above)[29]	
278/892	(30) Muḥammad b. al-Faḍl (as above)[30]	
	(31) Aḥmad b. 'Umar b. 'Abd Allāh, Abū Mālik[31]	
287/900	(32)'Abd Allāh b. Ibrāhīm b. Aḥmad, Abū l-'Abbās[32]	
289/902	(33) Ziyādat Allāh b. 'Abd Allāh b. Ibrāhīm b. Aḥmad, Abū Muḍar[33]	'Abd Allāh II b. Ibrāhīm, Abū l-'Abbās
290/903	(34) Muḥammad b. al-Siraqūsī[34]	Ziyādat Allāh III b. 'Abd Allāh, Abū Muḍar (290–6/903–9)
	(35) 'Alī b. Muḥammad b. Abī l-Fawāris[35]	
	(36) Aḥmad b. al-Ḥusayn b. Rabāḥ[36]	
296/909	(37) 'Alī b. Muḥammad b. Abī l-Fawāris (as above)[37]	

Notes

1 List of Sicilian rulers is based on that of Amari's in *BAS*[2] It. II:723–5. The genealogy is not reproduced in the *BAS*[2] Arabic edition, the index of which is by no means exhaustive. References given here are to the earliest source for the start of each ruler's

period of power in the context of Sicily and south Italy. Significant discrepancies have also been noted. A list of the Aghlabid *amīrs* of Ifrīqiya can be found in C. E. Bosworth, *The New Islamic Dynasties* (Edinburgh, 2004), pp. 31–2; and G. Marçais, *Aghlabids*, in *EI*^{2} I:247.

2 Ibn al-Athīr, *BAS*^{2} Ar. I:271; *BAS*^{2} It. I:367 (frequently attested thereafter).

3 Ibn al-Athīr, *BAS*^{2} Ar. I: 272; *BAS*^{2} It. I:368. The name is uncertain and given in manuscripts of al-Nuwayrī and Ibn Khaldūn in several, equally plausible, forms.

4 Ibn 'Idhārī, *BAS*^{2} Ar. I: 409; *BAS*^{2} It. II:6–7. From al-Andalus, possibly an outlaw who had arrived via Crete. The only other source for him is al-Nuwayrī, who added his Berber tribal *nisba*, *BAS*^{2} Ar. II:486; *BAS*^{2} It: II:119.

5 Ibn 'Idhārī, *BAS*^{2} Ar. I:410; *BAS*^{2} It. II:7 (only source).

6 Ibn al-Athīr, *BAS*^{2} Ar. I:273; *BAS*^{2} It. I:369 (frequently attested thereafter).

7 Ibn al-Athīr, *BAS*^{2} Ar. I:273 ; *BAS*^{2} It. I:370 (frequently attested thereafter).

8 Ibn al-Athīr, *BAS*^{2} Ar. I:276; *BAS*^{2} It. I:375 (frequently attested thereafter). The reference to the 'Banū l-Fazāra', an old north Arabian tribe, later attested in north Africa, was added by Abū l-Fidā' *BAS*^{2} Ar. II:464–5; *BAS*^{2} It. II:86, and then picked up in the later, 'western', sources of Ibn Khaldūn, Ibn Wādirān and Ibn Abī Dīnar.

9 Ibn 'Idhārī, *BAS*^{2} Ar. I:413; It. II:12–3. A stop-gap, and possibly contested, appointment. Uncle of al-'Abbās b. al-Faḍl (8).

10 Ibn al-Athīr *BAS*^{2} Ar. I:281; *BAS*^{2} It. I:382.

11 Khafāja arrived in Sicily in August 862 and was killed on 15 June 869. His genealogy was given by Ibn al-'Abbār (*BAS*^{2} Ar. I:382; *BAS*^{2} It. I:527) as Khafāja b. 'Abd Allāh b. 'Abbād b. Muḥrith b. Sa'd b. Ḥizām b. Sa'd b. Mālik b. Sa'd b. Zayd Manāt b. Tamīm. According to al-Nuwayrī, his killer was a Berber from the Hawwāra tribe (*BAS*^{2} Ar. II:488; *BAS*^{2} It. II:123). After Khafāja, the main chroniclers become muddled and diverge significantly. The progression of rulers mentioned by Ibn al-Athīr was: 11, 12 (murdered by his eunuchs), 13 (dies quickly), 21, 24. According the Ibn 'Idhārī the order was: 11, 12, 13, 15, 21 (murdered by his eunuchs), 22 (overthrown), 23, 24 etc. For al-Nuwayrī, whose account was the most lacunose, it was: 11, 14, 17 (dies after a month), 18, 19, 20, 32. He claimed that al-Ḥabashī ('the Ethiopian') ruled for twenty-six years (probably confusing him with his contemporary, Ibrāhīm II, in Ifrīqiya r. 875–902).

12 Ibn al-Athīr *BAS*^{2} Ar. I:281–4; *BAS*^{2} It. I:382–7. Attested from the 860s as an active leader of raids in eastern Sicily, including the conquest of Malta.

13 Ibn al-Athīr *BAS*^{2} Ar. I:285; *BAS*^{2} It. I:389. A short-lived governor, appointed and sent from Ifrīqiya. According to Ibn 'Idhārī, *BAS*^{2} Ar. I:414; *BAS*^{2} It. II:15, the ruler of the mainland, was his brother 'Abd Allāh, contrary to the claim of al-Nuwayrī who may have confused Rabāḥ with Aḥmad.

14 Mentioned only by al-Nuwayrī (*BAS*^{2} Ar. II: 488; *BAS*^{2} It. II:123), who states that he was chosen locally after the murder of Muḥammad b. Khafāja (12), but was replaced from Ifrīqiya by Rabāḥ (16).

15 Ibn 'Idhārī, *BAS*^{2} Ar. I:414; *BAS*^{2} It. II:15.

16 Al-Nuwayrī *BAS*^{2} Ar. II:488; *BAS*^{2} It. II:123. Rabāḥ was attested in Sicily as early as 852 (Ibn al-Athīr, *BAS*^{2} It. I:377), but was briefly *wālī* of Sicily during 871, the year of his death. Al-Nuwayrī also recorded that his brother, 'Abd Allāh, was appointed at the same time as *wālī* of the mainland after the fall of Bari.

17 Al-Nuwayrī, *BAS*^{2} Ar. II:488; *BAS*^{2} It. II:123.

18 Al-Nuwayrī, *BAS*^{2} Ar. II:488; *BAS*^{2} It. II:123, the only source to suggest this governor in this period. For Ibn 'Idhārī's view, see note 23

19 Al-Nuwayrī, *BAS*^{2} Ar. II:488; *BAS*^{2} It. II:123.
20 Al-Nuwayrī, *BAS*^{2} Ar. II:489; *BAS*^{2} It. II:124.
21 Ibn al-Athīr, *BAS*^{2} Ar. I:288; *BAS*^{2} It. I:396 on the conquest of Syracuse which Ja'far led. For his murder, see Ibn Idhārī, *BAS*^{2} Ar. I:414; *BAS*^{2} It. II:16.
22 Ibn 'Idhārī, *BAS*^{2} Ar. I:415; *BAS*^{2} It. II:16. Alleged in this source only to be a coup leader who briefly held sway at Palermo during 878 before being ousted in what was clearly a period of some confusion after the conquest of Syracuse.
23 Ibn 'Idhārī, *BAS*^{2} Ar. I:415; *BAS*^{2} It. II:16.
24 Ibn al-Athīr, *BAS*^{2} Ar.I:289; *BAS*^{2} It. I:397, and Ibn 'Idhārī, *BAS*^{2} Ar. I:415; *BAS*^{2} It. II:17.
25 Ibn al-Athīr, *BAS*^{2} Ar. I:290 (twice); *BAS*^{2} It. I:398 and I: 399; Ibn 'Idhārī, *BAS*^{2} It. II:17 and II:19.
26 Died in 884/5. Ibn al-Athīr, *BAS*^{2} Ar. I:290; *BAS*^{2} It. I:399, and Ibn 'Idhārī, *BAS*^{2} Ar. I:415 *BAS*^{2} It. II:17. Possibly not the same person as (15), unless he had stepped down some years before.
27 Ibn al-Athīr, *BAS*^{2} Ar. I:399; *BAS*^{2} It. I:399, and Ibn 'Idhārī, *BAS*^{2} Ar. I:416, *BAS*^{2} It. II:17. Both authors added the *nisba*, al-Tamīmī, after the old Arab tribal confederation. Deposed from office.
28 According to Ibn 'Idhārī, *BAS*^{2} Ar. I:415, *BAS*^{2} It. II:18, he held office briefly around 887.
29 Ibn 'Idhārī, *BAS*^{2} Ar. I:415, *BAS*^{2} It. II:18.
30 Ibn 'Idhārī, *BAS*^{2} Ar. I:416; *BAS*^{2} It. II:19.
31 Ibn al-Athīr, *BAS*^{2} Ar. I:291; *BAS*^{2} It. I:400. Attested during the year 900. As Amari suggested (Amari-Nallino, SMS^{2}II:718), this may have been the person al-Nuwayrī called al-Ḥabashī (20).
32 Ibn al-Athīr, *BAS*^{2} Ar. I:287; *BAS*^{2} It. I:393 (see also, Amari's note 1). Also attested in the *Cambridge Chronicle* (*BAS*^{2} Ar. I:190, *BAS*^{2} It. I:280) as having arrived in Mazara on 24 June, taking Palermo on 8 September 900. Also, see list of Aghlabid *amīrs* of Ifrīqiya.
33 Ibn al-Athīr, *BAS*^{2} Ar. I: 288; *BAS*^{2} It. I:395. Also Aghlabid *amīr* of Ifrīqiya.
34 Ibn al-Athīr, *BAS*^{2} Ar. I:294 It. I:405; al-Nuwayrī, *BAS*^{2} Ar. II:489; *BAS*^{2} It. II:124.
35 *Cambridge Chronicle*, *BAS*^{2} Ar. I:194 ; *BAS*^{2} It. I:280–1; al-Nuwayrī, *BAS*^{2} Ar. II:489; *BAS*^{2} It. II:124–5.
36 *Cambridge Chronicle*, *BAS*^{2} Ar. I:194 ; *BAS*^{2} It. I:281; al-Nuwayrī, *BAS*^{2} Ar. II:489; *BAS*^{2} It. II:124.
37 As n.35.

2 Rulers of Sicily during the early Fatimid period

297/910	[Al-Ḥasan b. Ahmad] Ibn Abī Khinzīr
299/912	ʿAlī b. ʿUmar al-Balawī
300/913	[Aḥmad b. Ziyādat Allāh] Ibn Qurhub
304/916	Mūsa b. Aḥmad Abū Saʿīd al-Ḍayf
305/917	Sālim b. Rashīd
325/937	Khalīl b. Isḥāq b. Ward Abū l-ʿAbbās
329/941	Ibn ʿAṭṭāf

3 The Kalbid dynasty in Sicily

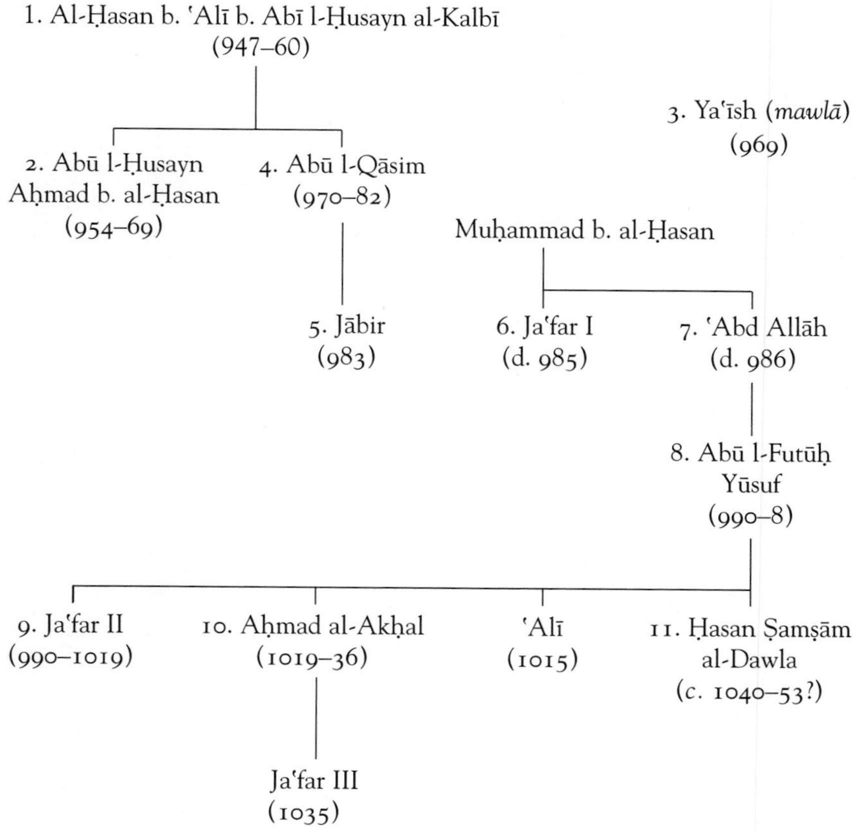

4 Norman and Staufen rulers of Sicily and south Italy (1057–1268)

Muriella = Tancred of Hauteville = Fresenda

William 'Iron Arm' count of Apulia (1042–6)
Drogo count of Apulia (1046–51)
Humphrey count of Apulia (1051–7)
Geoffrey count of Capitanata (d. 1063)
Serlo

Alberada = **Robert 'Guiscard'** = Sichelgaita
duke of Apulia (1057–85) of Salerno (d. 1090)
6 other children
1. Roger I count of Sicily (d. 1101) = (1) Judith of Évreux = (2) Eremburga of Mortain = (3) **Adelaide of Vasto** (Regent 1101–12; d. 1118)

Bohemond I prince of Antioch (1099–1111)
Roger Borsa duke of Apulia (1085–1111)
9 other children
(illeg.) Jordan (d. 1092)
(3) **Simon** count of Sicily (1101–5)
(3) **2. Roger II** count of Sicily (1105–28) duke of Apulia (1128–30) king of Sicily (1130–54) = (1) Elvira of León-Castile = (2) Sybil of Burgundy = (3) Beatrice of Rethel
(1, 2 & 3) 15 other children

Bohemond II prince of Antioch (1111–30)
William duke of Apulia (1111–27)
(1) **Roger** duke of Apulia (d. 1148)
Alfonso prince of Capua (d. 1144)
Tancred prince of Táranto & Bari (d. c. 1139)
(1) **3. William I** king of Sicily (1154–66) = Margaret of Navarre Regent (1154–66) (d. 1183)
(1) 2 other children
(illeg.) **Simon** prince of Táranto
Frederick I German Emperor (1152–90)

Sybil of Acerra = **5. Tancred** (illeg.) king of Sicily (1190–4)
Roger duke of Apulia (d. 1161)
Robert (d. c. 1159)
4. William II king of Sicily (1166–89) = Joanna of England
Henry prince of Capua (d. 1172)
7. Constance Queen of Sicily (1195–8) = **Henry VI** German Emp. (1190–7)

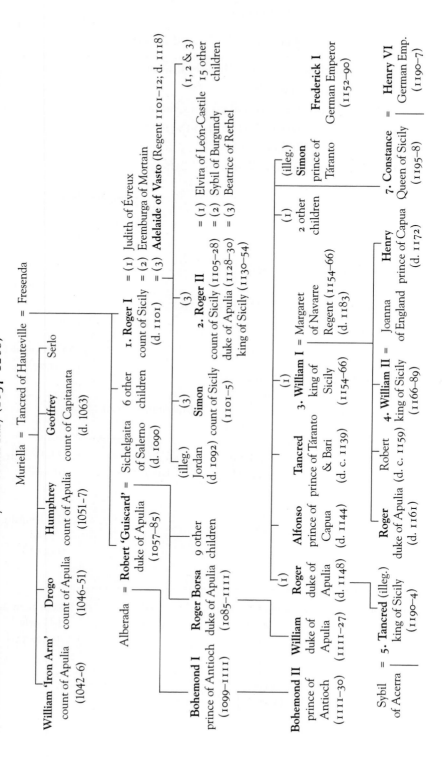

4 Norman and Staufen rulers of Sicily and south Italy (1057–1268) (*cont.*)

Sybil of Acerra = 5. **Tancred** (illeg.) king of Sicily (1190–4)

6. **William III** king of Sicily (1194)

Roger duke of Apulia (d. 1161)

Robert (d. c. 1159)

4. **William II** king of Sicily (1166–89) = Joanna of England

Henry prince of Capua (d. 1172)

7. **Constance** Queen of Sicily (1195–8) = **Henry VI** German Emp. (1190–7)

8. **Frederick II**
king of Sicily (1198–1250)
king of Germany (1212–50)
Emperor (1220–50)

Henry (d. 1141)

Conrad IV king of Sicily (1250–4)

Conradin (d. 1268)

Manfred king of Sicily (1258–66)

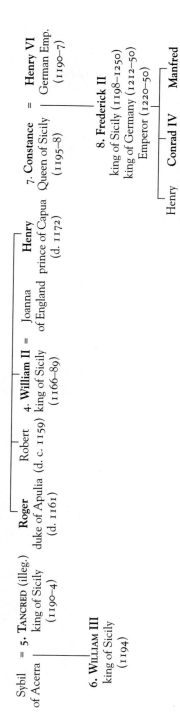

Maps

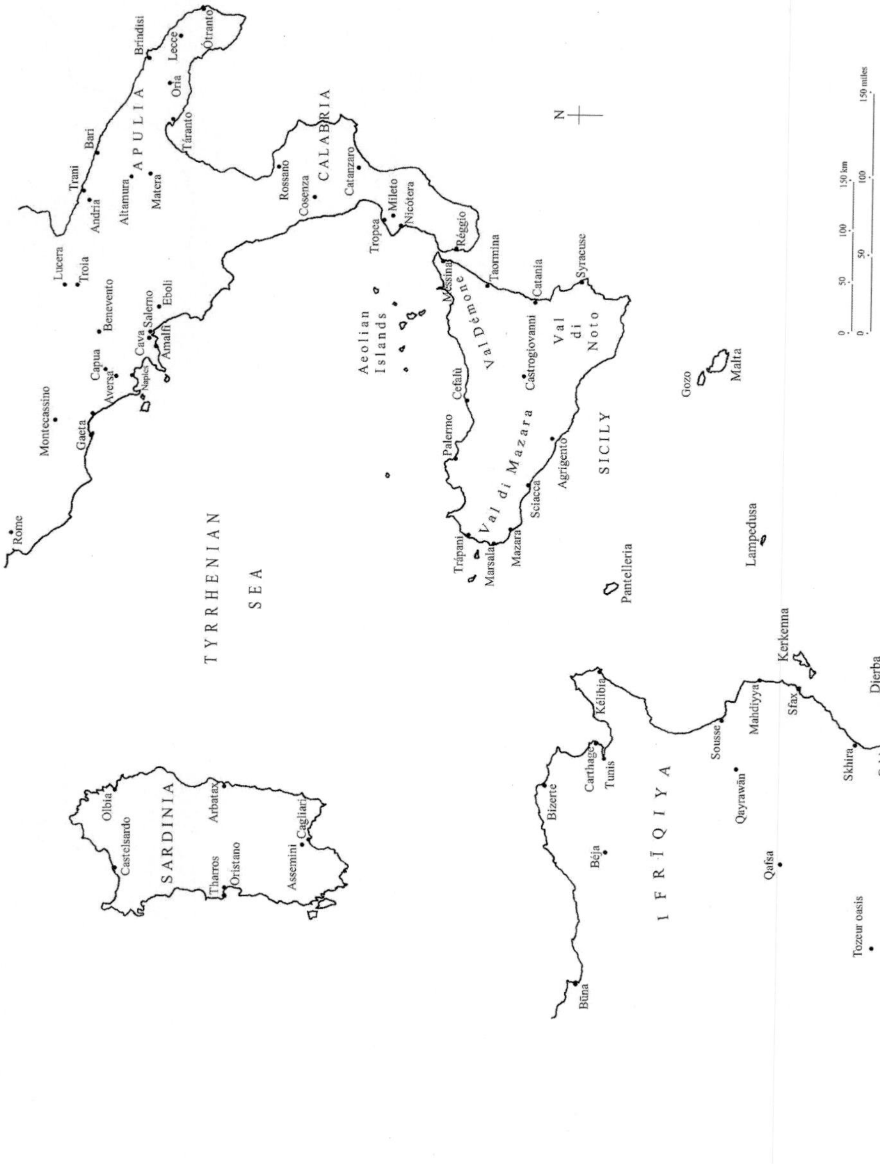

Map 1 The central Mediterranean in the medieval period

Map 2 Main towns and settlements in medieval Sicily

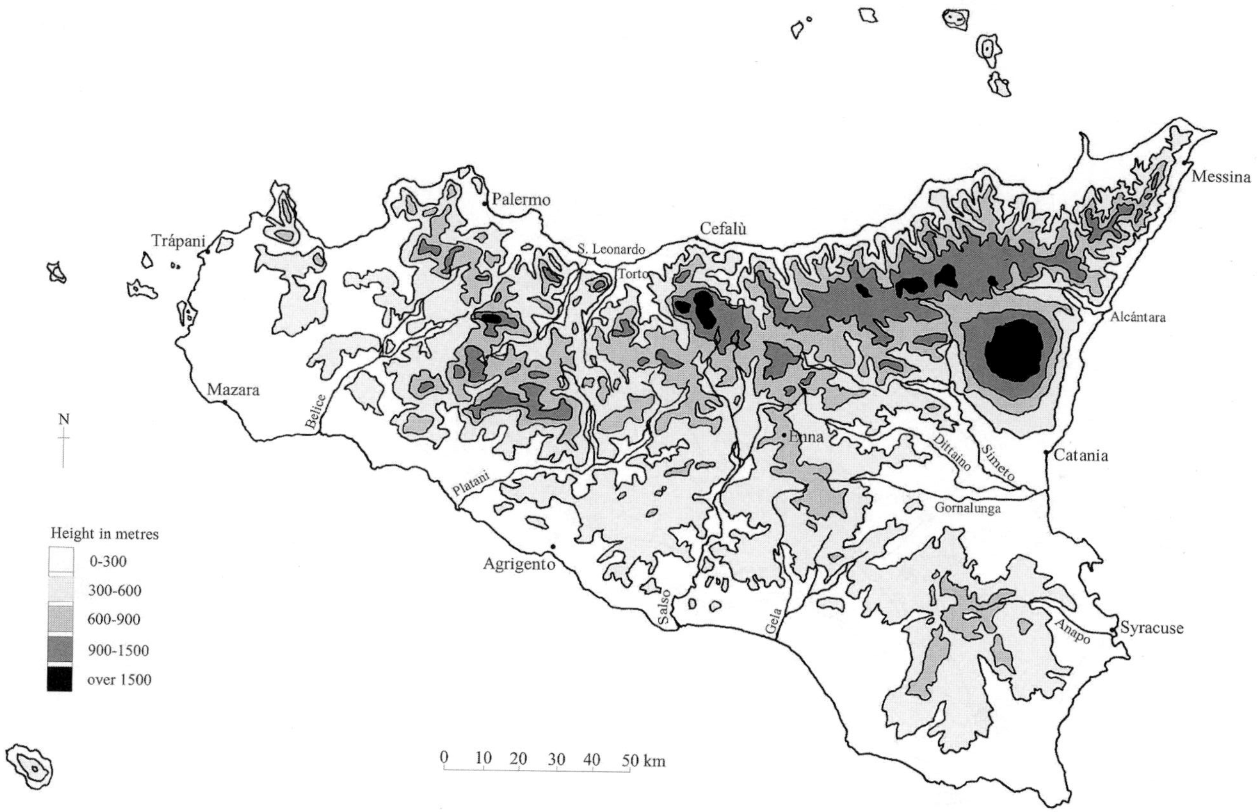

Map 3 Physical relief map of Sicily

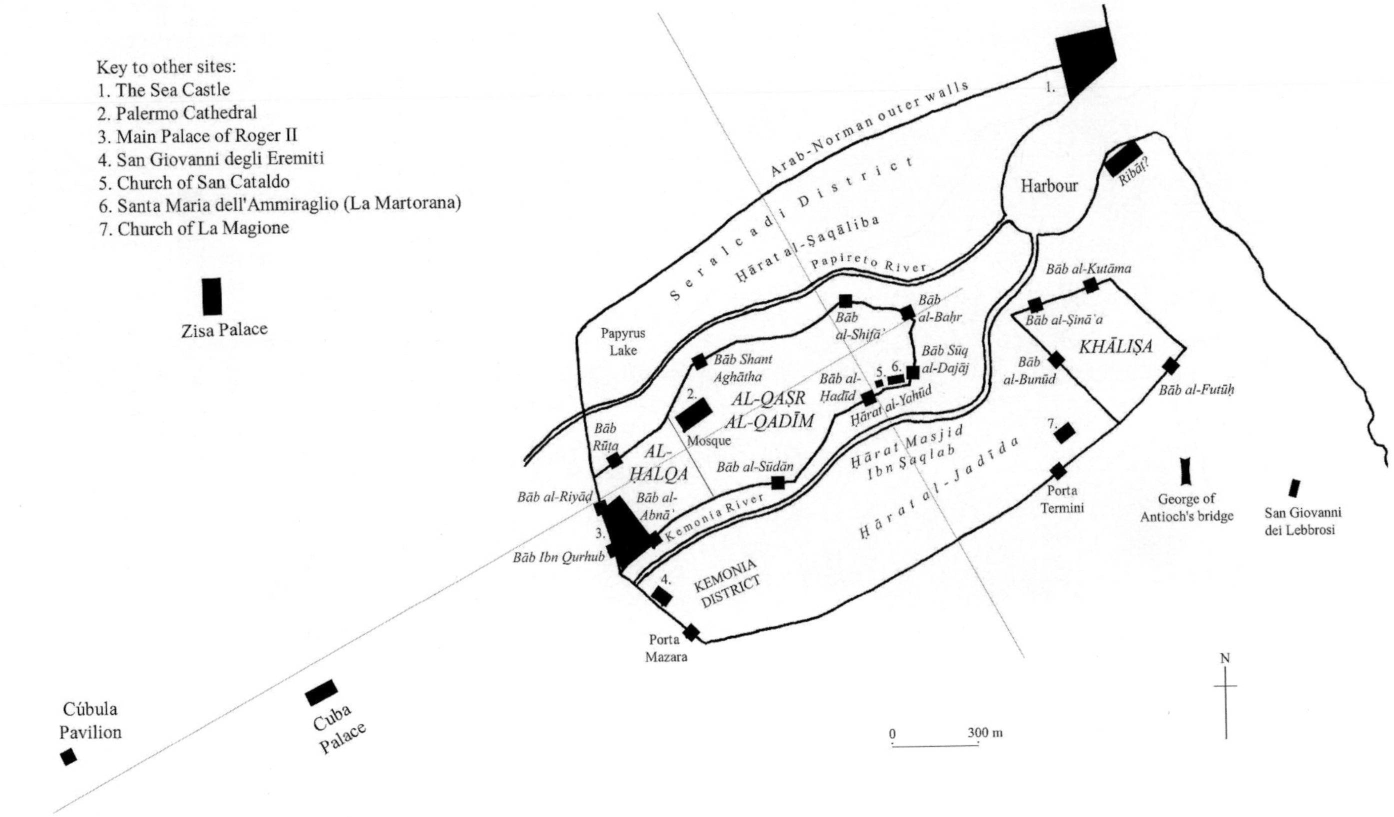

Key to other sites:
1. The Sea Castle
2. Palermo Cathedral
3. Main Palace of Roger II
4. San Giovanni degli Eremiti
5. Church of San Cataldo
6. Santa Maria dell'Ammiraglio (La Martorana)
7. Church of La Magione
Zisa Palace
Cúbula Pavilion
Cuba Palace
Arab-Norman outer walls
Seralcadi District
Ḥārat al-Ṣaqāliba
Papireto River
Papyrus Lake
Harbour
Ribāṭ?
Bāb al-Kutāma
Bāb al-Ṣinā'a
KHĀLIṢA
Bāb al-Bunūd
Bāb al-Futūḥ
Bāb al-Baḥr
Bāb al-Shifā'
Bāb Sūq al-Dajāj
Bāb Shant Aghātha
Bāb al-Ḥadīd
Ḥārat al-Yahūd
AL-QAṢR AL-QADĪM
Mosque
Bāb Rūṭa
AL-ḤALQA
Bāb al-Sūdān
Bāb al-Riyāḍ
Bāb al-Abnā'
Bāb Ibn Qurhub
Kemonia River
Ḥārat Masjid Ibn Ṣaqlab
Ḥārat al-Jadīda
KEMONIA DISTRICT
Porta Mazara
Porta Termini
George of Antioch's bridge
San Giovanni dei Lebbrosi
N
0
300 m

Map 4 Palermo in the later Islamic period (with Norman additions)

Introduction

This book traces a history of consequence: repeated invasions that triggered the collapse and reconfiguration of age-old frontiers between the continents of Africa and Europe; the advent of new states, laws and systems of governance; the exchange of religious beliefs between Islam and Christianity; the transformation of arts, culture, science and learning; and fundamental shifts in the social and economic dynamics of the central Mediterranean. Above all, this is a study of people and power.

The primary focus is the pivotal role that Muslims played in Sicily and parts of south Italy during a tripartite shift from Byzantine Greek to Arab-Muslim to Latin Christian. These were periods and places in a state of constant, and often violent, flux. Very little survived unscathed by the changes wrought by competing factions, whose ambitions successive Sicilian rulers struggled to limit. Irrespective of religion, the most ruthlessly determined of all were the island's conquerors themselves, each of whom sought an essentially different form of recognised authority to justify their status, conduct and actions.

This is a history largely devoid of heroes: by the end of Muslim rule, Byzantine Greek culture had been all but obliterated. Thereafter, Latin Christian rule all but obliterated Arab-Muslim culture. The high points in the Islamicisation of Sicily followed by its 'Europeanisation' are rare and worth treasuring. Those precious moments are well remembered, especially when they are understood as evidence for tolerance and interfaith harmony. The best remaining examples can be found in the Arab-Norman art and architecture, along with their multilingual court and administrative offices. These, however, were hybrid products of a curious, deceptive and experimental kingship; co-operation and goodwill between a select few occurred in a context of tension and insecurity for many others.

The geographical and chronological reach of this book extends across and beyond the south Italian peninsula between 800 and 1300, with particular emphasis on the island of Sicily during the central 300 years of that period. Rich, diverse and widely recognised as this history is, it remains relatively unexplored, particularly so for questions of Muslim power and society. It is not as familiar as the Iberian peninsula or Syria-Palestine, but is it sufficiently compact to make a more coherent regional study than Spain, and is far better furnished with surviving charter materials than the Crusader states.

For the most part, works on medieval Sicily up to 1300 tend to begin with the Norman conquest and then make chronological divisions according to dynastic eras: Norman; Staufen; and Angevin. This approach has unfortunate consequences for the Italian Muslims. Even if Muslim rule was limited to a mere 250 years prior to the Normans, Muslim settlement extended for almost five centuries across all these periods. Such a split correspondingly marginalises the importance of the Muslims to the extent that, in some accounts, they make only cameo appearances. This work seeks to link the political and social history of these periods through the medium of Arab-Muslim colonisation, institutions, culture and communities. The intention, therefore, is to offer a fresh, integrated perspective which may be read as both a survey and a monograph.

For much of this history, we are at the limited mercy of the sources, and not all the surviving Latin, Greek and Arabic documentary sources have been accurately transcribed, translated and indexed in modern, scholarly editions. In recent years, new materials have come to light, and more of these may do so in future. In the meantime, archaeologists have barely scratched the surface of an island stacked with Greek, Punic and Roman sites as well as medieval ones. For the Islamic period, the annalistic chronicles are almost all distant in time and place from that which they describe, although some were able to draw on much older, and apparently well-informed, material. Even so, the sources quickly become confused when recounting the bare events of the long Muslim conquests or relating the transition of the island's governors in colourless prose. The histories can, however, be supplemented from a fragmented range of other written media, largely in Arabic and Greek. These include geographical descriptions, travelogues, merchants' letters, biographical dictionaries, poetry, legal opinions (*fatwas*), and saints' lives. For the Islamic period especially, it is these sources which breathe life into the history.

From the Norman period, Latin sources begin to come to the fore. Apart from the period of 1100–30, we are furnished with details from an array of materials including charters, archaeology and art history. Indeed, most aspects of the Norman and Staufen kingdoms in Italy not only have been well-researched, but are also supplied with ample secondary literature. The same can be said of the wider Mediterranean. My approach, therefore, has not been to retell the intricate dynamics of south Italian politics, the north Italian maritime states, the papacy, Byzantine and German empires, but instead to give sufficient background information in order to contextualise the relevant points under discussion. The same course is adopted when introducing the complexities of Arab-Muslim north Africa.

The reader is otherwise exposed to the earliest and most reliable source materials as far as is sensible or feasible, rather than become embroiled in modern historiographical debates. While it would have been useful to give more extensive footnotes to illuminate historiographical trends, it is simply not possible to do justice to the body of literature in the interrelated fields which a study of Sicily necessitates. As such, attention has been drawn to a selection of seminal and up to date works in which readers will find extensive bibliographical references. Wherever possible, I have pointed to translations of the Arabic, Greek and Latin sources, giving equivalents rendered into more commonly known languages, particularly English and French. Even with the resurgence of interest in this subject in recent years, the nineteenth-century works of Michele Amari, and his translations of the Arabic sources into Italian, remain indispensable for non-Arabists.

For certain sections of this work, I have drawn heavily on a number of articles and monographs produced by the current generation of scholars. Indeed, the list of those who have shaped my understanding of Sicily and the medieval Mediterranean is now considerable; I have been especially influenced by the scholarship and diverse knowledge of David Abulafia, Dionisius Agius, Henri Bresc, Michael Brett, Adalgisa De Simone, Vera von Falkenhausen, Graham Loud, Annliese Nef and Ferdinando Maurici. All of these I have had the pleasure of meeting and I am grateful for their kind thoughts and encouragement. I have also spent many hours in fruitful conversation with talented emerging scholars, such as Ewan Johnson, Paul Oldfield and Giuseppe Mandalà. Particularly evident in this book – and it is perhaps no surprise – is the influence of my former supervisor, Jeremy Johns, whose outputs on art history and the Arabic administration of Sicily and Calabria continue to redefine the subject area.

I

Muslim expansion into the central Mediterranean

From the fall of Rome to the rise of Muslim Africa

At the height of Rome's power, long after the great enemy of Carthage had been absorbed into vast imperial provinces, their ancient rivalry reduced to mere legend, it was still attractive to imagine that the origins of empire were intimately bound up with the fate of Africa. In Virgil's epic poem, the *Aeneid* such dim historical memory found literary expression in the figures of the resolute colonist Aeneas, and his smitten and spurned lover Dido, the queen of Carthage, driven to suicide by divine conspiracy. As in the *Aeneid*, the island of Sicily was the stepping-stone from Africa to Italy, but by Virgil's day it was something of a rural backwater in the middle of the Mediterranean, far from the empire's frontiers. Links to non-Latin African elements persisted in Sicily, but they did so at only a minor cultural level, visible in the decoration of funerary steles and audible in the neo-Punic dialects of its western ports like Lilybaeum (Marsala). The island's strategic importance to the Italian peninsula had also faded with the Romans' domination over a sea they had grown accustomed to call their own.

In the fifth century, when this control was partially undermined by the incursions of Vandal fleets, the challenge to the central Mediterranean islands and Italian mainland originated from the same coasts of north Africa. The riposte of the Eastern Roman Emperor Justinian (d. 565) and his illustrious general, Belisarius, was to break Vandal power in Africa. This allowed the Byzantines a platform for victories over the Ostrogoths in Sicily, and from there to make their own advance north into the Italian peninsula. The Eastern Empire's gains were famously short-lived and, in the face of Lombard and Frankish expansion southwards, a montage of statelets emerged, which constantly reconfigured Italy's amorphous political geography throughout the early medieval period. In amongst these states, Byzantine power was concentrated mainly around Ravenna in the north-east, across Apulia and Calabria in the the far south and on the islands of Sardinia and Sicily.

When Arab-Muslim armies expanded into Byzantine Syria and Egypt from the 630s and across north Africa from the 640s, the first raid against Sicily was launched from the new Arab province of Syria, probably in the year 652, only twenty years after the death of the Prophet Muḥammad. In Constantinople, the rise of Muslim power and early incursions against south Italy were catalysts for a tactical redeployment. Against a background of political machinations at court, the risk of further Byzantine losses and only fragile truces with the Arabs, Emperor Constans II transferred his residence to Syracuse in 663, to where he also contemplated shifting the political hub of the empire. But if Sicily had been intended as central to the geopolitical defence of the region, its role was curtailed by Constans' assassination five years later and the partial reversal of naval policy under his successors. More lasting arrangements, however, were implemented in response to the contraction of the empire's borders. Towards the end of the 600s, probably in response to the fall of Carthage in 698, the *theme* (θέμα) of Sicily was created as part of a wider social, defensive and administrative reorganisation of the provinces in which civil and military authority were combined and placed in the hands of a governor (*strategos*).[1]

The potential risk to Constantinople of further territorial loss on the western border represented a serious threat. Initially, the Arabs in Africa were concerned with the consolidation of the continent and, later, expansion into the Iberian peninsula, but they now securely held the launch-pad of the old Roman province of Africa – or Ifrīqiya as it was renamed in Arabic. If Sicily and south Italy were to fall to forces bent on destroying Byzantium, there was little to prevent a domino effect across the Adriatic into Dalmatia and through the Balkans to the metropolis of Constantinople itself.[2] Indeed, this was exactly the route adopted by the Normans in the eleventh century under Robert Guiscard, who died in Greece at the head of a south Italian army. Muslim consolidation of Ifrīqiya thus affected the dimension and distribution of power in the central Mediterranean for which control over the Ifrīqiya–Sicily–south Italy axis was essential.

From the late-seventh century, the south Italian *themes*, and particularly the main urban centre of Syracuse, were receivers and transmitters of cultural, literary and religious influence, spearheaded by Hellenised, Greek-speaking civil and military officials, bishops and literati. Connections to the Byzantine east were strengthened when the ecclesiastical jurisdiction of Calabria and Sicily was transferred under Leo III from Rome to the Patriarch of Constantinople in the mid-eighth century, nourishing a monastic and eremitic tradition that produced Sicilian-born saints, popes and religious scholars, who helped fashion early medieval Christian thought and doctrine.[3] However, Byzantine Sicily's assets were not evenly spread around the island. Culturally and politically, its orientation was towards the Italian mainland and beyond to the eastern Mediterranean. Correspondingly, power and wealth tended to be more concentrated in the eastern parts of the island, partly reflected in the distribution of its population and the towns which were the seats of its bishoprics. To the east were Messina, Taormina, Syracuse, Leontini (Lentini), Catania, Tindari, Lípari, Mylai (Milazzo) and Malta; in the west were Thermai (Termini), Palermo, Lilybaeum, Trokalis (Triocalà) and Agrigento.[4]

Early medieval Sicily was home to vast, rural imperial and ecclesiastic estates (*latifundia*) dotted with small, undefended hamlets. However, the island had also maintained a number of its ancient urban centres, most of which could already trace their origins back a thousand years. Many worship sites had been transformed from pagan sanctuaries into churches which retained their external appearance as ancient temples. Alongside these, larger settlements had preserved elements of their classical architecture, including their defensive walls. The conjecture of al-Qazwīnī in the 1200s that Sicily was depopulated until it was resettled with displaced peoples from the Muslim invasion of Ifrīqiya was only half right on both counts.[5] There *were* a few refugees from north Africa, but not enough to make a significant impact overall. On the other hand, the population of the Sicilian towns had sharply declined in number, but had not collapsed, since the heyday of the classical period.[6]

Both Sicily and Sardinia were targets for Muslim raids. Not all the dates given by the various (and late) sources for attacks are secure, and there is a genuine risk of conflating some accounts. From around 704, each island was plundered numerous times, particularly during the 730s, culminating in an aborted invasion of Sicily in 739–40, to which we shall return shortly.[7] Later, in 752–3, both islands seem to have made a large tribute payment, referred to in Arabic sources as the *jizya*. For its part, Sardinia had been very peripheral to the Byzantine exarchate of Africa and, like Sicily, both were considered safe havens for those fleeing north since the days of the Vandal attacks. This may account for the choice of Cágliari on the southern coast as a site for the translation of the body of Saint Augustine, who had died during the Vandal siege of Hippo Regius (later called Būna, now ʿAnnāba). Long before the fall of Rome, the island was considered a remote place: at the centre of the Mediterranean, yet in the back of beyond. However, by the time of the Muslim raids, Cágliari was not thought remote enough for Augustine, prompting another translation to Pavía in northern Italy between 721 and 726 when the saint's relics were purchased by the Lombard king, Liudprand.[8]

One poorly attested effect of the Muslim raids may have been to cause the coastal population of Sardinia to contract towards the mountainous centre. If it did, then it is likely to have introduced a conclusive phase of Christianisation in the semi-pagan hinterland that had so greatly concerned Gregory the Great. Otherwise, Sardinia's ports were relatively few and were always more parochial targets than Sicily's. Anecdotes of Muslim raids in Arabic sources share this view, telling how the hostile and crafty locals buried their treasure beneath the sea or hid it in church rafters before discovery could be made: there was booty in Sardinia, but it was hard to come by. The added perception that the island was difficult to reach safely from Africa was supported by an initially successful mission which was wrecked on its return leg in 816–17. Sicily, on the other hand, lay on the 'Sicilian channel' and ships sailing from Ifriqīya never passed out of sight of land.[9] It not only offered a relatively safe passage and an accessible target, but the island was also richer and more populated than Sardinia. Once the invasion of Sicily had begun in 827, Sardinia was rarely raided thereafter, and remained unexploited and sparsely populated until it became the object of Muslim–Christian rivalry again in the eleventh century.

Historical background to the conquest of Sicily

During the course of the eighth century, a distinctive pattern emerged in which Muslim expeditions in the central Mediterranean were conditioned, if not determined, by the situation in north Africa. On the one hand, the need to find new slave resources, together with the success of previous missions, impelled further raids. On the other hand, overseas operations were distracted when simmering discontent at home broke out into open revolt.

The grievances of the local populations stemmed from the Arab conquests of north Africa in the seventh century. Disparate and pagan tribesmen, who were spread over vast and varied regions, were referred to pejoratively by the Arabs – like the Romans had before them – as 'Berbers'. Their initial subjugation resulted in their provision of tribute rendered in terms of slaves. Thereafter, large numbers of Berbers had been willingly recruited for the conquest of the western regions of north Africa (the Maghrib) and Spain.[10] However, the vital roles they played in the Arab armies, and their conversion to Islam did not redress their inequitable status after the conquests. Rather than submitting themselves to the leadership of Arab governors appointed by the caliph and sent into north Africa from the east, the Berbers used their adopted religious identity as the vehicle to seek power by selecting a leader considered the best among the Muslim community as a whole. Resistance to the Arab governors and army commanders was led by the sectarian movements of the Berber Ṣufrī-s ('the Yellows') and the Ibāḍī-s ('the Whites'), and was thus articulated in both ethnic and politico-religious terms. To their Arab enemies, these Berber rebels were called 'Kharijites' ('outlaws'), a label with profoundly negative connotations for those associated with it. Indeed, in Arab-Muslim historiography, the term 'Berber' was so closely linked to ideas of rebelliousness that it can sometimes be taken to refer to a behavioural category as much as an ethnic affiliation.

In 740, Arab-Berber antagonism erupted in the western Maghrib where local tribes, led by their own 'caliph' Maysara al-Maṭgharī, rebelled against the

Arab governor, ʿUbayd Allāh ibn al-Ḥabhāb, who had attempted to tax the Muslim Berbers by rigidly enforcing the original terms of their capitulation, pressing them into service as if they had been slaves or conquered pagans. The Maysara rebellion helped to initiate a generation of violent conflicts which spread east, threatening the basis of Arab rule and even the city of Qayrawān itself in 742. As for Sicily, the recall of troops scuppered their first bid to invade the island, complete with cavalry, during which – an Arabic source retrospectively imagined – the Muslim commander had made his mark on the besieged gate of Syracuse by hammering on it with his sword before retiring.[11] Indeed, a similar redeployment from Sicily had to be made in 752–3 to quell another Berber revolt which, as the Arabic chroniclers noted, allowed sufficient respite for the Byzantines to fortify defensive hilltop sites across Sicily.[12] For over half a century few Muslim raids were launched into the central Mediterranean.

In Sicily, there is a limited amount of archaeological evidence for at least some defensive restructuring during this period of calm, most notably a Greek inscription commemorating fortifications built by the *strategos* of Sicily, Constantine, at Castelmola overlooking Taormina.[13] There are, however, doubts about the extent and effectiveness of the defences, particularly on the western side of the island. At the ancient and medieval site of Selinunte, for example, there can be seen the remains of hastily constructed ramparts (see fig. 1 on p. 138). These may not have been intended to withstand sustained attacks from a determined enemy, but were instead designed to shelter the community from an initial onslaught, allowing them time to negotiate surrender terms. More complete, and not dissimilar, structures can be seen at Byzantine Sbeïtla in Ifrīqiya, which had fallen two centuries earlier. The measures taken by the Sicilian *theme* remain open to question, but its organisation into smaller units may also have partially reversed the ruralisation of the preceding centuries and begun to fragment the great estates. At the same time, empowerment and effective organisation at a local level ensured that any future invasion was likely to be a time-consuming series of assaults conducted against one stronghold after another.

The turmoil in the Muslim west coincided with a wider political reconfiguration of the Islamic world as the Umayyad empire collapsed in the mid-eighth century after the civil war (*fitna*), which escalated following the violent death of the caliph, Walīd II. The subsequent defeat and dissolution of the dynasty, and eastward shift in the centre of political gravity from Syria to Iraq under the Abbasids, loosened the bonds of control between the core and the peripheries of the new-found empire. In the extreme west, across the Iberian peninsula (al-Andalus), an independent, breakaway dynasty of Umayyad *amīrs* emerged by 756. After a generation of insurrection across north Africa, during which the Berber revolts had failed to establish any widespread authority, their sects were dispersed to the oases and towns on the desert fringe. Politically marginalised as these peripheries were, they were connected into, and accommodated by, lucrative, trans-Saharan trade routes which formed key links in the transportation of slaves and gold, feeding the burgeoning demands from towns further north.[14]

A further consequence of the Berber revolts, combined with the Abbasids' attempts to restore stability, was the emergence of powerful, new and increasingly independent commanders in Ifrīqiya with strongly anti-Berber perspectives. Rising to prominence, first as governor of the strategically important Zāb region in what is now central-eastern Algeria, was Ibrāhīm ibn al-Aghlab. Like most of the army (*jund*) in late eighth-century Ifrīqiya, the Banū l-Aghlab were originally Arabs from the eastern province of Khurāsān (in modern Iran), a region favoured by the Abbasids for its political and military support, and one which had been instrumental in bringing about the downfall of the Umayyads. Professional soldiers of Arab and Persian Khurāsānī origin formed the trusted core of the early Abbasid armies, and under the caliph al-Manṣūr (d. 775), large detachments had been sent west to Ifrīqiya in 772. From a position of power in the military and as a key provincial governor, Ibrāhīm ibn al-Aghlab built on his authority, putting down a revolt in 799 and, having assumed control of Qayrawān, was invested the next year as *amīr* of Ifrīqiya by the Abbasid caliph, Hārūn al-Rashīd. In return, Ibn al-Aghlab recognised the caliph's authority and agreed, in theory, to make tribute payments. In practice, he ruled as he saw fit and passed on his own dynastic power without further recourse to Baghdad.[15]

The changing political landscape across north Africa is particularly important for understanding how and why certain socio-political, military and ethnic tensions were transferred into the central Mediterranean with the Aghlabid conquest of Sicily and parts of south Italy. For their part, the *amīr*s doubtless wished to avoid any repetition of unrest in Ifrīqiya. Thus, as a product of ninth-century Aghlabid political thought, the colony of Sicily was probably intended to be fashioned in its rulers' own image from the outset: Arabic-speaking; Muslim; nominally Abbasid; anti-Berber; and run by dependable governors (*wālī*-s), loyal to the dynasty and reliant on those families of the military (*jund*) considered faithful. As conquest commanders, the Aghlabids were effectively the dividers of the spoils and counted heavily upon support from trusted factions within the army, who expected to be rewarded with the proceeds of expansion into zones already famed for their spoils. The development of Aghlabid Sicily for the entire period of the ninth century was, therefore, driven by the restrictive demands of a 'booty economy' and remained closely tied to the wants and needs of the military and the colony's governors.

The Aghlabids' reliance on their sources of power in Ifrīqiya was not always secure, and the decision to launch a full-scale invasion of Sicily in 827 was informed by particular pressures they faced from within the army itself and from opposition articulated through the medium of religious scholars. Their problems were exacerbated by economic concerns. From the time of the Arab conquests, certain sectors of the rural economy in Ifrīqiya had depended on low-cost labour as slaves had been put to work on large estates in the hands of the governors and local strongmen of the Arab *jund*.[16] By the beginning of the ninth century, parts of that economy were weakened, and the slave supply, once gained by conquest, was now limited. The pressing need to open up new slave resources was, therefore, an important motive for expansion northward into the central Mediterranean.

The *jund*'s privileged status was itself a cause of simmering tension, resentment and shifting regional allegiances – all the more so because different towns hosted particular garrisons of soldiers, each loyal to their own commander. Revolts of the *jund* at Tūnis in 802 and 809 were put down successfully, but the insurrection instigated from 824 by the governor of Tripoli, Manṣūr al-Ṭunbudhī, a local strongman with his own fortress outside Tūnis, was not. This revolt was so widespread that it was not quashed until two years later. Tacitly anti-Aghlabid support was lent by religious scholars of the Ḥanafī and particularly the Mālikī 'schools' (*madhhabs*) of Islamic law from their base in the holy city of Qayrawān, the most important focus of religious scholarship in the Muslim west. In their capacity as legal experts, the jurists wielded both moral and political power, condemning the Aghlabids for their worldly pursuits and dissolute lifestyles in an attempt to undermine the authority of secular leaders who presumed to rule over the Muslim faithful. In addition to their support for rebel factions within the *jund*, the jurists also sided with popular opinion against the levying of 'illegal' taxes with the introduction of fixed, rather than proportional, taxes on produce. The possibility of conquering Sicily in 827 thus offered the Aghlabids great opportunities and pretexts. By undertaking a *jihād* to expand the frontiers of Islam at the expense of the infidels by conquest – the first major undertaking since the invasion of the Iberian peninsula from 711 – they could silence the criticism of the jurists. At the same time, they could redirect the destructive energies of a restless *jund* across the Ifrīqiyan–Sicilian channel to secure new sources of manpower and wealth.

The annexation of western Sicily (827–59)

As the legendary turncoat Count Julian was to Visigothic Spain in the eighth century, so Euphemios – a rebel divisional officer in charge of the fleet – was to the *theme* of Sicily in the ninth: both allegedly offered invitations to Muslim forces to invade. In 826, Euphemios rose up and killed the island's *strategos*, Constantine, pronouncing himself ruler at Syracuse where he possibly even claimed imperial powers.[17] His motives are not clear. They may have been purely personal or perhaps opportunistic in attempting to seize power after the unavenged loss of Byzantine Crete to rebel Andalusi Muslims in the same year. The situation was also said by Ibn al-Athīr to have arisen in the wake of a naval attack he had led against the Ifrīqiyan coast, again in the same year. However, Euphemios' position within the *theme* was undermined by a counterattack led by a subordinate officer whom he had initially favoured. This character was known in Arabic as Balāṭa, a name which perhaps recalls the Byzantine honorific title *kuropalatēs* or master of the palace. The little that can be said of him is that he was acting in league with the governor of Palermo. Euphemios' struggle to overcome internal opposition suggests that his subsequent appeal to the Aghlabids aimed only at raising auxiliary forces. Indeed, his personal presence in Ifrīqiya immediately prior to the Muslim conquest implies that he may even have lost control in Sicily.

The dilemma whether or not to invade and colonise Sicily, rather than simply raid it, prompted great debate among the jurists, generals and leading families at Qayrawān. With the wisdom of hindsight, qualms about the legal and geopolitical pitfalls of an invasion were articulated in a set-piece debate, recorded (with variations) most fully in the eleventh-century *Riyāḍ al-Nufūs*.[18] Towards the end of the discussion, as reported in al-Nuwayrī's much later version, a wise jurist was made to enquire about the distance between the island and the Italian mainland compared with its distance from Ifrīqiya. On hearing the response in terms of days' travel, he replied, 'If I were a bird, I wouldn't fly over there.' Raiding Sicily from overseas was not the same as holding it as a colony from Ifrīqiya: control could be maintained only so long as forces in southern Italy were weak and disunited. Until the mid-eleventh century, they were precisely that.

Had the Aghlabids looked to the conquest of Sicily to solve several of their own internal problems simultaneously, the expedition's overall command was not to be placed in their hands. From the time of the earliest Arab-Muslim conquests, regulating the just distribution of spoils had proved a perilously divisive issue. The early raids on Sicily had been no exception. In Arabic sources, sorties were remembered for the fabulous booty and slaves that could be ferried away by the army and its commanders, but they had already provoked an unusual variant of the spoils' controversy. Saintly Byzantine icons had been shipped to India via Baṣra by the Syrian governor and soon-to-be Umayyad caliph, Muʿawiya. As al-Birūnī and others critically noted, the sale of effigies to idol worshippers could only promote polytheism and was hardly befitting for God's self-proclaimed deputy on earth. So, to ensure that all the delicate tasks of conquest, both spiritual and mundane, were undertaken in accordance with the emerging body of legal opinion, the most respected religious authority in the Muslim west, Asad ibn al-Furāt, was put in charge of the Aghlabid invasion force. As *qāḍī* (magistrate) of Qayrawān and author of an eponymous treatise, the *Asadiyya*, his legal credentials were impeccable: a lifetime of study across the Islamic world included instruction from Mālik ibn Anas himself while in Medina. This enormous experience was reflected in his advanced age, for at the time of the invasion he was already in his late sixties.

In mid-June 827, a large force of infantry and mounted soldiers was launched from Sousse and landed at Mazara in western Sicily. After initial, local plundering operations, the army set off across the island, probably following the old Roman road through the Val di Noto, to besiege the capital Syracuse. There, the resistance of the defenders (helped by the arrival of a Byzantine fleet), combined with an outbreak of disease among the Muslims and the death of Asad, brought the expedition to the brink of disaster. The conquest of Sicily was to be quite unlike the rapid collapse of Visigothic Spain, and at no point did the Byzantines risk all by putting a massed army into the field.

One of the striking characteristics of the invasion was how slow and disjointed it became. The conquest sequences, sketchily recorded in very much later sources, do not resolve neatly into defined campaigns according to either region or period. Rather, after the ignominious retreat west from Syracuse, and coming close to destruction at Mineo where they were besieged, the Aghlabids concentrated their operations on gaining control of the western third of Sicily – the Val di Mazara. The forces which did so were a coalition, comprising the Aghlabid Arab *jund*, the *Ṣaqāliba* (slaves of central European/Balkan origin, after whom the largest quarter in tenth-century Palermo would be named), as well as contingents of non-Arab Ifrīqiyans, troops from sub-Saharan Africa, and an Andalusi force from Tortosa led by a Berber adventurer, Aṣbagh ibn Wakīl, nicknamed Farghalūsh, who arrived to relieve the Muslims when they were besieged at Mineo. From the year 859, if not from the first engagements, a party of Cretan Muslims also joined the fray. These had originally been anti-Umayyad rebels expelled first from Córdoba and then from Alexandria in Egypt, but who had taken to seaborne conquests, capturing Crete in 826.[19]

Of the Christian forces allied with the Aghlabids through Euphemios, precious little is known. The stereotypical characterisation of Euphemios in the Arabic sources as an unreliable figure distorts his relationship with the Muslims, whose help was required to defeat Balāṭa in western Sicily after which the latter fled to Castrogiovanni (modern Enna), and from there on to the mainland where he was killed. The military input of Euphemios into the earliest phases of the conquest, such as at Mineo and Agrigento in 828, is reported in the Arabic sources, but appears undervalued. No mention was made of his expertise as a guide or his provision of local knowledge and support. Moreover, his forces offer evidence of early Christian co-operation until his death in 829 at Castrogiovanni where the local Christians seemed unsure which side to support. It is not known whether the forces with him dispersed thereafter or continued to fight alongside their Muslim allies.

By September 831, the coalition forces had brought about the capitulation of Palermo after a debilitating siege lasting almost a year, during which, according to Ibn al-Athīr, the indigenous population was dramatically reduced from 70,000 to barely 3,000. The figures are impressionistic, but there is little evidence for the widespread continuity of Christian institutions at Palermo thereafter. Indeed, when the city fell to the Normans in 1072, the Greek archbishop they found was operating in a small church not even within the city walls. Known to the new locals as al-Madīna ('the city'), Palermo was repopulated and blossomed for over four centuries as one of the wealthiest and largest cities in what is now considered part of modern Europe. As such, Palermo is easily the greatest surviving legacy of Muslim rule in Sicily. It soon came to assume the role of the colony's political and cultural centre and was overseen by the robust presence of leading Arab-Muslim families from the Aghlabid *jund*, after whom some of its quarters were named. It had never been Byzantine Sicily's foremost town, but under Aghlabid leadership its political, religious and cultural life were steered strongly towards their preferred models of governance. Material evidence for change was quick to appear: the first coinage with the Arabic legend *Ṣiqilliyya* were struck at the siege of Castrogiovanni as early as 829 and, within four years of the fall of Palermo, the first coins bearing the name of its governor are attested.

By the early 840s, with the surrender of inland strongholds such as Platani, Caltabellotta and Corleone, as well as the port of Trápani, the wider region of the Val di Mazara could be carved up by the Aghlabids as their own personal estates and benefices (*qaṭā'ī'*) allocated to the leading families of the *jund*. This, at least, is the assumption, although an almost total absence of evidence obscures the dynamics of any such arrangement, for example, whether taxes and/or obligations were, or were not, to be rendered. The size of these allocations is also unknown. However, the Aghlabids may have considered that reproducing the large, landed estates of Ifrīqiya was neither desirable nor practicable. Instead, evidence from later periods indicates that they had encouraged the intensification of farming, concentrated in smaller estates on which settlers from Ifrīqiya were added to those among the local population who had not fled or been taken captive. The fertile lands in the west and south-west thus came to be the earliest sites of Muslim settlement in Sicily.

Outside the Val di Mazara, Aghlabid successes in the early phases of conquest were more scattered and sporadic. Messina had fallen as early as 842–3 in an attack co-ordinated with forces from Naples, but the Muslims made few inroads into the mountainous, north-eastern section of the island – the Val Démone. On the other hand, the south-eastern third of the island – the Val di Noto – saw significant incursions with the fall of Módica, Lentini and Ragusa between 845 and 849, although many of the key strongholds in the east, such as Taormina, Catania and Syracuse, remained firmly in Greek hands.

Most of Byzantine Sicily was taken piecemeal and not as a result of open, pitched battles. Frequently, such as at Cefalù in 838 and several times at Castrogiovanni, the preliminary assaults failed and a considerable passage of time elapsed before they could be brought under Muslim control. When a citadel did not fall, it was the surrounding villages and countryside which were noted in the sources to have borne the brunt of summer raids (*ṣā'ifas*). The campaigns under the leadership of Palermo's talented governor and army commander, al-ʿAbbās ibn al-Faḍl (r. 851–61) in the early 850s, particularly in the eastern parts of the island around Taormina, Catania and Syracuse, resulted in the fall of the strategically important fort of Caltavuturo in 852 and a five-month siege of Butera the following year, in which large numbers of Christian prisoners were taken as part of a peace accord.[20] Similar expeditions and annual summer sorties were organised and led, for the most part, by the Aghlabid rulers of Sicily themselves. The campaigns around this time are significant because of the details given about the army's conduct which, apart from widespread burning and destruction, suggests that they were sometimes less interested in payment as a form of negotiated settlement than taking captives. At Qaṣr al-Jadīd, in the following year, the army turned down an offer of 15,000 dinars in return for peace. Cash and the generation of wealth from ransoming prisoners may therefore have been only one consideration: finding a source of labour was another. If so, then apart from their transportation overseas, we might cautiously infer that some Christians were put to work on estates in western and central Sicily with its burgeoning rural economy and recent Ifrīqiyan colonists.

In the case of Cefalù, where its defence had been aided by the rare appearance of a Byzantine fleet, it would be another twenty years before it yielded to Muslim rule. Its capitulation paved the way for another attack against the fortress at Castrogiovanni which, until that point, had proved impregnable. After the fall of Palermo, the Byzantines had raised Castrogiovanni's strategic and political importance to rank alongside that of Syracuse, thus pinning their hopes on the defence of the island's centre. Without bringing it under their control, the Muslims were not able to capture and consolidate towns further to the east without the risk of losing their gains in counteroffensives. During the 830s and 840s, five assaults against the town were recorded, and, although its outer defences were sometimes breached and booty taken, the Muslim forces did not manage to capture the stronghold itself. Its fall, followed by its comprehensive sacking and the slaughter of its defenders on 24 January 859 was thus, in military terms, the crowning achievement of the early Aghlabids in Sicily since the fall of Palermo, and was celebrated by the immediate construction of a mosque (or the conversion of a church into one). A counteroffensive of minor revolts across western Sicily, spurred by the arrival of Byzantine ships sent to Syracuse the following year, amounted to little and, by the early part of the 860s, the Muslim commanders had consolidated all their early gains and won strategic control over the centre of the island too. They were also now in a position to attack targets in the eastern part of the island without having to fall back to safer positions in western Sicily.

The transmission of authority

For the ninth century, we are furnished with details from later Arabic annalistic histories about the transmission of authority between governors. In this respect, a preferred pattern emerged from the death of Asad in the field when a new commander had been appointed on the spot. We frequently find the phrase in the chroniclers that, 'the people (*ahl*) chose for themselves as governor...'. An appointment, or in some cases, a removal, was retrospectively confirmed by Ifrīqiya. To imagine 'the people' in any modern sense is mistaken: the term refers only to 'the people who mattered'. The celebrated Sicilianist, Michele Amari, first hypothesised that this deliberation among the leading families presupposes the existence of an ancient institution, the *jamāʿa*, which has continued in various forms in north Africa into the modern period.[21] As a traditional, informal assembly or council of notables, the *jamāʿa* was convened to decide on key areas of civil, political and sometimes judicial affairs, and a late reference to it is to be found in Ibn al-Athīr, who mentioned that the Banū l-Ṭabarī were a dominant force in the Palermitan *jamāʿa* in the mid-tenth century.[22] Amari's assumption, however, is problematic because this institution was a tribal Berber one – an unlikely governing mechanism of choice by the Arab *jund*. Some further illumination may be found in the Cairo Geniza documents in which reference was made to a Palermitan *shūrā* ('council') during the 1000s. This may relate to a similar, or even the same, institution. However, along with the late reference to the supposed *jamāʿa*, this was probably the most convenient way of describing some ad hoc mode of government in the absence of anything more bureaucratically organised.[23] In the case of the Geniza, the reference pertains to Palermo in the mid-eleventh century when whatever central authority existed, had, by then, collapsed.

Otherwise, the city's 'elites' or 'notables' were occasionally attested as the *khāṣṣa* or *aʿyān* in Arabic sources, but the terms are far too vague to be of help in establishing their relationships with any constitutional framework. That said, the degree of self-determination which can be seen in the decision-making processes at Palermo accounts for the origins of tension that interdependence fostered between centre and periphery, colony and mainland, and between the emerging new force of 'the people of Sicily' and those in and from Ifrīqiya. The immediate appointment of governors locally, later to be confirmed centrally, had an important practical dimension because it guaranteed at least a stop-gap solution to the problem of continuity of authority, thus tempering any notions that this might be interpreted as evidence for incipient autonomy in Sicily in this very early period. Rather, it was in the interests of both Sicily and Ifrīqiya to appoint quickly and locally in the first instance, thereby stifling the hopes of would-be usurpers tempted to exploit any, even temporary, power vacuum.

The Muslims on the south Italian mainland (832–71)

The first half-century of invasion was a disjointed and poorly recorded affair, and no less so than operations launched against the south Italian mainland. Sometimes known in Arabic as 'The Big Land' (*al-'arḍ al-kabīra*), the Italian peninsula and especially its southern parts were otherwise referred to as Qillawriya, Qalawriya or Qalūriya, after the name of the Greek *theme*, Kalavría (Calabria), where the Christian population had maintained close contacts with their Sicilian co-religionists. The allure of the mainland had attracted Muslim raiders from the 830s, in part because only five kilometres of sea across the Straits of Messina separate it from the north-eastern tip of Sicily. In addition, south Italy was itself in political turmoil, susceptible to attack and open to outside interference. For adventurers, it also offered the possibility of operating beyond the control of the Aghlabid commanders whose ambitions on the Italian mainland were at times stymied by setbacks on the island. However, there was to be no sustained or systematic attempt to consolidate territory in Calabria or to establish defensible bridgeheads which would have facilitated a wider invasion. Instead, Muslim raids tended to fulfil the immediate aims of acquiring quick booty or to act as a distraction for the disaffected among their ranks. Occasionally, loose alliances were formed with local factions but, with the exception of settlements at Bari, Táranto and later at the mouth of the Garigliano river, bases were limited and campaigns scattered. The devastation they wrought on the population and rural economy was not recorded in detail by the Arabic chroniclers, but it was etched into the minds of the local peoples fearful of enslavement, and remembered with bitterness by Greek and Latin sources.

At the time of the Muslims' arrival in Sicily, the dominant (albeit unstable) political unit on the south Italian mainland was the duchy of Benevento, which had emerged in the wake of the Lombard invasion of the peninsula from the north in the latter half of the 500s. Within a century, its succession of dukes had come to be the most powerful force in the region, but they had never conquered Rome or all the Byzantine areas to the south. Greek rule in Apulia and on the tip of Calabria was thus pressed from the north, while in Campania and along the Tyrrhenian coast to the north and west, the three maritime duchies of Naples, Amalfi and Gaeta were only nominally considered part of the empire by the early ninth century. These maintained frequent contacts with the Muslims, notably via a mutual interest in overseas commerce and the need to form alliances due to their weakness relative to the power of the Lombard princes inland.[24] For similar motives, they had found it convenient from time to time to seek support from the Byzantines.

Of the intermittent raids and poorly documented events of the 800s, three episodes stand out as having made a significant impact on the development of Muslim–Christian relations in the south Italian peninsula and which also serve to epitomise its political and military modalities. First, the role that Muslim forces played in the split of Benevento, secondly, the economic, political and propagandist effects of their raiding activities, which included naval attacks on Rome and thirdly, the foundation of Muslim amirates at Bari and Táranto.

As early as 832, Naples, when besieged by the Beneventan prince, Sicard, had appealed to the Muslims for help, leading to the first of several alliances. Three years later, a combined Muslim and Neapolitan force attacked Bríndisi. In the 870s and 880s, such political fraternising resulted in the excommunication of its bishop-prince, Athanasius; but the amount of gold and gold coinage found in the Amalfitan port towns reveals the high level of commercial exchange from this period and strengthens the perception that Muslim–Christian relations were not exclusively hostile.[25]

One of the most important events in which the Muslims came to be involved, and one with lasting consequences, was the decade of civil war and division of the duchy of Benevento into two (later, three) parts. Latin sources recorded how, in 839, Sicard was murdered by his treasurer, Radelchis, leading to a fiercely fought civil war between himself and the prince's brother, Siconulf. During the 840s, Radelchis maintained a power base at Benevento and was said to have employed north African Muslims; Siconulf's support centred on Salerno where he initially sought the help of Andalusi Muslims, possibly Cretans. With a couple of exceptions, the Arabic sources are silent about these warlords, so it is through the medium of hostile Latin sources, such as Erchempert, a ninth-century chronicler from Montecassino, and the anonymous tenth-century sources of the *Chronica Sancti Benedicti Casinensis* and *Chronicon Salernitanum*, that most of our information is drawn.

A handful of names have come down to us relating to the leading Muslim actors in the split of Benevento, insufficient to gain any clear ideas of their personalities, but enough to infer something of their motives, their relationships with the Lombard princes and their (dis)connection with the Aghlabids in Palermo and Qayrawān. From the Latin sources, we learn of a certain 'Apolaffar' or 'Apoiaffar' at Táranto. His name appears to be a Latinised version of the name Abū Ja'far. First attested in 843, he allied himself, initially at least, with Siconulf against Radelchis. In addition to Abū Ja'far, we find 'Massar' (possibly a Latinised rendition of Abū Ma'shār, a relatively common medieval Arabic nickname which might be loosely translated as 'group leader'), who was in league with Radelchis and had troops under his command at Benevento. The Latin sources imply that these mercenaries had, at times, close relations with their paymasters, as shown by the levels of hospitality offered them, although this did not preclude double-dealing and treachery.

In addition to raids and mercenary deployments came a serious attack on Rome in August 846, when a Muslim expeditionary force sailed up the Tiber to sack the Basilica of Saints Peter and Paul where they were said to have carried off the altarpiece above the tomb.[26] The Rome raid was no worse than raids elsewhere, but the attacks on the holy city were carried forward into later memory, whereas similar ones on Capua, Bari or Réggio never fired Christian imaginations in quite the same enduringly bitter way. At Rome itself a defensive circuit of the Leonine wall was constructed, named after Pope Leo IV (847–55), and within three months of the raid an appeal was issued 'to fight the enemies of Christ – Saracens and Moors'.[27] Hence, an army of Frankish, Burgundian and Provençal soldiers under the command of Carolingian Emperor Lothar I's son, Louis II (d. 875), set out for Benevento 'without pillaging the Christian population' on the dubious pretext that the Muslims were about to invade a great part of Italy. The main achievement of this campaign was more political than military in that it eased the separation of Benevento into two. For his part, Louis II would become a major player in south Italian politics, launching two more expeditions in 852 and 860, and eventually destroying the Muslim amirate at Bari in 871.

Rome was again threatened in 849 in a naval encounter, which would be recalled by Raphael's famous fresco from 1514–15 of the battle at Ostia in which a Muslim fleet, possibly operating from Sardinia, was defeated and scattered by a combined naval force from Rome, Naples and Gaeta. In the same year, a treaty was signed which formalised the split of Benevento. Significantly, the agreement bound the parties to expel Muslim mercenaries and not to employ them in future. While not suggesting that the mercenaries were the cause of the conflict, their expulsion was seen at the time as a necessary ingredient for a peaceful and lasting solution. For their part, the Byzantines had played only minor roles in halting the Muslims, who within a few years of their arrival, had become ensnared in south Italian politics along with a number of other, often rival, players in the continual reshaping of alliances. It was clear to medieval Latin chroniclers that the military leverage which the Muslim warlords provided, and which both sides sought, served to aggravate wider instability and, more specifically, to exacerbate the conflict in Benevento. However, before the signing of the separation and the bilateral agreement to terminate their employment, the Muslims had already found footholds in Apulia and Calabria which would lead to the establishment of powerful strongholds.

The amirate of Bari (847–71)

Concurrent with the Aghlabid invasion of Sicily and further raids on the mainland, was the establishment of Muslim control at Bari, a major port formerly under Byzantine control on the Adriatic coast. The principal source for the 'amirate of Bari' is the Muslim chronicler, al-Balādhurī (d. *c.* 892) whose *Kitāb Futūḥ al-buldān* ('Book of the conquests of lands') is not only a valuable and rich history of the early Muslim conquests, but also makes rare mention of the campaigns on the Italian mainland in what was, to his contemporary Muslim audience, an extremely minor episode in the wider scheme of early Islamic history.[28] Many of the details about Bari then found their way, sometimes verbatim, into Ibn al-Athīr's history. Minimal as the sources are for the occupation of Bari, they make for a fuller history than that of Táranto, which was under Muslim control by 846 when it was taken for a second time, and from when some presence was maintained until 880.

Bari had been the target of an unsuccessful attack in 840 but, once established there seven years later, the Muslims were able to launch a number of attacks across and beyond Apulia. In 841, Capua was sacked and, under Bari's three *amīrs*, raids were attested around Naples during 856; Conza was attacked twice in 858 and 862, Ascoli and the abbey of San Vincenzo al Volturno were raided in 861, the following year Venafro was sacked, while the abbeys of Montecassino and San Vincenzo were each required to pay 3,000 gold coins to the raiders.[29] Arguably, by unlocking wealth from the vaults of great abbeys such as Montecassino and by not exporting the wealth, this redistribution contributed to an increased circulation of resources in the south. Even if this is accepted only with caution, any economic benefit was compensated by the negative effects of crop burning, unproductive warfare and depopulation by slave-taking, which more typically characterised the Muslims' presence in south Italy. Without exception, the non-Arabic sources were hostile to 'the Saracens'. The letters of Pope John VIII (872–82) routinely associated the 'wicked Muslims' (*impii Sarraceni*) with 'wicked Christians', while other sources referred to the Muslims as a 'most devious people' or 'the wicked people of the Hagarenes'. In spite of this, there is no clear sense that the Muslims were much different from any other type of threat to physical or spiritual well-being at that time. Terms of reference in Latin and Greek sources such as 'Saracen' and 'Hagarene' were standard usages drawn from a medieval repertoire of appellations derived from Biblical narratives in Genesis in which there appear Sarah (Abraham's wife) and Hagar (his concubine and the mother of Ishmael).

The first attack on Bari was conducted by a 'client' (*mawlā*) of al-Aghlab with the unlikely name of Ḥabla.[30] However, it was under the rule of three *amīrs* that we are better informed. The first of these to emerge was Khalfūn al-Barbarī ('the Berber'), known in the Latin sources as Kalfon, who conquered Bari and ruled over it for five years until 852. He was said by al-Balādhurī to have been another 'client', this time attached to the Arab tribe of the Rabīʿa. The minor and sniping details of Khalfūn's presumed ethnicity and social status were also applied to subsequent rulers of Bari, supporting the notion that these warlord adventurers were originally attached to, but were not acting in accordance with, Aghlabid forces on Sicily itself.

Khalfūn's tactics and rapport with other local forces are supplied by Latin sources, but again they mark him out as a mercenary continuing disruptive raids and forming fragile alliances. Thus, for example, in 848, he was in alliance with Radelchis and Beneventan forces in an attack against Capua. Muslim control of Bari also allowed considerable influence to be exerted over Apulia by forming a permanent and defensible base in a strategically important location on the Adriatic, although there was never any attempt to form a political axis between Bari and Palermo. Balādhurī appeared to be only dimly aware that the Muslims were now coming into contact with different peoples and stated specifically, but incorrectly, that the people of Bari were not Byzantine Greeks (*al-Rūm*). It is presumed that the local Christians became part of a tribute-paying population theoretically living under Islamic law, but there seems to have been very little tangibly Islamic infrastructure. Any administrative business that was done in Bari appears to have been conducted on an ad hoc basis in which tribute payments were exacted from particular towns in line with what would be expected in a booty economy reliant on conquest and plunder rather than trade or regular forms of taxation for its continued survival.

By the time of the second *amīr*, al-Mufarraj bin Sallām (r. 853–6), some twenty-four forts (*ḥuṣūn*) were under Muslim control. A level of wider politico-religious awareness and a greater level of ambition and diplomatic sophistication was shown by a request submitted to the communications and intelligence chief (*ṣāḥib al-barīd*) in Egypt to the effect that neither he, nor any of the Muslims with him, could expect to receive benefit from prayer unless he were confirmed governor of the region, and therefore not considered an unlawful usurper. Having built a congregational mosque, Mufarraj was killed when his comrades rose up against him for reasons about which we are ill-informed. Unlike another breakaway Muslim amirate of this period, Crete, where the rulers came with their wives and families, hereditary rule was not established at Bari. Indeed, the actions of the rulers there appear to be those of single, male soldiers as scions from the Muslim army. Nor were they free of internal instability, which is shown in the successful and violent revolt by his comrades leading to Mufarraj's death and the rise of a third and final ruler. It is tempting to link the fall of one with the rise of the other.

The last *amīr* of Bari held sway between 857 and 865 and was the bearer of another unusual name: Sawdān. In Latin sources, he is known as 'Seodan' or 'Saugdan'.[31] His name was rendered in different forms, but there is an implication in it that he was originally from sub-Saharan Africa. A problematic reference to him in an unedited text, which can be read as 'Sawdān al-Māwrī' ('the Moor', ultimately from the Greek, *mavros*, 'black'), again suggests that, like the previous commanders of the Muslim forces in Bari, they were not Arab Aghlabid commanders, but their 'clients'. If the term 'moor' was applied to him, then it was most likely a Latin or Greek loan word, and was thus probably acquired while in Italy. An alternative reading would give 'al-Māzarī', indicating a Sicilian provenance.[32] Sawdān continued the strategy of regional plundering and at least five major raids were conducted, including those against the abbeys of Montecassino and San Vincenzo al Volturno. However, it was also under his leadership that a request for recognition was made directly to the caliph al-Mutawakkil in Baghdad. The demand was recorded by al-Balādhurī, who was a well-known figure at the court of the Abbasid caliph in Baghdad, so it is possible that his information relating to the Bari *amīrs* came from the emissary himself or from a source who had been close by. Although the request was eventually granted, Balādhurī's emphasis of their Berber associations perhaps reflected a grudging attitude toward the caliph's investiture of a warlord at the end of the earth. The timing of the request was unfortunate in that the emissary was unable to leave before the caliph was murdered in December 861. He may have received confirmation of his legitimacy only shortly before Bari was retaken by Louis II in February 871, after which Sawdān was taken as a prisoner to Benevento, where he remained for four years until his release with the help of the Muslims at Táranto.

After the fall of Bari in February 871, the appointment of two governors was announced by Aghlabid Qayrawān: one to rule over Sicily, the other to oversee 'The Big Land'. This appears to be an attempt by the Aghlabids to fill the void left by the Bari *amīrs* and may explain the motive for a twelve-month siege of Salerno, which began late in the same year. The siege failed, but it was a clear attempt by the Aghlabids to flex their muscles on the mainland. What is unclear is whether a powerful Muslim fort at the mouth of the Garigliano river was instigated by the Aghlabids or by another band of breakaway soldiers, operating on their own account. Throughout the obscure events of the early Aghlabid period, Sicily and parts of the mainland were unable to escape the region's characteristically haphazard dynamics, now exacerbated by raiding, conquest and the processes of colonisation. The Italian continent continued to attract those in search of a quick profit, but a full generation after the launch of the invasion, the piecemeal Muslim conquest of Sicily was far from complete.

Notes

1 The date for the creation of the Sicilian *theme* is controversial, although it is not thought to pre-date 687, and the term *strategos* is not attested before 701. See N. Oikonomidès, 'Une liste arabe des stratèges byzantins du VIIe siècle et les origines du Thème de Sicile', *Rivista di Studi Bizantini e Neoellenici*, 1 (1964): 121–30. On the wider context, T. S. Brown, *Gentlemen and Officers: Imperial Adminstration and Aristocratic Power in Byzantine Italy* A.D. 554–800 (Rome, 1984).

2 For this argument, and an incisive assessment of seapower in the central Mediterranean (which prefigures Pirenne), see J. B. Bury, 'The naval policy of the Roman Empire in relation to the Western provinces from the 7th to the 9th century', in *Centenario della nascita di Michele Amari*, vol. 2 (Palermo, 1910), pp. 11–34.

3 Several works in French and Italian include good surveys of Byzantine Sicily and south Italy, including Jules Gay, *L'Italie méridionale et l'Empire byzantin* (Paris, 1904); Vera von Falkenhausen, *I Bizantini in Italia* (Milan, 1982), pp. 1–136 and Ferdinando Maurici, *La Sicilia occidentale dalla tarda antichità alla conquista islamica. Una storia del territorio ca. 300–827 d. C.* (Palermo, 2005); T. S. Brown, 'Byzantine Italy *c.* 680–*c.* 876', in *New Cambridge Medieval History II, c.700– c.900*, Rosamund McKitterick (ed.) (Cambridge, 1995), pp. 320–45. See also the valuable collection of twenty-nine reprinted articles by André Guillou, *Studies on Byzantine Italy* (London, 1970) and *Culture et Société en Italie Byzantine VIe–XIe siècles* (Aldershot, 1978). For modern accounts of the emergence and historiography of the early medieval Mediterranean, complete with extensive bibliographical essays, see Peregrine Horden and Nicholas Purcell, *The Corrupting Sea. A Study of Mediterranean History* (Oxford, 2000), in addition to Chris Wickham's *Framing the Early Middle Ages: Europe and the Mediterranean, 400–800* (Oxford, 2005). For more northerly parts of the Italian peninsula, see Wickham's, *Early Medieval Italy, Central Power and Local Society 400–1000* (Basingstoke, 1981).

4 André Guillou, 'L'habitat nell'Italia bizantina: exarchato, Sicilia, Catepano (VI–XI sec)', in *Atti del colloquio internazionale di archeologia medievale*, 1974 (Palermo, 1976), p. 173, reprinted in *Culture et Société en Italie Byzantine*. For the Muslims in Sicily, indispensable but dated are the revised volumes of Michele Amari, *Storia dei Musulmani di Sicilia*, 2nd rev. edn, Carlo Alfonso Nallino (ed.), 3 vols (Catania, 1933–9). Henceforth, Amari-Nallino, *SMS*².

5 Al-Qazwīnī, *BAS*² Ar. I:152 ; *BAS*² It. I:238.

6 For a clear survey of long-term population change, see Roger J. A. Wilson, 'Changes in the Pattern of Urban Settlement in Roman, Byzantine and Arab Sicily', in *Papers in Italian Archaeology*, 6 (1985): 313–44.

7 Raids on Sardinia are predominantly attested in moveable dates of the Islamic calendar which equate to AD 703–4(?), 705–6, 707–8, 710–11, 732, 735–6, 737(?), and 752–3. On Sicily: 705, 710–11, 720–1, 727, 727–8, 729–30, 732–3, 735–6, 739–40, 747–8(?) and 752–3.

8 Bede, *Chronica majora*, C. W. Jones (ed.), *Bedae Opera de didascalica*, 3 vols, CCSL

123A–C (Turnhout, 1975–80), II:463–544, (§ 593, p. 535). Jan T. Hallenbeck, *The Transferal of the Relics of St. Augustine of Hippo from Sardinia to Pavia in the Early Middle Ages* (New York, 2000). For both Bede and the slightly later *Historia Langobardorum* of Paul the Deacon, these events were either contemporary or had taken place in recent living memory.

9 See the useful discussions on sea travel in S. D. Goitein, *A Mediterranean Society: The Jewish Communities of the World as Portrayed in the Documents of the Cairo Geniza*, 6 vols (Berkeley, 1967–93), I:301–26 (p. 326).

10 For the unification of north Africa by Islam and its subsequent Arabicisation, see Michael Brett and Elizabeth Fentress, *The Berbers* (Oxford, 1996), pp. 81–154.

11 Al-Nuwayrī, *BAS*[2] Ar. II:483; *BAS*[2] It. II:113.

12 For Byzantine *incastellamento* from the mid-700s, see Ibn al-Athīr, *BAS*[2] Ar. I:269; It. I:363, and al-Nuwayrī *BAS*[2] Ar. II.483; It. II:113.

13 Ferdinando Maurici, *Castelli medievali in Sicilia: Dai bizantini ai normanni* (Palermo, 1992), p. 27.

14 Michael Brett, 'The Islamisation of Morocco from the Arabs to the Almoravids', most easily accessible in *Ibn Khaldun and the Medieval Maghrib* (Aldershot, 1999), among several articles linking issues of north African economy, its people and the formation of Arab-Muslim states.

15 For the Arab conquests and rise of the Aghlabids, see Michael Brett, in *The Cambridge History of Africa*, J. D. Fage (ed.), vol. 2, pp. 490–555. On the Aghlabid dynasty, see also Mohamed Talbi, *L'Émirat aghlabide, 184–296/800–909: histoire politique* (Paris, 1966).

16 Mohamed Talbi, 'Law and economy in Ifrīqiya (Tunisia), in the Third Islamic century: agriculture and the role of slaves in the country's economy' in *The Islamic Middle East 700–1900: Studies on Economic and Social History*, A. L. Udovitch (ed.) (Princeton, 1981), pp. 209–49.

17 The fullest accounts of Euphemios' revolt are found in Ibn al-Athīr, *BAS*[2] Ar. I:270–1; *BAS*[2] It. I:364–6 and al-Nuwayrī, *BAS*[2] Ar. II:484–5; It. II:113–4. For the important discussion of Amari-Nallino, see *SMS*[2] I:367–81.

18 For the discussion about whether to raid or conquer Sicily, see al-Mālikī's *Riyāḍ al-Nuūs* in *BAS*[2] Ar. I:212–13; It. I:304–8; al-Nuwayrī, *BAS*[2] Ar. II:483–4; It. II:114–15.

19 A reference to Andalusi contingents appears in the *Kitāb al-amwāl* ('The Book of Finances') by the jurist al-Dāwūdī in which he related that they had landed properties in Sicily. It is possible that either they, or the Tortosan Andalusis, lent their name to the open estate of al-Andulsīn in western Sicily attested in Norman sources. Such was immigration from the Muslim west that most attempts to corroborate settlement links end in speculation.

20 As part of the pact concluded at Butera, 6,000 slaves were taken according to Ibn 'Idhārī, *BAS*[2] Ar. I:411; It. II:10. Ibn al-Athīr also recorded significant numbers of captives, *BAS*[2] Ar. I:279; It. I:378.

21 Amari-Nallino, *SMS*[2] II:13–16.

22 The notables of the 'council' at Palermo (*min a'yān al-jamā'a*) are attested in Ibn al-Athīr, *BAS*[2] Ar. I:300 and 302; *BAS*[2] It. I:416.

23 Moshe Gil, 'Sicily 827–1072, in the light of the Geniza documents and parallel sources', in *Italia Judaica. Gli ebrei in Sicilia sino all'espulsione del 1492, Atti del V*

convegno internazionale, Palermo, 15–19 giugno 1992 (Rome, 1995), pp. 96–171 (p. 116).

24 Barbara Kreutz, *Before the Normans: Southern Italy in the Ninth and Tenth Centuries* (Philadelphia, 1991) and Armand O. Citarella, 'The Relations of Amalfi with the Arab world before the crusades', *Speculum*, 42/2 (1967): 299–312.

25 The evidence that the Muslim and Neapolitan forces were fighting together at this point derives from a highly problematic passage in Ibn al-Athīr, *BAS*[2] Ar. I:276: 'In this year [842–3], al-Faḍl bin Ja'far al-Hamdanī travelled by sea and landed at Messina where he spread out detachments and took a great deal of booty. The people (*ahl*) of Nāb.l [other manuscript readings are: Bāb.l or Nāt.k] sought a treaty from him and set out with him'.

26 See the excellent work by Giosuè Musca, *L'emirato di Bari 847–871* (Bari, 1964), p. 28, for fuller bibliographies and also for extensive quotations from primary sources. Also, Amari-Nallino, *SMS*[2] II:506 for the Rome raid, and II:492–530 for the expeditions against the mainland. For analysis of events on the mainland in this period, see also G. A. Loud, *The Age of Robert Guiscard: Southern Italy and the Norman Conquest* (Harlow, 2000), pp. 12–59.

27 *Hlotharii, MGH, Leges, Capitularia regum Francorum* II, 9, p. 67. For further discussion, see Musca, *L'emirato di Bari*, pp. 28–31.

28 Al-Balādhurī, *BAS*[2]Ar. I.183–4; *BAS*[2] It. II:268–70; English trans. Philip K. Hitti, *The Origins of the Islamic State* (New York, 1916–24; reprinted, 2002), pp. 371–2. Ibn al-Athīr, *BAS*[2] Ar. I.285–6; *BAS*[2] It. I.390–1.

29 For an important discussion of the impact of Muslim raids in the region, see Armano O. Citarella and Henry M. Willard, *The Ninth-Century Treasure of Monte Cassino in the Context of Political and Economic Developments in South Italy* (Montecassino, 1983).

30 The name is clearly problematic. Ḥabla means a rope-like grapevine. Ibn al-Athīr gives the name as Ḥayā. The outline of the two names might easily be confused and the manuscript text of the latter presents a difficult reading.

31 For ease of reference, extracts from the principal Latin sources for the Muslims on the mainland such as Erchempert, the Salerno Chronicle, John the Deacon and the Chronicle of Saint Benedict are reproduced in *Gli Arabi in Italia*, pp. 706–24.

32 On his identity, see the useful discussions in Musca, *L'emirato di Bari*, pp. 62 and 116, n. 50.

2

The consolidation of Muslim authority in Sicily

On Sicily, after the capture of Castrogiovanni (modern Enna) in 859, the Aghlabids dominated the central regions of the island, enabling them to push into its south-eastern third or Val di Noto. Spurred by the loss of Castrogiovanni, Byzantine forces arrived from overseas to save the remains of their authority in the east. Their advent coincided with an uprising of towns in the south-west including Agrigento, Caltabellotta and Platani which, until now, had remained largely quiescent after their conquest. If the Byzantines had attempted a combined operation, or had wished to foment revolt across the island, then their hopes were soon wrecked when the revolt was put down, and they were reduced to venting their frustration by exhuming and burning the corpse of the long-serving *wālī*, al-ʿAbbās, who had died near Caltagirone in summer 861. Aghlabid Sicily was not to produce such a long-serving leader again. They were, however, not short of capable governors, such as Khafāja ibn Sufyān (r. 862–9) who arrived from Ifrīqiya after two brief interregnum periods in which local candidates from al-ʿAbbās's family aspired to the office of *wālī*. Under Khafāja, annual expeditions against the Christians focused on towns in the south-east. A number of these, Ragusa in 849 for example, had already capitulated at least once before, but some appeared to have slipped out of their tribute-paying obligations, thus justifying their renewed subjugation. Noto, for instance, was reportedly taken twice in successive years between 864 and 866. When sieges failed to break the major towns such as Catania, Taormina and Syracuse, which were repeatedly targeted, it was the countryside and villages around them which were again pillaged. And when a Byzantine naval expedition arrived to assist the relief of Syracuse, under attack in 868 for the third time in as many years and its outskirts sacked, the Greeks were unable to translate moral and physical support into anything resembling an incisive counterattack.

On his return from a summer raid against Syracuse in 869, Khafāja was killed by a soldier, said in the Arabic sources to have had a Berber name. The reasons for his murder were not reported, but it is tempting to suggest a connection with tensions over the division of spoils between different sections within the army. The killer found refuge in Syracuse and Khafāja's body was translated to Palermo rather than being buried en route, perhaps so as not to risk desecration at the hands of the Christians.[1] His son, Muḥammad was locally acclaimed successor and shortly afterwards received robes of honour from Ifrīqiya to confirm his investiture. He too was murdered in obscure circumstances, this time by his eunuch slaves in 871. In fact, there was rarely a period in Aghlabid Sicily's history when it did not exhibit the signs of a wild frontier, attracting the ambitious, the adventurous and the lawless into areas where the vicissitudes of annual raiding had become normalised. Between the murders of its governors, one of the relatively few successes of the Aghlabids in this period was to occur in an entirely new field of operations.

The expeditions against Malta and Syracuse

Reported in a haphazard manner by Arabic sources, Malta, which had been raided in the mid-830s, was devastated in August 870 by an expedition launched from Sicily. A Byzantine relief effort was to no avail and the island's governor was killed, its bishop taken to Palermo, its fortress levelled and its wealth carried away.[2] Not all the plunder was transported to Sicily. Aḥmad ibn al-Aghlab (*c.* 874–8), known by his nickname al-Ḥabashī ('the Ethiopian'), had his Ifrīqiyan palace near Sousse propped up with columns of Maltese marble taken from its main church.[3] After the failures of expeditions to consolidate all south-eastern Sicily, and the capitulation of only lesser towns to satisfy the income requirements of the *jund*, the symbolic value of such demolition and recycling, which had been common in early Arab Ifrīqiyan architecture, assumed added significance. Confirmation of the magnitude of the Maltese victory and its link to the re-use of its bountiful plunder was commemorated in a triumphant inscription at Ḥabashī's palace.[4]

The celebrated acquisition of a new and strategically placed island for Islam was not a victory which the Aghlabids developed in other respects. In part, this may have been due to the renewed instability which the violent death of Khafāja's son and successor, and a spate of six governors in three years, suggest. Their terms of office are muddled in the sources, significantly so because it implies that political concerns at Palermo had distracted attentions away from all but the most pressing of engagements. Against this background, Malta may have been quickly forgotten. Ifrīqiyan involvement in the attack may also help to explain why there was little interest in the island thereafter, since Malta lay outside the main Sicily–Ifrīqiya passage.

On the Italian mainland, the Muslims had lost ground after the failed siege of Salerno and fall of Bari, whose eventual restoration to Byzantine rule was an important factor in the subsequent reawakening of Greek power in Apulia. Significantly, the Arabic sources have little to say for the period in Sicily between 872 and 878 except to note the unusually high turnover of governors, and an attack on Syracuse in which tribute payment was secured in return for a release of Muslim prisoners.

As for Muslim Malta, its pre-Norman social history remains something of a conundrum. It is at least partially solved in a detailed account by al-Ḥimyarī (d. 1329) in which he claimed that 'after [the raid], the island of Malta became desolate (*khirba*), without inhabitants'.[5] This view is also supported by Ibn Ḥawqal's tenth-century account.[6] If the depopulation theory is accepted, then the island continued with no detectable, permanent settlement for almost 180 years during which it was said to have been visited only by fishermen or by those in search of timber or honey. The account is a controversial one since it suggests a scenario of complete, and for some, uncomfortable, disjuncture with the distant past. The religious history of an island once visited by the shipwrecked Saint Paul, but whose population's language is derived from Arabic, appears to recommence in earnest with its repopulation by Muslims in the mid-eleventh century and, as we shall see in Chapter 5, its capture by the Normans.

Half a century after the Muslim invasion of Sicily had begun, the western parts under Aghlabid rule were settled with a mixed Muslim–Christian population where the locals were exposed to processes of Arabicisation and Islamicisation, their numbers boosted by Ifrīqiyan colonists; the Val di Noto largely comprised Christian tribute-paying towns and villages. Thus, the region of most concentrated Christian settlement became the Val Démone in the north-east. Above all, Syracuse remained beyond Muslim control. Its capture would not only guarantee enormous booty and keep up the conquest momentum, but it would also secure the Val di Noto and displace the sites of Christian opposition further into the hills of the north-east. In 877, the city, which juts out on a spit of land, was subjected to a prolonged blockade by land and sea, and was unable to be relieved by a Byzantine fleet. Unlike predatory summer raids or regularly conducted attacks to exact tribute, the siege became a determined effort to break the resistance of the city. Sophisticated techniques of siege-craft were employed, including an innovative form of mangonel which had perhaps first been used at the siege of Salerno.[7] An eye-witness account of the withering blockade and fall of Syracuse is contained in a dramatic letter penned by the monk Theodosios.[8] Even allowing for exaggeration, the images he described portrayed an insider's view of the deteriorating conditions: the inhabitants reduced by starvation and disease; the hyper-inflationary prices paid for paltry amounts of staple foods; and the miserable humiliation and discomfort of the survivors.

Cracking Syracuse was a huge and long-anticipated victory for the Muslims, both materially and psychologically. When the city's defences were breached after nine months in May 878, those Christians and Jews who were not massacred, were rounded up and led to Palermo where Theodosios himself was taken and died. The remainder were released – but only when ransoms were negotiated and paid seven years later, according to an anonymous, probably tenth-century Sicilian, source commonly known as the *Cambridge Chronicle*.[9] Much of the material infrastructure of Syracuse itself – its walls, churches and houses – was damaged, and the city was stripped of its transferable wealth in two months of post-conquest looting.

The civil wars of 886–900

One might have expected the generation following the triumph at Syracuse to have been Aghlabid Sicily's finest. It was not. Rather, it was marked by internal discord revealing profound crises within the army and ruling elites, exacerbated by the colony's frontier status as a place of continual warfare. In the same year as the siege of Syracuse, the governor of Sicily, Jaʿfar ibn Muḥammad was murdered by his slaves (*ghilmān*) acting on the orders of his imprisoned uncle and brother. They then seized power before being deposed in an uprising against them at Palermo in September, after which they were returned to Ifrīqiya and executed by the Aghlabid *amīr*, Ibrāhīm II (r. 875–902).

Ibrāhīm's appointment of his own son was short-lived, and under a new, local governor, Ḥusayn ibn Rabāḥ, campaigns were renewed against the eastern Christian strongholds of Rometta, Catania and Taormina. The latter in particular would come to be the focus of large-scale, but ultimately unsuccessful, engagements, and the town was attacked in the following year too. A naval campaign conducted against the Byzantines in the eastern Mediterranean resulted in a counterattack and in Greek forces landing in Sicily, where they were able to secure positions and make raids themselves in the mountainous north-east. Further attacks on Taormina in 881–2 and 889–90 did not break the stronghold either. Indeed, the lack of success was notable, even in terms of the acquisition of booty and prisoners which were a vitally important part of the political economy on which the principal Arab families of the Sicilian and Ifrīqiyan *jund* thrived.

A Muslim force led by a *jund* commander, Abū l-Thawr was virtually annihilated in 881–2, and, with Sicilian governors changing on an almost annual basis, a Muslim army was raised by a wider call to arms, a sign of the severity of the military crisis following their failure to make further headway with the conquest.[10] The army marched successfully against Catania, Taormina and then 'the king's city' as Ibn al-Athīr probably called Polizzi. Rometta and Catania were again the targets of attacks the following year and, under yet another new governor, Sawāda ibn Khafāja dispatched from Ifrīqiya in 885, more campaigns against Catania and Taormina yielded further booty, in the sense that the army was at least paid off, since the towns did not fall. The taking of prisoners by both sides attests to the defensive strength of the Byzantines, who were then able to secure the release of their Syracusan prisoners from 878 in exchange for 300 captured Muslim troops. Ibn al-Athīr's reference to 'the great army' which was involved in the campaign hints that it had been recruited from an unusually wide cross-section of the population or had included forces brought from Ifrīqiya. In either case, a larger army required a wider distribution of spoils – if the campaigns were successful. Such tensions and mixed triumphs, underpinned violent events among sections of the army in the years of the 880s. The dividing lines came to be simplified in later sources as a conflict between ruling factions and rebels, which was frequently phrased in terms of an ethnic struggle between Arabs and Berbers.

On the south Italian mainland during 885–6, the Muslim forces suffered serious setbacks at the hands of a Byzantine army under the command of Nikephoros Phokas, and it was in this context of failure that civil strife between the Arab *jund* and the 'Berbers' first broke out on the island during December 886. Ibn 'Idhārī described how 'the people of Palermo' forcibly dismissed Sawāda and his supporters sending them back to Ifrīqiya, and electing for themselves a (short-lived) governor of their own choice. The imposition by Ibrāhīm II of another new governor, the rapid success of raids and the defeat of a Byzantine fleet off Milazzo, followed up by ravaging attacks in Calabria and against the port of Réggio during 888–9 appears to have taken the heat out of the feuding factions while, in the following year, Sawāda reappeared from Ifrīqiya at the head of an army leading a failed attack against Taormina. In March 890, a revolt erupted at Palermo. This time, it was described in the *Cambridge Chronicle* as an uprising of the Sicilians against 'the people of Ifrīqiya', most likely indicative of the friction between local Arab families of the *jund* and those troops who had come with Sawāda from Ifrīqiya. The events as vaguely reported by the sources formed part of the simmering three-way tensions of late Aghlabid Sicily: between Muslims and Christians; between Arabs and non-Arab factions within the army; and between Sicilian and Ifrīqiyan interests. It also demonstrated how continual military successes, or raids conducted in the name of a *jihād*, were essential for the political stability of Sicily where it was becoming increasingly difficult to find a suitable or lasting governor.

Across northern Ifrīqiya, too, a widespread rebellion of disaffected parties among the *jund* and landholders broke out during 893, who directed their hostility towards Ibrāhīm II. This was such a serious insurrection that it could not be quelled until the following year. The Arabic sources for Sicily during these years are virtually silent as the expeditions against the Christian towns were halted and a truce agreed during 895–6. The unusual details for the peace are striking: four times a year, over the course of forty months, the Christians released a total of 1,000 Muslim prisoners, by turns, a group of Arab captives and then a group of Berbers. Not only does this show the extent of Christian military success against the Aghlabids in eastern Sicily, but it may also have been deliberately aimed at exacerbating tensions within the Muslim army by playing off one faction against another in negotiating their staggered release. During 898, by which time most, if not all, of the prisoners had been set free, serious fighting broke out between 'Arab' and 'Berber' factions within the Sicilian Muslim army. The response from Ifrīqiya was decisive and forceful: the ringleaders were rounded up, but the general peace which was offered was not heeded. The task of restoring order was given to Ibrāhīm II's own son, Abū l-'Abbās 'Abd Allāh, who had been instrumental in suppressing the powerful Ifrīqiyan rebels of 893, and now commanded an army that set out to reconquer the island. By the time the Ifrīqiyans had arrived at Mazara and laid siege to Trápani at the beginning of August 900, a clear regional dimension to the civil strife had opened up with engagements between Palermitan and Agrigentan forces. The reasons for this were never made explicit in the sources, although historians in the modern era have been tempted to consider it as an extension of the Arab–Berber tensions on the island: the Berbers being associated with settlement around Agrigento, whereas the Arab parties in the *jund* were Palermo-based. As we shall see, landholdings around the Agrigento area had long been a matter of dispute and were only to worsen in the tenth century where they can be seen more clearly as playing a role in sparking serious violence. Strikingly, the Arabic sources did not cite ethnic tensions as the cause of the strife in the year 900, nor did they frame the fighting in such terms either.

The events narrated or alluded to in differing degrees of detail are conveyed by the *Cambridge Chronicle*, Ibn 'Idhārī, Ibn al-Athīr and Ibn Khaldūn. The seriousness of the situation threatened to rupture Sicily from Aghlabid Ifrīqiya, and also to fracture Sicilian Muslim polity through civil war. The sources agree that both the Palermitans and the Agrigentans sent delegations to Abū l-'Abbās claiming fealty, but Ibn Khaldūn was alone in suggesting that the Palermitans and Agrigentans had resolved their differences and stood united against the Ifrīqiyans. When the negotiations broke down, the Palermitans launched a failed attack. The Ifrīqiyan army then marched against Palermo, occupied its outskirts and, after inflicting significant numbers of casualties, brought about its surrender on 18 September 900. Many families were reported to have fled for Taormina while the commander of the fleet, an Arab Sicilian, Rikmawayh (his Persianesque name associates him with the Aghlabid *jund*), sought refuge with his supporters further afield in Constantinople beyond the reach of the Ifrīqiyans. The ructions on the island did not escape the notice of the Byzantines, as noted by a contemporary mainland source, John the Deacon of Naples, and they took the opportunity to strengthen their positions in Calabria. The enforced restoration of peace in Sicily by an army from Ifrīqiya was followed by the immediate resumption of the *jihād*, making initially ineffectual attacks against and around Taormina and Catania. The following year, Demona was besieged but did not fall, while the Muslim fleet sailed from Messina and made a devastating attack on Réggio in summer 901, where Byzantine forces had mustered, taking a vast booty, large numbers of prisoners and compelling the city to pay the religious poll-tax or *jizya* in return for peace. A Byzantine counterattack by sea against Messina resulted only in their retreat and the reported impounding of at least thirty Greek warships. The continual conflicts had produced no major success for almost twenty-five years. This, however, was soon to change with an unexpected impetus from Ifrīqiya.

The campaigns of Ibrāhīm II in Italy

The last days of the *amīr* of Ifrīqiya, Ibrāhīm II, were spent campaigning overseas in Sicily and on the Italian mainland. Ironically, his successes marked the high point of Aghlabid Sicily, but his character and leadership proved both a strength and a weakness for the dynasty as a whole. He was remembered in the Arab-Muslim sources for his fearsome reputation in exacting justice and for vengefully suppressing all opposition. This opposition had been considerable, but his reign had also seen significant military successes in Ifrīqiya, notably its defence against incursions from Tūlūnid Egypt, but also in his campaigns against the Ibāḍīs in 879–80, the Berbers of the Zāb in 881–3, the great landholders in 893 and the rising of the Berbers of Jabal Nafūsa in 896–7. To some degree, Ibrāhīm was a victim of his own success, the historical memory of his deeds and his reputation exaggerated by posterity, stoking opposition from diverse quarters which ultimately contributed to his dynasty's downfall and eased the rise of their successors and conquerors in Ifrīqiya, the Fatimids.

His last actions were to come in a south Italian context. In June 902, Ibrāhīm stood down as *amīr* in Ifrīqiya, effectively exchanging offices with his son Abū l-ʿAbbās ʿAbd Allāh in Sicily, for motives which the sources claimed were an attempt to lead a life of pious atonement in the form of *jihād* against the Byzantines in place of making the pilgrimage to Mecca. Ibrāhīm moved swiftly across the island from Trápani to Palermo and then to the eastern towns at the head of a joint Sicilian–Ifrīqiyan expedition. The Arabic sources give only the sketchiest outline of the capture of Taormina on 1 August 902, although further details, including the martyrdom of its bishop, are found in a Greek source, the Life of Saint Elias.[11] The fall of Taormina was followed by the capitulation of other strongholds in the Val Démone, notably Rometta, which agreed to pay the *jizya*. In effect, for the first time after seventy-five years of almost constant campaigning, the Aghlabids could claim that all Sicily was under Muslim rule. From the island, Ibrāhīm crossed the Straits of Messina, leading the *jihād* onto the Italian mainland where the army's success was limited by Ibrāhīm's own (nonviolent) death while besieging the Calabrian town of Cosenza in October 902.

Al-Nuwayrī concluded his section on the Aghlabids in Sicily with the observation, 'each of the governors … led raids, military detachments and the *jihād* against the enemy'.[12] Such a succinct postscript framed exclusively in terms of the military is befitting as a memorial to their historical legacy on the island. It is unfortunate that the sources have provided so little for the reconstruction of other aspects of this period, such as the administration and social history. Of this, the slim offerings which have appeared since the mid-1800s are hypothetical and remain contentious.

Local Christians under the Aghlabid Muslim rulers

Of modern, secondary sources which cover Islamic rule in Sicily, Michele Amari's three-volume work, the *Storia dei Musulmani di Sicilia*, first published between 1858 and 1872, is a rare example of a history which was founded on the pioneering scholarship in Arab-Islamic studies of the nineteenth century (of which Amari was himself a key figure), and which has largely stood the test of time. Its academic value was greatly enhanced by a revised edition published in Catania during the 1930s, which included extensive and erudite notes made by Carlo Alfonso Nallino. It is this edition of almost 2,500 pages which remains an essential foundation in its subject area to this day.

For the Aghlabid period, Amari proceeded on the assumption that the conquest, division of spoils and, hence, the subsequent patterns of settlement, land tenure and taxation had followed a 'classical' Islamic system as articulated by later medieval jurists such as al-Māwardī (d. 1058) for whom lawful conquest could occur in two ways: 'by force' (*ʿanwatan*) or 'by treaty' (*ṣulhan* or *ʿahdan*). So-called *fay'* lands were those which were taken by force or abandoned by their occupants and therefore became the property of the Muslim community. A rightfully appointed war commander was entitled to keep for himself one-fifth of this immovable booty, while the remainder was subject to division among the Muslim community by him into fifths. However, if the indigenous people had surrendered to Muslim rule and negotiated a treaty, then they were allowed to remain in possession of their land and retained the right to pass it on to their offspring. Had the imposition of such a clearly schematic distinction been made in practice, then this should also have determined the ways in which lands came to be settled or continued to be settled. Correspondingly, this would be reflected in the revenues collected from the lands and the people on them: for example, non-Muslim monotheists who had submitted to Muslim authority 'normally' paid the religious poll tax or *jizya* whilst also paying a land tax (*kharāj*). The presumed distribution of lands into allocations of variable size as part of the division of spoils to supporters would also be similarly affected by the ways in which the lands had come into the possession of the Aghlabid commanders. But, from the very outset, the conquest of Sicily had been a contentious affair. At the first siege of Syracuse, the Byzantines had, according to al-Nuwayrī, sued for peace by asking for a treaty (*amān*). Rather than oblige them as the legal expertise of Asad had prompted him to do, the army generals had disagreed. When Asad died, their first action was said to have been to tighten their grip on the city. Thus, after Asad's death at Syracuse, there was little to prevent the division of booty according to the will of the Aghlabid army answering to itself, its commanders and the exigencies of the situation on the ground.

It is possible to see a murky transition in the historiography as later sources struggled to arrange the legal history into a convenient order. The gravest concerns of all were expressed by a contemporary source. The Mālikī jurist and greatest legal authority in the Maghrib, Saḥnūn (d. 855), bluntly claimed that 'nothing in Sicily was conquered [legally] by the Muslims'.[13] This alone would seem to serve as the starkest possible warning against the assumption that a classically Islamic model could ever have been implemented. Concerns about the past, though still evident, had yielded somewhat in the hypothetical approach of the jurist al-Dāwūdī (d. 1011), whose ignorance of what had actually happened did not prevent him from giving opinions based on how he believed the law *should* apply in the light of the controversies presented to him by those seeking legal counsel – and some incidents to which they referred dated back almost 200 years. By the time that all resulting reports had passed into the chronicles of the twelfth and thirteenth centuries – and even later in some cases such as al-Nuwayrī (d. 1333) – it was possible for each to relate the history which underpinned any legal considerations of the here and now with a casual and unjustified certainty.

For most of the Aghlabid period, whenever the *jizya* was attested, it appeared in the context of the capitulation of an entire non-Muslim community: in effect, on such occasions it seems to have served as a simple, collective tribute payment. Those who submitted to Muslim authority paid the *jizya* and became *dhimmīs* – non-Muslim monotheists protected under Islamic law. The strong and reasonable assumption is that, in return, they preserved their religious autonomy within the parameters of usual Islamic practice. However, from Dāwūdī's later account (which may be referring to any period or place in the ninth or tenth centuries), more finely drawn distinctions can be inferred, and these appear to have been made irrespective of any difference between conquest by force or by treaty. First were those who paid the *jizya* as a capitation tax, but who could pass on or sell lands as they wished if they had rights over them. In other cases, Dāwūdī speaks of those who paid an unusual, split *jizya*. On the one hand, as non-Muslims, they paid a *jizya* as a head tax and, on the other, they paid a *jizya* on their lands which they were not free to sell. The aim may have been to discourage the Christians from abandoning (fertile?) lands completely or benefiting excessively from their sale. Given the absence of evidence to suggest to whom, when or where these distinctions applied, not to mention our ignorance of the levels at which the taxes were set, then beyond establishing the basic principle of the *dhimmī* system, further debate to separate semantics from substance is hypothetical – all the more so since most of the arrangements had probably been subject to bargaining on a local, ad hoc, basis in the first instance. None the less, in all cases, one immediate benefit of conversion to Islam (nominal or otherwise) was that the *jizya* was remitted, and for those who paid the *jizya* on their lands, these could be disposed of as the convert pleased. The likely overall result, corroborated by the later confusion related by Dāwūdī, was a strong tendency towards variety and diversity, the status of the land complicated further by religious conversions, tax evasion, non-observance of previous agreements and continual upheavals caused by local revolt, population displacement and returning refugees attempting to reassert their rights, of which we shall hear more later.

Both assessment for, and collection of, the *jizya* was likely to have been an erratic and problematic affair, particularly if there was little or no regular, centralised infrastructure to co-ordinate the collection of revenues. Evidence of written records cannot be inferred until the Fatimid period in the tenth century, but the implementation under the Aghlabids of at least a crude mechanism by which proof of *jizya* payment could be demonstrated is shown by the discovery of a small group of wearable *jizya* seals datable to *c.* 856–907.[14] Much later, the Cairo Geniza documents shed further light on the *jizya* as they revealed the complaints that Jewish merchants made to each other about high rates of taxation imposed on them in Sicily. However, these letters date mainly from the eleventh century when authority at Palermo (at least) had developed to a much higher level of administrative complexity, if not subtlety and competence, prior to its fragmentation and collapse into civil strife.

Legal theories aside, there were practical problems of governance in Sicily: not least how best to manage a frontier colony with a fractious, diverse and changing population. As Byzantine resistance showed, many of the larger towns had been reluctant to surrender to the conquerors, and, wherever capitulation occurred, a new set of challenges faced the Aghlabids. In a century of conquest driven by a 'booty economy', and in the apparent absence of any form of Sicilian Aghlabid 'state' or evidence of a regular administration, it is strongly presumed that there was widespread continuity of Byzantine practices – at least at the outset, and especially at a local level. Of this, even before the conquest, we know little, but we can infer that nothing could otherwise have intervened in any place which had not yet made its surrender. Thus, long after the launch of the invasion, many Christians were still theoretically under Byzantine control, but lived with the prospect of gradually encroaching Muslim rule, their responses to the situation determined by varying degrees of defensive and diplomatic ability. As ground was lost to the Aghlabids in the west, the Christians became more concentrated in the east, particularly in the mountainous strongholds of the north-east, the shortest distance from Byzantine south Italy with which there was always some communication, at least detectable through the remaining monastic houses.

From a Christian perspective, biographies of Sicilian saints' lives composed in Greek survive from the ninth and particularly the tenth centuries, including those of Leo of Catania (d. 780), Elias the Younger (d. 903), Leo-Luke (d. *c.* 910), Elias Speleotes (d. 960), Vitale (d. 990), Sabas the Younger (d. 990/1), Luke of Demenna (d. 993) and Neilos (d. 1005).[15] Most of these monks eventually fled and were in self-imposed exile in Calabria and beyond. Migratory movements can be detected within Calabria too as the Christian population later moved further north or into the hills in order to avoid falling victim to Muslim raids. Many of these saints had been associated with important monastic centres on the island, such as San Filippo at Agira, and came to play leading roles in the foundation and proliferation of important Greek-rite communities in south Italy especially around Mount Mercurion and later at the monastery of Rossano, contributing to the 're-Byzantinisation' of southern parts of the Italian peninsula from Sicily.[16] The status of monks as leaders and representatives can only have worked against the complete disintegration of Christian communities via religious conversion. Their role as intermediaries is shown by their high-profile diplomacy with the Muslims. For example, the *Cambridge Chronicle* recorded for the year 953–4 that a monk concluded a treaty resulting in the return of troops to Ifrīqiya. A more famous example is found in the tenth century, when a letter sent by Saint Neilos to the Christian secretary of the *amīr* secured the favourable release of a group of captured monks.

The gradual but steady diaspora of Sicilian holy men carried their ideas and influence far beyond Sicily, but they left behind the remains of an ecclesiastical infrastructure which had fallen into severe crisis under Muslim rule. However, its near total destruction outside parts of the Val Démone over the course of the Islamic period was not matched by the collapse of the population professing to be Christian. Thus, Christianity survived even if the number of functioning monasteries and churches fell to critical levels outside the north-east. Indeed, in spite of the long-term, socio-cultural processes of assimilation towards the language and religion of the new rulers, it is clear from evidence found in later periods that many local Christian communities were less resistant to cultural change than to religious change. By the mid-tenth century, the north-east of the island still retained communities in which Christian identities were conspicuously upheld. Arabic culture and Arabic as a lingua franca, however, increasingly came to predominate for the vast majority of the island's burgeoning population.

The emerging society of Islamic Sicily

The tensions of Islamic Sicily were interlinked religiously (Muslim–Christian), ethno-politically (Arab–Berber), regionally (Sicily–Ifrīqiya) and locally (Palermo–Agrigento and between the Val Démone, Val di Noto and Val di Mazara). These complex dynamics find muted expression in the partial and gradual transformation of Sicilian toponymy from its Latin and Greek precedents into Arabic. The clearest indicator which links the evolution of the society to the distribution of authority and settlement is to be found in north-eastern Val Démone, where Christian settlement and resistance was strongest and where there were the least number of Arabic placenames. The Val di Noto was more mixed, whereas the most dense clusters of toponyms of Arabic origin are to be found in the south-western third of the island – the Val di Mazara. Particularly striking in the western parts are placenames beginning with the Arabic noun *Qalʿa(t)* 'fort of', suggesting settlements with at least minimal defences or occupying a defensive site. In the modern period, these Arabic names are still easily recognisable with the prefix *Calta-*, *Calat(a)-*, *Cauta-* and *Carta-*. Predominantly, such forms are found in the Val di Mazara where there are approximately twice as many as there are in the Val di Noto and about six times as many as in the Val Démone. Not dissimilar proportions can also be seen in the terms *Qaṣr* (in the sense of a fort) and *Burj* (referring to a tower).[17]

There was a tendency for some forts in western Sicily to include Arabic personal names, as in Qalʿat Bū Samra, Qalʿat ʿAbd al-Mu'min, Qalʿat ʿAlī and Qalʿat Abī Thawr. In the apparent absence of bureaucratic offices to oversee grants of land to Aghlabid supporters, it is tempting to assume that these were names of army commanders to whom defensible locations and their surrounding areas had been initially awarded in the form of benefices. However, not all these forts were necessarily linked to the Aghlabid *jund*. For example, Qalʿat al-Ṭrazī (near modern Calatrasi), is reminiscent of the name of Palermo's *qāḍī* in the late Aghlabid period, Abū l-Qāsim al-Ṭrazī. From earlier times, the abbreviated name, Fīmī, as in Qalʿat Fīmī (modern Calatafimi), matches that used by the Arabic chroniclers to refer to the Sicilian rebel Euphemios.

The names of settlements, particularly open estates, are found mainly in documents supplied by the Arab–Norman bureaucracy of the twelfth century, but the vast majority of these villages can be presumed to have been established much earlier. There are obvious methodological problems with this type of retrospective reconstruction using names and settlements, not least the almost insurmountable task of ascertaining *when* a particular place was settled, and whether or not the name had changed to reflect later landholders. Moreover, key issues over their size, proliferation, period of indenture, or how many 'forts' were actually fortified in the Islamic period, remain unresolved. The lack of evidence reduces us to further generalisation and conjecture, but it is possible that some of these lands were granted free of all tax liability, effectively turning the population who lived on them into the landholder's own tenants. In which case, such lands were probably managed indirectly through the landholders' own agents.

Although power and wealth were inevitably more concentrated in some of the larger walled towns, there is no evidence in the Aghlabid period that urban sites developed into administrative centres or formed part of organised provincial structures. Such a movement in that direction can be detected for the first time only in the tenth century. Archaeological excavations in future will confirm or deny the physical extent and activities of some of these settlements, but it is not generally assumed that the existence of fortified sites led to a type of 'feudal' lordship in the countryside either. The leading families derived wealth from the land and from taking booty in military forays, but they continued to live in the cities, especially Palermo, which was always the focus of political power, and in which they played conspicuous roles. In this respect, the Aghlabids in Sicily appear to have avoided replicating the worst excesses of the *jund* in Ifrīqiya, where their control over the countryside had occasionally threatened to destabilise overall Aghlabid authority. Rather, it was farmer-colonists from Ifrīqiya, along with indigenous Christians, who lived and worked on the land itself. As we shall see, in some areas, for example around Agrigento, there was considerable competition over resources and over claims to various rights.

Outside the bigger towns, toponyms prefixed with *raḥl*, *manzil* or *qarya* (all referring to open, unwalled settlements), supported by archaeological finds and later medieval documentation, confirm the existence of a network of small, open settlements in the countryside. Indeed, if inheritance laws had been applied in the same way in which they were in Ifrīqiya, then we might expect the subdivision of land with successive generations, giving rise to a proliferation of small (perhaps very small) plots, such as perhaps those to which a tenth-century eye-witness, Ibn Ḥawqal, alluded in a cursory description of the outskirts of Palermo.

It was not untypical among the Arabic names of villages and estates to find the inclusion of a personal name probably echoing that of the landholder or colonist. Examples attested in later periods include Raḥl 'Abd al-A'lā, Raḥl 'Ammār, Raḥl 'Amrūn, Raḥl Ibn Sahl, Raḥl Ibn Baraka, Raḥl Bū Furīra, Manzil 'Abd Allāh, Manzil 'Abd al-Raḥmān, Manzil al-Amīr, Manzil Naṣr, Manzil Ṣāliḥ, Manzil Yūsuf and Manzil Qāsim.[18] Later references to plots of land (*ribā'*, singular *rab'*) also tended towards the use of personal names. For instance, and again in western Sicily, we find the plots of Bū 'Ajīna, the sons of 'Abd Allāh, the people (*ahl*) of Manzil 'Abd Allāh and Ibn 'Uqāba. Many rural estates and strongholds were known by Arabicised versions of Greek or Latinate names, most probably indicating that they were pre-Islamic settlements, rather than that they had been conceded to local Christians. Indeed, non-Arabic names associated with estates and towns, founded or renamed in the Islamic period, are conspicuous by their absence. Only in rare instances, for example *rabʿ Qusanṭīn* ('Constantine's plot of land'), can a non-Arabic name be found in western Sicily. Again, this late evidence comes from the 1100s and must, therefore, be used with the utmost caution when applied to earlier periods.

Some Sicilian toponyms evoke clan names, particularly those of Berber tribes and their branches. Assuming that the names of these places can be taken as dim indicators to illuminate something of settlement patterns, then native north African colonists can be inferred to have been more concentrated in unwalled estates on the agricultural lands of the west and south-west. Among the less controversial examples which match Berber tribal names and confederations are: Karkūd (from the Karkūda tribe); Melilli (Malīla tribe); Micchinesi (Miknāsa tribe); Manzil Zammūr (Zammūr tribe); al-Maghāghī (Maghāgha tribe); Ḥajar al-Zanātī (Zanāta tribal confederation); and Sinagia (attested in Latin but referring to a spring, perhaps named after the tribal confederation of the Ṣanhāja).[19]

Evidence from the Norman period provides a number of Berber personal names referring to tribes or clans from witness lists, the names of signatories and registers of men settled on lands. In the case of the latter, when individuals were later recorded by a third party in that period, tribal affiliations counted for little: such names are very rare in comparison with names that indicate a relationship with immediate family, a profession, a local place or a personal physical characteristic in the form of a nickname. For those required to identify themselves as witnesses or signatories, there was an aggrandising tendency to provide names that included a reference to a tribal confederation, usually some ancient Arab tribe or a Berber one. The most prevalent references to Berber tribes are to the Hawwāra, Zanāta and Lawāta and can be found mainly among private documents from the twelfth century. That a phenomenon like this should occur as late as the twelfth century suggests that such distinctions still mattered in the minds of their authors, even if these identities had long since ceased to play any obvious role in the politics or culture of the islanders.

The immigration of 'Berbers' and the roles they played during both the Aghlabid and subsequent Fatimid periods are ill-defined. First, there were those who had arrived as part of the original Aghlabid forces, and, as we have seen, within a decade of the fall of Palermo, some fought on their own account on the Italian mainland and founded the amirate of Bari. Later, with the accession to power of the Fatimids in Ifrīqiya in 909, and their conquest of Tāhart, Ibāḍī sources such as the *Kitāb al-Siyar* of al-Wisyānī and al-Shammākhī suggest some emigration to Sicily and settlement in the central area around Castrogiovanni. Indeed, several Berber tribal groupings attested in Sicily, such as the Barqajāna, Hawwāra, Lawāta, Nafzāwa, Zanāta and Zuwāwa, are attested and also known to have been involved at various times and in various places with the Ibāḍī movement across north Africa. Significantly, it was only briefly in the Aghlabid period that the Berbers in Sicily were conceived collectively and acting in concert, and even then, they feature momentarily in the slippery historical context of ructions within the army towards the end of the 800s. After this, neither Berber nor Ibāḍī immigration into Sicily made any political or cultural impact of consequence, bar contributing numbers to the growing Muslim population. For their part, the highly exceptional Kutāma Berbers served to fulfil specific military and political functions of the Fatimids and their viceroys during the tenth and early eleventh centuries.

The strongly Arabised and Arabicised island which the Normans found in the mid-eleventh century suggests that the effects of acculturation had gradually and relentlessly worn down any Arab–Berber ethnic distinction as the steady trickle of incoming migrants were absorbed into the background culture of the island. Thus, had Berber dialects ever been widely spoken in Sicily, they appear to have become muted quite quickly in the face of competition. This is also implicit in the observation of the eleventh-century Sicilian poet Ibn Ḥamdīs, who described his former homeland of Sicily as 'paradise', using the Arabic word *janna*, but when speaking of Ifrīqiya as his new paradise, he used a Berberised form (*tajanna*), indicating that Berber was spoken in Ifrīqiya in a way which it was not in Sicily.[20] If language use is to be linked to 'Berber' ethnic identity as one of its distinctive and persistent features, then the decline of Berber in Sicily might be taken as an indicator of assimilation towards Arabic as the prestigious tongue of the rulers and the island's lingua franca. Terms of Berber origin or usage are extremely rare in Sicily, although a small handful of Arabicised Berber words and usages exist.[21]

Whether the socio-political dynamics of Islamic Sicily were first and foremost ethnic is uncertain, and the extent to which it was tribal or supra-tribal remains an open question. There is, however, no doubt that important socio-political networks operated at the level of extended families or kin groups. Politically, only a fraction of the old Arab–Berber ethnic tension of the African continent was ever echoed in Sicily as these identities came to be dissolved by rivalries between layer upon layer of settlers and newcomers, and by power struggles between 'local' inhabitants whose blurred identities the Arab historiographers increasingly came to resolve into 'the people of Sicily' in contradistinction to 'the people of Ifrīqiya'. Indeed, by the end of the Islamic period, divisions over local political interests and issues of the day cut across all ethnic, sectarian and religious lines.

At the furthest reaches of Muslim rule – in the Val Démone in particular – later evidence for language and anthroponyms suggests that the indigenous population doggedly tried to maintain their own dialects and naming traditions, as well as their Christianity as badges which signalled defiance and, indeed, celebrated their very survival. Otherwise, the status of Arabic as the prestigious, cultural and inter-communal spoken language of the island gave rise to bilingual Christian communities (attested in later sources), affording them connectivity without conversion. Overall, for the Islamic period, the diverse shreds of evidence point to a range of reactions across the island from religious conversion to resistance or flight, but with many immersed in an assimilative 'melting pot'. Christians' knowledge and understanding of their new Muslim neighbours was relative to the degrees of separation between them; acculturation was, therefore, contingent on levels of social association and intermingling. Put crudely, the closer they were together physically, such as in western Sicily and some of the main towns, the more Arabicised and Islamicised they became over time.

Long-distance diplomacy: Bertha of Tuscany and the Caliph al-Muktafī

Neither Greek nor Arabic sources reveal the extent to which Christians allied themselves politically with Muslims at a local level. However, we are unusually well informed about a longer-distance relationship, as a remarkable and early example of diplomatic contacts and exchanges between Muslim and Christian powers shows. The so-called Bertha correspondence at the beginning of the tenth century between Lucca and Baghdad was first recorded in a little-known Arabic source, al-Awḥadī.[22] It originated from Bertha of Tuscany (d. 925), daughter of Lothar II of Lorraine and wife of Adalbert 'the rich'. In the year 906, Bertha sent a letter and gifts to the caliph, al-Muktafī (r. 902–8), in Baghdad. There, the letter, which was said in Arabic sources to have been composed in characters 'resembling Greek writing, but more regular', was translated into Greek by a non-specialist 'Frank' who was working in the caliph's robing store. From the Greek, it was rendered into Arabic. The gifts were conveyed by a certain 'Alī, a captured eunuch and commander of a naval detachment of the Aghlabid *amīr* Ziyādat Allāh III (r. 903–9). They included fifty swords, fifty shields, fifty spears, twenty garments woven with gold, twenty white eunuchs, twenty slave girls, ten large and fierce dogs, seven hawks, seven falcons, a silk tent, a multicoloured woollen garment, beads that drew out arrowheads and lance points and, finally, three Frankish birds which called out and beat their wings when presented with poisoned food.

The eunuch envoy also bore a confidential message which was to ask for friendship and a marriage alliance. Clearly, nothing came of this for the ambitious Bertha, who had optimistically described herself as 'queen of the Franks'. The incident, however, reveals her ignorance of the political dynamics of rule in Ifrīqiya and the Mediterranean by supposing that the Abbasid caliph in Baghdad had anything but theoretical influence in the region.

Certainly, this was an expensive attempt on Bertha's part to ingratiate herself with the caliph, offering objects that north Italians considered worthy and wondrous. The gifts would have allowed the caliph to participate in outdoor Tuscan life, but the conspicuous largesse was somewhat underwhelming by contemporary Abbasid standards. And a woollen jacket might have sent particularly confusing messages to a Muslim caliph. It also shows how ineffectual long-distance, inter-state diplomacy in this period was, since Bertha's mission had failed to engage in a sufficiently appropriate way with Islamic state machinery to be taken seriously. The only reason that the incident was recorded at all was the curious format and Latin palaeography of the letter itself, rather than the silk tent, eunuchs, hawks or spears that accompanied it.

Notes

1 Ibn ʿIdhārī, *BAS*² Ar. I:413–14; *BAS*² It. II:14.
2 On Muslim Malta, see Joseph M. Brincat, *Malta 870–1054. Al-Ḥimyarī's Account and its Linguistic Implications* (Valletta, 1995). Anthony Luttrell, *The Making of Christian Malta: From the Early Middle Ages to 1530* (Aldershot, 2002). See also the important review of Luttrell's volume by Jeremy Johns, *Journal of Islamic Studies*, 15/1 (2004): 84–9.
3 See Talbi, *L'Émirat aghlabide*, pp. 475–6 including references to other Arabic sources.
4 Recorded by Ibn al-Jazzār. See Talbi, *L'Émirat aghlabide*, p. 476.
5 See Brincat, *Al-Ḥimyarī's Account*, pp. 8–9 for parallel Arabic–English texts.
6 Ibn Ḥawqal, *Opus Geographicum (Ṣūrat al-Arḍ)*, J. H. Kramers (ed.), 2 vols (Leiden, 1938–9), II:204.
7 Talbi, *L'Émirat aghlabide*, p. 487. Amari-Nallino, *SMS*², I:583.
8 Only the opening section of the letter survives in Greek; see C. O. Zuretti, 'La Espuganzione di Siracusa nell' 880. Testo greco della lettera del monaco Teodosio', *Centenario di Michele Amari*, vol. 1, pp. 164–73. B. Lavagnini, 'Siracusa occupata dagli Arabi e l'epistola di Teodosio monaco', *Byzantion*, 29–30 (1959/60): 267–77. R. Anastasi, 'L'Epistola di Teodosio Monaco', *Archivio storico siracusano* (1978/9): 169–82. For an English translation of the Theodosios letter (in an otherwise quirky history), see F. M. Crawford, *The Rulers of the South: Sicily, Calabria, Malta*, 2 vols (London, 1900), II:78–98. For Amari-Nallino's discussion, see *SMS*² I: 541–51.
9 The *Cambridge Chronicle* (more correctly titled, the *Ta'rīkh jazīrat Ṣiqilliyya*), in *BAS*² Ar. I:190–203 (p. 193); *BAS*² It. I:277–93 (p. 279).
10 On Abū l-Thawr's defeat, see Ibn al-Athīr, *BAS*² Ar. I:289–90; *BAS*² It. I:398. No mention is made of Caltavuturo, although it is later attested as Qalʿat Abī Thawr by al-Idrīsī. See also Amari-Nallino, *SMS*² I:562.

11 Vasiliev, pp. 125–9. On the impact of saints and condition of the Sicilian Christians, see Amari-Nallino, *SMS*[2] I:606–63.

12 Al-Nuwayrī, *BAS*[2] Ar. II:489; *BAS*[2] It. II:125.

13 For the relevant passages in al-Dāwūdī in Arabic with a French translation, see H. H. Abdul Wahab and F. Dachraoui, 'Le Régime foncier en Sicile aux IXe–Xe siècles', *Études d'Orientalisme dédiées à la mémoire de Lévi-Provençal*, 2 vols (Paris, 1962), II:401–44 (p. 411).

14 Paul Balog, 'Dated Aghlabid lead and copper seals from Sicily', *Studi Maghrebini*, 11 (1979): 125–32.

15 For a survey of Sicilian Greek saints during the Islamic period, see G. da Costa-Louillet, 'Saints de Sicile et d'Italie méridionale aux VIIIe, IXe et Xe siècles', *Byzantion*, 29/30 (1959/60): 89–173. For the remarks of Amari-Nallino, see *SMS*[2] II:371–5 and II:456–75.

16 Léon-Robert Ménager, 'La "Byzantinisation" religieuse de l'Italie méridionale (IXe–XIIe siècles) et la politique monastique des Normands d'Italie', *Revue d'Histoire Ecclésiastique*, 103 (1958): 747–74.

17 See the especially useful discussion of fortifications and toponymy in Maurici, *Castelli medievali*, pp. 62–72.

18 By far the richest resource for these and other toponyms in western Sicily comes from the royal grants of lands and men made for the benefit of the church of Monreale in the 1170s and 1180s: see Cusa, *Diplomi*, pp. 134–286. See also the valuable resource of Girolomo Caracausi, *Dizionario Onomastico della Sicilia*, 2 vols (Palermo, 1993).

19 These examples of Berbers exclude the Kutāma, who were closely associated with the Fatimid dynasty. If the Latin toponyms Cutemi, Cutema and Gudemi are to be linked with them in Sicily, then they are unlikely to pre-date the tenth century. At least some Kutāma came to dwell on estates in western Sicily; three families are attested in the Corleone area in 1178. However, these are exceptional examples and not illustrative of wider settlement. On Berber toponyms, see Nallino's footnotes in Amari-Nallino *SMS*[2], II:53–5, and Leonard C. Chiarelli, 'The Ibādī Presence in Muslim Sicily', *Bulletin of the Royal Institute for Inter-Faith Studies*, 7/1 (2005): 69–89 *passim*. Chiarelli's article builds on Amari-Nallino's observations and ascribes important political and economic roles to the Sicilian Ibāḍīs, expressing less scepticism than some over questions of Siculo-Berber language and identity generally. For an alternative perspective, see Alex Metcalfe, *Muslims and Christians in Norman Sicily: Arabic-speakers and the end of Islam* (London and New York, 2003), pp. 60–7.

20 The poem was composed between 1121 and 1133 in honour of the Zirid *amīr* of Mahdiyya, al-Ḥasan, by Ibn Ḥamdīs, *BAS*[2] Ar. II:683; *BAS*[2] It. II:404.

21 The least controversial Berber term attested in Sicily is *farṭās* meaning 'mangy', which was frequently used as a nickname. Examples of Maghribi Arabic are better recorded, including *zawj* ('two'); *rayḥān* (meaning 'myrtle', not 'basil') and *ijjāṣa* (not *injāṣa*, for a pear orchard).

22 Several articles now deal with the Bertha correspondence. These include: M. Hamidullah, 'The Embassy of Queen Bertha of Rome to Caliph al-Muktafī billāh in Baghdad', *Journal of the Pakistan Historical Society*, 1 (1953): 272–300; G. Levi della Vida, 'La corrispondenza di Berta di Toscana col Califfo Muktafī', *Rivista storica italiana*, 66/1 (1954): 21–38; G. Inostrancev, 'Note sur les rapports de Rome et du Califat abbaside au commencement du Xe siècle', *Rivista di studi orientali*, 4

(1911–12): 81–5; C. G. Mor, 'Intorno ad una lettera di Berta di Toscana al Califfo di Bagdad', *Archivio storico italiano*, 112 (1953–4): 299–312; C. Renzi Rizzo, 'Riflessioni sulla lettera di Berta di Toscana al califfo Muktafi: l'apporto congiunto dei dati archeologici e delle fonti scritte', *Archivio storico italiano*, 159/1 (2001): 3–47.

3

Fatimid rule in Sicily

The Fatimid regime in Ifrīqiya and Sicily

In sharp contrast to the Aghlabids or, indeed, to any Sunnī Muslim regime, the revolutionary Fatimid dynasty pressed a claim to both worldly and spiritual authority drawn from a line of imāms descended from the Prophet Muḥammad's cousin and son-in-law, ʿAlī ibn Abī Ṭālib. They came to be called after ʿAlī's wife, Fāṭima, although some Arabic sources preferred the appellation of 'the ʿUbaydiyyūn', or followers of the Mahdī, ʿUbayd Allāh (more correctly, ʿAbd Allāh). Otherwise, they are generally referred to as Shīʿa, being followers of the *shīʿat ʿAlī* or 'faction of ʿAlī'. The Fatimids were Ismāʿīlī-s, deriving their more immediate lineage from Ismāʿīl, the son of the Sixth Imām, Jaʿfar al-Ṣādiq (d. 765), hence also their designation as 'Seveners'. The majority of later Sunnī sources speak of the Fatimids from a standpoint of politico-religious hostility. Rare, contemporary works, such as those of the Fatimid *qāḍī*, al-Nuʿmān; the memoirs of the eunuch administrator, al-Ustādh Jawdhar and the Cairo Geniza documents of Jewish merchants thus serve as an important counterbalance.[1]

The obscure circumstances of the Fatimids' rise in Syria and their links to other non-orthodox movements of the 800s and 900s need not be explored here. Suffice to note that their 'missionary' (*dāʿī*), Abū ʿAbd Allāh, was operating in Ifrīqiya from the summer of 893, and won the backing of the Kutāma Berbers in the hills of the Lesser Kabylia in eastern Algeria. To these tribesmen, the appeal of the messianic figure of the Mahdī carried more weight than any wider ideological opposition of the aspiring imāmate to the Sunnī Abbasid caliph in Baghdad. Kutāma support was not only central to the Fatimids' initial success in Ifrīqiya in 909, but also to their continued success in Egypt to where both they and the imām-caliph transferred after its conquest in 969. However, in Sicily, their privileged status and military roles marked them out as potential rivals to the old Aghlabid *jund*.

Fatimid Ismāʿīlī doctrine was not for the masses: on the contrary, it was open only to a select few. Very little can be said about Fatimid recruitment in Sicily itself, but a brief and lacunose entry in the *Cambridge Chronicle* for the year 960–1 recorded that Sicilian notables (*wujūh al-Ṣiqilliyyīn*) were taken to Ifrīqiya to be inducted into the 'school' (*madhhab*) of the imām-caliph.[2] Indeed, the intricate and distinctive aspects of Fatimid ideologies made no deep impression on Sicily. Ironically, it was the Norman kings of Sicily, with their hybrid notions of kingship, who led a revival of Fatimid art and administration in the twelfth century.

Even under Shī'īte Fatimid rule, both Sicily and Ifrīqiya maintained a strong presence of Sunnī Mālikī jurists. The origins of enduring Mālikī influence can be traced back to rivalries which developed during the Aghlabid period when the Ifrīqiyan *amīrs* on occasion preferred religious scholars of the Ḥanafī law school over their Mālikī rivals.[3] In Asad's day, a double election to the key position of *qāḍī* of Qayrawān served as a compromise but, more contentiously, in the early part of the ninth century, the Aghlabids followed the lead of the Abbasid caliph by favouring jurists with Mu'tazilite leanings. This controversial choice became a source of direct and sometimes deadly resentment as the politico-religious struggle in Iraq between ruler and religious scholars over issues of who was to interpret the law and scriptures was reproduced in provincial Ifrīqiya. It was a contest which the Mu'tazilites, with their rationalist philosophical interpretations of Islam, were to lose in both regions. The celebrated Mālikī scholar Saḥnūn had his predecessor, the Mu'tazilite *qāḍī* of Qayrawān, slowly beaten to death in an uncharacteristic act of vengeance. The victory for the Mālikīs strengthened their position across the Maghrib and later left them sufficiently steadfast in Sicily to sustain and build on their influence, even under the Fatimid dynasty, whose Ismā'īlī law and doctrines they firmly rejected, and whose keenly felt hostility they recorded in writing. Although Mālikī Palermo lived in the shadow of Mālikī Qayrawān, the island produced a number of religious scholars, particularly specialists in Islamic jurisprudence (*fiqh*), the *ḥadīth* or traditions of the Prophet, and Qur'anic recitation (*tajwīd*). Such alumni are known to us primarily from entries in biographical dictionaries (*ṭabaqāt*).[4] Religious scholars with experience in both Sicily and Ifrīqiya were not uncommon in the Fatimid period; for example, the chief magistrate of the appeals' court (*maẓālim*) in Qayrawān, Abū 'Amr al-Mal'ūn (d. 928/9), later became *qāḍī* of Sicily. The trend was a continuity from the Aghlabid period as shown by the example of the *qāḍī*, Abū l-Qāsim al-Ṭrazī, who had formerly held the important post of market inspector (*muḥtasib*) at Qayrawān.[5]

Shortly after the accession of the Mahdī in Ifrīqiya, a pro-Fatimid Sicilian faction emerged in Palermo which eased, at least initially, the transfer of power into the hands of a local choice and former governor, Ibn Abī l-Fawāris, in April 909. As in the Aghlabid era, the leading men of the island looked first to appoint their own choice as governor and then to seek retrospective approval from Ifrīqiya – which in this case they received until he was unexpectedly arrested in Ifrīqiya while travelling to see the Mahdī. According to al-Nuwayrī, the Mahdī had initially sent Ibn Abī l-Fawāris a letter urging him to launch raids by land and sea. This is probably the same letter (*kitāb*) quoted verbatim in the *Iftitāḥ al-daʿwa* ('The Beginning of the Mission') of the *qāḍī*, al-Nuʿmān (d. 974), in which the Fatimid hierarchy specifically addressed the 'people of the island of Sicily' also in the year 909. The aim of the Fatimid state to uphold its religious duty as defenders and extenders of the faith was unequivocally set out, in this case by pursuing an aggressively expansionist policy against the Byzantines:

> in virtue of your land's proximity to that of the Christians (*dār al-mushrikīn*), and for your struggle (*jihād*) against unbelief and oppressors, if God wills, I shall fill your island with cavalry and infantry of the faithful who will wage holy war for God and the duty of His *jihād*. Through them, God will empower the faith and the Muslims. Through them He will overcome polytheism and the polytheists![6]

The letter may have had a mixed reception in Palermo in spite of al-Nuʿmān's claim that it spread reassurance. On the one hand, it implied a military course of action which favoured the *jund*; but on the other hand, they were not to be alone in their endeavours, but supplemented by forces from Ifrīqiya.

Fatimid rule over Sicily began confidently and optimistically with the imposition of at least three appointments from Ifrīqiya. In 910, there arrived a new governor, Ibn Abī Khinzīr, originally from Mīla and formerly the governor of Qayrawān, where he was already a figure of hate for the Mālikī scholars. On arrival in Sicily, he directed the Sicilian Arab *jund* in destructive and successful raids against mainly Christian towns in the Val Démone. Around the same time, the first Fatimid *qāḍī* of Sicily, Isḥāq ibn Abī l-Minhāl, was appointed. He appears to have aroused less hostility and later served as *qāḍī* in Qayrawān. At Palermo, a high-ranking, and evidently unpopular, tax official bearing the title of *ṣāḥib al-khums* ('lord of the fifth') had been installed.[7] The inference from his title was that he was charged with the collection of a fifth of the taxes on all revenues, according to Shīʿīte law.[8] The Fatimids' ambitious plans for Sicily were interrupted when the Palermitans rose up around 911–12 against Ibn Abī Khinzīr, whose officials (*ʿummāl*) had 'oppressed the people'. Thus, what appears to have been a tax revolt forced his withdrawal from the island, and the *ṣāḥib al-khums* was put in charge for the interim until the arrival of another *amīr* appointed from Ifrīqiya in August 912, ʿAlī al-Balawī. Described as old and ineffectual, he soon appears to have lost control in Sicily: the violent death of the *ṣāḥib al-khums* in Palermo early in the following year for uncertain (but presumably tax-related) reasons and the expulsion of Ibn Abī Khinzīr's brother from Agrigento, opened the way for the emergence of a powerful rebel leader – Aḥmad Ibn Qurhub.

The revolt of Ibn Qurhub

Under the Aghlabids, Ibn Qurhub had been the governor of Tripoli. His clan name recalled both that of 'Uthmān Ibn Qurhub, who had taken over as governor from Abū Fihr in the 830s, and that of a certain Muḥammad Ibn Qurhub, an army commander who had orchestrated the siege of Syracuse in 878 and who may have been his father.[9] If these figures were all part of the same kin group of the Banū Qurhub, then they most likely had support from within the old Aghlabid *jund*, whose former privileged status was threatened by the new regime. However, there were wider political dimensions to Ibn Qurhub's revolt, which became apparent when he successfully appealed to the Abbasid child caliph, al-Muqtadir, and in return received regalia as visible proof of approbation and investiture. Thus, the revolt can also be interpreted in terms of a loyalist uprising playing on the Sunnī–Shī'a divide. Moreover, local support for Ibn Qurhub suggests a specifically Sicilian attempt to free itself from colonial rule from Ifrīqiya, against which two naval assaults were launched. In the first of these, Ibn Abī Khinzīr was killed. Ibn Qurhub's forces were also sent against the Italian mainland and secured a truce with the Byzantine *strategos* of Calabria by which the Sicilians were paid off with a substantial tribute payment in return for suspending the *jihād*.

As a local political phenomenon, the uprising had few of the essential cultural and anti-Arab ingredients of the *shu'ūbiyya* movements which had faded in the East in the previous century, but would re-emerge in al-Andalus in the next. Nor should it be mistaken for a movement for absolute Sicilian independence either, since some form of caliphal authority, or claim to caliphal lineage, was essential for Sicily's legitimate existence as a political entity. Thus, there could never have been a caliphate of Palermo following the model of Córdoba. Rather, Ibn Qurhub had opted for greater autonomy by seeking to put himself under the theoretical control of a distant ruler. The revolt also lacked a pan-Sicilian appeal in the sense that he did not attempt to gain support from the Christians, as his son's three-month siege of Taormina showed when it had shaken off rule from Palermo after its conquest by Ibrāhīm in 902. This failure further weakened Ibn Qurhub locally and his influence waned over a restless *jund* unable to raid the mainland. A Sicilian faction – about which we are told nothing – lost confidence and appealed to the Mahdī, who dispatched a new pro-Fatimid governor from Ifrīqiya with a force of Kutāma troops that landed at Trápani. Following a ruthless, six-month siege of Palermo, the revolt collapsed in 917 and Ibn Qurhub, his son, and Sunnī *qāḍī* were hauled off to Ifrīqiya where they were tortured over Ibn Abī Khinzīr's grave prior to their mutilation and public execution. The Banū Qurhub's legacy was not entirely snuffed out: when Ibn Ḥawqal visited Palermo in 973, he noted that one of the town's gates was named after them. However, in the immediate aftermath of the revolt, the power and status of the old Aghlabid Sicilian *jund* was significantly undermined with their partial disarmament, heavily punitive fines, and the new presence of a Kutāma garrison. The Fatimids' reissued their peace treaty (*amān*) to the island. This time they acted from a position of greater and lasting strength, as the ensuing twenty years of relative stability under the *amīr* Sālim ibn Rashīd shows.

Early Muslim contact with north Italy: Fraxinetum and Genoa

The Muslims' footholds at Táranto and Bari on the mainland had long since slipped away and, by 915, the fort known as *ḥiṣn Ghalyāna* had also been lost. Built under the Aghlabids by 883, it was strategically located at the mouth of the Garigliano river to the south of Gaeta. It was from here that raids had been launched against the monasteries of San Vincenzo al Volturno and Montecassino.[10] A Muslim presence was occasionally felt in the far north of the peninsula, although it was unconnected to either Sicily or Ifrīqiya. The town of Fraxinetum (modern La Garde-Freinet in southern Provence) had been founded by the late 880s and survived until the early 970s. It was said by Liudprand of Cremona to have been settled by a small group of Andalusi Muslims. They had established themselves sufficiently well to bind and loosen the bonds of regional power through alliances and by profiting from their ideal location to carry out sorties across the wider Provence area, including the Rhône valley.[11] By the end of the 920s they had been able to extend eastwards to occupy some of the Alpine passes of Piedmonte and to raid into Liguria.

Their raiding activities, potential for local disruption and the belief that the Umayyad caliph in Córdoba could exert influence over them, provided motives for the famously unproductive exchanges between the German Emperor Otto I (d. 973) and the Umayyad Caliph ʿAbd al-Raḥmān III al-Nāṣir (d. 961) in 953 when John, the abbot of Gorze, was dispatched to Córdoba. There, he was detained until being granted an audience three years later, by which time a Córdoban mission had also been to Germany and back. The catalyst for conclusive action, however, was not inter-state diplomacy, but the combined efforts of Church and nobility. The capture of the abbot of Cluny, Majolus, while traversing the Great Saint Bernard pass in the Alps in 972, and his subsequent ransoming spurred into action a coalition force of French barons led by William I of Provence, which decisively defeated the Muslims at Tourtour the following year.[12]

In Sicily, until the late 930s, the focus of Fatimid military operations had been away from its shores. The long governorship of Sālim gave rise to successful operations on the south Italian mainland and contributed to the perception that the frontier with the infidel was to be found somewhere on the continent, rather than in the Val Démone. The major campaigns of the 920s in Apulia, and particularly in Calabria, not only renewed the possibility for the *jund* to procure revenue from attacks, but also followed more coherent strategies of raiding than previously undertaken, aiming at specifically Byzantine territories in the south. Indeed, the reception of Bulgar emissaries at Mahdiyya may have prompted fears that a Fatimid–Bulgar alliance might have led to Constantinople's encirclement with hostile forces in the Balkans and south Italy had they not been intercepted on their return journey. The campaigns of the 920s were a great success for the Muslims. Among their victories was the capitulation of Táranto, Oria and their surrounding villages during 926, which were relieved from further advances only when an outbreak of disease forced a retreat. It is notable that the Fatimid fleets returned to Mahdiyya, not Palermo, with much of their human booty: behind the lines of the Muslim–Christian frontier, the island's colonial masters could also benefit substantially from successful expeditions on the Italian mainland.

A lasting truce concluded in 931–2 between the Mahdī and the Byzantine emperor represented a double victory for the Fatimids, who acquired the material benefit of gold payments in exchange for the deferral of further raids on south Italy, in addition to the kudos of forcing the first diplomatic recognition of the regime by Constantinople. As often, such a lasting truce had political consequences closer to home since it brought to an end the *jund*'s forays into Calabria and Apulia. In part, this explains an ambitious overseas operation in which a large Fatimid fleet plundered the north Italian port of Genoa and raided Corsica and Sardinia on its return leg during 934, showing the range and audacity of their naval power in the Tyrrhenian Sea. Imagined to be an island by the tenth-century Muslim cartographer Ibn Ḥawqal, the nascent Ligurian maritime state of Genoa would rapidly extend its influence in the eleventh century to become a pivotal player (along with Pisa) in the distribution of south Mediterranean power and commerce in the twelfth century.

Settlement, administration and disputes: the case of Agrigento

As noted in the *Cambridge Chronicle* for the years 926–7 and 931–2, Sicily had experienced the intervention – without major revolt – of officials from Ifrīqiya co-ordinating the collection of taxes. Another five years later, after two difficult seasons in which extreme rainfall caused widespread flood damage at Palermo, followed by a year of crop failures, a serious revolt against the *amīr*'s provincial official erupted in the Agrigento area. The ensuing siege of Agrigento was broken by the defenders, and the soldiers were pursued across the island where the insurrection rallied support among factions in Palermo, which now found itself under siege. An army led by the Qayrawān *jund* commander, Khalīl ibn Isḥāq, was dispatched to Sicily in autumn 937, and it was in the midst of this strife that a fortified governmental district, known as the Khāliṣa, was constructed at Palermo. The siege was eventually lifted but not before the revolt had spread across many of the key strongholds of western Sicily, including Mazara, Caltavuturo, Caltabellotta, Collesano and Platani. Notable too was a successful appeal by the rebels to the Byzantine emperor for assistance and supplies, though it was insufficient to prevent a severe famine recorded for the year 940, the same year in which Agrigento, the last fort to yield to Khalīl's forces, capitulated after a long siege. A triumphant Khalīl returned to Ifrīqiya in the following year, leaving behind a trail of destruction. To complete the victory, all the rebel Agrigentan leaders, who were obliged to accompany him, drowned en route when their ship happened to sink.

The direct cause of the insurrection may have been sparked by a tax-related issue. However, if the scrambled account of Agrigento reported by the jurist al-Dāwūdī is credible, then it had deeper roots which touched on sensitive questions of rival settlement on the land. Dāwūdī's account is rich in convoluted detail: it is useful, but treacherous. Even so, the long-running disputes at Agrigento illustrate a number of points about the haphazard nature, cause and proliferation of disputes conflict on the island. In addition, it highlights the difficulty of reconstructing aspects of such a history in the absence of detailed and reliable sources.

The discourse of those who presented their case to Dāwūdī in return for his legal opinion can be summarised as follows. First, the town was said to have been abandoned after its initial conquest. This was itself a significant claim given the implications of the crucial 'by force'/'by treaty' distinction in Islamic law by Dāwūdī's day. Moreover, Agrigento had been taken in 828–9 by an army under the Byzantine *Christian* rebel Euphemios, when fighting with the Aghlabids. These points aside, Dāwūdī was then informed that the town came to be occupied by a group of Muslims who were said to have done well for themselves on the land. After some unstated period of time had passed, the town attracted another group of settlers, whose cattle grazed on lands over which their owners allegedly had not been granted rights. These were joined by even more people using the land as pasturage. A conflict arose and the 'original' inhabitants defeated the newcomers. As a consequence, the dispossessed appealed to the island's (unnamed) ruler and the army was sent in. The original inhabitants were either killed or fled and the town was given over to the newer settlers. No mention of Christians was made, so all involved are presumed to be Muslim. This is broadly consistent with later charter evidence relating to Agrigento, which suggests that Christian settlement in this area was light until the 1190s. A long period of peace ensued until the settlers were required to cut wood for the *jihād* to help build a fleet. Having refused to supply the wood, which was normally plentiful on the island, Agrigento was repeatedly set upon by the army, who established a tight and devastating siege. Afterwards, the occupants of the town fled leaving it so seriously depopulated that the (unnamed) governor of the island ordered it to be resettled. And it duly was – with a *new* set of colonists from around Sicily as well as Ifrīqiya, who were drawn from a wide range of socio-economic backgrounds.

At this point, the descendants of those who had been evicted, reappeared. Along with some of the 'original' settlers, they attempted to re-establish their claim to rights over it. Some said they had bought land there from a man known only as al-Ṭiflī. Others, from a certain kin group, the Banū ʿAbd al-Ṣamad (who are most probably to be identified with a clan from the *jund* at Mīla in Ifrīqiya), claimed that they had agreed to buy it from Ibrāhīm II with their share of the booty after the fall of Taormina in 902, but the deal had fallen through and was in limbo. Unable to substantiate their claim, the land was declared to be the property of the Muslim community as a whole by the irate governor. At this same inquiry, one of the oldest *shaykhs* in Sicily recalled that his father had been the local official (*amīn*) for the town and was responsible for the *khums* and the *kharāj*, referring to two types of land/tax distinctions. His father had kept a tax register of the lands, until it was apparently burned during the revolt of 937–41 – a convenient and common device for retrospectively justifying a particular version of events. Dāwūdī's report then proceeded to speak of Taormina's evacuation and destruction (datable to 969) along with other Christian strongholds of Rometta and Aci in north-eastern Sicily, which the jurist's informants described as ruined, hence there was an attempt to repopulate them. In this case, men from Agrigento, who had been caught deserting from campaigns waged on the mainland, were compulsorily required to relocate. Ibn al-Athīr noted that the repopulation of Rometta occurred in the year 976–7 though, in the event, the Agrigentans objected to going there and were allowed to live in Syracuse instead. It was in the recent light of this final complication that the inquiry seems to have been convened, perhaps by then around the late 970s or early 980s, which is not too late to accord with the account given by the elderly *shaykh* who recalled his father's job of *amīn* forty years earlier, *c*. 937–41.

When situated in their wider historical context, these anecdotal reports – by far the most complete evidence available – add to a skeletal account of parts of the evolving Muslim administration. At the heart of this was, from the late 930s, the new district of the Khāliṣa, whose construction under Khalīl ibn Isḥāq had come at the grudging expense of the locals during the siege of Palermo.[13] Literally meaning 'the pure', the Khāliṣa has given rise to the name of the modern Kalsa district in Palermo, and was a term associated with early Ismāʿīlīsm. The name also carried a fiscal connotation, especially in the eastern provinces where it referred to lands held as the personal property of the ruler. This aside, it was not exceptional in the Islamic world to find fortified areas within a major political centre. The Palermitan version was described by Ibn Ḥawqal as an enclosed, stone-walled, trapezium shape, whose four gates comprised the Bāb al-Bunūd ('Gate of the Regiments'), the Bāb al-Ṣināʿa ('Gate of the Dockyard'), the Bāb al-Futūḥ ('Gate of the Victories' as in that of later Fatimid al-Manṣūriyya and, more famously, Fatimid Cairo) and, finally, there was the Bāb al-Kutāma, named after their Ifrīqiyan tribal soldiers.[14] The Khāliṣa was also furnished with a congregational mosque, an arsenal, prison, bath-houses and barracks. To describe it as a city within a city is slightly misleading since it risks exaggerating its (unverified but modest) size and degree of self-sufficiency. Besides which, although it was situated within the wider conurbation of Palermo, it lay outside the central space of the walled al-Qaṣr and al-Ḥalqa districts.[15] The fortified and isolated Khāliṣa housed and protected the nerve-centre of Sicily, the governor, his retinue, officials and bodyguard.

The division of labour in the Palermo administration remains obfuscated by lack of evidence, but it centrally oversaw an evolving, but evidently fragile, provincial structure managed in the regions by local tax officials who kept their own written records of different lands and the revenues due from them. It is not known whether these men were implanted in the provinces from the capital, or whether they were representatives formed from the old Aghlabid class of rural administrative 'agents'. Either way, they were evidently unpopular figures who were occasionally expelled during uprisings, perhaps suggesting that they were not themselves local to the areas they oversaw.

The little of the administration we can glimpse is derived largely from the problematic scenarios surrounding Agrigento: the extent to which such arrangements were reproduced elsewhere is unknown, although we shall revisit the question of provincial structures shortly. However, it is clear that the central administration and their designated representatives maintained at least a theoretical distinction between the *khums* ('fifths') lands on which the tithe of the *ʿushr* was paid on produce, and the *kharāj* lands on which the *kharāj* or 'land tax' was paid. The distinction matches, or was made to match, the legal difference between lands taken 'by force' (which were supposed to have been divided into fifths and belonged to the Muslim community as a whole), and those taken 'by treaty' with the indigenous population, who were entitled to stay on the land.

There is thus evidence of greatly increased bureaucratic activity in the Fatimid period, and clearer support for the existence of a regular administration in the tenth century which is absent in the ninth century. What is equally clear from Dāwūdī's account is the extent of radical change which competing cohorts of inhabitants had experienced. These changes were compounded over time by the arrival and departure of yet more new settlers who had a range of motives and aims for their move, and who could come from diverse regional, economic and religious backgrounds. We can only guess at the impressions which layer after layer of settlement had made on local identities, such as a sense of being 'Sicilian', as opposed to 'Ifrīqiyan'. However, this was to become an explosive issue bound up with taxation in the countryside in the following generation.

The Banū l-Ṭabarī revolt and rise of the Kalbids

In Ifrīqiya, the Fatimids were almost destroyed by a Kharijite uprising led by a Berber rebel, Abū Yazīd. This culminated in a siege during most of 945 of the imperial centre, al-Mahdiyya, bringing the imāmate close to outright defeat. In 948, the main palace and administrative centre moved to al-Manṣūriyya (near Qayrawān), which took its name from the imām-caliph, al-Manṣūr. It was against this backdrop of political insecurity at home and a Palermitan rebellion overseas, which gave rise to the Arab-Ifrīqiyan Banū l-Kalb as the Fatimids' viceroys in Sicily.

An uprising in 947 at Palermo highlights an important relationship between the Arab-Sicilian nobility and the Italian mainland. Truces with the Byzantines in south Italy provided leading families with material compensation for not being able to raid, or conduct the *jihād*. The Byzantines had stopped paying this peace payment (*māl al-hudna*), yet the *amīr* of Sicily was unwilling to pursue the matter. The *jund* were thus denied a key source of revenue, and violent disturbances against the governor and his soldiers broke out in Palermo at the end of Ramaḍān in April 947. They were led by the Banū l-Ṭabarī, a powerful kin group in Palermitan political circles. Their name suggests that they were originally from the eastern provinces of the Abbasid empire, linking them to the old Aghlabid *jund*. To quell the revolt, al-Ḥasan ibn ʿAlī, a former governor of Tūnis from the Arab clan of the Banū l-Kalb, who had distinguished himself in countering the Abū Yazīd uprising (with which al-Manṣūr was still occupied), was dispatched to Sicily. He arrived at Mazara in the spring of the following year.[16] It was into this safe pair of hands – a tried and tested Arab-Ifrīqiyan governor backed by the *jund* and Kutāma – that the amirate itself was to be entrusted until his death in 960. Thereafter, the arrangement became dynastic.

From 950, Kalbid relations worsened with the Byzantines whose military build-up in south Italy preceded a Fatimid–Kalbid expedition to Calabria. It is striking that even at the height of Islamic Sicily's power, the *amīrs* often had recourse to military assistance from Ifrīqiya. It is also notable how such campaigns resulted in mixed success other than securing payments from the besieged (for example at Gerace in 950 and 952) which was thought sufficient by the Muslim forces. Unusually, after this campaign a decision was taken to build a mosque at Réggio. An explicit account given by Ibn al-Athīr recorded its construction:

> [Al-Ḥasan] built there a large mosque (*masjid*) in the middle of the town. At one of its corners he constructed a minaret. He imposed conditions on the Byzantines (*al-Rūm*) that they should not prevent the Muslims from frequenting it, performing prayers there or giving the call to prayer; that no Christian should enter it; that any Muslim prisoner would be safe there regardless of whether he was an apostate or had persisted in his faith; and that if [the Christians] smashed a single stone of it, then every church of theirs in Sicily and Ifrīqiya would be demolished. The Byzantines met all of these conditions with mean-spirited humility. Al-Ḥasan remained in Sicily until [the imām-caliph] al-Manṣūr died [in 953].[17]

The choice of Réggio was significant as a site to carve out and defend a sacred space and place of sanctuary from the religious 'other'. The town, with its strategic location, had often been a bone of contention and had been besieged or sacked on at least five occasions between 918 and 930. On the other hand, to plant a symbol of the faith on the very tip of the Italian peninsula was a modest contribution to expanding the frontiers of Islam. Indeed, the reference to apostates among the south Italian Muslims implies that either captive Muslims had been converted, or that isolated pockets of Muslims on the continent had been absorbed into Calabria's background religious culture.

The short and successful mainland campaigns of the early 950s were sufficient to secure the Kalbids as capable and loyal Arab governors of Sicily. Their dynastic ambitions were sealed with the succession of Ḥasan's son, Aḥmad. It was under Aḥmad (r. 953–69/70) that Islamic Sicily would build on its bases of power, stability and wealth for which it was famed in the second half of the tenth century. Palermo's metropolitan development was enhanced with the building of two new city gates promoting connections and improving security.

It was the Kalbids' revenge attack on the south Andalusi port of Almería, following the Umayyads' chance interception of an Ifrīqiyan ship carrying diplomatic documents from Palermo in mid-955, that sparked a brief conflict between the Sunnī Spanish Umayyads in league with the Byzantines against the Fatimids, during which the Greeks sought to strengthen their positions in south Italy. Had the Kalbid mosque been intended as an indicator of their early efforts to stake a claim on a formerly non-Muslim area, then it was a short-lived venture, and one which was not to be repeated. The destruction of this religious boundary marker by the Byzantines, recorded in the *Cambridge Chronicle* for the year 955–6, was thus an act of deliberate retribution that consciously broke the unilaterally declared stipulations of sacrosanctity.[18] The hard fought campaigns between the Kalbids and Byzantines on the mainland over the course of the next two years thus maintained their religious edge and formed part of a wider, intermittent series of conflicts and truces.

The fall of Taormina and proposed reforms of the 960s

Byzantine power in south Italy, which had been restricted to southern parts of Calabria and Apulia, experienced an appreciable resurgence during the 960s. The fall of the Muslim amirate of Crete in March 961 to the energetic Greek general, Nikephoros II Phokas (d. 969), shortly followed by the capture of Cyprus in 965, substantially reduced the range of Muslim seapower in the eastern Mediterranean. The Fatimid–Kalbid raids on the mainland caused local disruption and a more northerly population displacement, but the Calabrian Greeks they targeted were by now increasingly secure in well-fortified, defensible, hilltop sites, even if raids from Sicily continued to be a hazard of south Italian life into the early eleventh century. The imām-caliph, al-Mu'izz (r. 953–75) had been unable to respond to the Byzantine attack in time to save Crete which, alongside Cyprus and Sicily, figured in medieval Muslim maps as three great circles across the Mediterranean. The loss of Crete and perception of a threat against Sicily may have prompted the Muslims to press for an outright conquest of Sicily by attacking the vital Christian stronghold of Taormina in the Val Démone. After a thirty-week-long siege, the fall of Taormina at the end of 962 was commemorated by the renaming of the town as al-Mu'izziyya. But unlike al-Mahdiyya and al-Manṣūriyya before it, al-Mu'izziyya was not to become an imperial city. Rather, the imām-caliph received a booty of 1,570 prisoners, perhaps one-fifth of the remaining population, after which the town was resettled – for the time being – with Muslim colonists.

In August of the following year, the stronghold of Rometta, the last bastion of Christian-led resistance on the island, was under attack in what was becoming a definitive struggle for control of the north-east. Nikephoros Phokas, now emperor, ordered a huge Byzantine relief operation, possibly with the aim of retaking Sicily. Landing at Messina in October 964, its initial success resulted in the town's capture and that of other sites around the Val Démone, only to be defeated at Rometta itself. The Byzantines retreated first to Messina, then to Calabria, but when they tried to cross back to Messina in 965, the army was cut to shreds at a celebrated victory known as the 'Battle of the Straits' (*waqi'at al-majāz*). This expensive disaster came during a rare period when Constantinople had turned its attention away from protecting Thrace from the Bulgarians or their south-eastern borders from the Muslims, and had prioritised the defence of the central Mediterranean sufficiently to dispatch a major force. Their defeat ended in a truce favourable to the Fatimids, perhaps convincing them that the Byzantines were weaker than they actually were. Indeed, it may have been a dangerous delusion given the relative ease with which the Muslims had lost control of Messina. This alone should have sounded a warning since it was the obvious point of entry for any invasion force arriving from south Italy.

Between April and early May of 962, Sicily's population benefited from the decision of al-Muʿizz to celebrate the circumcision of his three sons by distributing largesse to families across the empire. Thousands of children were operated upon in a huge propaganda exercise to bind the community closer to the Ismaʿīlī imām-caliph.[19] The claim in later sources, such as in the *Book of Gifts* and al-Maqrīzī, to the effect that Christians and Jews were also required to be circumcised is unlikely. Figures cited in the sources also appear exaggerated (and are inconsistent anyway), but there is no doubt that the event involved a vast drain on central treasury resources. More importantly, a census was held in order to calculate expenditure and some half a million gold dinars were transferred to Sicily and given to families in proportion to their wealth. Unlike Ifrīqiya, where the en masse proceedings had been conducted centrally in Mahdiyya, the distribution of funds in Sicily had been made via regional officials, which suggests that they had convened many local events. If the sources can be trusted on this, and assuming that all the largesse reached its intended recipients, then Sicily's capability to organise such events presupposes a certain degree of administrative co-operation and information gathering in the regions for which there is only slender evidence otherwise.

The mid-960s was also a period in which there was widespread resettlement after the successful campaigns in the Val Démone. This affected at least some of Christian-dominated towns such as Taormina, Rometta and Aci. Taormina, for example, had been repopulated with Muslims after its fall in 962, but within two years was razed and evacuated, probably as part of the accord with the Byzantines. It was not resettled until at least the summer of 976.[20] In the meantime, and coinciding with the Fatimids' preparations to transfer their seat of power from Ifrīqiya to Egypt, there had been a centrally imposed effort towards strengthening the system of provincial administration in Sicily. According to al-Nuwayrī (the only source to record this), in the year 967, al-Muʿizz sent a mandate to the Sicilian *amīr* Aḥmad ordering him to set about the immediate rebuilding and strengthening of the walls of Palermo.[21] In addition, in each province (*iqlīm*) of the island, he was told to construct a fortified city with a mosque and *minbar* (pulpit), and to encourage the inhabitants of each province's satellite villages to settle in the cities. Aḥmad was said to have immediately dispatched *shaykh*s around the whole island to oversee the reforms. The report confirms the view that some form of provincial government existed prior to the order, but it also shows that it did not amount to much in terms of defensive or religious infrastructure. Indeed, the absence of congregational mosques in some of the island's main towns – almost a century and a half after the fall of Palermo – suggests a retarded development of religious institutions outside the metropolis. Alternatively, and quite plausibly, the Fatimid Sicilian provinces were small in size and large in number. In any case, al-Muqaddasī, writing in the late 980s, made no mention of mosques except the one in the Khāliṣa. He did, however, note that within the walled fortress of Petralia there was a church.[22]

However, the evidence also corroborates the move away from the booty economy of the Aghlabid period towards a more integrated system of central and regional government under the Fatimids. Such proposed reforms were consistent with the type of domestic policies that al-Muʿizz had been pursuing throughout the 960s, yet it is unclear whether his order was ever implemented effectively in Sicily as the proposed building work has left barely a trace in the way of discernible archaeology. Of the principal, fortified towns listed by al-Muqaddasī, most had ancient and/or Byzantine origins anyway, and relatively few were far inland, as one might have expected in a provincial network intended to envelop the whole island.

Even if the provincial centres were walled, the dynamics of this reform were not analogous to the *incastellamento* movement on the south Italian mainland, and did not give rise to 'feudal' lordships or local strongmen with private militias in the regions.[23] On Sicily, the secular officials who managed the provinces did not have parallel military obligations, nor were they involved with the dispensation of justice, which was the preserve of trained Muslim jurists. Rather, the greatest effect of this reform was to empower the provincial officials entrusted with the co-ordination and collection of taxes from local *shaykh*s on behalf of the governor. It is probable that, by overestimating tax returns, they were able to absorb some of the revenues for themselves before passing the rest up to the central administration in Palermo. There was thus a delicate relationship of interdependency between the central administration, their regional officials and the local *shaykhs*. It was one which relied on mutual trust, co-operation and tacit understandings.

In part, the Byzantines' truce with the Fatimids in 967 came as a response to the presence of a German Ottonian army in south Italy and the rare coincidence of perceived mutual interests. For their part, the Byzantines were unwilling to allow the Germans to take a hold in areas where they too harboured ancient claims to rule. For the Fatimids, an orderly Sicily and peaceful relations with their old Byzantine sparring partners on the mainland suited their preparations for the final transition from Ifrīqiya to Egypt between 969 and 973, taking with them the amassed wealth of their treasuries, regiments of the Kutāma and some of their most capable administrators. The intention in Sicily and Ifrīqiya was to leave these regions in the hands of trusted dynastic rulers: the Kalbids in Sicily and the Zirids in Ifrīqiya. Both these regimes were able to govern with an unprecedented degree of independence as viceroys. However, the move introduced a fundamental change in the relationship between Ifrīqiya and Sicily. Formerly motherland and colony respectively under the Aghlabids and Fatimids, these two regions had experienced high levels of *inter*dependence. Now, with the gradual, long-term loosening of the bonds between them and their masters in Cairo, relations between Sicily and Ifrīqiya became increasingly ambivalent and, at times, antagonistic.

In 969, the *amīr* Aḥmad, along with his entire extended family and all their wealth, were favourably recalled to Ifrīqiya, depriving them (at least for a brief while) of the opportunity to make Sicily their own personal amirate when the Fatimids moved to Egypt. Such was Fatimid confidence that the island had been consolidated and made safe – and perhaps to avoid a strong, independently minded, military ruler – that they put it in the hands of a bureaucrat, called Yaʿīsh, who was a Kalbid 'client' (*mawlā*). Fighting broke out at Palermo which spread to Syracuse. In both cities, it was the Kutāma and their *mawālī* supporters who absorbed the brunt of the violence and were said to have suffered great losses in the process. Unable to gain any control or to rein in those who were illegally attacking Christian strongholds which were still under the peace agreement, al-Muʿizz intervened to depose Yaʿīsh as administrator and restore Kalbid dynastic rule with the appointment of Aḥmad's brother, Abū l-Qāsim, as *amīr* in 970.

From his accession until his death in 982, the lack of dissent towards Abū l-Qāsim's authority indicates that he had neutralised the opposition of the island's key factions. He was also quick to return to the old strategies and politico-economic dynamics of raiding. Thus, a Kalbid army commander, rather than a trusted bureaucrat, was invested with power over the frontier colony. Until the early 1000s, when storm clouds began to gather, Kalbid control held firm during a period which, with hindsight, was Muslim Sicily's finest. However, it was also a time when commercial opportunities to establish control over the central Mediterranean trade routes were on offer; when nascent Italian maritime city-states were only beginning to gain in reach and confidence, and when the Italian mainland was still relatively weak. Kalbid Palermo, which Ibn Ḥawqal described on his visit in April 973, was close to its peak, but even at such heights, it was underdeveloped and its rulers appeared unwilling, then increasingly unable, to capitalise on Sicily's geopolitical strength by imposing their control over a much wider range.[24]

The development of urban space

The greatest city of Christian unbelief in Italy – *Rūmiya* or Rome – and the home of its imām (that is, pope), was imagined by Muslim authors to be perfectly round, just as the carefully planned, circular cities of the Islamic world, notably al-Manṣūriyya of the Fatimids and its precursor, Abbasid Baghdad.[25] Casually confused with 'the other Rome' (that is, Constantinople), intellectualised accounts by authors such as al-Harawī (d. 1215) and al-Qazwīnī (d.

1283) blended accurate experiences with legendary and metaphorical elements. However, the city's circularity bore only a superficial similarity to the harmoniously proportioned, Islamic ideal. Rather, it was an inferior, even perverse, counterpart and was depicted as an escapable maze with only a single entrance and exit. An explanation for this curious arrangement can be found in al-Birūnī's, *History of India*, written by 1030 and, therefore, the earliest known account of its type. Rome, it was claimed, had become confused with a fortress that existed at the cupola of the earth (the Laṅkā) to where the Hindu devil, Rāvaṇa, retired after he had carried off Rāma's wife. This circular, labyrinthine stronghold was called Yāvana-koti (from the Sanskrit for 'the fort of the Greeks/Europeans'). According to the exceptionally well-informed Birūnī, it was mistakenly believed by Muslims to refer to the city of *Rūmiya* itself.[26]

For its part, Kalbid Palermo, like many of the larger cities on the island whose growth had accelerated under Aghlabid and Fatimid rule, was partly superimposed over the outline of an old Byzantine town. Over time, it had swollen into the shape of a gnarled rectangle, encompassed by two rivers, regulated by seasonal flows, which spliced its suburbs roughly along a south-west, north-east axis. In the Islamic period, when political and commercial expansion focused on burgeoning western Sicily closest to Ifrīqiya, the rise of Palermo was accompanied by the resurgence of western coastal towns such as Trápani, Marsala, Mazara, Sciacca and Agrigento. New settlements of varying sizes were also found in fertile rural areas inland, especially in western Sicily, where Christians were inconspicuous. On the other hand, the eastern cities such as Syracuse, Catania and Messina featured less prominently in the political, cultural or economic revival, and those in the hills, such as Taormina and Rometta, are mentioned almost exclusively in the context of conflict with the Christians. It is no surprise that most visitors from Islamic lands sojourned mainly in the metropolis itself.

In 973, eight months after al-Muʿizz's relocation from al-Manṣūriyya to Cairo, the celebrated cartographer, traveller, merchant and Fatimid spy, Ibn Ḥawqal, witnessed Arab-Muslim Palermo at its prime. Such was his vitriolic criticism and unrelenting gibes at both the place and its people, that the account was not a glowing endorsement. Nor was it wholly reliable, even if he had met men of consequence like one of his named informants, 'Uthmān bin al-Kharrāz, the head of their judges (*wālī quḍā'i-him*). Ibn Ḥawqal's pro-Fatimid sympathies account for many of his hostile perspectives, especially his criticisms of the Mālikī jurists and educated classes, whose ignorance of doctrine and general dim-wittedness he sought to ridicule with varying degrees of subtlety. The rapidity with which the arts and the Islamic sciences had flourished and successfully reproduced (but had not outshone) similar outputs of other great Muslim cities may have prompted his disparaging comments that their pretence to knowledge had no firm foundations whether acquired from books or from their daily lives. The extent of their ignorance was merely multiplied, in his view, by the proliferation of family mosques of which the city was full, and were more numerous than in any other except Córdoba – another bastion of Sunnī orthodoxy.

Throughout this period, Sicily tended to remind Muslim observers of the backwaters of the Islamic world. They did not intend this in terms of material wealth, but rather in terms of its population and their customs. Its Byzantine elements, from its large Christian minority to its remaining arts and architecture, were a mixed experience too. On the one hand, they were evidence of conquest and proved the successful, recent expansion of Islam, but they also marked out the island as being on the verge of unbeliever territory. Other Arabic sources, such as Yāqūt, who had consulted Ibn Ḥawqal's work, even thought Sicily was a society of converts.[27] For Ibn Ḥawqal, the pretentious and poor Arabic spoken by the urban elites and the 'incoherent deaf mutes' who populated the countryside was symptomatic of the deficient state of education and understanding. However, it may actually reveal something of the long-term processes of imperfect assimilation and acculturation. In an intriguing passage, and one of many later paraphrased in the anonymous compilation known as the *Book of Curiosities*, Ibn Ḥawqal reported that interfaith marriage was endemic outside the main cities: boys were brought up as Muslims like their fathers, but girls in the same families were Christian like their mothers.[28]

In some cases, visits to the supposed tombs of revered, ancient thinkers enhanced the island's interest for Arab-Muslim audiences. Ibn Ḥawqal told how Aristotle was somehow suspended in a wooden beam in the main mosque of Palermo in a rare, and implicitly reverential, Muslim view of a once, non-Muslim, religious space. The account serves as one of the earliest sources for the dissemination of similar, supernatural suspension legends in Arabic romances.[29] The same imagery was alluded to in the twelfth-century Byzantine Greek epic of the *Digenēs Akrítēs*.[30] The thirteenth-century traveller, al-Harawī, who set out to describe pilgrimage sites, stated emphatically that the visitor could find the tomb of the Greek physician Galen at Misilmeri on the Palermo–Agrigento road. However, such interest in the Greeks should not be overstated. Even if a translation of Dioscurides' treatise on botany and herbal remedies from Greek into Arabic for the Spanish Umayyad caliph, 'Abd al-Raḥmān III, was made with Sicilian Greek help, and Ibn al-Jazzār's medical treatise, the *Zād al-musāfir*, had been translated into Greek in the late-tenth century in Calabria, at no point did Sicily become a major transmitter of classical Greek or Latin knowledge to Arab-Muslim audiences. Nor was Fatimid–Kalbid Sicily the medium for the spread of Arabic works beyond Muslim lands. However, translations, including an Arabic and Greek version of Luke's gospel made in 1043 by a single Christian scribe, Euphemios, provide important evidence for Arabic–Greek bilingualism during the Islamic period.[31] Whether this extended beyond the Christian community is doubtful: Theodosios' implication that a Muslim commander had threatened the humble bishop of Syracuse in Greek when he had taken refuge in the siege of 878, bears the hallmarks of a literary fiction. Indeed, there is scarcely any evidence that the Sicilian Muslim elites absorbed cultural influences 'from below'.

The evolution of the *ribāṭ* system

Al-Muqaddasī was among those who noted Sicily's reputation as a frontier zone and a place of continual holy war. Indeed, the island in the late 900s still bore the scars of civil strife, as a deserted village outside the capital perhaps suggested. One of the results of Sicily's place as a war zone was the development under the Aghlabids of military fortifications known as *ribāṭs*. These were, initially at least, a type of fortified monastery designed to attract dutiful benefactors and to house men for the *jihād* as well as to protect the frontiers. The surviving *ribāṭs* at Sousse, for example, from where the Sicilian invasion force was launched, had been substantially refitted in 821 a few years before the conquest. This fortification system was transferred to Sicily where *ribāṭs* were said by Ibn Ḥawqal to be a notable feature of coastal military architecture. They were perhaps especially common along the northern seaboard warning Palermo of Byzantine attacks coming from the Italian peninsula. They are also likely to have served as focal points of frontier communication and exchange. In addition, they can be presumed to have attracted inalienable grants and pious endowments of property to the extent of achieving a high degree of self-sufficiency.[32] Sicily's numerous *ribāṭs* provoked bitterly hostile opinions from our pro-Fatimid eye-witness of the 970s, Ibn Ḥawqal, who regarded them as places for the unemployed, the idle and the pseudo-pious. By this time, the *ribāṭs*, like those in Ifrīqiya, had become places of refuge for Sunnī opponents of the Fatimid regime, and had lost their original prowess and purpose. Indeed, it is significant that in Sicilian dialect of the 1500s, *murabitu* referred to someone who abstains from wine, suggesting an association derived from (Muslim) piety and asceticism, not a frontier defender or a *mujāhid* fighter.[33]

The coastal location of many *ribāṭs*, and their functional transition between the Aghlabid and Fatimid periods, account for why they played no significant combat role in either the fragmentation of the island from the 1030s, nor in its defence during the Norman conquest post-1061 when much of their remaining wealth and landed properties must largely have been broken up. Nor are they mentioned by al-Idrīsī in his mid-twelfth-century description of the island. However, lists of taxpayers from the 1180s from western Sicily contain names associated with them (for example, 'the *murābiṭ* at Calatrasi' and 'the shaykh *al-murābiṭ*'), signalling their survival under later Christian rule in western Sicily.

This is supported by the evidence of a famous Andalusi traveller, Ibn Jubayr, who visited Sicily during 1184–5 and stayed overnight at a certain Qaṣr Saʿd, located on the coast and possibly to be identified with Castello Sólanto, near Santa Flávia, to the east of Palermo. He reported that the building dated from the Islamic period, and he appears to have been describing a working *ribāṭ* complete with its own *imām*, high fortifications, a robust iron gate, fine mosque and well-appointed quarters for those who stayed there.[34] At Palermo itself, it is likely that the jail and garrison of the Sea Castle in Norman times, as well as the church of San Giovanni dei Lebbrosi (see fig. 4 on p. 139), called *chastel Jehan* by Amatus during the Norman siege of the city in 1071–2, were both formerly *ribāṭs*.[35]

Around the *ribāṭ* that Ibn Jubayr described, numerous tombs of the faithful, were sufficiently important to have attracted visitors. The entire area, including a nearby spring called ʿAyn al-Majnūna ('spring of the mad woman'), exuded a certain *baraka* or blessedness from all directions. Further descriptions of holy sites are included in al-Harawī's early thirteenth-century work on tombs of the pious and of famous warriors who had fallen in Sicily. Such *zāwiyas* as had survived were, therefore, still a distinctive feature of Siculo-Ifrīqiyan sepulchral architecture in the early 1200s. From around that same time, a boundary description relating to Paternò makes mention of a Muslim cemetery, including a *qubba* (here in the sense of a small mausoleum) and the enclosure of a *ribāṭ* or *zāwiya*.[36] Indeed, some type of *qubba* now forms part of the Capuchin monastery at Mineo. This is possibly connected to Asad ibn al-Furāt since al-Harawī reported that he was buried in a town between Catania and Castrogiovanni, suggesting that his body had been transported to Mineo, where the army had headed after his death at Syracuse. However, other surviving *qubbas* in Sicily are either very late (for example, Santa Crescenza at San Vito lo Capo), or they are linked to water, rather than interment (for example, La Cuba di Cíprina at Vícari: see fig. 3 on p. 139). A strikingly similar structure of a well in rural Sardinia (Mitza S'Orrù at Ortacesus) – possibly Byzantine, but certainly not Muslim – further obfuscates the diverse origins and functions of miscellaneous constructions referred to as *qubbas* in Sicily.

Trade, commerce and the economy

Sicily of the 970s was a place in which those wishing to avoid military service could pay the Kalbid rulers a tax instead. Ibn Ḥawqal noted with some disdain that they had put up for sale (*bāʿa*) their obligations set down by God, engaging more in the marketplace than on the battlefield where there were only raids, not a sustained *jihād* to open up new lands for Islam. The term *bāʿa* not only had commercial connotations, but also political ones since its root conveys the notion of concluding contracts, oaths and allegiances. Within a century, the implosion of Kalbid power and the rise of Palermo's last *amīr*, an overseas merchant, Ibn al-Baʿbāʿ, on the eve of the city's capitulation to the infidels, seems to bear out the consequences of Ibn Ḥawqal's prescient thesis.

For the time being, the metropolis of the 970s gave the impression of a well-populated, prosperous Arab-Islamic city. As he described, and as the Cairo Geniza documents amply corroborate, the many producers, middlemen and merchants gave Palermo its bustling character. They concerned themselves with taxes and prices, quantities and qualities and all the demands of local and long-distance markets. Indicative of the island's thriving and integrated economy, which linked rural supply with urban and overseas demand, Ibn Ḥawqal painted a lively picture of the varied markets that filled large areas around the capital. These included sections for olive-sellers, flour merchants, money-changers, pharmacists, blacksmiths, burnishers, grain markets, embroiderers, fish sellers, spice sellers, butchers, fruit and vegetable stalls, potters, bakers, rope-makers, perfume sellers, shoemakers, tanners, carpenters, joiners, woodworkers, cotton merchants and ginners.

The presence of a money-changers' market served a complex series of needs, providing mechanisms and media of exchange. Sicily had a robust bimetallic economy: that is, one based on the circulation of both silver and gold. The money-changers thus also supplied vital liquidity to the local and wider economy. The financial instrument of the *qirāḍ* (broadly equivalent to the Latin *commenda*) provided capital from investors, including the state and its officials, to merchants and speculators for the purpose of trade in which profit and risk were shared, significantly encouraging business associations and ventures.[37] These arrangements wove together the interests of those engaged in trade with those who operated in the political arena. Indeed, political stability and co-operation were prerequisites for a flourishing economy, and successful expansion into new markets via trade or conquest could return great profits. Conversely, political upheaval or excessive taxation were likely to result in the contraction or displacement of commercial activity.

After the failure of the Aghlabids to establish the gold dinar in Sicily, the Fatimids introduced a new, but smaller gold coin, the *ṭarī*. In Latin this was known as the *tarenus*, in Greek the *taríon* and, as this coin was equivalent to a quarter dinar, in Arabic it was also known as the *rubāʿī*.[38] Issued initially from the mint in Palermo, it was especially associated with production under the Fatimids in keeping with the greater level of fiscal complexity found in the region by the tenth century. During the same period, the *tarì* was also commonly found on the mainland, being first attested at Amalfi in 907, Salerno in 911 and Naples in 935. Although this phase of its circulation coincided locally with the Muslim fortress on the Garigliano prior to its destruction in 915, the coin is more closely linked to trade in the towns of the Amalfi coast where, from the ninth century and in spite of Muslim raids, there is ample evidence for commercial exchange. The *tarì* remained in wide circulation in Sicily and south Italy under the Normans and Staufen rulers until it was discontinued by the Angevins. For small transactions, glass jettons may have been used, partly at the expense of a payments in kind system of equivalence in a region which, by comparison to anywhere in the Latin West, was highly monetarised.

In spite of Sicily's economic prowess, according to a problematic passage in the *Book of Curiosities*, the personal wealth of the urban elites was limited and stood in contrast to the large amounts that were raised via customs duties, tithes and taxes.[39] These were reported as: the 'fifth' (*khums*); taxes on produce; a tax on wine; the poll tax (*al-jawāl*); a sea tax; general tribute payments; and a duty on fishing. If this data ultimately came from Ibn Ḥawqal, then it may have been drawn from his lost 'book' on Sicily, which he claimed to have written. Indeed, he had quoted similar information for the Maghrib, where he also had access to high-ranking informants.[40]

In the countryside, the so-called 'green revolution', that is to say, the processes by which the rural economy had been transformed by new technology, such as systems of hydraulic irrigation, is attested in both documentary and archaeological sources.[41] Water from streams, rivers, springs and wells – to which access rights were an important issue – was directed through ditches and channels which criss-crossed the countryside, supplying the fields, population and many watermills and market gardens. Watercourses also served as convenient points of reference in later boundary descriptions, which is our main source for establishing their existence. Cool water was channelled underground via excavated *qanāt* or canals, some of which can now be visited around Palermo. Terms of reference to hydro-technologies account for surviving Sicilian dialect terms of Arabic origin too. Examples which have not become entirely obsolete include, *gattuso* (from the Arabic *qadūs*, referring to an interconnecting, ceramic section of a water conduit); *saia* (a water channel from the Arabic *sāqiya*); and *gébbia* (Arabic *jābiya*, an artificial reservoir). The Islamic period also witnessed the introduction of new crops and plants, such as citrus fruits and date palms. Henna for dyeing was attested around Partinico and in western Sicily; mulberry trees on which silkworms fed were not uncommon. In addition, we find sumac seeds for cooking and tanning, as well as sugar cane. At Palermo, Ibn Ḥawqal had admired the papyrus plants which were cultivated within the city and used to manufacture rope and, more importantly, high-quality paper rolls for the administration. These, the first paper documents to be attested in medieval Europe, were technologically advanced, but were too fragile to stand the test of time.

The island's rich mineral resources and deposits were recorded by Yāqūt to include antimony, silver, iron, lead and ammonia salts in addition to alum and green vitriol, whose properties were known to alchemists and dyers.[42] Close, off-shore fishing for tuna and swordfish as well as stock-rearing can all be inferred to be important subsectors of the economy. The enormous potential of the Sicilian countryside, already rich in natural resources, not only satisfied internal demand, but was also the source of raw products which could be exported. In some cases, these were refined and then sold on at a premium. However, Sicilian industry was less prominent than its export of raw materials. In relatively few cases, such as the production of Sicilian ivory caskets, trade and industry were contingent on imported goods which craftsmen then reworked locally for the export market.

For their part, the merchants, by knowing their prices and constantly moving capital around the western and central Mediterranean between Spain, Sicily, Ifrīqiya and Egypt, were able to turn a profit through arbitrage and the satisfaction of supply and demand for different products in different places. This was in spite of incurring tax and customs duties, and risking loss, damage or confiscation of goods in transit. Regularly mentioned among the Geniza documents of the Jewish merchants (in addition to the material resources cited above) were the import–export of plants for medical and industrial purposes, precious metals and minerals, basic and luxury foodstuffs, spices, gums and resins and raw and finished textiles. More specifically, these included aloe, colocynth, asafoetida, celandine, flax, amber, cedar resin, coral, lapis lazuli, kohl, vermilion, pearls, rose oils, soaps, civet perfume, musk, myrrh, furs, leather, skins and hides, wax and honey, pepper, cinnamon, carobs, cumin, galangal, ginger, laurel, mace, mastic resin, sandalwood, diachylon, almonds, cherries, figs, gallnuts, nutmeg, saffron, tamarind, borax, sulphur, bronze, mercury, tin, copper, zinc, acorns, barley, rice, olives and olive oil, plums, prunes, raisins, wine, cloths and textiles, cotton, felt, muslin, tar and pitch, timber and ceramics. The cost of carry was reflected in the price; thus, the immense purchasing power of a state such as Kalbid Sicily in a location where several trade routes intersected, played a vital role in importing rare and expensive commodities which had been transported across long-distance trade routes, passing through the hands of several merchants along the way.

The site of origin and production of Sicilian commodities was largely in the countryside where there was little demand for their use. Rather, that demand was located in the cities and overseas. Thus, it was in Sicilian ports where the Fatimid–Kalbid state and its officials were best positioned to tax the outgoing flow of raw materials and incoming flow of refined goods. This they did with characteristic and unrelenting vigour. Where business and politics combined, we are afforded rare glimpses of what was undoubtedly a wider picture: namely, that the *amīrs* and their officials had their own commercial interests embedded in certain sectors of the Sicilian economy. This is most clearly seen in the example of the Ifrīqiyan administrator Jawdhar, whose logging business in the Val Démone is known to us from his letters.[43] In the following generation, the *amīr* Yūsuf, was said to have possessed at least 13,000 pack animals when he was governor in Sicily, but died a pauper when he transferred to Egypt.[44] Here it is possible to make a connection between Jawdhar's interests in the rural economy and Yūsuf's in stock breeding, since both were essential resources for the military and the *jihād* – timber for the building of warships, pack animals for the transportation of equipment. Such was the scale of investment in these cases, it is not unreasonable to infer that the Kalbid state, its *amīrs* and officials (from both Sicily and Ifrīqiya) had not only invested in, but had also perhaps monopolised, key areas of the internal economy. What we do not know is the extent to which Ifrīqiyan-based investors and concessionaires continued to uphold business interests in Sicily after the Fatimids had left for Egypt.

Of all goods destined for overseas that emanated from Sicily, one stands out as having a particular importance: durable Sicilian grain. This was exchanged for Ifrīqiyan gold on a grand scale. Not only was this big business, but it was also one that had a political dimension by virtue of Sicily's more robust agricultural sector than their Ifrīqiyan allies who, in frequent times of shortage, relied on importing provisions from their northerly neighbours. The division of the old Fatimid state may have left late Kalbid Sicily militarily indebted to Ifrīqiya, but Ifrīqiya, from the 1000s, would become increasingly reliant on Sicily's economic and agricultural wealth to sustain it.

Notes

1 No work exists which deals specifically and exclusively with the Fatimids in Sicily. On the Fatimids in Ifrīqiya, the following monographs provide detailed, scholarly accounts with full bibliographies: Heinz Halm, *The Empire of the Mahdi: The Rise of the Fatimids*, trans. M. Bonner (Leiden, 1996); Michael Brett, *The Rise of the Fatimids. The World of the Mediterranean & the Middle East in the Tenth Century* CE (Leiden, 2001). For the above-mentioned sources, Al-Nuʿmān, *Iftitāḥ al-daʿwa wa-ibtidāʾ al-dawla*, F. Dachraoui (ed.) (Tunis, 1975), translated by Hamid Haji as *Founding the Fatimid State: The Rise of an Early Islamic Empire* (London, 2006). *Sīrat al-Ustādh Jawdhar*, M. K. Husayn and M. A. Sha'ira (eds) (Cairo, 1954); trans. Marius Canard, *Vie de l'Ustadh Jaudhar* (Algiers, 1958). For a survey of contemporary events on the mainland, see G. A. Loud, 'Southern Italy in the tenth century', in *New Cambridge Medieval History*, T. Reuter (ed.), III:624–45.

2 *Cambridge Chronicle* in *BAS*[2] Ar. I:202; *BAS*[2] It. I:292.

3 William Granara, 'Islamic education and the transmission of knowledge in Muslim Sicily', in *Law and Education in Medieval Islam: Studies in Memory of Professor George Makdisi*, Joseph E. Lowry, Devin J. Stewart and Shawkat M. Toorawa (eds) (Warminster, 2004), pp. 150–73; G. Marçais, *La Berbérie musulmane et l'Orient au Moyen Age* (Paris, 1946).

4 Annliese Nef, 'Les élites savantes urbaines dans la Sicile islamique d'après les dictionnaires biographiques arabes', in *MEFRM*, 116/1 (2004): 451–70. See also M. De Luca, *Giudici e giuristi nella Sicilia musulmana – Notizie e biografie estratte dal Tartīb*

al-Madārik (Palermo, 1989), and (in Arabic) Ihsan Abbas, *A Biographical Dictionary of Sicilian Learned Men and Poets* (Beirut, 1994); and Granara's article (above, note 3) for a summary.

5 Al-Mālikī, *Riyāḍ al-Nufūs*, *BAS²* Ar. I:219 and 222; *BAS²* It. I:313 and 317; Amari-Nallino, *SMS²* II:7.

6 *The Founding of the Fatimid State*, pp. 182–3. The Arabic text, translation and comments are also found in Antonino Pellitteri, 'The historical-ideological framework of Islamic Fāṭimid Sicily (fourth/tenth century) with reference to the works of the Qāḍī al-Nu'mān', in *Al-Masāq*, 7 (1994): 111–63 (pp. 147–8).

7 Jeremy Johns, *Arabic Administration in Norman Sicily: The Royal* Dīwān (Cambridge, 2002), p. 24.

8 Halm, *Empire of the Mahdi*, p. 177.

9 Ibn 'Idhārī, *BAS²* Ar. I:412; *BAS²* It. II:7. Talbi, *L'Émirat aghlabide*, p. 487, n. 2.

10 For a survey of contemporary events on the Italian mainland in general, see G. A. Loud, 'Southern Italy in the tenth century', in *New Cambridge Medieval History*, T. Reuter (ed.), III:624–45.

11 Book 1 of Liudprand of Cremona's, *Antapodosis*, in *MGH*, *SRG*, 41:3–6; translated into English as *The Complete Works of Liudprand of Cremona*, trans. Paolo Squatriti (Washington DC, 2007), pp. 41–8, 94–5, 142, 176, 181, 221 and 225.

12 On the Fraxinetum Muslims, see Gabriele Crespi, *The Arabs in Europe* (New York, 1979), pp. 63–74; for the Fatimid context of relations with Spain, see Brett, *Rise of the Fatimids*, pp. 226–31.

13 Ibn al-Athīr, *BAS²* Ar. I:299; *BAS²* It. I:413–15.

14 On the Khāliṣa and its gates, see al-Muqaddasī, *The Best Divisions for Knowledge of the Regions (Aḥsan al-Taqāsīm fī Ma'rifat al-Aqālīm)*, trans. Basil Collins (Reading, 2001), p. 192, and Ibn Ḥawqal, *BAS²* Ar. II:121–2; *BAS²* It. I:19–20. After the Norman conquest of Palermo in 1072, the 'Gate of the Victories' came to be incorporated into the chapel of Santa Maria della Vittoria where it has partially remained until today. For the unusual, purported, customs of Kutāma hospitality, see the reprinted and expanded Jaubert translation of *Idrîsî, La première géographie de l'Occident*, Henri Bresc and Annliese Nef (eds) (Paris, 1999), pp. 174–5.

15 For an updated account of medieval Palermitan topography and its twelve gates, see Jeremy Johns, 'Una nuova fonte per la geografia e la storia della Sicilia nell' XI secolo: il *Kitāb Ġarā'ib al-funūn wa-mulaḥ al-'uyūn*', in *MEFRM*, 116/1 (2004): 409–49, (pp. 419–20). For a later, revised article by the same author with important new observations, see 'The new "Map of Sicily" and the Topography of Palermo', in *Nobiles Officinae: perle, filigrane e trame di seta dal Palazzo Reale di Palermo*, Maria Andaloro (ed.) (Catania, 2006), II: 307–12. Still highly valuable for its map and detailed description of medieval Palermo is G. M. Columba, 'Per la topografia antica di Palermo', in *Centenario della nascita di Michele Amari*, G. Bestia *et al.* (eds), 2 vols (Palermo, 1910), II:395–426.

16 For a genealogy of the Kalbid *amīrs*, see C. E. Bosworth, *New Islamic Dynasties* (Edinburgh, 2004), p. 33.

17 Ibn al-Athīr, *BAS²* Ar. I:303–4; *BAS²* It. I:421.

18 *Cambridge Chronicle*, *BAS²* Ar. I:201; *BAS²* It. I:291.

19 Al-Nu'mān, *al-Majālis wa-l-musāyarāt*, al-Ḥabīb al-Faqqī, I. Shabbūḥ and M. al-Ya'lawī (eds) (Tunis, 1978), p. 291.

20 On the repopulation of Rometta in 976–7, see Ibn al-Athīr *BAS*² Ar. I:310; *BAS*² It. I:432.

21 Al-Nuwayrī, *BAS*² Ar. II:494–5; *BAS*² It. II:134–5.

22 Muqaddasī, *Best Divisions*, pp. 191–2.

23 For an introduction to *incastellamento* (or the lack of it) in Islamic Sicily with a good bibliography to several works published in conference proceedings, see Ferdinando Maurici, *Castelli medievali in Sicilia. Dai bizantini ai normanni* (Palermo, 1992), pp. 13–89.

24 For a compressed form of this economic argument, see Brett, *Rise of the Fatimids*, pp. 360–3.

25 For Italian translations and bibliography, see Adalgisa De Simone and Giuseppe Mandalà, *L'immagine araba di Roma: I geografi del Medioevo (secoli IX–XV)* (Bologna, 2002). In English, see the older article by R. Traini *Rūmiya* in *EI*² VIII:612.

26 For the observations of al-Birūnī in English translation (omitted in the above works), see *Alberuni's India*, trans. Edward C. Sachau, 2 vols (London, 1888. Reprinted in a single volume, Delhi, 1989), pp. 306–7.

27 For the idea that Sicily's population were converts to Islam, see Yāqūt, *BAS*² Ar. I:124; *BAS*² It. I:202–3.

28 Book 2, chapter 12 in the 'Book of Curiosities' gives a description and map of Sicily. See Emilie Savage-Smith and Yossef Rapoport (eds.), *The Book of Curiosities: A critical edition*. World-Wide-Web publication at: www.bodley.ox.ac.uk/bookofcuriosities (March, 2007) (accessed on 2 April 2008).

29 For suspension legends, see H. T. Norris, 'The suspended "superhuman" in medieval Christian and Muslim legend and romance', in *al-Masāq* 6 (1993): 77–94. The Palermo experience may possibly have also inspired the dangling of the ruler of Gurgan in Iran in the celebrated mausoleum of Gunbad-i Qabus, built in 1006–7.

30 'May you come to Palermo, see the mosque (το μασγιδίον)/May you worship, Emir, the Hanging Stone (τὸν κρεμάμενον λίθον)/Be found worthy to adore the Prophet's tomb', *Digenes Akrites*, ed. and trans. John Mavrogordato (Oxford, 1956, reprinted 1999), ll. 101–2, p. 9.

31 Vera von Falkenhausen, 'The Greek presence in Norman Sicily', in *The Society of Norman Italy*, G. A. Loud and A. Metcalfe (eds) (Leiden, 2002), pp. 256–7.

32 On Ifrīqiyan *ribāṭ*s under the Fatimids, see Heinz Halm, *The Empire of the Mahdi. The Rise of the Fatimids*, trans. M. Bonner (Leiden, 1996), pp. 221–38. For a survey, see G. Marçais, 'Note sur les Ribàts en Berbérie', in *Mélanges d'histoire et d'archéologie de l'Occident musulman, I, articles et conferences de Georges Marçais* (Algiers, 1957), pp. 23–36.

33 *Il Vocabolario siciliano-italiano di L. C. Scobar*, Alfonso Leone (ed.) (Palermo, 1990), p. 182, and also Caracausi, *Arabismi*, p. 297.

34 For the description of the *ribāṭ* at Qaṣr Sa'd, see Ibn Jubayr, *BAS*² Ar. I:90–1; Eng. trans. Broadhurst, pp. 345–6. If the Sicilian *ribāṭ*s were like those in Ifrīqiya, they may have been particularly busy during Ramaḍān: see Hady Roger Idris, *La Berbérie orientale sous les Zīrīdes Xᵉ–XIIᵉ siècles*, 2 vols (Paris, 1962), II:689.

35 Amatus, VI:16, p. 156. Amari-Nallino, *SMS*², III/1:119–20. Maurici, *Castelli*, p. 62. The existence of the modern Sicilian surname 'Morabito' might also be interpreted as an indication of the obscure Muslim–Christian transition from the late 1000s. Intriguingly, this surname is strongly and almost exclusively associated with Messina and southern Calabria.

36 '*tendit per viam cumbe* [i.e. *qubba*] *et redit ad murum marabotti*', see C. A. Garufi, 'I de Parisio e i de Ocra nei contadi di Paternò e Butera', *Archivio Storico Sicilia Orientale*, 10 (1913): 346–73 (p. 370).

37 On the overlapping relationships between the commercial and political in Fatimid Ifrīqiya and Egypt, see the important discussions in Brett, *Rise of the Fatimids*, pp. 235–56. For an introduction to the *commenda* in the Islamic world, see A. L. Udovitch, *Ḳirāḍ*, in *EI*[2] V:129.

38 S. Stern, 'Tari. The Quarter Dinar', *Studi Medievali*, 3/11 (1970): 177–207. Vincenza Grassi, *ṭarī* in *EI*[2], X:238. On medieval Sicilian coinage, see Lucia Travaini, *La Monetazione nell'Italia normanna* (Rome, 1995), also P. Grierson and L. Travaini, *Medieval European Coinage*, 14 Italy III (South Italy, Sicily, Sardinia), (Cambridge, 1998).

39 www.bodley.ox.ac.uk/bookofcuriosities (accessed on 2 April 2008).

40 For an overview of the imām's revenues in Ifrīqiya, see Halm, *Empire of the Mahdi*, pp. 355–65.

41 Andrew M. Watson, *Agricultural Innovation in the Early Islamic World* (Cambridge, 1983), and 'A medieval green revolution. New crops and farming techniques in the early Islamic world', in *The Islamic Middle East, 700–1900*, A. L. Udovitch (ed.) (Princeton, 1981), pp. 29–58.

42 For the island's mineral resources, see Yāqūt, *BAS*[2] Ar. I:125; *BAS*[2] It. I:203–4.

43 *Sīrat Jawdhar*, pp. 119, 121, 127–8 and 136–7; French trans. M. Canard, *Vie de l'Ustadh Jaudhar*, pp. 180, 183, 194–5 and 209 (letter nos. 53, 56, 67 and 77).

44 Al-Nuwayrī, *BAS*[2] Ar. II: 497; *BAS*[2] It. II:140.

4

The civil war and Sicilian *ṭā'ifa* period

The origins of political, economic and military crisis

According to the *Book of Curiosities*, the constellation of Leo rose obliquely over Sicily. The malign celestial influence this exerted on the mundane rendered the island's population difficult to govern and given to rebellion. The anonymous Arabic author of this particular section of the Sicily account was most probably writing towards the end of the debilitating rebellions-cum-civil strife which engulfed Muslim Sicily from the mid-1030s. Yet, this disastrous state of affairs appears unavoidable only with the benefit of hindsight, and had taken almost two generations to manifest itself in repeated crises. Given its apparent economic and military strength, the atmosphere of the Kalbid golden age in the late 900s was reminiscent of the halcyon days which preceded the downfall of the Spanish Umayyads in a near contemporary period. However, both the late Kalbid economy and the military were held in a delicate balance and required careful handling.

Analogy and horoscopic speculation aside, the Fatimids' move to Egypt by the 970s not only distanced Sicily from Ifrīqiya from a political standpoint, but it also removed high-minded, politico-religious ideologies from the western and central Mediterranean. In addition, it displaced the economic centre of gravity away from the entrepôts of exchange, supply and consumption further towards the east. In so doing, it revealed, for a brief time, the potential for a politico-economic reconfiguration of the south-central Mediterranean. This opportunity also presented risks for both Sicily and Ifrīqiya. With regard to their allegiances, the Kalbid *amīrs* remained faithful viceroys of the Fatimids. Indeed, the horizons of their economic aspirations remained as limited as their political outlook, and they failed to seize the opportunity to profit from controlling a wider ebb and flow of goods, or to develop industries to higher levels, preferring instead to appropriate the island's wealth via taxation and to whittle it away on their own lifestyles and palaces. As such, the late Kalbids continued to oversee the island in its role as a great producer and supplier of materials, but they did not become involved in the profitable carriage of goods across the Mediterranean and to Egypt, even if, in some cases, they had awarded themselves concessions over the source of supplies. Nor did they attempt to expand into new regions via conquest, favouring instead a strategy of raid and retreat operations against the south Italian mainland. When the *amīrs* eventually began to experience financial crisis in the early 1000s, they resorted to firmer control *internally* over the island's terminals of production, where their direct power was at its weakest. In order to empower the centre and generate greater revenues for the treasury at Palermo, they exerted fiscal pressure down the lines of supply and into the countryside. The attempted central imposition of tax reforms unsettled the *shaykhs*, tenants and sharecroppers of rural Sicily, which resulted in violent and repeated revolts of both the great and the small, significantly undermining the *amīrs*' political credibility, and ultimately loosening their grip on power. Similarly, when they looked to tighten control over the points of exchange in the marketplace with increased taxation, the effect was detrimental to the commercial economy which relied on the circulation of wealth. Over time, the *amīrs*' central power and aggressive strategies in the markets and ports appears to have oppressed the traders. Thus, when merchants briefly achieved self-government in Palermo, they did so only in the late 1060s, when central authority had collapsed. The sources barely allude to these indicators of impending crisis, but concentrate on the disintegration of the army, the crises in the countryside and conflict beyond the island. Indeed, the Kalbids' lack of imperialistic ambition had another consequence for this history because, unlike the Zirids, they did not nurture their own dynastic historians. As such, the sources also tend to view the decline into civil war in terms of Ifrīqiyan–Sicilian political relations.

The late Kalbid dynasty experienced pressures from both internal dissent and external assault, but there was no single point at which these were to prove insupportable. Nor was the island's eventual downward trajectory constant, and, even in crisis, dangerous attacks could still be inflicted by land and sea. In the twenty-five years up to 1040, by which time the political unity of the island had begun to fracture and would not reset, the Kalbids had survived three serious rebellions, two Greek-led invasion attempts, the arrival of large numbers of Ifrīqiyans and the presence of a hostile Zirid army. Viewed in this wider context, the 'Norman conquest' of the island from 1061 – often considered as a point of radical disjuncture by European historians – merely continued processes of political change as Kalbid power crumbled in the midst of socio-economic upheaval while a new leadership and politico-religious dynamism slowly emerged. Assessing nascent Christian rule over the Sicilian and, later, the Ifrīqiyan Muslims is best undertaken from the perspective of the preceding civil war, albeit with its many uncertainties, together with the ways in which Muslim factions struggled to empower themselves at each other's expense by resorting to alliances with the Zirids, Byzantines and, eventually, the Normans themselves. Each of these parties found themselves willingly lured onto the island by the prize of controlling Sicily which – even in times of turmoil – was still considerably richer than any other area of the Latin West.

Prior to the increasing difficulties on the island, Kalbid rule in the later tenth century was not without its successes, notable amongst which was a victory over an Ottonian army. Following his coronation in Rome in February 962 with the imperial title, the German king, Otto I, sought alliances with Capua–Benevento in an attempt to extend his rule into Byzantine south Italy during the campaigns of 967–8. His son and heir, Otto II, married into the ruling house of the Byzantines sealing a fragile peace, but he found a pretext for another conquest attempt in the Muslim campaigns waged in Apulia and around Calabria from 976 under the Kalbid *amīr*, Abū l-Qāsim. Otto's offensive followed the death in March 981 of his southern ally, Pandulf I 'Ironhead', the prince of Capua and Benevento, but resulted in a German defeat at the hands of a Muslim army in southern Calabria in July 982. The Kalbids retired with the death on the battlefield of Abū l-Qasim, and so let slip any chance to build on their victory. The battle was perhaps all the more significant given Otto's untimely death the following year, which put the German throne in the hands of a minor, effectively halting, for the time being, their ambitions in south Italy.

The following generation witnessed periods of political stability, especially under its popular *amīr*, Yūsuf, who was given diplomatic investiture and the title 'Confidence of the State' from the Fatimid imām-caliph al-ʿAzīz on the death of Yūsuf's father, Jaʿfar, in 990. The narrative sources recorded Yūsuf's peaceful command over the island until he suffered a stroke in 998 which left him paralysed down the right-hand side of his body. The memory of him as a wise and respected ruler has been unfairly preserved in Arabic sources, perhaps to highlight the contrast with the antagonistic tendencies of his offspring who succeeded him. In their different capacities, Yūsuf's four sons would oversee the final descent of Islamic Sicily into civil war, after which the Kalbids do not appear to have played any further political role on the island.

There were signs even in Yūsuf's day that the Kalbids had already gained an unpopular reputation for their elaborate court life, and also as parasitical extractors of the island's taxable wealth who were reluctant distributors of it. A highly stylised anecdote in the biographical dictionary of Ibn Khallikān relates how a wandering Ifrīqiyan poet was paid off and bundled out of Palermo on Yūsuf's orders for fear that he was spreading malicious rumours about the *amīr*'s tight-fistedness. Certainly, financial considerations, especially concerning the army and the taxation of those who either held land or derived wealth from it, can be seen as intertwined with issues of political instability under Yūsuf's reviled successors.

With Yūsuf incapacitated, his son Jaʿfar (r. 998–1019) was nominated by his father, and received investiture from Cairo with the honorific title of 'Tāj al-Dawla, Sayf al-Milla' or 'Crown of the State, Sword of the Faith'. For the sake of clarity, Ja'far is sometimes referred to as Ja'far II to distinguish him from his grandfather (d. 985) and nephew (d. 1035) of the same name. There were two major revolts during Ja'far's time as *amīr* for which he is best remembered in the sources. Both revolts had serious consequences for the Kalbid army, its recruitment, funding and the tensions which emerged between the 'people of Sicily' and 'the people of Ifrīqiya', shortly before the Kalbids were to enter into an important alliance with the Zirids which introduced a period of Ifrīqiyan influence and intervention in Sicily.

Revolt and reform in the Kalbid army in Sicily

In January 1015, Ja'far's brother, 'Alī, led an unsuccessful rebellion which set in motion important changes in the basis of political and military power on the island. 'Alī was said to have gathered his army outside Palermo and to have been in league with 'Berbers and slaves (*'abīd*)', although we are not told either who they were or what the cause of this alliance was.[1] The *'abīd* in this context probably refer to sub-Saharan infantrymen; the reference to Berbers here implies that they were the remnants and descendants of Kutāma troops and their 'clients' (*mawālī*). After the battle, in which 'Alī's forces were defeated, all Berbers on the island were said to have been deported along with their families. The rebellious slaves were executed along with 'Alī himself, to the great pain of his hapless father. The evidence for continued Berber presence on the island post-1015 strengthens the idea that the expulsion of Berbers in this case referred specifically to Kutāma elements in the army. As a consequence, the army (*jund*) was reduced in size and comprised only 'the people of Sicily'. What the sources do not reveal is whether there was a re-allocation of benefices in the wake of their departure. However, from this time, future disaffection of the empowered 'people of Sicily' directed against the Kalbid *amīr*s undermined their central authority and their ability to deal with political and military threats. Furthermore, comments made by Ibn Ḥawqal in 973 in the wake of the Fatimid move to Egypt suggest that, even at that time, there were recruitment problems in the army and that the Sicilians preferred to pay an exemption tax rather than be called up for the *jihād*. He added that evading conscription was also the reason why there were so many schoolteachers in Sicily because this was considered as a type of 'reserved occupation'. The unpopularity of the *jihād* around this time was also confirmed by Dāwūdī's report of desertions from mainland campaigns. It is thus quite plausible that, throughout the later Kalbid period, without help from Ifrīqiya, the proportion of the Sicilian population capable of serving as effective soldiers was limited.

The question of Sardinia and control of the Tyrrhenian Sea

Significant geopolitical changes were beginning to exert pressures around Sicily, first of all to the north over the question of Sardinia. After the Byzantine and early Islamic periods, there remained only vague and vestigial links between the island and the African mainland. For example, it is unclear why there should have been a fort in tenth-century Ifrīqiya called 'Sardāniya' if there was no association of any kind between the two. Firmer evidence can be found in a handful of surviving Arabic coins and epigraphic fragments in Sardinia.[2] However, the haziness of former Sardo-African relations in the minds of later Muslim authors is itself telling. In the twelfth century, al-Idrīsī thought that the population of Sardinia was made up of Latin-speaking refugees from Ifrīqiya; similar notions two centuries later may have prompted Ibn Khaldūn to suggest a confused connection between them and the Nafzāwa tribes of the remote Tozeur oasis in southern Ifrīqiya where Idrīsī recorded that Latin-speaking Africans (*Afāriqa*) could still be found.[3]

But, as Idrīsī knew, Sardinia had great natural resources, particularly its material wealth such as silver and timber – to say nothing of its potential for manpower and agriculture, even if it had remained underexploited. The strategic importance of the island was heightened by the role it had begun to assume as a staging-post along trans-Mediterranean shipping lanes for Andalusi merchants and travellers, especially after the Muslim capture of the Balearic islands in 902 and the strengthening of the eastern Iberian coasts under 'Abd al-Raḥmān III from the mid-tenth century. Sardinia could therefore be used to establish naval control over a much wider area, not only in the western Mediterranean, but also over the Tyrrhenian Sea to the east, to which the Sicilian and Ifrīqiyan Muslims had enjoyed relatively unhindered access.

In 1015–16, it appeared as if the island had yielded to Muslim rule when a large conquest expedition was launched from the newly formed *ṭā'ifa* statelet of Dénia to the south of Valencia on the eastern coast of al-Andalus, created after the implosion of the Spanish Umayyad caliph's central authority in Córdoba. Recorded in Arabic, Pisan and Genoese sources, the expedition was led by Abū l-Jaysh Mujāhid al-'Āmirī, known in Latin sources as 'Mugeto'. Mujāhid was a convert and manumitted slave who had risen to power in Dénia and set out to take the island with a large fleet. He was said by Ibn Gharsiyya, a close but tricky Andalusi source, to have been originally from Sardinia itself.[4] The logic of expansion accords well with his capture of the Balearic islands the previous year, and can be understood as a concerted effort to forge a maritime state extending into the central Mediterranean from Dénia linking an island chain of Ibiza, Minorca, Majorca and Sardinia. Mujāhid was ousted by a powerful coalition of Pisans and Genoese who, with papal encouragement, defeated the Andalusis in two campaigns which defined an episode of regional history. This opened up Sardinia to Ligurian influence for the next 300 years, putting the island beyond the immediate reach of Muslim fleets until the Ottoman period. It also hastened the 'Latinisation' of the island, which marked the final separation of Sardinia from any lingering traces with the Byzantine Greek world, leading also to the advent of a more substantial Christian infrastructure in the central zones of the island with the foundation of many new churches.

Less than a century before, the Fatimids had been able to launch serious attacks against Genoa and Sardinia. Now, Muslim naval forces could operate only in a restricted area, whereas Pisan and Genoese commerce was expanding aggressively southward towards Sicily and Ifrīqiya. Thus, major Pisan raids on Būna were attested in 1016 and 1034–5. These were threatening portents which prefigured later assaults against Palermo in 1063, and a joint Pisano-Genoese attack on Mahdiyya itself in 1087.[5] In the twelfth century, under Norman rule in Sicily, privileged north Italian merchants would significantly increase their presence in the south Mediterranean and consolidate their grip over the profitable commercial routes which passed through there, contributing to the slow transition of wealth from the rich south to the developing north Mediterranean.[6]

The rural economy and tax revolt of 1019

Ifrīqiya and Sicily had both known many times of political crisis but, on the island, the rich and diverse economy with its sustained, high level of agricultural production at least ensured that serious food shortages were rare. In stark contrast, the agricultural history of eleventh- and twelfth-century Ifrīqiya was punctuated by a series of devastating crop failures. A particularly severe famine was recorded in the year 1004–5, which Arabic sources vividly described as causing extensive migrations of rural and urban populations into Sicily. So ruinous was this famine and depopulation of the countryside that it marked a tipping point in the fortunes of the Zirid dynasty. In the eleventh century, serious seasonal famines were recorded in Ifrīqiya in 1018–19, 1022–3, 1033–4, 1040–2, 1055–6 and 1076–7.[7] Thereafter, economic decline gradually began to undermine the political integrity of the region as it entered a downward spiral of crop failure, famine and the gradual depletion of the Zirids' gold reserves caused by importing grain from Sicily which they might otherwise have been able to produce for themselves.[8] The political and economic dynamics of the powerful landholders and their great estates which had emerged in the wake of the Arab conquests had long been broken down during the Aghlabid period in favour of smaller units and sharecropping. However, the Ifrīqiyan soil was overworked, increasingly thin and, in addition, the literal interpretation and implementation of inheritance practices as favoured by Mālikī jurists, whereby plots of land were continually split between all rightful heirs, had gradually rendered agricultural lands less viable to work. In turn, this had contributed to the rise of nomadic pastoralism, which served to compound the economic crises and fuel political instability across the region – a pattern that continued in the twelfth century.[9]

The accession of the child al-Muʿizz as Zirid ruler in 1016 also began ominously. His arrival in Qayrawān, the stronghold of Mālikī Sunnism, provoked widespread rioting and a coup attempt. This he survived, but not before anti-Ismāʿīlī massacres had been repeated beyond the city, their leaders rounded up only after further troubles the following year. Politically, relations with the Fatimids remained amicable until the 1040s, but financially, the preceding decades were characterised by the illusion of prosperity brought by conspicuous expenditure, set against the background of an ailing rural economy. This may help to explain al-Muʿizz's interests in an increasingly divided, but wealthy, Kalbid Sicily either through alliance with their rulers, or by directly assuming power from them. In the guise of settlers, economic migrants or, from the 1020s, as military personnel, ever more Ifrīqiyans were arriving in Sicily throughout the first half of the eleventh century.

Among the events of 1019 in Sicily, as recalled by al-Nuwayrī, was an attempted tax reform by Jaʿfar's secretary (*kātib*), Ḥasan b. Muḥammad al-Bāghā'ī. Judging by his name, the secretary – here the term can be understood as referring to his chief minister – was an Ifrīqiyan from Baghaï in the eastern part of modern Algeria. Acting on his advice, Jaʿfar proposed to introduce a variable rate of tax on produce for the tithe of the *ʿushr* (literally 'tenths'). The rationale for the reform was modernisation and conformity with other lands, but it doubtless masked an economic motive calculated to increase tax revenues for the treasury. We can only speculate as to why the treasury required additional funds at this time, but it is likely to be related to the change in recruitment for the army following the expulsion of the Kutāma in 1015.

In Sicily, the administration had previously upheld a distinction between lands on which the *ʿushr* tithe was payable, and lands on which the inhabitants paid the *kharāj* or land tax. One effect of maintaining this distinction was that it was the status of the lands, not the status of the population on those lands, that determined which type of tax was to be paid. In Fatimid Ifrīqiya, the tax rate of the *ʿushr* and the *kharāj* had been linked. To determine the level of the *kharāj*, the maximum and minimum amounts of the *ʿushr* (in years of bumper crops or failed harvest) were added together and divided by two. This movable average was then set as the *kharāj*, and could vary from year to year. Any change to the *ʿushr* (even a slight change) therefore affected the *kharāj*. In Fatimid Sicily, however, the administration used a fixed tax as the *ʿushr*, and they reckoned it using the ox-plough measure (*al-zawj al-baqar*), probably an old Byzantine practice that had never been discontinued. The introduction of a proportional *ʿushr* tax would not only affect those who paid it, but also those who paid the *kharāj* since the *ʿushr* was used in its calculation. Unlike local, political disputes, such a proposed centralised tax modification, therefore, had the potential to affect many people over a large area simultaneously.

The report of the reform attempt offers a rare glimpse into the fiscal administration of the island and indicates a certain degree of bureaucratic sophistication, with executive power concentrated in the hands of a professional and well-known functionary – his link with Ifrīqiya is likely to have counted against him in the minds of longer established 'Sicilians' on the island. If the motive for the reform were fiscal, it was to have serious political repercussions. The affected and aggrieved parties of the proposed changes were said by al-Nuwayrī to have been 'the people of Sicily' and the *shaykhs* of the towns (*bilād*) 'both great and small', who then marched on Palermo, besieging the Kalbids in their own palace. Such was the gravity of this revolt, which continued into the night of the 14 May 1019, that a part of the palace complex (or a suburban palace) was destroyed. With no armed forces apparently willing or able to quell the riot and looting, Jaʿfar's father, Yūsuf, was carried on a litter to the deferential rebels. He then pledged to remove Jaʿfar with immediate effect, and offered to entrust power to a leader of their choice. Another of Yūsuf's sons, Aḥmad al-Akḥal was thus installed.

Yūsuf and Jaʿfar in fear of their lives fled to Egypt where they were said to have died destitute in spite of taking with them a vast amount of whatever transferable wealth they could muster. Evidence from an unusual source corroborates the level of political and material damage directed at the very centre of Kalbid power. In 1062, the compiler of a detailed inventory known as the *Book of Gifts* interviewed a named source in the Egyptian town of Bilbays who had once been the *mawlā* ('client') of his master, Yūsuf.[10] According to this uniquely well-placed informant, Yūsuf had received a number of precious gifts from the Byzantine emperor, Basil II (d. 1025). These had quite possibly been received as a result of a diplomatic settlement following an unsuccessful Kalbid siege of Bari and naval defeat off Réggio in the first decade of the 1000s. However, the source commented that all Yūsuf's gifts and possessions had been plundered when he fled to Egypt. This claim was repeated with the added information that a ruby, extravagantly bought in Sicily for 11,000 dinars, was sold for 4,000 after the rest of his possessions were looted (*nuhib*) on his escape to Egypt. The ruby was said to have been bought by the imām-caliph al-Ẓāhir (d. 1036). Apart from the damage done to the Kalbid palace, this report shows how their court life had become a target for popular hatred which was unleashed when taxes were increased. In post-riot Palermo, Jaʿfar's Ifrīqiyan administrative officer, Ḥasan al-Bāghā'ī, bore the brunt of popular displeasure: he was decapitated by a mob and his corpse abused. Presumably, conservative Muslim Sicily continued with its traditional, fixed tax system as before. In addition, 'the people of Sicily' were further empowered at the expense of the Kalbid's own personal wealth and standing.

From the medieval to the modern period, historical memory has recorded Ja'far as a profligate failure. Michele Amari's verdict on him was particularly scathing, referring to him as 'the author of mediocre verses ... bone-idle, greedy and cruel'.[11] Above all, he is often blamed for steering Islamic Sicily into precipitous decline prior to the civil war. While Amari's view may be unduly emotive given the unfavourable, non-Kalbid, sources and the starkly drawn, even literary, contrast made between Ja'far and his father, support for it comes from his expensive military failures, such as the three-month-long siege of Bari in 1003–4 and the defeat at Réggio in the following year. Thereafter, mainland expeditions returned little booty and made no military gains. On the other hand, apart from the traditional Byzantine enemy, the Muslims were coming up against an array of new forces, often acting in coalition: Normans and the prince of Salerno in an attack around the year 999; Venetians and Greeks at Bari; Pisans and Greeks in the assault against Réggio.

Ja'far's lifestyle and reputation as the prodigal son is supported by a reference from the 1180s found in Ibn Jubayr's account of the island to Qaṣr Ja'far ('Ja'far's Palace') near Palermo, prompting the suggestion that at a time of financial crisis the *amīr* was responsible for its construction (or reconstruction). Given that there were three *amīr*s called Ja'far between the 980s and 1030s, this palace – perhaps to be identified with the Favara or Maredolce on the southern outskirts of Palermo – need not have been built on his specific orders. However, Ja'far may have been struggling with additional politico-economic problems in this period. According to the account of Sicily in the *Book of Curiosities*, it was claimed that 'fifty years ago [*c.* 1013–*c.* 1022] [Palermo] acquired a new quarter known as al-Ja'fariyya, in which there are 10,000 houses'.[12] The figure is, of course, impressionistic, but the dates concur with the final years of Ja'far's rule (r. 998–1019), when it would appear that the city embarked on a period of rapid expansion, the main cause of which may have been to accommodate the influx of economic migrants from Ifrīqiya wracked by famine and politico-religious strife.

The stinging criticisms of Ja'far may have been justified, but he was also battling to maintain order in an increasingly disorderly island. On the other hand, like other medieval Muslim rulers, he was a man of culture with a taste for literature; he was also a poet and a patron of the fine arts. When set against the profiles of the leaders that would soon emerge on the south Italian mainland, particularly the early Normans of the Robert Guiscard generation, whose reputations were forged almost entirely from martial life and for whom exceptional acts of violence were considered prestigious, the contrast might even show Ja'far in a favourable light.

Ja'far's successor was his brother Aḥmad (r. 1019–36), more usually known by his nickname, al-Akḥal, referring to one whose eyes were, or appeared to be, darkened with kohl. He was swiftly given the honorific title 'Ta'yīd al-Dawla' or 'Support of the State' in a diplomatic investiture by the Fatimid imām-caliph al-Ḥākim. The situation which faced al-Akḥal in 1019 was bleak, and yet, contrary to all expectation, his rule appears to have begun successfully. Partly, this was achieved through the traditional distraction of campaigning: not against the mainland, however. Rather, in this case, an easy, internal *jihād* was conducted against Sicilian Christians whose direct threat to the integrity of Kalbid power was presumably minimal, but who – according to Arab-Muslim sources – were attacked 'until all their [unnamed] strongholds recognised his authority'.[13] Given the Christian presence in the north-east, this politically inspired, domestic *jihād* reopened a dimension of religious and regional conflict which had remained largely dormant since the 960s. Implicit in the attacks is that some of these Christian towns had become increasingly autonomous, perhaps by slipping out of their tribute-paying obligations. In any event, the frontier with the infidel was again to be found on the island, and in future military operations, the Kalbids would require the help of allies.

Relations with Byzantine south Italy in the 1020s

On the Italian mainland, the balance of power was also beginning to shift with the decisive emergence of new forces – notably, the Normans – and the brief *re*-emergence of old forces – the Byzantines in Apulia and Calabria. Regular as Muslim incursions in these areas had been for 200 years, Sicily had rarely been threatened with invasion from this direction, and the previous attempt of the Byzantines in the 960s had failed disastrously, so the Sicilian Muslims' perceived need for defence was a secondary consideration compared with their desire to launch raids. By the 1020s, Byzantine power in south Italy had strengthened, albeit for the interim, until they succumbed to the Normans by mid-century. Indeed, the fortunes of the Byzantines in south Italy had undergone a significant shift after the failure of the revolt against them during 1017–18 led by Melus, a Lombard from Bari. The revolt also led to the rise of the catepan Basil II Boiannes, who consolidated Byzantine power in the south by constructing a series of fortified hilltop towns at Troia, Fiorentino, Montecorvino, Dragonara and Civitate. These then served to secure the frontier of Apulia. In addition, since the Byzantines in the east had subdued the Bulgars and consolidated territories in the Balkans, more effort could be expended on less immediate threats in the western Mediterranean. By the mid-1020s, this included another plan to recapture Sicily from the Muslims.

For his part during the 1020s, al-Akḥal had commanded expeditions on the mainland in alliance with an Apulian rebel known only as 'Rayca', as recorded in summary form by the Apulian chronicler, Lupus Protospatharius. The Byzantine source, John Skylitzes, referred to the leadership of a certain 'Apollophar', which is most likely a distorted version of Abū Jaʿfar ('the father of Jaʿfar') and thus refers to al-Akḥal himself since Jaʿfar was the name of his son who, in the Arabic sources, was attested as deputising for his father when he was away waging *jihād*. The Muslim–Apulian rebel coalition forces besieged and took Bisignano in Calabria and appeared outside the walls of Bari in 1023, and later Obbiano in 1029 and even Cassano as late as 1031.

In 1025, a large, composite Byzantine army crossed to Messina in an attempt to invade the island, but the campaign was quickly abandoned on the death of the Byzantine Emperor Basil II at the end of the same year. None the less, it was this attempted conquest which spurred the Sicilian Kalbids to forge a defensive alliance with the Zirid ruler al-Muʿizz.[14] The Kalbid–Zirid pact held for almost a decade, and Greek sources recorded naval raids in the eastern Mediterranean on Thrace and Corfù until 1032. The alliance also heralded the beginning of much greater Zirid influence and intervention in Sicilian affairs. Once factions in Sicily had the serious option of appealing to Zirid Ifrīqiya, a new and potentially destabilising factor was introduced into the Kalbid–Zirid relationship. At the same time, the Kalbids were effectively forced into making military alliances to defend against the threat from the Italian mainland at a time when the Zirids' political thinking was becoming increasingly independent. While Ifrīqiyan support brought temporary stability and military aid for al-Akḥal, by the mid-1030s peace had been concluded with Constantinople, and Sicilian–Ifrīqiyan relations cooled. Thereafter, the Zirids appeared to contribute to undermining, rather than buttressing, Kalbid power. On the other hand, al-Akḥal would begin to look towards the Italian mainland for allies.

'The people of Sicily' and 'the people of Ifrīqiya'

The chronological order of events between 1032 and 1036 as recorded in both Greek and Arabic sources is far from clear. None the less, Ibn al-Athīr and later Arabic sources recorded, in 1035–6, contentious attempts by al-Akḥal's son, Jaʿfar (here, Jaʿfar III), to reform the land tax system radically by introducing a type of regional identity as the basis for its payment. In a set-piece scene of theatrical improbability, he was said by al-Nuwayrī to have convened the so-called 'people of Sicily' and offered to remove 'the people of Ifrīqiya' from them on the grounds 'that they had become partners in their lands and wealth'.[15] The Sicilians were said to have replied that there was no meaningful difference between the two groups as they had intermarried for so long, at which point Jaʿfar made a similar offer, this time to 'the people of Ifrīqiya'. They accepted. As a consequence, the *kharāj* or land tax was thus imposed on only 'the people of Sicily'. If such an event ever happened, the implementation of a discriminatory fiscal policy on an already fractious island, served only to exacerbate existing political tensions. Also of note is that the power hitherto wielded by the representatives of the 'people of Sicily', who had enjoyed a political resurgence since the 970s, from this point, appears to splinter.

According to Skylitzes, around this same time, the ruler (*archon*) of Sicily, 'Apolaphar Mouchoumet' (probably for Abū Ja'far Aḥmad, that is, al-Akḥal), was in conflict with his (otherwise unattested) brother referred to as 'Apochaps' (Abū Ḥafṣ? Abū Ḥāfiẓ?) who was in alliance with the Zirids. This prompted al-Akḥal to appeal to the Byzantines, who then offered him the title of *magistros*, while his son was sent to Constantinople and the Byzantine general George Maniákes was dispatched to south Italy. For their part, Arabic sources offer an equally brief, but not inconsistent account, namely that a mission from among 'the people of Sicily' approached the Zirids in Ifrīqiya (between November 1035 and October 1036) and offered to submit to their authority with the threat that, if this were not accepted, they would turn the island over to the Byzantines. In response to the appeal of 'the people of Sicily', al-Mu'izz dispatched his teenage son, 'Abd Allāh, at the head of a Zirid army against al-Akḥal who was besieged in the Khāliṣa. The confusion of the sources for these important, yet fragile and fickle, alliances is rounded off by the Arabic chroniclers, who reported the dramaticised events of the revolt against al-Akḥal and the resulting siege in Palermo, during which he was killed by a group from within 'the people of Sicily', who then turned against one another and rose against 'Abd Allāh and the Zirid faction who were forced to flee the city. Beyond the sphere of regional politics, a lasting truce had in the meantime been signed between the Fatimids in Cairo and the Byzantines in Constantinople. In effect, with Kalbid power substantially reduced, the political coherence of Sicily was now beginning to disintegrate at Palermo where al-Akḥal's brother Ḥasan 'Ṣamṣām al-Dawla' ('Battle-axe of the State') now held sway, his loyalty to Fatimid Cairo shown by the issuing of coins that bore the name of the imām-caliph, but with power shared with a faction of 'the people of Sicily' who formed a type of ruling council (*shūrā*) with its leading *shaykhs*. Power in the metropolis was dissipated further by the emigration of some of its leading families. Meanwhile, the principal, perhaps the only, coherent and competent force left to 'defend' the island was the Zirid army. Yet, an explanation of civil strife is still not sufficient to account for the end of Muslim rule in Sicily. For that we must turn to the mounting external threat from the south Italian mainland.

The expedition of Maniákes and the descent into civil war

Chaotic and antagonistic as the internal socio-political dynamics on the island were, on the Italian mainland – and almost entirely beyond the range of the Arabic sources' vision – a far greater threat was looming. The Byzantine Emperor, Michael IV, had ordered his general, George Maniákes, to prepare a coalition force to capture the island. By 1038, Maniákes had arrived in south Italy to finalise the slow military build-up in the peninsula. To the Byzantines, Maniákes was already a famous figure, having made his name as the general who captured Edessa in northern Syria in 1031. Under his command, an army was assembled in south Italy which comprised contingents of Greeks, south Italians and Varangians including Harald Hardrada, the future king of Norway and Denmark, known also for his invasion of Saxon England and his defeat at Stamford Bridge in 1066. More ominously, for Sicily at least, the Maniákes' army included a group of Norman mercenaries – the first to be engaged in the island's history.

During the summer of 1038, the expedition was launched against Sicily calling first to join with forces at Salerno. The army landed outside Messina, which was quickly captured when the defenders were said to have fled. This then became the base from which other areas were attacked, including Rometta, its capture celebrated by John Skylitzes. Indeed, Greek sources speak of the capture of thirteen unnamed towns and the defeat of the Zirid forces under the command of ʿAbd Allāh in the Val Démone between Randazzo and Troina. This weakened the Zirids' ability to defend Sicily, but it did not undermine their resolve to intervene, as shown by their willingness to send an army to fight the Normans in the 1060s. The campaign was also the scene for new reputations for martial prowess to be forged: a Norman knight knocked a horse unconscious with a single strike of his fist before the animal was hurled off a cliff, and William 'Iron Arm' Hauteville earned his nickname for slicing down the *amīr* of Syracuse in a single blow.

Even when faced with an incoming, non-Muslim invasion threat, the Sicilian Muslims were unable to muster or maintain a united front. On the contrary, the ease with which Maniákes was able to take major cities and strongholds in the east and north-east of the island not only shows the disarray into which Islamic Sicily had sunk – to the extent that it was barely able to defend itself – but also it implies an unquantifiably high level of support among elements of the local population, who were further won over by the reconstruction of their damaged city defences. Significantly, the main areas of operation were set largely in the Val Démone and along the eastern coastal towns where Christian settlement was strongest and which had been subject to attacks in the previous generation at the hands of al-Akḥal's army. The new-found confidence among the indigenous Christian population may have rekindled ambitions of independence from the Muslims: on the heels of the invading army were Greeks who had travelled across the Straits of Messina from Calabria, prefiguring a movement of unknown scale that would occur after the Norman conquest of the island in the following generation.

The figure of Maniákes as a popular hero for the Sicilian Christians endured in spite of his order for the translation of holy relics to Constantinople, including the body of the fourth-century Saint Lucía from Syracuse and that of Saint Agatha from Catania. The plain and town of Maniace were both named after him, although Castello Maniace in Syracuse was a thirteenth-century fortress built by Frederick II. However, his popularity with the locals was not shared by all those among the multi-ethnic army. During the course of the invasion, Latin sources recalled that the Normans had become embroiled in disputes with him over the distribution of the spoils. Furthermore, while the campaign was still in full flow, Maniákes was recalled to Constantinople, and tensions within the army became more evident as the leadership of the expedition changed hands and the coalition forces acrimoniously split. This brought the campaign to an end and allowed the Muslims to recoup their losses in the north-east of the island, taking all towns except Messina, which remained in Byzantine hands until 1042.[16] That the overall effect of Maniákes' expedition had been to accelerate the destabilisation of Muslim Sicily is shown by its subsequent disintegration into *ṭā'ifa*-s or factionalised statelets, leading to the breakdown of centralised authority and control of the regions from Palermo.

As with much of the history of this particular period and region, the sources covering the civil war which led into the Norman conquest offer only a sketchy account, devoid of critical and unequivocal analysis. In good part, the patchy sources merely reflect the political fragmentation of central government on the island. As for the term *ṭā'ifa* ('faction'), this was used by medieval Arabic chroniclers to describe petty states which had resulted from the dissolution of central power. Most famously, it was applied to the contemporary disintegration of authority in the Iberian peninsula as the *mulūk al-ṭāwā'if* or *reinos de taifas* which followed in the wake of the death of al-Manṣūr in 1002, the unexpected sack of Córdoba by mercenary Berber troops from north Africa in 1013 and the break-up of the Spanish Umayyad dynasty in 1031. *Ṭā'ifa* was also applied in a Sicilian context by al-Nuwayrī when referring to the independent strongholds and their magnates which arose in the long period of turmoil following al-Akḥal's death.[17] In al-Andalus, the *ṭā'ifa* period produced a flourishing of the arts in the regions as new courts sought to emulate the prestige of major cultural centres and to attract the patronage of poets and artists. In Sicily, this movement – if it happened at all – did so on a very modest scale, perhaps with Mazara best placed to draw itinerant literati from Ifrīqiya, such as the poet Ibn

Rashīq, briefly displaced after the Hilālī 'invasion' of Ifrīqiya during the 1050s, about which more will be said in the following chapter.

On the wider political front, observing from the perspective of early-1200s Syria, Ibn al-Athīr was convinced of a connection between the wider southward movements of 'Franks' at the expense of the Muslims across the Mediterranean in three arenas: Sicily (with the fall of Palermo in 1072); Spain (after the fall of Toledo in 1085); and the creation of the Crusader states in Syria–Palestine following the fall of Jerusalem in 1099. The complex causes behind the decline of Muslim power in each of these regions were quite different, although during the eleventh and twelfth centuries both the Iberian peninsula and Ifrīqiya–Sicily would undergo substantially changed relationships with the African mainland. All regions concerned witnessed a fundamental reformation of their indigenous power bases and the emergence of new regional forces. In Sicily, the Arabic sources for the 1040s and 1050s focus on the interplay between the two main protagonists – Muḥammad b. Ibrāhīm Ibn al-Thumna and 'Alī b. Ni'ma Ibn al-Ḥawwās, who were related by marriage. These episodes are characterised by literary touches and give a histrionic account of the final years of independent Muslim rule on the island. Each of the main, city-based rulers had some military and even limited naval forces at their own disposal but, as there is no remaining trace of any centralised administration, it is reasonably supposed that this was operational only at a provincial level or less. At least one of the *ṭā'ifa* rulers minted coins locally to promote himself, boost liquidity and stimulate local circulation.

The idea that the island had come to be divided into spheres of control raises a number of problems. Large areas, for example along the north coast, in the south-east Val di Noto and around the hinterland of the north-west, are unaccounted for, and it is unclear under whose control these parts were – if indeed, they were under any control which was not purely reduced to town and village level. The broad divisions, however, reflected an east–west split. Inland, the fortress of Castrogiovanni dominated the centre of the island, which in time of conquest, regained its strategic importance. This, along with Agrigento, Castronuovo and the smaller towns around them was in the hands of Ibn al-Ḥawwās. In charge of the western coastal towns of Mazara, Trápani, Sciacca, Marsala and Castelvetrano was a certain Ibn Mankūd (or Ibn Mankūt), possibly from a Berber tribe. At Palermo, Ḥasan Ṣamṣām al-Dawla may have continued until as late as 1052–3. His fate thereafter is unknown, but the city appears to have reverted to government by a council of leading *shaykh*s until (and probably beyond) the arrival of a Zirid force in 1063. A certain Ibn al-Maklātī was in control of Catania and was married to Maymūna, the sister of Ibn al-Ḥawwās. She was widowed when the leader of Syracuse, Ibn al-Thumna, defeated him, took charge of Catania and then married her himself, apparently with the permission of Ibn al-Ḥawwās. This rare appearance of a named, female character, stereotypically portrayed as calculating and divisive, who was now married to a leader who was said to be a drunkard (read: a bad and misguided Muslim), when combined with the relative absence of hard history in the sources, does little to engender trust in the narratives. A fierce argument with Maymūna was recorded in dramatic detail by Ibn al-Athīr in which a drunken Ibn al-Thumna ordered that her wrists be cut. Saved by her son, she eventually managed to persuade her remorseful husband to visit her brother with gifts, but he would not allow her to return, so Ibn al-Thumna prepared his troops to march against Ibn al-Ḥawwās. By this time – although the chroniclers are no less vague about these episodes than about the civil war generally – Ibn al-Thumna was said to have gained control over most of the island, to the extent that he was recognised in the Friday sermon in Palermo. It is possible that Ibn al-Thumna was the leader of a pro-Fatimid faction as he had either invested with, or had simply adopted, the Fatimid title of *al-Qādir bi-llāh* ('He who is powerful through God'). Against this, the western towns seem to have had closer ties with the Zirids who had sought to distance themselves from the Fatimids during this period. However, there is no clear sense that there was a genuinely ideological or wider political dimension to this conflict. Indeed, Ibn al-Ḥawwās was eventually killed by the Zirids, undermining the argument that he could have been their representative on the island. Rather, the evidence that at least three of the main protagonists were related by marriage suggests that the civil war was characterised by a political power struggle and in-fighting between local kin groups.

The final phase of the strife prior to the entry of forces from the Italian mainland occurred when Ibn al-Thumna marched against his brother-in-law, Ibn al-Ḥawwās, but suffered a calamitous defeat at Castrogiovanni. As a result, he left for the mainland to hire mercenaries from among 'the Franks' (*al-Faranj*) – at which point the histories of the island and the mainland intersect with the much better documented Norman conquest of Muslim Sicily.

Notes

1 The earliest source for the army revolt of 1015 is al-Nuwayrī (d. 1333), *BAS*[2] Ar.II: 496; *BAS*[2] It. II:137–8.

2 On Sardinia, see G. Oman, *Sardāniya*, in *EI*[2] IX:49–50; for the Arabic sources, see Maria-Giovanna Stasolla, 'Arabi e Sardegna nella storiografia araba del medioevo', *Studi Maghrebini*, 16 (1982): 163–201. For a historiographically-based study, see Luigi Pinelli, *Gli arabi e la Sardegna: Le invasioni arabe in Sardegna dal 704 al 1016* (Cagliari, 1976), superseding the dated work of Pietro Martini, *Invasioni degli arabi e delle piraterie dei barbareschi in Sardegna* (Cagliari, 1861; reprinted Bologna, 1963). Two Arabic toponyms in Sardinia (Arbatax, from *al-rābi'at 'ashra*, 'the fourteenth', and Assemini, from *al-thāmina*, 'the eighth', translations of ordinal numbers from Latin relating to coastal watchtowers of classical antiquity) imply some settlement

or control at some time by Arabic-speakers. In the case of Arbatax, these may have come from al-Andalus after the mid-eleventh-century foundation of Santa Maria Navarrese, 6 km across the bay to the north.

3 For Idrīsī on Sardinia, see *BAS*² Ar. I:35; *BAS*² It. I:45–8. For the bilingual *Afāriqa* of southern Ifrīqiyan oases, see Tadeusz Lewicki, 'Une langue romane oubliée de l'Afrique du Nord', *Rocznik Orientalistyczny*, 17 (1958): 415–80, and Halm, *Empire of the Mahdi*, pp. 98–9.

4 References to the Mujāhid expedition to conquer Sardinia are scattered across a number of sources, including Pisan, Genoese, Andalusi and the Arab chroniclers. G. Larsson, *Ibn García's Shu'ūbiyya Letter: ethnic and theological tensions in medieval al-Andalus* (Leiden, 2003), and James T. Monroe, *The* Shu'ūbiyya *in al-Andalus: the Risāla of Ibn García and five refutations* (Berkeley, 1970). For a brief introduction (with wider references), see Travis Bruce, 'The politics of violence and trade: Denia and Pisa in the eleventh century', *Journal of Medieval History*, 32/2 (2006): 127–42.

5 H. E. J. Cowdrey, 'The Mahdia campaign of 1087', *English Historical Review*, 92 (1977): 1–29.

6 The classic account of Pisan and Genoese commercial and political involvement with south Italy is that of David Abulafia, *The Two Italies: Economic relations between the Norman Kingdom of Sicily and the Northern Communes* (Cambridge, 1977).

7 For an introduction to the transitions in Ifrīqiya from Roman to Arab to Islamic, see Michael Brett and Elizabeth Fentress, *The Berbers* (Oxford, 1996), esp. chs. 2–4, pp. 50–153.

8 Idris, *La Berbérie orientale*, p. 655. However, see the caveats of the gold for grain argument in Brett, 'Ifriqiya as a market for Saharan trade', pp. 347–53.

9 On the socio-economic and political effects of Ifrīqiyan agriculture, see Mohamed Talbi, 'Law and economy in Ifrīqiya (Tunisia), in the Third Islamic century: agriculture and the role of slaves in the country's economy', in *The Islamic Middle East 700–1900: Studies on Economic and Social History*, A. L. Udovitch (ed.) (Princeton, 1981), pp. 209–49.

10 Ibn al-Zubayr, *Kitāb al-Dhakhā'ir al-tuḥaf* (Arabic), M. Hamidullah and S. Munajjid (eds) (Kuwait, 1959), pp. 83–4 and 193. For an English translation, see *The Book of Gifts and Rarities*: Kitāb al-Hadāyā wa-l-tuḥaf, trans. G. al-Ḥijjāwī al-Qaddūmī (Harvard, 1996), pp. 115 and 193.

11 For Amari's criticism of Ja'far, Amari-Nallino, SMS² II: 406.

12 Book 2, chapter 12 in Savage-Smith and Rapoport, *Book of Curiosities*: at www.bodley.ox.ac.uk/bookofcuriosities (accessed on 2 April 2008).

13 Al-Nuwayrī, *BAS*² Ar. II:497; *BAS*² It. II:140. Al-Nuwayrī is an important, but very late, source for the early 1000s in Sicily, offering details of what appear to be defining episodes in the run-up to the *ṭā'ifa* period which are not found elsewhere.

14 Ibn al-Athīr recorded that the large Zirid fleet sent to Sicily in January 1026 was wrecked off Pantelleria. However, this serves as a reminder that the narrative of events in this period is highly questionable. Not only does a reference to 400 ships in the fleet seem a gross exaggeration, but also Ibn al-Athīr may have confused this with 1052, when the Zirid fleet also went down off Pantelleria: cf. Ibn al-Athīr, *BAS*² Ar. I:314–15; *BAS*² It. I:440, and al-Nuwayrī, *BAS*² Ar. II:499; *BAS*² It. II:144.

15 The only source for the attempted land tenure reform of 1035–6 is al-Nuwayrī, *BAS*² Ar. II:497; *BAS*² It. II: 140–1.

16 Maniákes was recalled to Constantinople by Emperor Michael IV (d. 1041), who was succeeded by Michael V, who had him return to Byzantine Italy as catepan in April 1042, but who was deposed as emperor shortly after. Maniákes then rebelled against the newly installed Emperor Constantine IX and died on campaign in the Balkans in February 1043.

17 See al-Nuwayrī, *BAS*[2] Ar. II:498, for the rare use of the Arabic term *ṭā'ifa* in a Sicilian context.

5

The Norman conquest of Muslim Sicily

The rise of the Normans in south Italy

The third time during the eleventh century that invasion forces from the south Italian mainland landed on Sicily came with the Norman conquest from the 1060s. The enduring consequences of this phase for central Mediterranean history are hard to overstate. By 1072 Palermo had fallen; by 1091 the conquest was complete; and in 1130 Sicily and the south Italian peninsula were fused into a single political entity that retained a declining Muslim population for almost two centuries. The kingdom came to be split with the Treaty of Caltabellotta, ending the Wars of the Sicilian Vespers in 1302, but it survived, more or less, as a political unit until 1861 when it was incorporated into the unified kingdom of Italy in the wake of the *Risorgimento* movement.

The bulk of the forces that the Norman knights faced in Sicily were Muslim, but the conquest is not generally considered to be a crusade. Apart from the fact that it pre-dated the call for the First Crusade in 1095, there were no overtly religious motives for the Normans' intervention in Sicily in the sense that they did not set out to conquer the island *because* it was Muslim. Warfare was to occur between people of different religions, but it was not religiously inspired warfare. However, given the regular raids from Sicily against the mainland for the past 200 years, religious pretexts for war were already well established in the region.

Unlike Maniákes, the Normans showed no interest in the recovery and translation of relics, nor were there holy sites in Sicily to recoup and defend of the magnitude of Jerusalem. Rather, only a few Greek houses of any note had survived, and the island was not yet on a Christian pilgrimage route. The papacy's long-term aim to 'Latinise' south Italy and Sicily implied the establishment of new Latin churches where there had previously been none, although churches of the Greek rite were also supported, providing they recognised the primacy of Rome. For the non-Christian subject population, there was no suggestion that they would be required to change their faith en masse. None the less, it is possible to speak in terms of a nascent proto-crusader consciousness in the years prior to the First Crusade and Spanish *Reconquista*, and many ingredients were present in south Italy which lent the conflict a religious edge, not least the involvement of the papacy and its tacit approval of annexing a region which was once Christian, but had long since been under Muslim control. Even if the Normans were perceived by many in south Italy as 'wicked Christians', they were at least still nominally Christian and, when set against the backdrop of Islamic Sicily, it was now the Muslims who were vulnerable to being cast in the role of the politico-religious 'other', thereby helping to ease the Normans' accommodation as a new and, at times, confrontational power to the south of Rome.

Compared with the literature available for the island of Sicily, a substantial body of primary and secondary material exists which relates to the south Italian mainland and, in particular, to the rise of the early Normans. Important as that history is, its direct bearing on the Muslims of Sicily is limited, and so that which is offered here aims merely at introducing the so-called 'Normans in the South', and contextualising the political dynamics of the wider region. Key issues in recent times have come to focus on ethnogenesis, Norman-ness and how culturally and institutionally Norman the *gens Normannorum* and kings of Sicily actually were. Indeed, many now question the very existence of a 'Norman World' as imagined in previous eras, and have sought to point to the differences, rather than the similarities, between Normandy and Anglo-Norman England on the one hand, and south Italian Normans on the other.

There is also an important diachronic dimension to this debate. It has been estimated, largely from onomastic evidence, that between two-thirds and three-quarters of first generation south Italian Normans can be described as Norman in the sense that they hailed from Normandy.[1] However, with the passing of a second and third generation of Norman settlers, such assessments become increasingly evaluative and raise questions about the whole issue of ethnicity, the unreliability of its indicators, and the concept of a 'race' or 'people' as understood by medieval sources, or as epitomised by kings who had never ventured further north than Ceprano, located between Naples and Rome, some 1,500 kilometres overland from Rouen. Thus, to locate the kings – whose power centre was firmly rooted in Palermo – within a northern European frame of reference, without at least some serious qualification, would be mistaken. As we shall see, an argument could be made that the appellation 'Norman' might be less appropriate than 'Sicilian' when referring to the unique kingship which emerged in the twelfth century. On the other hand, in the Muslim sources, there is no impression that the Normans – or 'Franks' as they were called in Arabic – posed any threat at all prior to the actual conquest. Rather, they appear at the point of invasion from almost nowhere, there being little or no sense of who they were, or of the profound military and political impact they had brought to bear on the south Italian mainland from the beginning of the eleventh century.

The consolidation of Norman power and rise of the Hautevilles

On the turbulent and politically fragile mainland, the Normans had found ready employment in the duchies to the north of Byzantine Apulia and Calabria. Amatus of Montecassino reported that a group of forty Normans returning from pilgrimage to Jerusalem shortly before the turn of the millennium had assisted in fending off a Muslim raid on Salerno in the year 999. Certainly, Monte Gargano to the east of Fóggia, where the archangel Michael was said to have appeared, was, by 1016, an important place of pilgrimage. Whether or not the pilgrims can be identified with the same Normans involved in defending Salerno is another matter, but there is less doubt about the ways in which they came to gain power through their mercenary tactics. In this respect, there is much to be said for the three-phase division of the rise of the Normans, which corresponds to similar processes towards a rudimentary unification of south Italy. During and after the unsuccessful revolt of Melus against the Byzantines in 1017–18, the Normans had found themselves hired by both Lombard and Byzantine forces; in the 1030s, Normans, in the pay of the duke of Naples, had been vital for the defence of the duchy against Capua and, in 1038, the Norman leader Rainulf was appointed and confirmed as the count of Aversa, giving them an important territorial foothold in the area. Indeed, the town would remain closely associated with the Normans. As we have seen, in the same year, 300 Norman knights were said to have participated in the Maniákes expedition and crossed the Straits of Messina for the first time. Taxes raised by the Byzantines to fund this heroic failure may have fuelled serious revolts in Apulia during 1040–1, which not only undermined the campaign, but ultimately enhanced the leadership of the Normans under William of Hauteville, who was made count of Apulia the following year. Prior to this, it was William who had acquired his nickname 'Iron Arm' fighting the Muslims on the Maniákes expedition. The rise of William, who like his brothers came from Normandy, marked the beginnings of the Hauteville-led domination in the Byzantine provinces of Apulia and Calabria. Later, this remarkable extended family would produce successive counts and dukes of Apulia, the princes of Antioch and, most notably, the counts and kings of Sicily.

From the 1040s, and under their leadership, the Normans can be seen acting in a less disjointed manner, and beginning to make gains as a loosely affiliated group with a clearer set of mutual interests, their successes in Aversa and Apulia forming the basis for further cycles of conquest and political change. Norman dominance was confirmed by an important victory over a coalition of papal and Byzantines forces at the battle of Civitate in 1053, after which the papacy adopted a more pragmatic approach in recognition of the Normans' progressive military strength in the region. This grudging accommodation was turned to the advantage of a reform-minded papacy whose own position had been particularly uncertain at the end of the 1050s, but whose long-term aims of consolidating their own sway and working towards a reorganisation of the church in south Italy were more likely to be achieved with Norman military support. Papal investiture with titles and lands served to legitimise the Normans' presence even if some remained available for hire as mercenaries.

From the late 1050s, two of William of Hauteville's brothers, Robert (d. 1085) and Roger (d. 1101), emerged as his successors who would eventually lead the coalition campaigns in Sicily.[2] Robert was known by his nickname, 'Guiscard', from the Old French *viscart*, 'cunning'. His biographer, Malaterra, said that he had been given this name at birth, so we cannot safely infer anything of his character from it. It had, however, gained in popularity as a first name in south Italy by the twelfth century. In his adult life, Guiscard had a fearsome and negative reputation – like many of the early Normans in south Italy – for plundering that wrought devastation on the countryside. Campaigning in Calabria and Apulia, from 1057, he assumed the leadership of the Norman forces in the region and conquered most of the former Byzantine provinces by 1060 with the capture of Réggio, leaving only a handful of strongholds, such as Bari, beyond his control until its fall in 1071. During these campaigns, the Normans had also gained Capua when Richard of Aversa took the town in 1058.

At the Synod of Melfi convened by Pope Nicholas II in the summer of the following year, Guiscard swore formal allegiance to the pope and, in return, was invested with banners and titles.[3] The specific reference to him as 'the future duke of Sicily' almost two years before the invasion of Sicily and thirty years before its completion is particularly noteworthy. Not only was he being conceded lands which had not yet been conquered – and which were arguably not the pope's to grant – but also, by implication, the conquest of Muslim Sicily had already been envisaged as an extension of the gains made in Byzantine Calabria and Apulia during the late 1050s. Further evidence that the papacy had contemplated how a Christian Sicily might one day be organised is shown by the appointment of Humbert of Mourmoutiers as the (theoretical) archbishop of Sicily in 1050 by the pope's predecessor, Leo IX. Humbert was later to become the cardinal-bishop of Silva Candida and the legate to Constantinople who laid the papal bull on the high altar at Hagia Sophia which excommunicated the Patriarch of Constantinople leading to the schism of 1054. As such, it is possible that the papacy had considered him as a compromise candidate for Sicily, who was acceptable to both Rome and Constantinople, as part of an attempt to narrow the gap between the Latin and Greek Churches in that period.[4] None the less, the clear implication is that discussions had taken place in Rome at the highest level concerning the potential role Sicily might play in present and future politico-religious debates should it ever fall out, or be prised out, of Muslim hands. Although it was not specifically mentioned in the context of Sicily, the papacy was likely to have proceeded on the assumption that it had territorial rights over these areas anyway. According to the 'Donation of Constantine' – an eighth-century forgery, widely presumed until the 1400s to be valid – the Byzantine Emperor had purportedly granted to Sylvester I (d. 335) and his successors legal entitlement to lands around the central and eastern Mediterranean, including 'Africa, Italy and various islands' (*vel diversis insulis*).

Guiscard, in contrast to his brother, was to play relatively minor roles in the conquest of Sicily, and he died on campaign against the Byzantines in Kefalonia in 1085. His dynastic legacy in Italy was limited, although his son Bohemond (d. 1111) and grandson of the same name (d. 1131) became the first princes of Táranto and, more famously, Antioch after its fall in 1098 during the First Crusade. In Sicily, it was Guiscard's brother Roger – sometimes referred to as 'the Great Count' or more accurately, Count Roger I of Sicily – who was instrumental to most of the campaigns and was particularly important in the period after the fall of Palermo until his death in 1101. It was Roger's direct descendants who would become the first kings of Sicily.

To suggest that the Normans had completed the unification of south Italy prior to the conquest of Sicily would be misleading: it was not yet a recognised political unit, and it was still divided between warring lords. This fractious instability prevented Guiscard and his sons from establishing a more powerful, mainland platform on which to build and pass on their authority, since the regions were not pacified until almost a decade after the creation of the kingdom of Sicily in 1130. Even then, stability was far from guaranteed. Nevertheless, the areas formerly under the control of Lombards and Byzantines were sufficiently well cobbled together, politically speaking, to make the Muslims' tenuous control of insular Sicily even more precarious. Moreover, the Muslims' defence of Sicily was compounded by the coincidence of civil strife with a significant weakening of their strongest potential ally – Ifrīqiya.

The Hilalian invasion and break-up of Zirid Ifrīqiya

By the end of the 1040s, the Zirids under al-Mu'izz had decided upon political disengagement from the Fatimids in favour of recognising the Abbasid caliph. This bold strategy resulted in one of the most famous, and contentious, episodes in medieval north African history: the so-called Hilalian invasion. The events that followed, recorded most notably by Ibn Khaldūn and in later romances, have both literal and figurative elements. Legend casts the Banū Hilāl as unruly nomads, encouraged to migrate westwards from Egypt by the Fatimids in order to inflict revenge on the Zirids, hence Ibn Khaldūn's theatrical imagery of the Hilalian invasion as a swarm of locusts descending on the Ifrīqiyan countryside.

Rather more prosaically, the Banū Hilāl were semi-sedentary tribesmen from the western oases of Egypt who first appear in an Ifrīqiyan context as Arab contingents in the army of al-Muʿizz in Tripolitania before they turned against him.[5] In a major engagement at Ḥaydarān in April 1052, they defeated the Zirid forces, and in winter of that same year, a large Zirid fleet sank off Pantelleria as it was heading to Sicily in response to an appeal from eminent migrants fleeing the troubles on the island. Ibn al-Athīr was quite adamant that it was this catastrophe which undermined the Zirids' capacity to overcome the Hilālīs thereafter.[6] The Zirids renewed their fealty to Fatimid Cairo in 1054–5, but by the end of 1057, their power in Ifrīqiya had been significantly reduced. Al-Muʿizz and his son, Tamīm, had been forced to take refuge in the old Fatimid stronghold of Mahdiyya, while the Hilālī's sacking of Qayrawān marked the decline of one of the great cities of the early medieval Islamic world. By the death of al-Muʿizz in 1062, Zirid Ifrīqiya was politically and economically in disarray. Meanwhile, in Sicily, the Norman conquest of the island had begun in earnest. For the next century, Zirid political control over the cities of Ifrīqiya would remain unsure and weak as the Hilālī kin groups formed political alliances and took power in the fragile city-states across the region.

By virtue of their perception as Arab nomads, later historiography and romance attributed to the Banū Hilāl the cause of twin cultural and socio-economic change with which their political ascendancy had coincided. As nomads, their presence in Ifrīqiya came to represent the climax of the long-term and continuing evolution from an agrarian to a pastoral economy. As Arabs, they were credited with introducing a new and decisive phase of a linguistic shift: from a Berber-speaking to an Arabic-speaking region.[7]

Ibn al-Thumna and the Norman conquest of Sicily

Arabic sources were particularly ill-informed about the Norman invasion, and provide only fragmentary, often erroneous, data. Ibn al-Athīr, for example, made the unlikely claim that Ibn al-Thumna had sought assistance from 'the Franks' in Mileto as early as 1052, when Roger was still on the French side of the Alps. An early date, briefly believed to have been confirmed by the Cairo Geniza documents, has not overturned the standard dating of the Norman conquest from the Latin sources and cannot, therefore, be used to recalibrate the dates of the civil war and invasion period.[8] Indeed, it is the principal Latin sources for the conquest, namely Geoffrey Malaterra, Amatus of Montecassino and William of Apulia that are depended upon to reconstruct the narrative history of the wider conquest period from 1060 to 1098.[9] From them, we can also infer a great deal about Norman leadership, relations with the papacy and the military manoeuvres of the campaigns, although less can be gleaned about Norman involvement with the Muslims. As far as Ibn al-Thumna's initial contact with Roger was concerned, this can be reckoned to have taken place toward the end of February 1061, according to Malaterra. In the following month, raids were conducted around Rometta, Milazzo and Messina. This version of events consistently fits with the expansionist logic of the Normans in that precise period. Indeed, Malaterra recalled that after the conquest of Calabria by the spring of 1060, Roger had begun to explore the practicalities of a Sicilian invasion. Besides, in early autumn of the same year, he had already raided around Messina, perhaps to reconnoitre the area. As a primary landing site and base for the Norman forces, Messina was again taken with only limited opposition from within the city itself, although this did not curtail the reported slaughter. From here, the Norman forces retraced some of the steps that the Maniákes expedition had taken through the Val Démone, and quickly established important garrison bases at Petralia and Troina: in effect, guarding the passage through to Messina between the Nébrodi and Madonie mountain ranges and mount Etna to the south-east.

The conquest, which took almost thirty years to complete, was characterised by sporadic campaigning and numerous skirmishes rather than a series of open battles or extended sieges. The relative manpower of the armies and numbers cited in the narrative sources should be treated with caution, but the Norman leaders, barons and knights were repeatedly said to have been in a very small minority. On their leadership, Malaterra emphasised the Normans' ruthless determination (*strenuitas*). However, his account misleadingly underplays the roles of their Muslim allies, and says little of the rapid capitulation of many Muslim towns or the seemingly effortless incorporation of defeated Muslims into the Norman-led army. In addition, the Norman forces rarely appear to have sustained anything other than low rates of casualties throughout, and often enjoyed high levels of co-operation from both Muslims and local Christians. Thus, those among the island's population who fought against the Normans came to accept subordination by negotiation and agreement, with Muslim contingents actually contributing to the invasion effort. Amatus recorded that, even prior to the main conquest, both Muslims and Christians in Réggio enthusiastically and conspicuously lent their support to Robert Guiscard, although he added that that was done in order not to raise suspicions about their trustworthiness. Until the violent death in 1062 of Ibn al-Thumna during an ambush in the hostile territory of western Sicily near Entella, his forces were working in close collaboration with the Normans. And while the latter regarded their campaigns as a conquest in which their leader had already been invested as the island's future ruler, Ibn al-Thumna's perspective was presumably that he was now able to recommence the civil war which he had been waging: the Norman reinforcements would allow him to overcome Ibn al-Ḥawwās in the centre and west of the island. In spite of differing agendas, such was the importance of Ibn al-Thumna to the Normans that on his death they withdrew their garrisons from Petralia and Troina in the Val Démone back to Messina itself. His death was mentioned in passing in a Jewish merchant's letter dated to 12 August 1062 in which the news was regarded positively, in part because many Jews had died at the hands of the Normano-Muslim coalition forces during the capture of Messina.[10]

It can be presumed with a reasonable degree of safety that Ibn al-Thumna's forces continued their support for the Norman coalition after his death. A family member was perhaps even granted control over Catania in the 1080s. By then, Malaterra claimed that the Muslim soldiers in the Norman army were reckoned in their thousands and that they constituted the majority.[11] Indeed, after the conquest many Muslims continued to find employment in the standing army of the Hautevilles, particularly as personal (and trusted) bodyguards as well as infantrymen and archers, at least some of whom were highly skilled. So prized were the latter that when Roger's widow, Adelaide, was to be married in 1113 to the king of Jerusalem, Baldwin I, she was accompanied by a detachment said to have been unparalleled experts in the art.[12] Often described in terms of the horror and fear that they instilled, Muslim contingents were attested in campaigns on the Italian mainland, appearing at the sieges of Salerno in 1076, Cosenza in 1091, Castrovillari in 1094 and Amalfi in 1096. Their deployment in action was often only noted outside the island. As we shall see, their use by Christian rulers of Sicily was always controversial, yet it continued throughout the twelfth century and into the thirteenth century, when many of the primary functions of the Muslim colony at Lucera were related to the military.

Muslim responses to the conquest: resistance and collaboration

The final Zirid intervention in Sicily came in the form of an army led by Ayyūb and ʿAlī, the sons of the *amīr* Tamīm b. al-Muʿizz (r. 1062–1108). In 1063, Ayyūb headed for Palermo where he appears to have assumed command. ʿAlī, meanwhile, gained control of Agrigento and, at some point before 1068, came into conflict with Ibn al-Ḥawwās and killed him. Clearly, western Sicily was still in turmoil during this period even without the help of the Normans. In the north-east of the island, the Normans sealed their control with a victory in open battle on the plain of Cerami in 1063, for which they received absolution from their sins from Pope Alexander II. The sources, however, are unclear as to who was leading the opposition in this engagement. The Muslims were commanded in battle by the awe-inspiring, armour-clad figure of 'Archadius' from Palermo. 'Archadius' was not a personal name but the noun used by Malaterra to describe Muslim leaders (cf. a certain Archadius of Syracuse, probably deriving from *al-qā'id'* 'leader' rather than *al-qāḍī'* 'magistrate'). However, his relationship to other Muslim forces, and the extent of their co-operation are unknown. Following their later calamitous defeat at Misilmeri in 1068 and the withdrawal of the Zirid army from the island, the remaining Sicilian Muslim opposition appeared to have been even more fragmented and was thereafter organised on a purely local basis.

When describing the army that the Normans faced in battle, Malaterra juxtaposed the 'Arabs and Africans' and 'Africans and Sicilians', presumably in reference to various Zirid contingents as well as Sicilian Muslim soldiers. More significantly he referred to 'the pagans and the Sicilians' and, on one occasion, to 'Africans and Arabs with Sicilians', which could be taken to mean that there were Sicilian Christians who had joined forces with the Muslims.[13] This scenario was by no means improbable. For example, when the Normans first reached the town of Troina in 1061 with its mixed Muslim and Christian inhabitants, the Norman soldiers were said to have been joyfully welcomed. Later, when they returned amid a suggestion of maltreatment of the local girls at the hands of those billeted in their houses, both the Muslims and the Christians joined forces to besiege the Normans, including Count Roger and his wife, during the depths of winter before they were able to break out. In addition, there were genuine fears that rebel Normans, such as Roger's illegitimate son, Jordan, might ally themselves with Muslim opposition forces.[14]

However, the involvement of treacherous 'Greeks' at Troina – playing to their stereotypical depiction in the Latin sources as untrustworthy – was unusual. Elsewhere, the indigenous Christians were attested as helping the invaders and were promised benefits in return. Overall, the effect of the Norman conquest, like that of the Maniákes expedition, had been to exacerbate indigenous Muslim–Christian tensions on the island, regardless of any socio-political links that existed between the two communities. It is impossible to calculate how dense local Greek Christian settlement across Sicily was, but it was unquestionably very localised, and their numbers were increased by immigration from Calabria in the post-conquest period.[15] Their traditional strengths in the Val Démone were well known and, during the conquest, they were even attested as far west as Agrigento where they were sufficiently confident to lend their open support to the Norman invaders. The implicit socio-political proximity of the local Greeks to the Muslims is alluded to on several occasions. For example, we hear of bilingual spies, and early in the invasion at Petralia – whose population like many of the towns in Sicily comprised Muslims and Christians – both communities were said to have discussed the terms of surrender.[16] It is unfortunate that we do not know whether the terms of surrender were the same for both communities. Indeed, if the conquered peoples of a particular town had agreed to pay tribute to the Normans collectively, there may have been little or no change from the Islamic to the early Norman period in terms of the overall tax burden that the indigenous Christians were required to pay.

The battle of Misilmeri and the rise of Ibn al-Baʿbāʿ

The second, and final, pitched battle of the conquest was a pivotal victory for the Normans outside Misilmeri in 1068. This laid open the way to the metropolis. As the stronghold was only eight miles from Palermo as the crow flies, and double that by road, there was a sense that the Muslims' eventual defeat was inevitable by this stage. After the battle, the invaders' psychological grip was further tightened by the grim dispatch of blood-soaked carrier pigeons, who returned to Palermo bearing no written message, stoking political tension yet further and anticipating the complete withdrawal of the Zirid army from the island. Fear of raids and the risk of capture by the Normans were often signalled in the Latin sources, and Malaterra even stated that these were major factors which urged the Muslims to a speedy surrender. Moreover, the battle-hardened Norman knights had spent most of their lives engaged in campaigns, whereas the youth of the Sicilian Muslims during the 1060s had considerably less experience of combat or of withstanding siege warfare during the civil war period.

The Normans' brutality as well as the Muslims' fear of it were shown in an unusual gesture reported by Malaterra at the fall of Messina, when a Muslim killed his sister rather than leave her to the mercy of the troops. Generally, the early Normans were dogged by accusations of rape by their many detractors. So persistent and widespread were the claims that they cannot be casually dismissed as hostile propaganda. That rape accompanied defeat was made abundantly clear by Hugh of Flavigny when describing the conduct of the Norman troops in the sack of Rome in 1084.[17] A couple of years later in Sicily, it was also implied by Malaterra, who reported the specific orders given by Roger *not* to rape the wife of the *amīr* of Castrogiovanni after her capture at Agrigento. The impression, even in a relatively non-hostile source such as Malaterra, is that the early generations of Normans were fiercely determined men of the sword and, as he put it: 'addicted to hunting and hawking'.[18]

Political changes that had occurred in Palermo during the latter phases of the Norman conquest are abstruse and made more so by the limited and confused nature of the sources. Numerous references in the Cairo Geniza point to the emergence of a certain Abū ʿAbd Allāh Muḥammad ibn ʿAbd al-Raḥmān, known as Ibn al-Baʿbāʿ, as ruler of Palermo by the late 1060s. He appears to have governed through, and with the support of, its leading merchants and *shaykhs*. What is known of Ibn al-Baʿbāʿ is immensely important, even if his political affiliations remain open to question. His rise to power by May 1069 was not unopposed, and probably post-dates the return of the Zirid army to Ifrīqiya after their defeat at Misilmeri.[19] His close connections with overseas merchants, including the many Jews in Sicilian ports, are signalled in the Cairo Geniza letters, to the extent that Moshe Gil has suggested, not implausibly, that the family may have once been converts to Islam from Judaism.[20] References to all three generations in the Geniza letters indicate that the family may originally have been jewellers and/or goldsmiths (hence reference to them as al-Ṣā'igh), and that they came from Spain (hence his alternative appellation of al-Andalusī). Linking Ibn al-Baʿbāʿ to a wider kin group, however, remains problematic since the name al-Ṣā'igh, or indeed, Banū l-Ṣā'igh, was not uncommon.[21] By the 1020s in Sicily, the family were prominent as merchants in Mazara and Palermo, plying trade in commodities between Sicily, Mahdiyya and Alexandria. Sound and ample evidence for their mercantile activities comes again from the Geniza, in which we see the merchant ships of Ibn al-Baʿbāʿ in operation from around 1052. On occasions they had also acted as trusted couriers of substantial amounts of gold and silver coin.[22]

The Geniza documents point to the crushing effect that the civil strife was having on the economy by the 1050s and 1060s. Merchant shipping had been interrupted; in one case, a boat had been intercepted and attacked by the forces of Ibn al-Thumna off Agrigento.[23] Deteriorating conditions had generally led to a stricture of supply and signs of hardship were reported. The remains of the central authorities had channelled their revenues into the war; at the same time, the once most powerful purchasers in the market could no longer operate as before. Indeed, to raise funds to alleviate their cash crises, the Kalbid authorities had decided to impose and enforce even higher import duties on goods, much to the chagrin of the merchants. All of this adversely affected trade in and out of Sicily. Significantly, we begin to detect Ibn al-Babāʿ and Palermitan merchants becoming more involved in political dealings, particularly from the 1060s. In a brief passage by Ibn al-Athīr, it appears that Ibn al-Baʿbāʿ had sought to undermine the power of the Zirids by playing off Tamīm against his Ḥammādid rival over issues of control at Bougie (Bijāya), and had, in addition, resisted Zirid interference in Sicily, allying himself instead with the Fatimids. As conditions worsened, supply and demand was strangled and profits were reduced by increased taxation, so the grasp of Ibn al-Baʿbāʿ strengthened over commerce/political affairs at Palermo, particularly when the last vestiges of authority slipped away after Misilmeri. Eventually, the merchants took matters into their own hands: Ibn al-Baʿbāʿ appointed his old Palermitan business associate, Zakkār ibn ʿAmmār, as leader (*nagid*) of the Jewish community, as well as the supplier to his soldiers, which he had deployed against the local *qā'ids* in order to become Palermo's 'sultan'.[24]

The brief ascendancy of Ibn al-Baʿbāʿ in the guise of a relative political outsider from a mercantile background introduced a significant change to previous dynastic arrangements. Had the Normans not conquered Palermo, it seems from its political trajectory that it might have fallen even more fully into a form of self-government by merchants in much the same way as other maritime states that had emerged around the Mediterranean. Unfortunately, but for his commercial relations, Ibn al-Baʿbā's political involvement with other factions remains largely shrouded from view. Gil's conclusion that he could not meet Fatimid tribute payments and had therefore handed Palermo over to the Normans who put him to death, is based on the laconic (and slightly anachronistic) passage in Ṣibt ibn al-Jawzī's, *Mir'āt al-Zamān*.[25] The alternative scenario is that he fled to Alexandria prior to the Norman siege, as implied in a Jewish merchant's letter. In either case, he had disappeared from view by early 1072. The Jewish merchants' role and position in all this was uncertain. It is possible that they may have found themselves out of favour with the Normans, especially if Jewish opposition to Ibn al-Thumna had been transferred to his allies. Many seem to have cut their losses and run, judging by the relative silence of the Geniza letters from this period until the 1120s. By the time of their return, the ports of Norman Sicily had begun to thrive with Christian merchants from around Italy.

The fall of Muslim Palermo in 1072

From a Norman perspective, the conquest of the island would have been swifter had its leaders not been distracted by commitments on the mainland, particularly in Apulia, which was still not entirely subjugated. Thus, while Roger was preparing for the critical battle at Misilmeri, Guiscard's forces were engaged in a long blockade of Bari which lasted for three years. Only when Bari had fallen in 1071, were the Normans freer to continue in Sicily with their joint siege of Palermo by land and sea in the autumn. Victory on the mainland was shortly followed by the fall of Palermo itself, when the Muslim capital of 240 years, capitulated on 10 January 1072 after a five-month siege.

On early Normano-Ifrīqiyan relations, Malaterra revealed an important bilateral understanding of non-aggression when he reported that Roger had refused to join the Pisans in their attack on Mahdiyya in 1087, citing that he was unwilling to break the peace he had made with Tamīm.[26] Thus, any lingering Zirid hostility had effectively been neutralised by diplomacy and treaty sometime between 1068, following their defeat and withdrawal from Sicily (but presumably post-dating their assault against Mazara in 1075), and the Pisan attack of 1087. As we shall see, the Normans' relations with overseas Muslim powers were complex and delicate, yet, in many respects, they were more consistent and less mutually threatening than relations with the German or Byzantine empires. The danger of a counter-attack on Sicily from any Islamic region was minimal until the early 1160s when the Almohads may have contemplated an invasion prior to the death of their energetic caliph, ʿAbd al-Mu'min, in 1163.

Throughout the entire Sicilian campaign, there had been a number of exploratory forays and raids, most of which were successful and some of which were major undertakings. The long period after the fall of Palermo witnessed mopping-up operations and short sieges resulting in the capitulation of Trápani and Castronuovo (in 1077), Cinisi (in 1079), Syracuse (in 1085), Castrogiovanni in 1086, followed by Caltanissetta and ten other towns around the south-central region in the same year, and Agrigento in the next. Towards the very end of the campaign, in 1090, a rare overseas operation was launched to capture Malta. Meanwhile, stubborn resistance persisted only in the south-eastern Val di Noto, around Syracuse, Noto and Butera where the remaining forces of a certain 'Benarvet' (also known as 'Benevert', possibly a corruption of Ibn al-Ward or Ibn ʿAbbād), who had been killed at Syracuse, were not subjugated until February 1091. Although revolts were few, serious tensions surfaced within some Muslim-held towns. At Castronuovo in western Sicily, its ruler, a certain Bechus (Abū Bakr?), failed to put down a local revolt, said to have been inspired by a miller (a *mawlā*?) whom he had unjustly treated, thus suggesting personal motives for action. None the less, if the episode can be credited, then the rebel was consequently rewarded for his actions by the Normans.[27] It also suggests that the broken remains of central authority in Muslim Sicily had, in some cases, been reduced to the level of autonomous towns and villages, rather than provinces. Also worthy of note was a short-lived alliance forged between Serlo and a certain Muslim called Ibrahīm in which they were said to have taken each other as brothers. Although this pseudo-familial partnership – a Sicilian Muslim custom also noted in the following century by the Latin chronicler Falcandus – turned out to be treacherous, leading to Serlo's death, it provides evidence for further and open Muslim–Christian collaboration. Elsewhere, such as at Pantálica in the Val di Noto, a truce-breaking insurrection was stamped out a year after the final surrender of Noto.[28]

All parties in the conflict brought with them a crude awareness of religious difference. In the narrative of Malaterra, completed in the years after the launch of the First Crusade, certain episodes even appear to have either coloured – or been coloured – with imagery found in early crusader narratives.[29] Indeed, anecdotal battle accounts circulating around south Italy might account for this. The prime example is Malaterra's timely apparition of Saint George on a white charger, carrying a white banner and with a cross fixed to his lance, at the battle of Cerami in 1063, leading the Norman army into the fray. Roger's own lance was party to a divinely positioned banner and cross arrangement. This is comparable with an account in another south Italian source, the *Gesta Francorum*, of ethereal, holy warriors outside Antioch during the First Crusade. Otherwise, ceremonies such as taking Communion prior to battle were standard among the Norman soldiers, and when Malta was captured, the prisoners there flagged up their Christian credentials by holding up makeshift crosses and singing the *Kyrie Eleison*.[30]

Triumphantly recorded by both Malaterra and William of Apulia, the famous main mosque of Palermo – formerly a Byzantine church, and before that, an ancient Greek temple – was converted into a church immediately after the fall of the town. In the words of William of Apulia:

> glorifying God, he destroyed every structure of the temple of vice; and where there was previously a mosque, he constructed a church of the Virgin Mother; that which had been the seat of Muḥammad and the demon, he made a house of God and a gateway to Heaven for the deserving.[31]

This was later rebuilt from scratch, while the mosque at Catania was later known to have been converted into a church. However, conspicuous conversions of congregational mosques are seldom attested. The Normans sometimes built their churches into the shell of ancient Greek temples (such as at Syracuse), or sometimes directly on top of them (such as the chapel of San Biagio at Agrigento). The royal foundation of San Giovanni degli Eremiti at Palermo was also built over some previous, unidentified, structure. Indeed, many mosques had formerly been Greek churches, adding to the problem of distinguishing the archaeological remains of a mosque from the ground plan of any rectangular building with a niche in one wall, which leaves us with regrettably little to say about these vitally important transitions. Yet, if we do not assume that many other, minor mosques were destroyed, changed into churches or fell into disuse over time, then it becomes difficult to account for why so few were attested in later periods.[32]

There is no evidence whatsoever that the Normans attempted to convert the Sicilian Muslims en bloc away from Islam. However, on at least one occasion, a leading individual was obliged to convert. After the fall of Castrogiovanni in 1086, its ruler, called 'Chamut' or 'Chamutus' by Malaterra, was compelled to abandon Islam for fear that his wife and children who had been taken hostage at Agrigento would be killed. There was at least significant material compensation for his spiritual compromise – he was given lands in Calabria on his request. 'Chamut' is one of Malaterra's less garbled renditions of an Arabic name, and probably corresponds to the common Arabic personal name 'Ḥammūd', rather than to the kin group name of al-Ḥammūdī or Ibn Ḥammūd. The theories surrounding this clan and its leadership will be taken into account below, in Chapter 11.

The conversion to Christianity of Chamutus at Castrogiovanni appears to have allayed some of the reservations the Normans had about the loyalty and trustworthiness of the Muslims, but the act of conversion raised a greater risk that, if imposed, it might unleash forces of religious antagonism around which opposition could grow. Clearly, this was not in the Normans' interests if they were to take the island without the nagging threat of rebellion. The backlash caused by conversion is seen in another incident at the same siege in Castrogiovanni. Here, Malaterra recorded the case of an important convert referred to as Elias Cartomensis, who had helped co-ordinate the raising of local military forces.[33] On refusing to take up the offer of reconversion to Islam, he was killed by his co-religionists. These examples of conversions, both of which occurred in the same town, may have been recorded precisely because they were notable as exceptions to the rule. Indeed, there is some, albeit problematic, evidence for the Normans' active preservation of Islam.

Recorded in Eadmer's *Life of Saint Anselm*, Count Roger I at the siege of Capua in 1098 specifically forbade the conversion of his many Muslim troops.[34] Willing as they were said to have been, the biographer's well-meaning piety might itself be a distorting factor in the account. However, a strategy of segregation between divisions within the army had several advantages, not least that it was in keeping with tradition. Moreover, maintaining the discipline and allegiance of a few key leaders within each unit was instrumental to matters of exerting control over the army as a whole. Indeed, the stratified and isolationist arrangement within the army – the successful organisation of which the Normans knew very well – may provide illuminating examples of how they applied mechanisms of command and control over a diverse population via a hierarchy of compliance, responsibility and obligation. Thus, in spite of a clear sense of religious 'otherness' on both sides, preserving essential elements of the religious *status quo ante* was vital for the early Normans' rule over the Muslims.

Terms and conditions of the Muslims' surrender

The Normans had practised their negotiating skills in Calabria where they had concluded surrender treaties. On Sicily, Malaterra's account preserves details of numerous negotiations that determined the early conditions under which the Muslims agreed to live. The first attested pact relates to the fall of Rometta in 1061, where emissaries were dispatched from the town to conduct the dialogues: 'handing themselves and their city over, they confirmed their fealty by swearing on their books of superstitious law'.[35] The same episode was also recorded by Amatus, who noted that the envoys were the leaders (*qā'ids*) of the town itself.[36] Similar arrangements were made after the fall of Palermo, where more details were given about the terms that the Muslim leaders accepted. Two *qā'ids* led the talks, corroborating the absence of Ibn al-Baʿbāʿ by this point. On interrelated issues of obedience and religious freedom, they made their position perfectly clear, informing the Normans that:

> in no way did they intend to contravene or forsake their own faith (*legem*); but, if they were sure that they would not be constrained nor oppressed by unjust, new laws (*legibus*), then, since they were forced by their present circumstances to surrender the city thus, they would uphold their fealty in service and render tribute. They pledged to corroborate this with an oath of their own law (*legis*).[37]

Malaterra also recorded in verse that formal treaties were reached after the fall of Trápani and Taormina.[38] On other occasions, it is possible to infer that treaties had taken place about which we are only subsequently informed. For instance, at Iato in 1079, in one of the rare Muslim rebellions after the fall of Palermo, the local population (probably from the wider area) refused to pay tax and give services 'which had been agreed'.[39] At the same time, crops were burned around the rebel town of Cinisi, after which they were forced to come to terms. Similarly, when Syracuse fell in 1085, a treaty was attested but we are given no further details.

The most explicit and important example of surrender occurred after the fall of Malta in 1091, again recorded by Malaterra. As the Aghlabids had once launched a fleet to take Malta, as an extension of flagging campaigns they were conducting in the south-east of Sicily, so too had the Normans two centuries later. Since the devastating Aghlabid attack on Malta, the island had been depopulated, or had an inconsequential population, for the next 180 years. However, in 1048–9, it was unexpectedly repopulated and rebuilt.[40] No source mentions from where this influx had arrived or why, but presumably these people hailed either from Sicily and were escaping political turmoil, or from Ifrīqiya and were escaping economic malaise. A few years later, in 1053–4, its main, or perhaps only, settlement was besieged by a Byzantine fleet and saved by the combined efforts of the Muslims and their domestic slaves (*'abīd*), who all gained their freedom in return for their loyal support. Of these earliest Maltese inhabitants, we can infer that the first generation of battle-ready colonists, counted as 400-strong, along with their slightly more numerous retainers – who feared capture by the Greeks and were to be permitted to marry their former masters' daughters – were mainly Muslim, or they probably became Muslim on manumission. Secondly, that after the siege, the earliest population were all free men. Both Malta and nearby Gozo clearly prospered in the following two generations under the rule of a local *qā'id*, and were said by the Latin chronicler Malaterra not to have been suited to fighting in the least. Their wealth was remarkable and, when easily captured by an expedition led by Count Roger, the compliant *qā'id* offered horses, mules, weapons and cash. After agreeing on an annual tribute payment, they again made 'oaths according to their own law, and bound themselves to him'.[41]

By the time of their surrender, the Maltese islands had acquired a minority of Christians, quite probably captives from the Italian mainland, possibly from Benevert's seaborne attack on Nicótera, Réggio and around Squillace in 1085.

They were sufficiently small in number to have been rounded up at very short notice by the Muslims and taken hostage. A not dissimilar situation of hostage-taking had occurred at Syracuse too. The Maltese captives were all gratefully set free by the Normans, but could not be tempted to relocate to Sicily permanently, even with the most generous possible terms of tenure that had been specially granted to attract them. Rather, once in Sicily they returned across the Straits of Messina to their diverse lands in order 'to see their own fields'. Muslim Malta then came to be included as part of Count Roger's personal demesne. Whether the tribute was actually collected until 1127 when the island had to be 'reconquered' by Count Roger II is open to question. But ironically, as Anthony Luttrell noted, with the evacuation of some of its Christian population, the initial effect of the Norman conquest was to leave Malta 'more Muslim after 1091 than before'.[42]

Although patterns, protocols and procedures emerge from the surrenders, there was no guarantee for Muslim towns that this formed a fixed and consistent model because there were differences in terms from different negotiations. For example, at Noto the inhabitants were granted exemption from tribute payments for two years.[43] Given that Noto had become the last stronghold of the Muslim resistance leader Benevert, this offer was particularly generous and may reflect the Normans' desire to bring the conquest to a close without risk of further rebellion.

It is striking that when a key centre fell and agreed to pay tribute, the towns around it did not always follow suit without also having to be conquered by force, implying that they were (or had become) politically, fiscally and administratively independent. This is most clearly shown in the south-central zone of eleven towns including Caltanissetta, Licata and Naro, which are likely to have been in the orbit of the Agrigento–Castrogiovanni axis, two major towns known to have been politically connected from the time that Ibn al-Ḥawwās had assumed power in both. A generation later, Chamutus/Ḥammūd also appeared to have had important links with both centres since his wife was captured in one while he was at the other.

Some towns negotiated their own surrender; others were not afforded that luxury, and the population or sections of it were taken captive and either relocated or sold as slaves. To some extent this may be a reflection of the Normans' need to maintain a steady flow of booty for the troops campaigning with them, although some of the knights were described as being in receipt of stipends. This helps to account for the imbalance before and after the fall of Palermo, such that slave-taking was better attested in the earlier period, whereas treaty-making was more prominent in the period after the city's capture. Some of the recorded incidents were notably harsh and highlight how different the experiences of the Norman invasion were for different segments of the Sicilian Muslim population. For example, when Robert Guiscard was returning from the mainland in 1064, he marched straight to Palermo to which he laid siege with a group of 500 knights.[44] The decision to head for the metropolis had probably been prompted by the Pisan naval attack on the harbour the previous year. Malaterra recorded how, during the siege, the Normans camped on a hillside infested with insects which had given them an irresistible and perilous flatulence about which more details are offered than were recounted about the events of the siege proper. By inserting this distracting tale, Malaterra draws a veil between the reader and the Normans' lack of success after three months of besieging the city. Indeed, this failure most likely accounts for the raids to the south-west which followed directly in its wake in order to generate booty for the soldiers. These indiscriminate attacks included the entire depopulation of the walled town of Bugamo, where the townsfolk were unwilling to put up a fight, so the Normans razed the town and took the entire population captive along with their property.[45] Thereafter, they were forcibly resettled at the abandoned town of Scribla in northern Calabria which had once been Guiscard's base. The Normans' strategies towards the local population were not necessarily predictable or equitable, but could be determined by short-term exigencies alone.

The unsavoury effects of medieval raiding, which the mainland had experienced at the hands of the Muslims for over two centuries, were now directed towards unfortunate sections of the Sicilian Muslim population. However, it should also be noted that although crop burning and depopulation were a feature of Norman raids in Sicily, there were no accounts of serious food shortages, perhaps because the majority of the population in the countryside were marginal to most of the fighting. None the less, spoils appear to have been taken at almost every engagement. Captives were recorded after raids around Butera in 1062; in 1076, the *castrum* of Zótica (also called Judica) was not only razed to the ground and its menfolk slaughtered, but also its women were sold into slavery in Calabria.[46]

The regional role of Calabria as a place of exile to which the conquered might be sent is striking. Not only do we know of the important example of Chamut/Ḥammūd, who went to live near Mileto so that he might not instigate a revolt on the island itself, but the Muslim leaders of Butera were also sent to Calabria, fearing that if they were left in Sicily they might foment revolt.[47] In the latter case, although it is not explicit, it does not appear as if these leaders had been sold as captives. The great irony of this is that Butera would, indeed, become a centre for repeated and very serious resistance – from disaffected Latin Christian lay lords in the reign of William I. A small Muslim presence in Calabria was known prior to the conquest, and later charter evidence suggests that it may have continued for at least a generation afterwards. These Calabrian Muslims were presumably either converted or otherwise assimilated by the local Christian population, which already had converts among them from as far back as the tenth century.

The formation of indirect rule for the Muslim communities

After the surrender of Noto in early 1091, such was the complexity, or perhaps the sensitivity, of negotiations that Muslim envoys from the city were taken to Mileto in Calabria to conduct the discussions in person with Count Roger, implying that an interim cessation of hostilities was in place that allowed surrender arrangements to be settled. The impression gained from the examples of both Palermo and Noto is that the Muslim leaders were able to take a robust stance, particularly over the interrelated questions of religious continuity and leadership of their own communities. By and large, the same people who appeared to rule the towns led both the fighting and the post-conflict resolutions. In most cases, these leaders were maintained in their positions, thereby reducing the risk of rebellion since they had personally sworn to be bound by the treaty in the first instance.

The basis of interfaith diplomacy to guarantee peace and security was made *on* terms imposed by the Normans, but *in* terms proposed by the Muslims because the treaties, such as that at Malta, were specifically drawn up 'according to their own [Islamic] law'.[48] The Muslims paid the *tributum* or the *censum*, equivalent to that of the *jizya*, while the term 'subjects' (*confoederati*) which the Maltese Muslims agreed to become in relation to Count Roger, can be taken as the counterpart for the *ahl al-dhimma* ('people of the protection'). In effect, what emerged was a type of indirect rule, not inconsistent with the constitutional and fiscal regulation of government of the Muslim *dhimmī* system under which the island's Christians and Jews had been permitted to continue to worship freely, to use their own laws within their own communities, and to pay tribute in return for such guarantees.

The circumstances of the invasion, in which an alien religious minority had conquered a different religious majority that was liable to rebel at the slightest future disaffection, necessitated the inclusion of terms favourable to the majority. Thus, the Muslims had given ground, but this was not necessarily an irreversible or permanent state of affairs either. That said, payment of tribute to infidels would undoubtedly have raised prickly legal problems, as would questions of obedience to infidel authority and the extent to which dissent was valid or resistance necessary. No source now reveals how such legal points were debated at that time, but similar issues *were* raised and partially resolved in the twelfth century. It is worth reiterating that the *qā'ids* (leaders) of the towns, not the *qāḍīs* (judges) of the law courts and mosques, negotiated the surrender terms of the eleventh century, the conditions of which would continue to apply to the Muslims of the twelfth century when the Mālikī jurists sought and found legal justifications for the position in which they found their community.

It may be too schematic to assume that a fully-fledged version of the Islamic *dhimmī* system was adopted by the Normans. The lingua franca of agreement, brokering the broad principle of subordination, could have had little to say about the practicalities of indirect rule between faith communities, the all-important minutiae of which carried connotations that were undefined and open to interpretation. The illiterate mercenaries who were the early Normans, in spite of access that they may have had to the expertise of local Muslim jurists and bilingual interpreters, could have had no idea of Islamic *sharī'a* law, its functions or its knotty ramifications. Only much later in the twelfth century would a more formal and codified arrangement of indirect rule emerge in the form of the royal Assizes which could be applied across the kingdom to any of its Muslim communities. But even then, it was not always obvious whether both sides were playing to the same set of rules.

An example which questions and qualifies the early formal relationships between the conquered Muslims and the Norman rulers is offered by the treatment and fiscal status of the substantial Jewish communities in Sicily. At Palermo, the Jewish quarter, or *ḥarat al-Yuhūd*, occupied a sizeable area of the city, and the activities of merchants and artisans are known through the Geniza documents, supplemented by later sources such as Benjamin of Tudela's *Itinerary*, in which he reported that in the 1170s there were some 1,500 Palermitan Jews or heads of Jewish families. There is clear evidence that Jewish settlement in the Islamic and Norman periods was significant and not exclusive to large, coastal, urban centres. Under the Normans, Jews – quite unlike Muslims – do not appear in positions of executive power, nor do they seem to have had access to the Norman rulers' entourage and palaces.

On the south Italian mainland, the Jews were treated as a separate faith community whose fiscal status was determined by their religious belief. Revenues from the community belonged to the dukes, but were often granted to churches.[49] Thus, for example, revenues from the Jews of Bari, Salerno and Melfi had been conceded by Roger Borsa to the archbishop in 1086, 1090 and 1094, respectively. This well-established practice was, from an early stage, transferred to Sicily. A sixth of the taxes from the Jews (*de redditivis Iudeorum*) of Palermo was granted by Robert Guiscard's wife, Sichelgaita, to the cathedral of Palermo where a new Latin archbishop had been installed.[50] After her death in 1090, the church was to receive all the Jews' taxes. In 1107, Roger's wife, Adelaide, granted the tithe of the Jews of Términi to the newly founded Latin church of San Bartolomeo of Lípari.[51] Similar echoes of this can be heard throughout and beyond the period, for example in Frederick II's donation of 1211 when the *redditus Iudeorum* was not only to be paid to the church of Palermo in perpetuity, but the archbishop was also to have jurisdiction over that community. Indeed, in the thirteenth century, a convincing argument can be made that Frederick's treatment of the Muslims had come to be informed by more formalised attitudes to the Jews which had crystallised and hardened since the inception of the crusades.[52] That particular argument, however, cannot be applied validly in retrospect to explain the eleventh century, and so the origins of the arrangements for the Sicilian Muslims ultimately remain unclear. Whether the Normans thought they had imported a practice which they understood primarily in terms of a mainland precedent, or whether they saw the negotiated arrangements as a continuity derived from the principles of *dhimmī* system of Islamic Sicily, they in any event came to link their authority over the Muslims and Jews to tribute payable according to religious conviction. Thus, as the society of Muslim Sicily had been divided by religion into two tiers: Muslims, then (Greek-rite) Christians and Jews, so the society of Norman Sicily was also to be divided according to nominal faith which, in turn, determined tax liability. The problem with dividing the conquered peoples according to religious practice was that it could not easily accommodate the local Christians. They had already begun to play important linking roles in the emerging, mixed society of the island, as a gateway community between the Muslims and Christians, but, to the Normans, they had the dubious distinction of being considered 'Greek' after the language of their liturgy. In the immediate aftermath of conquest, however, the most pressing issues as far as the island's peoples were concerned, were to ensure that the subject peoples agreed to pay tribute and would not rebel. Once peace had been established, the focus then shifted to the question of how best to distribute the Normans' new-found power and wealth.

Notes

1 L.-R. Ménager, 'Pesanteur et étiologie de la colonisation normande en Italie', in *Roberto il Guiscardo e il suo tempo* (Rome, 1975), pp. 189–390. Reprinted in Ménager, *Hommes et institutions de l'Italie normande*, (London, 1981); L.-R. Ménager, 'Inventaire des familles normandes et franques émigrées en Italie méridionale et en Sicilie (XI–XII siécles)', pp. 259–375, reprinted in the same volume.

2 For a detailed account and analysis of the early Normans on both the mainland and insular Sicily, see G. A. Loud, *The Age of Robert Guiscard. Southern Italy and the Norman Conquest* (Harlow, 2000).

3 For the Synod of Melfi, see *Le Liber Censuum de l'Église Romaine*, P. Fabre and L. Duchesne (eds), 3 vols (Paris, 1889–1952), I:422. For a translation and discussion, see Loud, *Robert Guiscard*, pp. 188–9.

4 For a gentle introduction to the schism in a south Italian context, see John Julius Norwich, *The Normans in Sicily* (London, 1992), pp. 97–105. For greater depth on early Norman–papal relations, see Loud, *Robert Guiscard*, pp. 186–233; in part, superseded by G. A. Loud, *The Latin Church in Norman Italy* (Cambridge, 2007), especially pp. 60–134.

5 See the important discussion in Michael Brett and Elizabeth Fentress, *The Berbers* (Oxford, 1996), pp. 131–42.

6 On the political crises in Ifrīqiya, see Ibn al-Athīr, *BAS*[2] Ar. I:319; *BAS*[2] It. I:448.

7 On the Banū Hilāl and the historiography of Ifrīqiya, see Michael Brett, 'Fatimid historiography: a case study – the quarrel with the Zirids'; 'The flood of the dam and the sons of the new moon'; 'The way of the nomad', and 'Arabs, Berbers and holy men in southern Ifrīqiya 650–750 H/1250–1250 AD'. All articles are reprinted and most easily accessible in *Ibn Khaldūn and the Medieval Maghrib* (Aldershot, 1999).

8 Moshe Gil dates the Norman conquest to 1056, in 'Sicily and its Jews', in *Jews in Islamic Countries in the Middle Ages*, trans. David Strassler (Leiden, 2004), pp. 535–96 (p. 555). See also Moshe Gil, 'Sicily 827–1072, in light of the Geniza documents and parallel sources', in *Italia Judaica. Gli ebrei in Sicilia sino all'espulsione del 1492. Atti del V convegno internazionale 1992* (Palermo, 1995), pp. 96–171 (p. 115). Discussions in these works remain important for their many observations on Islamic Sicily from the perspective of narrative sources and the Cairo Geniza documents. The dating of the Norman invasion, however, is not one of them. For Ibn al-Thumna's appeal to the Franks, see Ibn al-Athīr, *BAS²* Ar. I:318–19; *BAS²* It. I: 447.

9 Of the main Latin sources for the conquest period (Malaterra, Amatus of Montecassino and William of Apulia), an English translation by Graham A. Loud of *Malaterra: The Deeds Done by Count Roger of Calabria and Sicily and of Duke Robert his Brother* and *William of Apulia: The Deeds of Robert Guiscard* has been published online at: *www.leeds.ac.uk/history/weblearning/MedievalHistoryTextCentre/medievalTexts.htm* (accessed on 3 April 2008). This complements another recent translation by Kenneth B. Wolf, *The Deeds of Count Roger of Calabria and Sicily and of his Brother Guiscard* (Ann Arbor, 2005). In addition, see *The History of the Normans by Amatus of Montecassino*, trans. P. Dunbar and G. A. Loud (Woodbridge, 2004). The Latin texts of Malaterra, William of Apulia, Erchempert, Falcandus, Falco of Benevento, *Kalila e Dimna*, Lupus Protospatarius, Peter of Blois and Peter of Eboli *et al.* can be read at: www.intratext.com/Latina/Mediaevalis and www.thelatinlibrary.com/medieval.html (accessed on 4 April 2008). A hypertextualised Latin version (with word occurrences and concordances) which has been derived from the standard, Pontieri edition of 1927–8 is available at: www.intratext.com/IXT/LAT0870 (accessed on 4 April 2008). For Greek and Arabic sources from this period onwards, of note are two chapters in *Byzantines and Crusaders in Non-Greek Sources 1025–1204*, Mary Whitby (ed.) (Oxford, 2007): Vera von Falkenhausen, 'The south Italian sources', pp. 95–121, and Jeremy Johns, 'Arabic sources for Sicily', pp. 341–60.

10 For the relevant Geniza documents in English translation, see Shlomo Simonsohn, *The Jews in Sicily. Volume 1: 383–1300* (Leiden, 1999), p. 305 (no. 141) and p. 319 (no. 147).

11 On the relative numerical strength of the Muslims in the Norman army, 'quorum maxima pars exercitui intererat', see Malaterra, IV:26, p. 104 and IV:22, p. 101.

12 On the Saracen archers who accompanied Adelaide to Jerusalem, see Albert of Aachen XII:13. Parallel Latin–English text now to be found in *Albert of Aachen, Historia Ierosolimatana: History of the Journey to Jerusalem*, ed. and trans. Susan B. Edgington (Oxford, 2007), pp. 843–4. See also, Giovanni Amatuccio, 'Saracen archers in southern Italy' at: www.deremilitari.org/resources/articles/saracen_archers.htm (accessed on 13 May 2008).

13 Malaterra, II.33, pp. 42–4.

14 For the genuine fear that disaffected Norman knights might turn to the Muslims for support, see Malaterra, III:36, pp. 78–9.

15 Vera von Falkenhausen, 'Il popolamento: etniè, fedi, insediamenti', in *Terra e uomini nel Mezzogiorno normanno-svevo. Atti delle settime giornate normanno-sveve, Bari, 1985* (Bari, 1987), pp. 39–73 (pp. 47ff.).

16 For bilingual (Arabic-Greek) Christians spies, see Amatus, V:24, p. 142 and Malaterra, IV:2, p. 86. On the mixed-faith population of Petralia and their dealings with the Normans, see Malaterra, II:20, p. 35.

17 Hugh of Flavigny, *Chronicon*, in *MGH SS*, viii.462.

18 For a sobering portrayal of the early Normans' unbridled ambition and materialistic outlook, see Malaterra, I:3, pp. 8–9.

19 Establishing who was in charge at Palermo is complicated further by Roger's oration to his army before Misilmeri in 1068, which related that their enemies were still the same '(even) if they have changed their leader (*ducem*)'. See Malaterra, II:41, p. 50. If this refers to Ibn al-Baʿbāʿ and is not anachronistic, then it implies that he already held power at Palermo before the Zirid departure.

20 See the important discussion about Ibn al-Baʿbāʿ in Moshe Gil, *Sicily in the Geniza documents*, pp. 125–30. For further references and summaries of his appearances, see p. 127, n. 9. The relevant documents are translated into English in Simonsohn, *Jews in Sicily*.

21 One thinks, for example, of ʿAbd Allāh Ibn al-Ṣā'igh who was *wazīr* to Ziyādat Allāh III in Ifrīqiya at the end of the Aghlabid period. He fell foul of his master and others in the Aghlabid elite when accused of collusion with the early Fatimids around the same time that Ibn Qurhub, whom he also knew, was governor of Trípoli, (*Iftitāḥ al-Daʿwa*, pp. 150, 152, 168–70, 183–5). The escape route that Ibn al-Ṣā'igh had prepared was to set sail for Sicily, although there is no way of knowing if he or his family then suppressed their political aspirations for the time being, or if they were in some way tangled up in the Ibn Qurhub affair in Sicily. The appellation of al-Ṣā'igh was also quite common among Jewish merchants.

22 For Ibn al-Baʿbāʿ in the Geniza documents, see Simonsohn, *Jews in Sicily*, p. 177 (no. 93), pp. 207–8 (no. 104), p. 216 (no. 106), p. 224 (no. 109), p. 258 (no. 122), pp. 297–8 (no. 139), pp. 356 and 359 (no. 156), p. 366 (no. 158), pp. 387–9 (no. 162), pp. 381–2 (no. 163), p. 384 (no. 164).

23 On Ibn al-Thumna's attack on Jewish shipping, see Simonsohn, *Jews in Sicily*, p. 231 (no. 111); on increased import duty, p. 223 (no. 108), p. 226 (no. 109) and p. 380 (no. 162); for examples of deteriorating conditions, see pp. 302–5 (no. 141) and pp. 332–44 (no. 151).

24 Simonsohn, *Jews in Sicily*, pp. 381–2 (no. 163) and pp. 383–5 (no. 164).

25 For Ibn al-Baʿbāʿ opening the gates of Palermo to the Normans and his alleged death at their hands, see Ṣibt ibn al-Jawzī, *BAS*[2] Ar. I:380; *BAS*[2] It. I:524, relating to the year 463 AH (9 October 1070 to 28 September 1071).

26 For the Pisan suggestion to attack Mahdiyya, and the revelation of Norman treaties with the Zirids, see Malaterra, IV:3, pp. 86–7.

27 On a dispute between elements within the local Muslim population, See Malaterra, III:12, p. 64.

28 For the Pantálica revolt, see Malaterra, IV:18, p. 78.

29 For crusader sentiments in the Sicily conquest narratives, see Loud, *Robert Guiscard*, pp. 163–5.

30 On the first Norman conquest of Malta and Gozo, see Malaterra, IV:16, pp. 94–6.

31 On the Norman actions in the *urbs inimica Deo* (i.e., Muslim Palermo), see William of Apulia, III, lines 313–17.

32 Outside Palermo, mosques in the 1100s are attested at Catania, Termini, Qaṣr Sa'd (near Palermo), Alcamo, Trápani, Syracuse, Butera, Segesta and one near Corleone. Clearly, this represents only a fraction of surviving mosques. However, they are not otherwise conspicuous. Several *muezzin* are attested on lists of Sicilian 'villeins'. Unfortunately, the noun *mu'adhdhin*, when written in Arabic without diacritical points, is indistinguishable from the more common term, *mu'addib*, referring to a type of teacher .

33 On the conversion from Islam and subsequent killing of Elias Cartomensis, see Malaterra, III:30, pp. 75–6.

34 *The Life of Saint Anselm, Archbishop of Canterbury, by Eadmer*, ed. and trans. Richard Southern (London, 1962), II.33, pp. 110–12.

35 On Muslims' swearing allegiance to the Normans at Rometta, see Malaterra, II:13, p. 33.

36 Amatus, V:20, p. 140. Both Amatus and Malaterra concur over the roles of the *qā'ids* who led the fighting and were in charge of negotiations involving the surrender of towns.

37 See Malaterra, II:45, p. 53, for the stipulations of surrender at Palermo. Note the ambiguity of the Latin *lex* which could refer here to 'Sharī'a law' and/or 'the faith of Islam'.

38 At Trápani: 'they [the Muslims] surrender the town (*castrum*) and submit to his authority; they make a treaty in their accustomed way (*more suo*), but they do so lamenting', Malaterra, III:11, p. 63; at Taormina, 'a treaty is drawn up, the enemy laments', Malaterra, III:18, p. 67.

39 For the Iato and Cinisi revolts in 1079, see Malaterra, III:20–1, pp. 69–70. For the treaty at Syracuse in 1085, see Malaterra, IV:2, p. 86.

40 Joseph M. Brincat, *Malta 870–1054. Al-Ḥimyarī's Account and its Linguistic Implications* (Valletta, 1995).

41 On the Malta surrender terms, see Malaterra, IV:16, p. 95.

42 Luttrell, *Making of Christian Malta*, V:104.

43 On the surrender of Noto, see Malaterra, IV:15, p. 93.

44 For Guiscard's failed siege of Palermo, see Malaterra, II:36, pp. 46–7.

45 On the depopulation of Bugamo, see Malaterra, II:36, p. 47.

46 Malaterra, II:32, p. 42 and III:10, p. 62 for Butera and Zótica (Judica).

47 On the expulsion of the leaders of Butera to Calabria, see Malaterra, IV:13, p. 93.

48 See Johns, *Arabic Administration*, pp. 31–9, for more detail relating to the implications of Muslim capitulations to the Normans.

49 For the fiscal relationship of Jews to the Latin Church, see the important discussions in Loud, *Latin Church in Norman Italy*, especially pp. 316–20 and 512–13.

50 Simonsohn, *Jews in Sicily*, p. 387 (no. 166).

51 For the year 1107, 'I, Adelaide, Countess of Sicily and Calabria with my son Roger, have given to the church of San Bartolomeo, the tithe of the Jews who are at Termini'. For convenience of reference, see Simonsohn, *Jews in Sicily*, p. 391 (no. 170).

52 David Abulafia, 'Ethnic variety and its implications: Frederick II's relations with Jews and Muslims', in *Intellectual Life at the Court of Frederick II Hohenstaufen*, William Tronzo (ed.) (Hanover and London, 1994), pp. 213–24.

6

Muslims under early Norman rule: churches, charters and lordships

Fortifications and early instruments of command and control

From some distance in both time and place, Ibn al-Athīr (d. 1233) recalled the post-conquest situation in melodramatic fashion: 'Roger controlled the entire island and colonised it with Greeks and Franks alongside the Muslims; they left not a bath-house, shop, mill or oven to any of its inhabitants'.[1] This picture of absolute dispossession is exaggerated, even if the conquest had introduced a new set of dynamic forces to the island, the results of which, by Ibn al-Athīr's time, were plain to see. Central to understanding the transition of power is to account for the superimposition and privileging of certain groups over others on the island. Such an explanation is by no means straightforward, but Ibn al-Athīr's version of events will clearly not suffice on its own.

After the fall of Palermo in 1072, a garrison of soldiers had been installed and a Norman knight called Robert was appointed as governor of the city with the Arabic title of *amīr*. After his successor, Greeks were to occupy this important position until 1154. A deal was struck whereby, according to Amatus, Guiscard was to gain half of Palermo, half of Messina and half the Val Démone. The rest of the island was Roger's. Malaterra, however, suggested that Guiscard had retained all Palermo and given over the remainder.[2] In practice, once Guiscard had returned to the mainland, Roger was left to assume control of the entire island. It was thus under Roger, his wife, their sons and closest advisers that the rudimentary institutions and apparatus of control over the majority Muslim population initially, and slowly, came to be constructed. This infrastructure did not, nor could not, spring forth fully armed.

Both during and after the conquest period, areas of political and military sensitivity remained, some of which were around key Muslim towns that the Normans sought to shadow with the construction of new fortifications, or with the refortification of older defences. These included walls around a city and the fortification of a smaller town or settlement, usually referred to as a *castrum* or *castellum*. The latter terms carry some ambiguity since on relatively few occasions was an actual castle built. Roger's concessions of landed property included grants of both unwalled or open settlements (*casalia*) as well as walled villages, a number of which were located on easily defended hilltop sites. Such grants soon formed an important part of the distribution and partial devolution of power to ecclesiastical and lay lords, as well as serving to bolster his own comital authority.

During the conquest, defences of diverse types and degrees of permanency had appeared at Messina (1061), San Marco (1061), Petralia (1062) and Calascibetta (1074) – which guarded the stronghold of Castrogiovanni – as well as at Trápani (1077), Syracuse (1086), Agrigento (1087) and Noto (1091).[3] Petralia had been refortified by 1066, and Malaterra recorded how, after the fall of Palermo, a castle was built at Paternò which overlooked both the town and plain of Catania. In the same year of 1072, Roger constructed a castle at Ibn Mankūd's old centre at Mazara. This served as a base from which to raid the towns and villages around, and would provide an important defence against a sea borne attack from Ifrīqiya three years later.[4] The Norman period also saw the importation of the *donjon roman* form of defensive architecture such as at Paternò, Adrano and Motta, alongside older types from the Islamic period. Indeed, notable among the few loan words in Sicilian dialect which entered from Norman French is *bbággiu*, referring to an inner courtyard, which ultimately derives from the 'bailey' of military architecture.

New lordships in the late 1070s and early 1080s

Early instruments of rule and reward included Roger's division of lands and men to his knights and supporters. In turn, these formed the basis of new, lay lordships. Thus, embryonic structures of local control began to emerge as early as the 1070s. Malaterra recorded how Roger 'left Sicilian knights, to whom he had already granted possessions in as much of the island as he had conquered, around Partinico and Corleone. Sending them out in different directions, he ordered them to molest the people at Jato'.[5] The examples shown by a certain knight, Ingelmarius, who had attempted to build his own stronghold at Geraci, and shortly afterwards around 1083, Jordan's revolt in the Val Démone, may have been efforts by the potentially underprivileged to anticipate a distribution of lands by assuming local authority for themselves, setting dangerous precedents that highlighted the need for a clearer organisation and distribution of spoils to avoid a free for all land grab. By the 1090s, and after the final Muslim submission at Noto, Roger was said by Malaterra to have recompensed some of his followers with 'land and wide possessions, and others with diverse rewards for the sweat of their labour'.[6]

A salient factor that had empowered local lords on the mainland was so-called *incastellamento*, which refers to the enclosing of towns by walls. One of the many socio-economic effects of such concentrated centres was to enable local magnates to build up powerbases for themselves and their kin groups, which then became significant sites of political support or resistance. Indeed, on the south Italian peninsula, *incastellamento* had benefited the rise of the Normans. However, one of the key differences between the evolution of power on the mainland and that on the island was that this phenomenon was not widely reproduced in Sicily itself after its conquest. Rather, Roger and his successors were determined to avoid the proliferation of a potentially rebellious nobility. Therefore, they pressed their claim to rule over the entire island as directly as possible, while preferring to devolve power through the more stable agency of large church foundations. Thus, they guardedly parcelled out a limited number of much smaller grants to trusted individuals.

The creation of ecclesiastical lordships

By far the largest endowments were granted in order to create new institutions in the form of ecclesiastical lordships. The rapid development of richly endowed churches and monasteries would come to be a characteristic feature of Norman rule in Sicily.[7] As a result, very large numbers of Muslims of the post-conquest generation found themselves granted from the comital – later crown – demesne to churches along with the estates on which they lived.

Among the earliest foundations was the bishopric of Troina in 1079, which was granted two local *casalia* or walled estates shortly afterwards. Other early Latin foundations included the Benedictine abbey on the island of Lípari which was also endowed with landed property.[8] The end of the conquest gave even greater impetus to church foundations, so that between 1091 and 1093 bishoprics were founded, with papal approval, in the major cities of Catania, Syracuse, Agrigento and Mazara.[9] Prominent among the first generation of prelates on the island were an admixture of 'Latins', some, in this period, from 'beyond the Alps'. Thus, we find at Catania: a Breton called Ansger; Robert, a Lombard at Troina/Messina; Gerland from Besançon at Agrigento; and Roger from Provence at Syracuse.[10] At Palermo, the local Greek archbishop, Nicodemus, had been restored in the days after its fall. Thereafter, we find Alcherius, a Latin-rite prelate of unknown provenance. Throughout the twelfth century, high-ranking prelates were never far from the seats of power and influence, although many of their churches were later subject to substantial reorganisation.

A handful of towns that had been insignificant in the Islamic period rose to prominence in the early Norman period. The small town of Troina, for example, served as one of the earliest bases from which the nascent 'bureaucracy' could be organised, and was an early source for Greek administrators, such as the protonotary John of Troina, who supervised some of Count Roger I's earliest grants of men and whose signature appeared on a list of 'villeins' granted to Catania in

1095.[11] Troina may also have been the home of Eugenios, later to be known as the *amīr* Eugenios whose descendants would undertake a range of administrative duties. However, its significance in the late eleventh century was by no means matched by its status in the twelfth century. In 1096, the bishopric of Troina was joined to that of Messina and the bishop's residence moved with it, after which the town gradually lost its standing.

Although Roger required papal authorisation for all new church foundations and appointments to them, Urban's designation of Robert, the bishop of Troina, as papal legate without consultation with the count – in a church which Roger had apparently founded without consultation with the pope – resulted in the bishop's arrest. This brought to a head a dispute over the parameters of comital and papal authority in Sicily. Malaterra recorded the meeting of Roger and Pope Urban II at the siege of Capua in 1098 during which agreement was reached between the two, and his conquest narrative concludes with what is commonly and controversially understood to be the granting of the apostolic legateship to Roger, which formalised their mutual accommodation. In effect, Roger and his legitimate heirs were permitted to act in the place of a pope's personal representative in areas under Norman control.[12] The scope of the implied freedom in both practice and theory which this allowed has remained a matter of dispute ever since, but it gave the Normans unprecedented rights in dealing with new Latin churches to which they were making endowments and appointing loyal prelates of their own choice. Many of these empowering processes could now be done relatively free of papal interference. Ambivalent as the papal bull and its full implications were, it would continue to be of great, if not defining, importance for the relationship between the papacy and the Sicilian rulers. Its impact on the Sicilian Muslims was that the agreement gave the Normans greater possibilities for the use of churches on the island as political and administrative means of organisation, control and loyalty, in addition to their religious function and the gradual Latinisation of the island's ecclesiastical infrastructure.

The extent to which the fabric of the Greek Church had almost come to a point of collapse in western Sicily after almost 250 years of Muslim rule was highlighted by the description of the timid Greek archbishop of Palermo, Nicodemus, consigned to a small church which was not even located within the city walls. Partly to reinvigorate indigenous forms of Christianity and partly to reward the support of the local Christians, the early Norman rulers patronised and restored a number of old Byzantine churches whose condition had deteriorated but which had survived none the less. Among others, these included San Bárbaro at Demenna, San Filippo at Fragalà and Sant'Angelo at Brolo. Mirroring arrangements on the mainland, the Greek churches of Sicily recognised the primacy of the pope at Rome, but conducted their liturgy in

Greek. Roger's patronage of Greek houses continued into the early phases of the kingdom too, particularly with Roger II's foundation of San Salvatore *in lingua phari* at Messina between 1131 and 1134. This was then richly endowed with royal grants and made the archimandrite under which Greek-rite houses could then be organised, serving as a focal point for the revival of Greek monasticism on the island.

The Muslims of Catania and efforts to manage a displaced population

Fuller, detailed discussions of the intricate development of Latin- and Greek-rite houses in Sicily and the mainland have been undertaken elsewhere, but examples from Catania and Lípari-Patti here serve to illustrate the new modalities in eastern and north-eastern Sicily which early church foundations introduced.

The Benedictine abbey of Sant'Agata at Catania had been founded by 1091, twenty years after the city's initial fall to the Normans, but within a year of the final Muslim surrender. A grant made by Roger I the following year conceded the entire city with all its possessions to the church. The precise transition of power at Catania is murky: after Ibn al-Thumna's death, Roger's son-in-law, Hugh of Gercé, took over until he was killed in 1081 when, intriguingly, another member of the Banū l-Thumna took charge.[13] Notwithstanding this, the outcome at Catania thereafter was clear enough. The town with its surrounding lands and people, once under the secular leadership of the Muslim *amīr*, Ibn al-Thumna, now came under the sway of a Breton abbot-bishop of the Latin rite, who (unusually) bore a Norse name, Ansger ('God spear'). In the concluding stipulation on a surviving list of Muslims granted to the church, reference was made to an important meeting of lords that had been convened at Mazara two years earlier by Roger in 1093. It was at this assembly that the earliest lists of granted families were drawn up, most likely in Greek and Arabic, and then distributed as material proof of the concessions.[14] In the context of the chaos that marked the end of the Islamic period, followed by the Norman conquest, this was an important step forward in terms of command and authority in the absence of any remaining central administrative infrastructure over which they could assume power. The ad hoc issuing of documents 'in the field' was rudimentary and short term, but it was a solution that was repeated across the island as the main way of recording grants and the names of those registered on estates.

Possession of a written register of men thus came to form the basis of a lord's claim of rights granted over the people named on it. In the case of ecclesiastical lordships, the concessions contributed toward that foundation's ability to achieve a high degree of self-sufficiency. Indeed, churches also attracted trading privileges, concessions and tax exemptions.[15] Recording the names of heads of households to both a lord and a specific locality described a bilateral relationship that fixed the registered population to a particular place. In so doing, the registers also served as a basic bureaucratic response to the challenges posed by managing a population displaced by civil war, invasion and dispersal since those conceded as 'men of the registers' were tied to the place to which they were assigned.

As a tool that defined and regulated a lord's possessions and the movements of the population, the early lists or registers of men served primarily administrative and legal functions, but did not per se describe the named Muslims' fiscal status because the terms and conditions of service they owed to their lords were negotiated or decided upon separately. However, the registers (if accurate) could clearly be used for fiscal purposes as the basis for the collection of taxes. Indeed, a precedent from the era of Muslim rule can be seen since certain subsections of the names corresponded to that of a *jizya*-list. Thus, in the categories of those cited on the Catania list, distinctions were made between widows, slaves and the blind – precisely the groups who were exempt from paying the *jizya* under Islamic law. A subsection of Jews suggests that they had been liable to pay the *jizya*, again in accordance with the principles of Islamic taxation. Even if the information was not up to date, the lists did not necessarily become obsolete after an administrative slippage of a generation because the grants of 'men of the registers' also included the names of their sons, whose registered status was hereditary. The problem for much of Sicily, however, was that far more than a generation had passed with only little, if any, updating of records. Besides which, the disruption to settlement patterns had progressively worsened since the dissolution of power from the 1030s.

The relatively meagre amount of available evidence does not allow us to speak with any certainty about the burden of tax and services that the conceded Muslim families paid to their new Christian lords. However, it is quite clear from the evidence we do possess that there were great variations depending on particular circumstances. A combination of inference and assumption indicates that in cases where Muslims and Jews were granted to lords, the *jizya* payment they were required to make remained in the lords' possession. The lords did not transfer it to any treasury apparatus as was the practice in the Islamic period and in Muslim lands generally. In addition, when Muslims were granted to lords, labour services were required. This situation stands in contrast to what is known of the general practices in western Sicily on comital (later to become crown) lands where the *jizya* was accompanied by payment of a land tax, referred to in the Arabic of the Norman period as the *qānūn*.

An important, yet problematic, consideration is whether the *jizya* was levied collectively on the whole community or per capita. Evidence from the 'Rollus Rubeus' chartulary, the in-house records from the church of Cefalù, suggest that they were expecting to collect a total sum from the community, but that this amount was subdivided according to the relative means of each tax-paying family. The records are undated but claim to list Muslims donated in the time of Roger II as king (r. 1130–54). In other examples, all that is known to have been required was a simple figure, suggesting the amount was levied collectively. In cases where there was an established and known number of families in a community, but that community subsequently diminished, the same total amount was still required to be collected from the remaining families. One can only speculate, but if a vicious circle of gradual depopulation and constant tax demands were the scenario on lords' lands in eastern Sicily, an increasing per capita burden of taxes and services could help to account for the disintegration of Muslim communities there from the post-conquest period onwards, and their migration towards the lands of western Sicily where the landlords were the rulers themselves.

Two of the earliest lists of men, both originally dating from 1095, which recorded huge grants of mainly Muslim families, were made for Ansger of Catania. The first list is now lost, but survives in the form of a confirmation issued in 1145. On it were written the names of 525 'people (*ahl*) of Catania'. These were followed by the names of ninety-four widows; twenty-three slaves (*'abīd*) of the church, all of whom bore Arabic names; twenty-five Jews; and eight blind men.[16] The second list, also from 1095, survives in the Arabic original and partly also in a later confirmation from 1145. It recorded a grant to the church of 390 'Hagarene' families (that is, Muslims) from Aci Castello, a few kilometres to the north of Catania, whose names were written out in Arabic. An introduction and conclusion were added in Greek by a Greek scribe.[17] The prevalence of Greek and Arabic is best explained in pragmatic terms with the use of scribes familiar with the local languages and customs, and in the absence of a trained class of Latin notaries in the area. However, to speak of this brief burst of activity as the product of an 'administration' is premature, since Roger's stop-gap efforts to establish his lordship on the island and to deal with the problems raised by distributing the island's landed wealth were overseen by only a handful of scribes and were written in different places around the island, mainly Mazara, Palermo and Messina.

From this same period, another bilingual Arabic–Greek list of ninety-five 'Hagarenes' in western Sicily, who were conceded to Alcherius' cathedral at Palermo, also contained the names of twenty newly-weds, almost all of whom were the sons of named Muslims who had left their familial units to form separate, and therefore new, taxable households of their own.[18] From the internal prosopography of the list, it can be inferred to have been based on records compiled much earlier in the century. It is likely, therefore, that many – if not all – of these early lists of men from the 1090s were descended from older Arab-Sicilian models.

The pressing problem of how to manage or resettle a population that had been displaced by wars and was known only locally, if at all, is shown by what is thought to be a twelfth-century forgery, but which purports to be an authentic Latin copy.[19] In it, the abbot at Catania was allowed to retrieve from anywhere in Sicily all Muslims who formerly lived in the city at the time of the conquest but who had fled. Although the anachronistic references elsewhere within the document distinguish it as inauthentic, the right to recall Muslims who had vanished in the recent past was presumably part of the raison d'être of the forgery in the first place and hence supports the veracity of the situation which it addressed.

The combination of a newly founded Latin church, the immigration of new personnel to staff it, the attraction of immigrant colonists and the dispersal of the local Muslim communities can be clearly seen in the formative years of the abbey of San Bartolomeo.[20] Located on the arid island of Lípari, the abbey was founded by Robert Guiscard and Count Roger *c.* 1085, but was then joined with that of San Salvatore at Patti on the latter's foundation in 1094. Lying within Bishop Robert's newly formed diocese of Troina-Messina, the first abbot of San Bartolomeo, Ambrose (*c.* 1085–1119), received rich donations from Count Roger (and later from his wife and son), which initially included the seven Aeolian islands, as well as the *castrum* of Patti 'free of all services', along with satellite estates and those who lived and worked among the well-populated and fertile hills. The restored late-eleventh-century cloisters of San Bartolomeo serve as a good example of the simple, roughly executed architecture of the earliest Norman foundations, and stand in clear contrast to the better known and better preserved royal foundations of the twelfth century.

Several Norman or French families were attested as having made donations to the church and some were landholders in the vicinity. The little that is known of the early abbots and monks suggests that they were also a mix of 'Latin' immigrants. Perched on the crest of a hill which rises steeply from the coast, Patti itself was described as a *castrum* where only 'men of the Latin tongue, whoever they might be' were permitted to settle.[21] These were privileged, economic migrants who lived there on favourable terms. In return, they were required to defend the church from attack should the need arise. The town quickly drew colonists from across the Italian peninsula to where they were 'free' citizens, not vassals of the church like the indigenous population of Greek and Arabic speakers who, on linguistic grounds, were consigned to live on the outlying settlements in both open estates (*casalia*) and closed villages or towns (*castra*). A list of families from these settlements was drawn up, which was originally written in Greek and then transliterated into Latin script, to create a working document. The names were predominantly Greek, but some were of Arabic origin, consistent with the processes of intermingling and acculturation among Christian communities that had taken place during the Islamic period.[22] The church's 'Saracens' were listed separately, and interlinear notes between their Arab-Muslim names clearly show that the whereabouts of many were completely unknown: some were said to have fled, others had died along with their sons. Although the list bears no date, it was probably drawn up in the mid-1090s, then revised in the early 1130s, a generation later during a period of local disputes. The choice of language, rather than religion, as the determinant of settlement rights illustrates how, in this case at least, the plan to Latinise the town was designed to exclude the local 'Greek' Christians as well as the Muslims.

The problem of resettlement and the organisation, not only of lands, but of those who lived on the lands, can be seen by the assembly at Troina convened by Count Roger *c.* 1094 at which proclamations were made to the effect that landlords were required to hand over all illegally held families.[23] Any such people were to be settled at Focerò. As yet this locality remains to be discovered, but it is known that there was a watch tower which could relay signals along a chain of similar towers to Mileto, and so Focerò is probably located on some hilltop or coastal site near Patti. A sweep of the area was then made which, even though conducted over a relatively confined area, demonstrated the extent of the population displacement problem, since it was said to have yielded some 500 families. These were then resettled, with relief from taxes and services for the next five years. On Roger's death, however, this area was one of the focal points for a serious baronial revolt which flared up across north-eastern and north-central Sicily which saw the fort at Focerò destroyed and reconstructed three times between its foundation and 1140. The same revolt, or series of rebellious outbreaks, may also have been responsible for the destruction of Qalʿat al-Ṣirāṭ, which was rebuilt near Collesano. The inference of widespread and sustained damage in this area suggests that the traditional contrast between the order on the pacified island compared with the disorder of the rebellious mainland should not be drawn too starkly.

In terms of the *longue durée*, there is good reason to speak of the post-conquest period as a time of radical and irreversible change, and it is justifiable to point to key, institutional developments in this period in terms of originality, disjuncture and innovation. Even so, it is only in the grand scale of things that we can begin to describe distinct movements, and caution is still needed when identifying typical patterns, since that which had emerged was a confluence of unsystematically applied ideas. Given the extreme difficulty of the situation that the Normans faced, many of the solutions they fell back on were conservative in that they sought to preserve and revive existing structures, practices and traditions wherever possible. But if the broad objective of how to impose their rule had a dual focus: to retrieve and reconstruct whatever was extant from previous eras, while at the same time introduce new personnel and institutions, then the execution of this compatibilist strategy would prove to be problematic. The early comital documents of the 1090s were products of these tensions: they related to a local, largely Muslim population and were written out in Arabic and/or Greek by local and/or Calabrian scribes acting on the orders of a Norman count, mainly for the benefit of new Latin lords. All parties concerned were familiar with notions of administration, landholding, laws, customs and taxation. But they were not necessarily familiar with the *same* notions or terms of reference. For the time being, such details were of secondary importance, even if, in the absence of any overarching, coherent system of governance, the result was a breeding ground for confusion, disputes, disaffection, false claims and forgeries. In practice, justice remained a local matter, while socially, legally and politically, the magnitude of the new problems was just beginning to dawn, and was perhaps visible only to a few. Conquest had been a relatively straightforward matter. But how could any future ruler maintain political stability on an island where such a matrix of overlapping parameters and shifting spaces had been created within which a multi-faith, multi-ethnic, multi-lingual population competed, sometimes antagonistically, sometimes not?

Adelaide's regency: Latin settlement and Muslim emigration

On the death of Roger I in 1101, his third wife, Countess Adelaide (d. 1118), to whom he had been married since *c.* 1089, acted as regent for their son, Simon, who died in infancy in 1105, and thereafter as regent for their other son, Roger, until the year 1112 when he was old enough to assume rule in his own right.[24] Her regency was the first of four during the twelfth century in Sicily. Indeed, female rulership, the influence of wives and widows and alliances forged through marriage, form a striking feature of the 'Europeanisation' of Sicily in contrast to the previous period of Islamic rule of the *amīrs* in which powerful women were notable by their absence.

In Sicily, the circumstances of the regents differed greatly, but their political *modus operandi* was comparable in the way each was surrounded by close family members who introduced potent new influences. These would come to affect, often adversely, diverse elements within the Muslim communities. Adelaide was a patron of both Greek- and Latin-rite churches, and strengthened the movement towards re-Christianisation which had been set in motion in the post-conquest era across the island. Indeed, she followed her late huband in being referred to as 'helper of the Christians'. She was closely associated with the church at Patti – the bastion of Latin exclusivism – which she had endowed with families of Muslims, at least one largely Muslim estate and tax revenues from the Jews of Términi. Adelaide would also grant the newly founded settlement of Focerò to the church of Lípari-Patti where she chose to be buried. Her son, Roger II, later donated to it the estate of Raḥl Jawhar with its thirty Muslim families and their sons to help pay for the chapel in which she had been laid to rest.

Like many of those in ascendancy in south Italy and Sicily, Adelaide was not native to the area. Rather, she hailed from Savona in Liguria, about fifty kilometres along the coast to the west of Genoa. She belonged to the dynamic clan of the Aleramici, and made great use of these kin group connections, actively accelerating settlement into Sicily from mainland Italy, especially from the north-west. With her encouragement and that of her brother, Henry, large numbers of north Italians, or 'Lombards' as the sources referred to them, began to settle in the towns around, and to the south of, the wider Val Démone area.[25] These formed the origins of what has been described as a Lombard screen or wedge of towns which ringed the north-eastern third of the island such as Butera, San Fratello, Novara, Nicosia, Sperlinga, Piazza Armerina and Aidone – some of which appear to have conserved traces of Gallo-Italic elements in their present-day dialects.[26] Given the long-running and destructive baronial revolt conducted in parts of the Val Démone and across north-central Sicily, it is possible that Lombard support was vital in order to diffuse or to contain the spread of the insurrection. Such colonists were initially favoured, but during the second half of the twelfth century and especially in the transitional periods of the 1150s and 1160s, some of these Lombard towns became centres of active hostility to the king, his chief administrators and towards the Muslim population of eastern Sicily.

Many among the educated and wealthy Muslim population of the large urban centres, particularly Palermo, took the opportunity to follow the lead of those who had been leaving the island in waves since the 1030s. Some of these migrants are known because their achievements were recorded in Muslim biographical dictionaries, others are traceable overseas because they had adopted Sicilian *nisbas* or relative adjectives indicating a geographical origin, which they appended to their names. Funerary inscriptions from twelfth-century Ifrīqiya also yield a couple of individuals, each referred to as 'the Sicilian', the implication being that these people had once emigrated from there. For example, we find a certain Khalaf b. ʿAbd Allāh b. al-Ṣiqillī (d. 522/1127–8), and Muḥammad al-Qurashī al-Muqrī al-Ṣiqillī who died in 1147 in Monastir.[27] As so often with such evidence, there is no knowing the date of travel.

On safer ground, Sicilian literati are known to have found employment in the culturally burgeoning, provincial courts of the politically feeble *ṭāʾifa* statelets of al-Andalus, or else in Ifrīqiya and Egypt. Of these illustrious emigrants, perhaps the most famous was the poet, Ibn Ḥamdīs (d. 1132–3).[28] He had left Syracuse as a young man in 1078–9 and made his way in self-imposed exile to the court of al-Muʿtamid ibn ʿAbbād in Seville before transferring to Ifrīqiya in the early 1090s, where he stayed sufficiently long to witness the revenge defeat inflicted on the Norman expedition against al-Mahdiyya in 1123. The themes of his compositions were somewhat trite and self-indulgent, but they were also coloured by his unrelenting hostility to the Franks and his bitter-sweet reminiscences of a Sicilian homeland as a paradise lost.[29] Other important, but illustrative, examples of the Sicilian Muslim diaspora include the lexicographer and philologist Ibn al-Birr 'the Sicilian', who was at Ibn Mankūd's 'court' at Mazara during the *ṭa'ifa* period. He was then said to have been in Palermo until around the time of the Normans' victory of Misilmeri, and is best known for his transmission of works and his teaching. Among his famous Sicilian pupils was Ibn al-Qaṭṭā' (d. 1122). When the latter left the island, he made first for al-Andalus, and later became the personal tutor to the sons of al-Afḍal bin Badr al-Jamālī, the Fatimid *wazīr* in Cairo, counting among his distinguished pupils of grammar and lexicography, Ibn Barrī (d. 1187). Part of this same circle was Ibn Makkī 'the Sicilian', who emigrated to Ifrīqiya where he became a *qāḍī* and is thought to have died in 1108. Himself a pupil of Ibn al-Birr, his grammatical text *Tathqīf al-lisān* ('Education of the Tongue') is a rare source for the errors and mispronunciations he alleged were committed by Sicilian Arabic speakers, and which show elements of Maghribi dialect.[30]

The propensity for Sicilian Muslim notables to flee either south to Ifrīqiya or west to al-Andalus might also be taken as an unconscious indicator of the cultural direction Sicily faced vis-à-vis the rest of the Islamic world. That is to say, they did not generally migrate to the Levantine cities, and even less to the destinations of the Abbasid east. What is surprising, and indeed revealing, is how relatively few, such as the grammarian and religious scholar Ibn Faḥḥām (d. 1122), sought patronage in Fatimid Egypt. The flight to safety from the Normans of these tightly knit groups of men of letters would have far-reaching consequences. Not only did it bring about the rapid decline of intellectual and academic activity in Arabic on the island, but it also deprived the Muslims of important families who had been the primary transmitters of the island's identity as a place of Arab-Islamic culture. Ibn al-Qaṭṭā' cited 170 Arab-Sicilian poets from the Islamic period: only a handful are known from Norman times.[31] Those who emigrated presumably took as much transferable wealth as they could, abandoning any benefices, properties or landed estates over which they might once have had rights or control. We must again proceed on the assumption that these were incorporated into the comital demesne.

In political terms, the losses to the Muslim communities via emigration are hard to gauge, but one effect was most likely the creation of power vacuums into which stepped new elements alongside a reformed consolidation of older groupings. The result helps to account for the silence in the sources from this period over the political frictions which had characterised the past: we hear nothing further of 'the people of Ifrīqiya' and 'the people of Sicily', nor of rivalry between Sunnīs and Shī'a, nor Arab versus Berber. Thus, one effect of the Norman conquest was that such tensions dissipated with the formation of a more cohesive Muslim community at the expense of significant reductions in both its numerical size and political strength.

The influence of Christódoulos and George of Antioch

Historians remain divided over the extent to which the future king of the island, Roger's son (also called Roger), was a product of his environment, his upbringing, his own particular ideas, or the personnel around him. An equally sharp contrast can be drawn between those who describe his outlook largely in northern European terms, and those who see him as a south Mediterranean ruler. In recent years, the pendulum has swung ever more towards the latter view. Very little is known of Roger's early life, although his biographer, Alexander of Telese, reported that he had been brought up under the safe tutelage of his mother, Adelaide, when they were based mainly in Mileto in Calabria.[32] This may be an indication that he had little formal education, and he was certainly too young to have received any meaningful instruction from his father before his death. Roger's upbringing in formerly Byzantine Greek Calabria implies that he had been exposed to Greek language and culture. However, evidence for this, and for his subsequent contact with Arabic language and culture during his youth, while important, is entirely circumstantial.

The first move of a two-part shift accompanied the transfer of Adelaide and Roger's primary residence from Mileto to Messina in Sicily around the year 1109. Messina probably still had a majority Arab-Muslim population alongside a local Greek and migrant 'Latin' population from around the mainland. It was cosmopolitan by comparison with Palermo to where they moved in 1112, which was still strongly steeped in Arab-Islamic traditions. It was thus at an impressionable age that Roger came to be exposed to the full wealth of the old Muslim capital, vast by the standards of medieval Europe and easily the largest city Roger had ever seen – and would ever see. Even in a state of relative decline, it had much grander offerings than the commercial bustle of an entrepôt port like Messina. It was also far removed from the small, mountain retreats like Mileto or Troina of his Norman father, or Scribla and San Marco Argentano preferred by his uncle, Guiscard. Until the end of the 1130s, Roger rarely stayed for long in one spot, particularly after the turmoil of campaigning on the mainland. But thereafter, he effectively 'retired' to the city he had come to know as a youth. Indeed, by the time he had reached his forties, he barely seems to have left the comfort of the palace complexes.

One important long-term effect of this move was to secure the centre of political and cultural gravity in the extreme south-west of the future kingdom, far from its northern borders towards the Abruzzo mountains, the commercial ports of the Amalfi coast and far from the troublesome Achilles' heel of Apulia with its independently minded magnates and cities. It is misleading to speak of Palermo as a 'capital' city until a political nucleus formed around the royal palaces and central administration which developed quickly from the 1130s. None the less, from a geopolitical perspective, the adoption of a major political centre on the mainland might have given a greater strategic advantage in maintaining tighter, overall control across the wider region and the south Italian peninsula.

By the time Roger came of age in 1112, he was already surrounded in Palermo by some of the key advisers under whose influence the kingdom would come to emerge in 1130. The *amiratus* Christódoulos who, along with the two *protonotarii*, Nicholas and Bonus, was given the prestigious title of *protonobilissimos* by the Byzantine emperor, appears in the text of charters and chronicles between 1107 and 1125 when he is seen acting in collaboration with Roger and his closest advisers and administrators, in particular George of Antioch.[33] Christódoulos has long been linked with Calabria since it was there that he endowed Greek monasteries. This regional interest does not exclude the possibility that he was a convert from Islam, given the post-conquest relocation of Muslims to Calabria. However, what is known of his landed possessions connects him more closely with Sicily itself, as does his unusual name. Saint Christódoulos was linked to the late eleventh-century island of Patmos, but the name was not common in the Byzantine world. It was rarely attested on the Italian mainland either, and yet, it came to be popular among Christians on the island of Sicily. It is tempting to think that it may have had particular appeal to both Arab-Christians, who understood Greek, as well as to converts from Islam because the name in Greek means 'slave of Christ' and finds obvious equivalents in Arabic names beginning *'Abd al-*, which also mean 'slave of'. In the Arabic sources, Christódoulos was known as 'Abd al-Raḥmān al-Naṣrānī ('the Christian') – not a precise translation, but perhaps indicative of a dual identity of an Arabic-speaking 'Greek' Christian. While having two names was not untypical of Muslim converts, alternative Greek–Arabic names were common among indigenous Sicilian Christians of the period.

An essential source for our knowledge of the lives of Roger's early advisers is the chronicler, al-Maqrīzī, who resembled other very late Egyptian sources such as al-Nuwayrī in that he was able to draw on unique information not included in Ibn al-Athīr.[34] Maqrīzī said of Christódoulos that he 'shared absolute authority' with Roger from 1112, although he was to be arrested and killed on the orders of George of Antioch. This reversal of status is partially corroborated in other sources, in that as late as 1123, for example, in the failed campaign against Mahdiyya, George was subordinate to Christódoulos. The last mention of Christódoulos was in December 1125 when George was also first attested with the title of *amīr*, suggesting that the rise of one coincided with the fall of the other and may well be linked as Maqrīzī said.

The dominance of high-ranking Arab-Christian, and particularly Greek, personnel around Count Roger II is further supported by the presence of George of Antioch, one of the most important figures of Norman Sicily. His immediate assumption of power after his arrival in 1108 would eventually lead to his domination of political life as *amīr* of *amīrs*, archon of archons and chief minister (*wazīr*) until his own death in 1151. The paucity of specifically titled positions in this early period, while reflecting something of the relative lack of defined structure to medieval administrations is also, in the case of Sicily, an expression of the genuinely amorphous government of the young count, which was embodied by a few all-round functionaries. Maqrīzī's biography of George gives details of his wide-ranging responsibilities which place him at the very centre of power, not only as the chief architect of what would become the kingdom of Sicily, but that he, perhaps even more than Roger, held the tightest grip on the levers of power during the first half of the twelfth century. Indeed, to explain and account for George's influence is instrumental for understanding the formation of the multifaceted aspects of the kingdom and concepts of Sicilian kingship.

George's complex background and experience were by no means limited to Byzantine administration. Rather, he had spent most of his career working within an Ifrīqiyan, Arab-Islamic system of governance as he had been employed by the Zirid *amīr*,Tamīm, in Mahdiyya as a financial officer from *c.* 1087 until 1108. Maqrīzī claimed that he was forced to flee when Tamīm's son, Yaḥyā, assumed power, and he vaguely alludes to an internal conspiracy and personal attacks. However, if we accept that Christódoulos had sent a warship for his escape at George's request, then it is likely that he had already established diplomatic contacts with Palermo prior to 1108. Once in Sicily, he assumed a range of high-level responsibilities in the construction or continued reconstruction of Roger's comital administration, and maintained diplomatic contacts with Islamic chanceries. He was said, for example, to have acted frequently as Roger's envoy to the Fatimids in Cairo. His background gives us no reason to doubt al-Tījānī and Ibn Khaldūn's claim that he knew Arabic: not only would he have known it well, but George was at least bilingual. It is also thought that George was later the author of Roger's elaborate chancery signatures in Greek.[35]

In 1113, George was attested as the patron of an early and very conspicuous 'public' work, namely the construction of an impressive bridge outside Palermo over the Wādī ʿAbbās (Oreto river), which improved suburban and extramural connections, ingress, security and defence while, presumably, it allowed the raising of revenues through tolls (see fig. 5 on p. 140). Indeed, this is arguably one of the finest of Italy's many bridges. It also deserves to be among the most illustrious, since it was the site of the Garibaldi's victory over the Bourbons in May 1860 at the beginning of the *Risorgimento* movement.

Maqrīzī reported that George was put in charge of the Sicilian *dīwāns* (here, 'administrative offices') at the behest of Christódoulos. This overstates the structural level of the bureaucracy in this early period, but George was probably involved with the organisation of comital finances for which his experience and training in the administrations in Byzantine Antioch and Zirid Mahdiyya were invaluable. His first, specifically attested role was the management of the Muslim-dominated western province of Iato (Arabic: Jāṭū, around modern San Giuseppe Iato and Monte Iato), where he was attested as the *'āmil* (literally 'agent') or district governor in 1114. This raises a fascinating and important question. In 1079, Iato was said by Malaterra to have had 13,000 families, a figure which is unusually specific. If it is to be taken at face value, then it conceivably referred to the entire population of the whole province, rather than families within the town itself. Of greater significance is that data was already believed to exist for Iato which, when combined with George's known role as provincial governor in 1114, thereby allows a valuable trace of administrative continuity to be inferred between the late Islamic and early Norman periods. These lands, which lay relatively close to Palermo, passed directly into the hands of the count and would later become the property of the crown. It may not be coincidental that the Arabic and Greek records we possess from the 1170s and 1180s for the province of Iato and its estates are the fullest of their type and may, to some extent, follow the outline of an older Fatimid province.

George was the conspicuous benefactor of Greek-rite churches, most famously that of Santa Maria dell'Ammiraglio founded in 1143 in Palermo where he was buried. Now commonly known as the Martorana, the surviving internal decoration of the church reveals fleeting but important clues about George's outlook. Most notable are the church's mosaics, one of which depicts Roger as king, crowned directly by Christ (see fig. 8 on p. 231).[36] Also significant is the church's association with Arabic-speaking Christians of the Eastern Church. Thus, around a wooden drum in the cupola is found a Byzantine hymn transliterated into Arabic letters. Its young, Arabic-speaking Christian congregation, or at least the women among them, attracted Ibn Jubayr's eye as they entered the church at Christmas 1184. In spite of such evidence, we can conclude little with certainty about George's disposition towards the Sicilian Muslims. It may be a misreading of the evidence to interpret the other Arabic inscriptions in the church (even one with Quranic resonances) as specifically designed to attract or encourage converts from Islam although, of course, it may have had that effect. Indeed, if an ulterior motive of religious conversion were intended, then the church was ideally located: it was directly adjacent to the sizeable Jewish quarter (*ḥārat al-Yahūd*) along with its synagogue.

The Normans had not begun the conquest of Sicily with a fleet of their own, but, as William of Apulia described, they had acquired one from Calabria during the siege of Bari, and developed it thereafter when local Bariot ships and sailors were pressed into service. This increased potential immediately broadened their horizons and allowed them to contemplate taking Malta, rather than Palermo, as their next objective after Bari in 1071. In any event, and in order to defend Sicily effectively, they would require a substantial and locally based fleet. To this end, they had also inherited at least a vestigial fleet on the island and certainly had access there to dockyards, ship-building expertise and – in the figure of George of Antioch – a willing and able naval commander.

George remained militarily active to within three years of his death aged almost ninety; old by any standards and almost double the average lifespan of the three Norman kings of Sicily. Such was George's long dominance of Sicilian affairs that many of the Greek and Arabic personnel who had thrived while he was alive were unable to fill the power vacuum after his death.[37] If George had dynastic ambitions for his sons Michael and Theodore, then these amounted to little. Indeed, it is striking that no extended kin group could establish itself for long at the heart of government. George's death in 1151, followed by that of Roger himself three years later, would mark the resurgence of political momentum towards 'Latins' in high office and as the men of consequence around the kings.

George's life-long and varied knowledge of Arab-Islamic lands, regimes, cultures, languages and peoples, set him apart from other non-native settlers into the island, especially the 'Latin' lords and other incoming colonists who were arriving from around the Italian peninsula. It is fair to infer that their disposition towards the Muslims and local Greeks was fundamentally different. In George, it is possible to see many of the ingredients which comprised the essence of the kingdom-to-be under Roger. Indeed, over the course of the first half of the twelfth century, George played the crucial transitional role between post-conquest and kingdom; between comital and royal; between men of the sword and men of the pen; and between Arab-Muslim, Arab-Christian, Greek Christian and Latin-Christian elements. Above all, what George could offer to Roger's Sicily was the wide-ranging sophistication of south Mediterranean savoir-faire, the sources of which were more developed outside the island, and the conscious appropriation of which would come to distinguish the kingdom from other medieval 'Latin' regimes. The early Norman Sicily that George helped to fashion, was not so much the triangular space created by the intersection of its three great spheres of influence in the Mediterranean (Byzantium, Islam and the Latin West); rather, it was precisely the undefined space that remained *between* all three, equally peripheral to each and perfectly poised to import from around it that which suited the choice of its rulers and their closest advisers.

Abū l-Ḍaw' and the Banū Rajā'

In spite of the emigration of many of the leading Muslim families, we can discern the existence of at least one very important kin group, the Banū Rajā', whose prominence at Palermo in both secular and religious fields can be traced in charters and narrative sources with certainty from the early 1120s until the early 1160s. Four members of this extended family are attested over three generations as having held the key post of *qāḍī* at Palermo, with powers of jurisdiction over the Muslim community there. They are known to us from two deeds of sale in the city in 1137–8 and 1161. In addition, we have valuable scraps of information concerning another member of this same family, known by his common nickname of Abū l-Ḍaw', whose importance has recently been established as one of the early influences around the young Roger in the formative period after Adelaide's death and prior to his accession to the throne.[38] Overall, the extended period of influence which the Banū Rajā' held at the highest levels over the most important Muslim community on the island offers vital evidence for the continued collaboration of leading Sicilian Muslim families with the new leadership.

Details about Abū l-Ḍaw' ibn Rajā' have come down to us mainly via snatches of his own poetry cited by 'Imād al-Dīn, and in al-Maqrīzī's biography of George of Antioch. He was also in contact with Abū l-Ṣalt Umayya (d. 1134), the polymath historian and administrator of Zirid Ifrīqiya, who was on sufficiently good terms with Abū l-Ḍaw' to have sent him verses. In addition, both Abū l-Ḍaw' (described in the Greek of the petition with the general, honorific term *káïtos*), and his uncle, in his capacity as chief magistrate (*qāḍī*) of Palermo, were attested along with Christódoulos and a Calabrian Greek judge as having presided over a legal case from 1123 concerning usurped property near Ciminna.[39] The case is not only important for the legal history of the Norman period in its early and most experimental phase, but also remarkable in that the practices and procedures of this court resembled those of an Islamic *maẓālim* court to which appeals and petitions could be brought. This is all the more intriguing given Ibn al-Athīr's precise claim that '[Roger] set up the *dīwān al-maẓālim* to which plaintiffs could raise complaints'.[40]

The institutional framework through which a legal challenge to the ruling family could, theoretically, be brought was innovative and clearly impressed Ibn al-Athīr, who went on to comment that '[Roger] would administer justice [to the plaintiffs] even if it were against [the interests of] his own son'. It is possible that because this judicial hybrid of a court vaguely resembled something akin to proceedings in Islamic justice, Muslim observers unquestioningly assumed that it was a *maẓālim* court. It is also possible that this reference picks up the very lawsuit of 1123 which was, unsuccessfully, brought by a family of Muslims against Roger's own cousin. But after this episode, the sources fall silent. The testimony recorded at the court hearing is also significant in that it makes rare references to the destruction wrought during the widespread baronial revolt after the death of Roger I, but provides no details of who was involved.

The reference to Abū l-Ḍaw' in Maqrīzī's biography of George of Antioch by the specific title of *kātib al-inshā'* suggests that he was the author of diplomatic correspondence and dealt with legal petitions which arose from the *dīwān al-maẓālim*.[41] Although he was later said to have declined promotion to become George's head of the administration (*wazīr*), it should also be noted that a refusal to assume high office in a secular administration was commonly used in Muslim biographical writing as a pious topos. Notwithstanding this, the elegy Abū l-Ḍaw' wrote on the death of one of Roger's sons (probably either Tancred d. *c.* 1138–42 or Alfonso d. 1144) clearly demonstrates that his continued support for the crown into Roger's reign as king can be added to that of his family.

The Normans and the Muslim south Mediterranean (1117–28)

In, or around, 1117 Roger married Elvira, daughter of Alfonso VI (d. 1109), the king of León-Castile, conqueror of Muslim Toledo in 1085, and a leading player in the Spanish *ṭā'ifa* period. Alfonso had married a Muslim convert, who was presumably Arabic-speaking and had taken a Christian name, Isabella. Like the young and aspiring Roger, neither were in a position to conclude marriage alliances with major European dynasties, but both looked southward to carve out and append territories to their own – and both did so, in good part, at Muslim expense. Such was Roger's personal devotion to Elvira (who was remembered for her piety, almsgiving and little else) that, on her death in 1135, he locked himself away for so long that dangerous rumours spread that he had himself died.[42] He did not remarry for another fourteen years.

The relationship in all respects was rather more successful than that of his mother's attempt to remarry which had ended in a humiliating fiasco. Her dissolved marriage to Baldwin of Jerusalem has often been cited as the reason for Roger's reluctance to involve himself in crusader affairs in Outremer. However, in an apocryphal and anachronistic passage, Ibn al-Athīr related how a Frankish ruler of Jerusalem [Bardawīl] approached a Sicilian ruler [Rujār] with a plan to capture and jointly rule the coastal towns of Ifrīqiya.[43] Roger's advisers were spontaneously made to proclaim the benefits of converting the conquered to Christianity, whereupon the king lifted a leg and broke wind loudly at their counsel because they had not considered the risk of failure, the political cost of alliances with the crusaders, the economic costs of having to supply them, nor the diplomatic fallout of breaking existing treaties with the Zirids. The episode is pure theatre written from a long, retrospective distance, but to observers in the Islamic world, crafty Sicilian prudence was almost as legendary as the boorishness of the Franks. To later historians, his commercial and political acumen have been more perceptible than his religious zeal and, although Roger did not go on crusade, his expansion into the south Mediterranean posed a very serious threat to Muslim political and economic influence in Ifrīqiya.

Across the Sicilian channel, in the long aftermath of the Hilālian invasions, the old Fatimid capital of al-Mahdiyya had remained the political centre of the Zirid *amīrs*, with Zirid-appointed governors in both Sfax and Sousse. Exactly where the political orbit of the Zirids became too weak to maintain influence was a matter of contention, with several key cities under the sway of regional factions, particularly the extended kin groups that had emerged since the 'Hilālian invasion' of the mid-eleventh century. For their part, the Zirids, although in a long, slow, but not necessarily terminal, decline had retained their imperial aspirations to govern all Ifrīqiya, and were thus determined to defend their claim to control the flow of maritime trade in and out of Ifrīqiyan ports wherever they could. Set against this background, the standard interpretation of their attack in 1117–18 on the Banū Jāmiʿ, who controlled the powerful 'maritime oasis' of Gabès, when its governor sent out a merchant ship in his own name, is of a direct attempt from Mahdiyya to stamp Zirid authority over this trading centre and outlet which connected Saharan supply lines with the Mediterranean. As a result of Zirid intervention to stifle the commercial independence of Gabès, the latter sought assistance from Palermo, marking the start of worsening relations between the Normans and the Zirids under Tamīm's grandson, ʿAlī b. Yaḥyā (r. 1116–21). But as the Zirids attempted to consolidate and extend their commercial and political dominance along the Ifrīqiyan coast, so the Normans undermined their authority by forming alliances with the tribal governors in rival cities. Thus, as Zirid power gradually slipped over the course of the next generation, the disjointed Ifrīqiyan cities and islands were attacked by the Sicilians in a persistent but piecemeal fashion. Through his intervention in Ifrīqiya, Roger not only maintained his reputation and status as the region's supplier of grain, but he also gained control of the shipping lanes and, in so doing, enabled Christian merchants to assume a closer position relative to their market, seeking to dominate the lucrative and politically sensitive overseas trade that was plied between the two continents.[44]

As a direct result of the 1117–18 intervention, the first cities to submit themselves as protectorates of Sicily were Gabès and also, we can infer from a later reference, Trípoli. This introduced a new relationship into Norman–Ifrīqiyan affairs since attacks on the north African coast prior to 1118 had largely been conducted by the Pisans and/or the Genoese. For example, in 1114–15, large-scale attacks on Majorca had been undertaken by a joint Catalan-Pisan naval force in an attempt to carve out control of the Balearic islands for themselves. For motives most easily explained in terms of economic expediency and personal ambition of the protagonists involved, the years 1118–27 saw a number of Sicilian attacks launched against the Muslim south Mediterranean. Only in the loosest possible sense could these expeditions be considered as a species of crusader activity. They can, however, be understood as the precursor to the Normans' eventual extension into Ifrīqiya and the establishment of indirect rule there between 1148 and 1160.

In midsummer 1123 a fleet, with Christódoulos as admiral and George of Antioch as his second-in-command, launched a major attack from Marsala on Mahdiyya, but which managed to take only Pantelleria and the fort of al-Dīmās before the attackers were besieged themselves and retreated with heavy casualties. In part, the attack could be explained in terms of revenge for what may have been a joint Almoravid and Zirid raid on Nicótera conducted the year before. In which case, the causes of the Sicilian counterattack were not only direct and immediate, but they can also be linked to the deteriorating relations with their former allies. Even if the Normans had mistaken the identity of the raiders for the Zirids (as Ibn al-Athīr was convinced), the raid pre-dated by a matter of weeks, if not days, a Zirid appeal to the Fatimids in Cairo to use their influence in Palermo to prevent further raids against Ifrīqiya. While this shows a high level of warm diplomatic rapport between the Fatimids and the Normans at a relatively early date, as well as a renewed rapprochement between the Zirids and the Fatimids – probably out of the former's fear of an attack from Sicily – in the event, neither the mission which arrived in Palermo, nor subsequent diplomatic contact appear to have curbed the Normans' conduct towards Zirid territory in and around Ifrīqiya. Perhaps they were all the more ineffectual if George had acted as Roger's ambassador to the Fatimids, and there are hints in the Arabic sources of George's personal determination to destroy the capital of his former employers who had rejected him.

Sicilian naval activity in the late 1120s built on previous gains as well as extending the economic reach and potential of Sicily in the south Mediterranean. Thus, in 1127, Roger's (re)conquest of Malta in the wake of raids on Patti and Syracuse consolidated a base between Ifrīqiya and Sicily. In the following year, he concluded an agreement with the count of Barcelona to provide ships to raid the eastern Iberian coast 'in the service of God', that is, at the expense of Muslim shipping. Later in the same year, the Normans committed an impounded ship from Savona to help patrol the southern Mediterranean for pirates between 'Numidia' and Trípoli. In effect, it was to assume a policing role across the major part of the north African coastline. The increased Sicilian interest in north Africa and the south Mediterranean may have continued more vigorously had Roger not been required to act urgently over the question of his status on the Italian mainland.

The death of William, the duke of Apulia, in 1127 without an heir, prompted Roger to travel straight to Salerno in order to stake a controversial claim to what he regarded as his inheritance. Since the early 1120s, Roger had been looking to extend his power on the mainland, where he was in control of Calabria and where he represented the strongest force in an increasingly fragmented and disorderly region. Roger's supporters claimed that his rights to the duchy of Apulia derived either from an oral pledge allegedly given some years earlier by William to Roger, or by virtue of the fact that he was the surviving relative from the Hauteville clan. Besides which, he had been accepted as duke by the Salernitans and other major towns across the duchy. The view of the pope, Honorius II, concerned at Roger's growing power and relatively free hand that he had in his dealings with the Church in Sicily, was that Apulia should revert to the papacy, after which a candidate of their choice might be invested as duke.

The political repercussions resulted in Roger's excommunication and the remission of sins for all who fought against him. However, the raising of papal coalition forces against Roger, and their collapse outside Benevento, forced Honorius to grant investiture of the duchy of Apulia to Roger. By the spring of 1130, following campaigns in which Muslim troops were said to have been put to savage use, Roger had, in effect, much of south Italy under his authority by unifying Sicily with Calabria and Apulia. In the meantime, on the pope's death in February 1130, a double election brought into competition two rival popes: Innocent II (d. 1143) and Anacletus II (d. 1138). The latter had a power base at Rome, the former rallied support from France and Germany. The schism and Roger's support for the eventual loser, Anacletus, would have a lasting effect on his undertakings in south Italy and Sicily. While Anacletus' offer of a royal title, which he made in September 1130, led to Roger's coronation as king of Sicily, Calabria and Apulia in Palermo cathedral on Christmas Day of the same year, his actions thereafter were sanctioned by the dubious legitimacy of the anti-pope until the schism ended with Anacletus' death in 1138 and papal recognition of his royal status in the following year. However, much of Roger's work towards the reorganisation of the new Latin Church foundations in Sicily, such as the elevation of the abbot of Lípari-Patti to bishop, the lavish royal foundation of the cathedral of San Salvatore at Cefalù and the creation of Messina as metropolitan see, with both these and Sant'Agata at Catania as its suffragan bishoprics was not recognised as valid until later in the century. Papal approval of the sees of Lípari-Patti, Cefalù and Messina, for example, was given only as late as 1166.[45] Piecemeal as the complex process of legitimisation was, in little over a century after the fall of Muslim Palermo to the Normans, over fifty Latin abbeys would be founded which were divided among nine large dioceses: Mazara; Agrigento; Catania; Palermo; Lípari-Patti; Cefalù; Syracuse; Messina and Monreale.[46] Thus, under the Normans, the vast majority of the Muslim population lived either on crown lands or those of a Latin-rite church.

Notes

1 The Arabic chroniclers have relatively little to say about events on the island after c. 1030. After the Norman conquest, they speak largely of Sicilian–Ifrīqiyan affairs. On the post-Norman conquest period, see Ibn al-Athīr, *BAS*[2] Ar. I:320; *BAS*[2] It. I:449.

2 On the Latin sources' disagreement over the division of the island, see Amatus, VI:21, pp. 138–9 (and the observations on p. 139 n. 45), and Malaterra, II:45, p. 53.

3 The most systematic introduction to castle-building is Ferdinando Maurici, *Castelli medievali in Sicilia. Dai bizantini ai normanni* (Palermo, 1992). In addition, there are several articles by Henri Bresc, including: 'Terre e castelli: le fortificazioni nella Sicilia araba e normanna', in *Castelli. Storia ed Archeologia*, R. Comba and A. Settia (eds) (Torino, 1984), pp. 73–87; 'Les Normands, constructeurs de châteaux', in *Les Normands en Méditerranée dans le sillage des Tancrède*, P. Bouet and P. Nevueaux (eds) (Caen, 1994), pp. 63–75; and 'L'incastellamento in Sicilia', in *I Normanni: popolo d'Europa. MXXX–MCC*, Catalogo della Mostra, M. D'Onofrio (ed.) (Venezia, 1994), pp. 217–20. For an overview of the wider issues by the same author, see 'Féodalité coloniale en terre d'Islam: la Sicile (1070–1240)', in *Structures féodales dans l'Occident méditerranéen (X^e–XIIIe siècles), Actes du Colloque Internationale*, 1978 (Rome 1980), pp. 631–47.

4 For Norman castles (*castella*) at Paternò and Mazara, see Malaterra, III:1, p. 57; Maurici, *Castelli medievali*, pp. 92–4.

5 On early concessions to Norman knights and their harrying activities to the north-west and south-east of the Muslim stronghold at Jato, see Malaterra, III:20, p. 69.

6 Malaterra, IV:15, p. 94. On post-conquest defences and exemptions, see Malaterra, III:31–2, pp. 76–7 and IV:15, p. 93. For a recent survey of events post-1072, see Loud, *Robert Guiscard*, pp. 165–85.

7 Of secondary literature relating to the establishment and evolution of the Latin Church in Sicily, two works stand out: Lynn Townsend White, *Latin Monasticism in Norman Sicily* (Cambridge, MA, 1938) and G. A. Loud, *The Latin Church in Norman Italy* (Cambridge, 2007), which now largely supersedes it.

8 On the transition from pre- to post-conquest and early Church foundations, see Loud, *Latin Church*, pp. 10–134.

9 For the churches founded at Agrigento and Catania, see Malaterra, VI:7, p. 70.

10 On the early Church personnel, see Norbert Kamp, 'The bishops of Southern Italy in the Norman and Staufen periods', in *The Society of Norman Italy*, G. A. Loud and A. Metcalfe (eds), pp. 185–209. This volume also includes two other important articles on the Church, namely, G. A. Loud, 'The papacy and the rulers of southern Italy, 1058–1198', pp. 151–84, and Peter Herde, 'The papacy and the Greek church in southern Italy between the eleventh and the thirteenth century', pp. 213–51.

11 On the early scribes attached to the Norman leaders and the embryonic comital 'administration', see the important discussions in Johns, *Arabic Administration*, pp. 63–90.

12 The text of the papal bull awarding the powers to the apostolic legate, see Malaterra, IV.29, p. 107. On the implications for papal–Sicilian relations, see Loud, *Robert Guiscard*, pp. 231–3.

13 On Hugh of Gercé and the Banū l-Thumna at Catania, see Malaterra, III:10, pp. 61–2 and III: 30, pp. 75–6. 'Benthumen', as he was called by Malaterra, was referred to as a *paganus* and, therefore, was unlikely to have been a convert to Christianity as Amari and others after him have suggested.

14 For the context with corrected reading and translation from the Greek, see Johns, *Arabic Administration*, pp. 54 and 119–20. On the registers of men of the 1090s, see also Hiroshi Takayama, *The Administration of the Norman Kingdom of Sicily* (Leiden, 1993), pp. 38–40.

15 On the desiderata of granting exemptions to churches, and for an incisive survey of the Norman economy, see David Abulafia, 'The crown and the economy under Roger II and his successors', *Dumbarton Oaks Papers*, 37 (1983): 1–14.

16 Cusa, *Diplomi*, pp. 563–85. On the early administration generally, see Johns, *Arabic Administration*, pp. 51–62; and also, Takayama, *Administration of the Norman Kingdom*, pp. 24–46. Takayama's work is important for the kingdom as a whole, but that of Johns should now be preferred over questions of the Arabic fiscal administration of Sicily and Calabria.

17 Cusa, *Diplomi*, pp. 541–9 and 586–95.

18 Johns, *Arabic Administration*, pp. 46–51.

19 L.-R. Ménager, 'Notes critiques sur quelques diplômes normandes de l'Archivio Capitolare di Catania', *Bullettino dell'archivio paleografico italiano*, series 2–3, pp. 143–76 (pp. 150–2). For a discussion of the forgery, see Johns, *Arabic Administration*, pp. 39–41.

20 On Lípari-Patti, see White, *Latin Monasticism*, pp. 77–100. Some of the observations above are indebted to my collaborative work with Jeremy Johns in a forthcoming article 'A Latin register (*platea*) of villeins from twelfth-century Patti', which re-examines the defective edition of C.-A. Garufi's in 'Censimento e catasto della popolazione servile', *Archivio storico siciliano*, 49 (1928): 92–100. On the source materials, see Dieter Girgensohn and Norbert Kamp, 'Urkunden und Inquisitionen des 12 und 13 Jahrhunderts aus Patti', *QFIAB* (1965): 1–240.

21 For the Patti charter, see *Roger II diplomata*, no. 23, pp. 64–6.

22 For issues on onomastics as evidence for intercommunal mingling, see Metcalfe, *Muslims and Christians*, pp. 71–98.

23 For the Troina assembly and proclamations, see Cusa, *Diplomi*, pp. 532–5.

24 On Adelaide's regency and her patronage of kin groups and 'Lombards', see Ernesto Pontieri, 'La madre di re Ruggero: Adelaide del Vasto, contessa di Sicilia, regina di Gerusalemme (?–1118)', in *Tra I Normanni nell'Italia meridionale* (Naples, 1964), pp. 409–509; Hubert Houben, 'Adelaide «del Vasto» nella storia del regno normanno di Sicilia', in H. Houben, *Mezzogiorno normanno-svevo. Monasteri e castelli, ebrei e musulmani* (Naples, 1996), pp. 81–115; also Johns, *Arabic Administration*, pp. 40–1 and 63–5.

25 On Lombard settlement and their contribution to the formation of later Sicilian society, see the valuable analyses in Henri Bresc, *Un Monde Méditerranéen. Économie et Société en Sicile 1300–1450*, 2 vols (Palermo and Rome, 1986), II: 582–708 (p. 595). For a survey of their privileges in the context of the kingdom, see Abulafia,

'Crown and economy', pp. 11–14.

26 For Gallo-Italic dialects and linguistic arguments, see Alberto Várvaro, *Lingua e storia in Sicilia I: dalle guerre puniche alla conquista normanna* (Palermo, 1981), pp. 185–96.

27 See Slimane-Mostafa Zbiss (ed.), *Inscriptions arabes de Tunisie* (Tunis, 1955), p. 92, no. 78; and Slimane-Mostafa Zbiss (ed.), *Inscriptions arabes de Monastir* (Tunis, 1960), p. 86, no. 107.

28 William Granara, 'Islamic education and the transmission of knowledge in Muslim Sicily', in *Law and Education in Medieval Islam. Studies in Memory of Professor George Makdisi*, J. E. Lowry, D. J. Stewart and S. M. Toorawa (eds) (E. J. W. Gibb Memorial Trust, 2004), pp. 150–73.

29 For Islamic Sicily as paradise or a paradise lost, see Ibn Ḥamdīs, *BAS*[2] Ar. II:619 and 621; *BAS*[2] It. II:313 and 315; also the poet ʿAbd al-Ḥalīm b. ʿAbd al-Wāḥid in *BAS*[2] Ar. 705–6; *BAS*[2] It. II:434.

30 Dionisius A. Agius, *Siculo Arabic* (London and New York, 1996), pp. 123–57, draws on the works of G. Caracausi, *Arabismi medievali di Sicilia* (Palermo, 1983), and G.-B. Pellegrini, *Gli Arabismi nelle lingue neolatine*, 2 vols (Brescia, 1972), and observes the data from Sicily in tandem with later Maltese dialects, the first evidence for which dates from the 1500s.

31 For the remaining traces of Islamic sciences on the island, see Francesco Barone, 'Islām in Sicilia nel XII e XIII secolo: ortoprassi, scienze religiose e tasawwuf', in *Incontri mediterranei. Rivista semestrale di storia e cultura*, 6/2 (2003): 104–15.

32 Roger's safe tutelage at the hands of Adelaide suggests that he had not been exposed to much in the way of formal education. Alexander of Telese, I:3. pp. 7–8. See online English translation by G. A. Loud.

33 For Greek officials in the kingdom, see Léon-Robert Ménager, *Amiratus – 'Αμηρᾶς. L'émirat et les origines de l'amirauté (XI*[e]*–XIII*[e] *siècles)* (Paris, 1960). Also, Takayama, *Administration of the Norman Kingdom*, pp. 44–5, 49–53, 66–8; and Vera von Falkenhausen's 'Cristodolo', in *Dizionario biografico degli Italiani*, 31, pp. 49–51. On the use of Greek titles in this period, see Takayama, *Administration of the Norman Kingdom*, pp. 33–4.

34 For al-Maqrīzī on Christódoulos, George of Antioch and Roger II, see Johns, *Arabic Administration*, pp. 80–90.

35 On Roger's Greek signatures, see Vera von Falkenhausen, 'I diplomi dei re normanni in lingua greca', in *Documenti medievali greci e latini. Studi comparativi*, Giuseppe De Gregorio and Otto Kresten (eds) (Spoleto, 1997), pp. 253–308 (pp. 285–6).

36 Ernst Kitzinger, *The Mosaics of St. Mary's of the Admiral in Palermo* (Washington DC, 1990), especially pp. 189–97.

37 On the death of George, Ibn al-Athīr commented that 'the ruler of Sicily had no one who could fill his place after him': Ibn al-Athīr, *BAS*[2] Ar. I:336; *BAS*[2] It. I:476; Eng. II:32.

38 Adalgisa De Simone, 'Il mezzogiorno normanno-svevo visto dall'Islam africano', in *Il mezzogiorno normanno-svevo visto dall'Europa e dal mondo mediterraneo, Bari, 1997* (Bari, 1999), pp. 261–93. The importance of Abū l-Ḍaw' and the Banū Rajā' is explained in Johns, *Arabic Administration*, pp. 88–90.

39 Johns, *Arabic Administration*, pp. 73–4, 295; Cusa, *Diplomi*, pp. 471–2.

40 On the alleged Sicilian *dīwān al-maẓālim*, see Ibn al-Athīr, *BAS*[2] Ar. I:320; *BAS*[2] It. I:450.

41 For the important issue on whether or not there was such a defined office as the *dīwān al-maẓālim* in Norman Sicily, see Johns, *Arabic Administration*, pp. 255 and 292–5. Maqrīzī had clearly picked up the idea that the Normans had later copied the Fatimids, which to some extent they had. However, Maqrīzī's descriptions routinely overestimate the development of political structures of Roger's Sicily and should be treated with caution.

42 On Elvira's pious largesse and Roger's dangerously reclusive reaction to her death in February 1135, see Alexander of Telese, III:1, p. 59.

43 For Roger's reaction to the suggestion of a crusade, see Ibn al-Athīr, *BAS*² Ar. I:320; *BAS*² It. 450–2.

44 For a survey and analysis of events, see David Abulafia, 'The Norman kingdom of Africa and the Norman expedition to Majorca and the Muslim Mediterranean', in *Anglo-Norman Studies*, R. Allen Brown (ed.), 7 (1985): 26–49.

45 On this, see the detailed discussions in Loud, *Latin Church in Norman Italy*, pp. 223–54.

46 For an introduction to the development of these early Latin-rite foundations, see White, *Latin Monasticism*, pp. 3–73.

Figure 1 Byzantine defences over Temple 'O' at Selinunte.

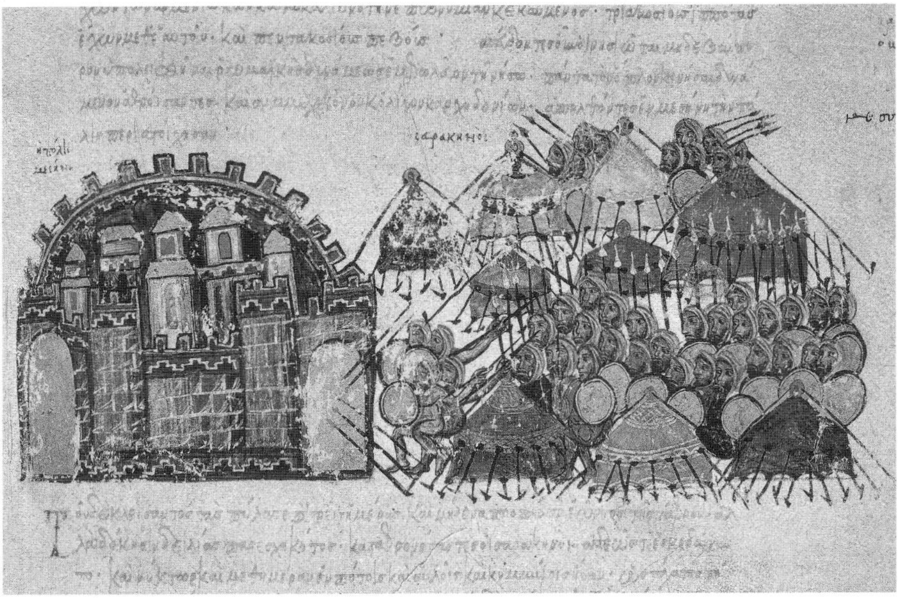

Figure 2 Muslim attack on Messina, taken from the chronicle of John Skylitzes copied in Sicily in the mid-twelfth century.

Figure 3 The Cuba Cíprina at Vícari.

Figure 4 San Giovanni dei Lebbrosi, founded by Robert Guiscard during the siege of Palermo.

Figure 5 George of Antioch's bridge outside Palermo.

7

The Muslims in the kingdom of Sicily

Overview and issues of periodisation

The kingdom of Sicily, with its Muslim majority population on the island, played a central role in the formation of medieval Europe during the twelfth and thirteenth centuries. The rich, mainly Latin, sources which describe the interlaced histories of north and south Italy, and the German and Byzantine empires, also outline relations with the papacy, the crusader states and the Norman, Mediterranean and Islamic 'worlds'. Given the clashes over the succession of rulers in which the national histories of Italy, France, England, Germany and Spain intersect, the standard periodisation of the twelfth and thirteenth centuries tends to fracture untidily along dynastic lines. The end of the Norman period is sometimes marked by the death of William II in 1189, bringing to an end the Hauteville line. However, it more usually includes the civil war which led to the coronation of Roger's illegitimate grandson, Tancred (r. 1190–4). It is sometimes extended to the chaos on his death from which Constance (r. 1195–8) and her German husband Henry VI (d. 1197) emerged as rulers. Hence, similarly indistinct origins initiate the Staufen period, dominated by the minority and rule of the German emperor and Sicilian king, Frederick II. Following Frederick's death in 1250, the search for a ruler, the struggle for Sicily under Manfred and the emergence of Angevin control then form the basis of accounts culminating in the twenty-year 'Wars of the Sicilian Vespers' between the Angevins and Aragonese. The Treaty of Caltabellotta, signed in 1302 at the end of the Vespers, came only a couple of years after the destruction of the colony at Lucera to where the remaining Sicilian Muslims had been deported. This serves as the obvious and definitive conclusion for Muslim settlement in the Italian peninsula in the medieval period.

The roles played by Muslims become increasingly peripheral in standard political histories of the region. This degree of eurocentricity is justifiable, not least because the kings' priorities were more often focused on the threat of invasion by the Byzantines from across the eastern Mediterranean or by German forces from the north, acting in league with discontented factions from within the kingdom. The Sicilian Muslims were not entirely divorced from these contexts even if, in the new, unified kingdom they represented a shrinking proportion of the overall population and lived in one relatively small, but important, area of it. As in previous centuries, there was no appreciable Muslim presence on the mainland during the 1100s, except for groups of merchants in port towns or the remaining trace of mixed communities in Calabria. Over the course of the century, the roles of Muslims in power came to be shared, tangential or eclipsed completely. As such, it would be relatively easy to overlook the history of the Sicilian Muslims were it not that the events of the twelfth and thirteenth centuries also hammered out a lasting Muslim–Christian frontier in the central Mediterranean with the progressive separation and crystallisation of Muslim and Christian power. From the 1160s, the Muslims' safety within the kingdom was compromised when disorder fuelled by revolt erupted into riots and massacres. Fear of further reprisals pushed them toward the crown lands of the west of the island where, like many of their co-religionists in the east in the century before, they were delivered into the hands of a new Latin church. On the death of William II in 1189, they rose up in a long revolt. Their eventual suppression, defeat and transportation to Lucera under Frederick II consigned their final days to a history of a single city as the fate of their former lands was decided among rival powers of the Latin West.

On the island itself, the Muslims probably comprised the majority of the population until the 1220s. As we shall see, even in the isolation of Lucera, they preserved the semblance of an Islamic society. The slowly dwindling Muslim communities thus provide key indicators of socio-religious, economic, demographic and linguistic change which invite comparison with the better studied regions of the Iberian peninsula and the crusader states. The Muslim population was vital to the island's economy, in both rural agricultural and urban trades and manufacturing, as well as providing skilled craftsmen, merchants and products for export. During the period of Norman state-building, Muslims maintained their roles as naval officers, foot soldiers and as bureaucrats charged with the management of the royal fiscal administration and palaces. Arab-Muslim influence made significant impressions on palace life, art and administration as well as on the outlook and lifestyles of the kings themselves. Above all, an Arab-Islamic facet was adopted as an element within the self-consciously tripartite, authoritarian and sacral kingship of Roger II. Protocols, ceremonies, clothes and the evolution of courtly behavioural codes complemented the art, architecture and recreational pursuits around the palaces. Moreover, royal patronage of scholars made Sicily a key link in the transfer of knowledge between the lands of Islam and Christian Europe. Within this wider historical context, the situation of the Muslims in Sicily becomes more apparent: influence from Arabic and Islamic sources were strongest when the kingdom was at its brief height, and the Muslims' subsequent decline helped undermine the peculiar construction of Latin, Byzantine and Islamic elements that made up the kingship. Viewed in this light, the fate of the Muslims was intimately linked with the fate of the Normans.

The conquest of the island and formation of the kingdom in 1130 were themselves remarkable achievements. Yet, commentators in the medieval period were divided in their opinions of Roger as king: an illegitimate, tyrannical usurper to many outside the kingdom; a wise, just and awe-inspiring ruler only to a more local and select audience.[1] In part, their verdicts were informed by how they had understood the legality and subsequent actions of the kingdom itself. His political triumphs were all the more noteworthy given that there was still very little central governmental machinery on the island prior to the formation of the kingdom, and there were nagging questions over the status of its ecclesiastical foundations. At the moment of Roger's coronation, almost a full century after the breakdown of central Muslim authority on the island, there was still no regular administration and no organised, permanent chanceries of which to speak. The promulgation of law codes, reforming of the coinage, the shaping and refining of the ruler's authority all lay in the future. One of the most striking features of the new kingdom, therefore, was how quickly and conspicuously these structures emerged – especially those relating to kingship and statecraft in the post-1130 period.

A distinctive feature of that kingship, and the organisation of the realm, was that vast swathes of crown lands and men in Sicily and Calabria were managed directly through centralised forms of control. These mechanisms stood in contrast to government through vassals on the south Italian mainland, which had been forged from a mishmash of independent or semi-independent principalities, duchies and former *themes*. Royal administration across the peninsula developed from the mid-1130s, but especially post-1139. None the less, the striking contrast between the two areas endured. On the mainland, not only was far more power in the hands of the nobility, who objected to encroaching control from Palermo and aspired to greater degrees of autonomy, but also there was a history of insurrection in areas far from the capital where revolt could easily be sparked by forces outside the kingdom. Indeed, it required most of the period from 1132 to 1139 to quell rebels in a series of fierce mainland campaigns, where Roger's deployment of Muslim soldiers did little to enhance his reputation in the eyes of his detractors as a mercenary upstart. He was, after all, carving out authority in dominions some considered to be the patrimony of the pope at Rome; others argued they should revert to the Byzantines, but which others still claimed they were the possession of the German kings as Holy Roman Emperors and successors to the caesars of classical antiquity. In any case, threats to the survival of Norman rule in Sicily were considerable. A serious illness and rumours of the king's death in 1134–5 was sufficient to spark a major revolt in

Capua. Apulia was again exposed as one of the kingdom's weak spots during the invasion attempt led by the German Emperor, Lothar III, in 1137 in which Roger lost both Bari and Salerno, and the duchy of Apulia was given over to Count Rainulf of Alife (or more correctly, 'of Caiazzo'). Only after campaigns conducted until mid-1139, and after the deaths of both Rainulf in spring and the pope in the previous year, was Roger able to restore his full authority on the mainland, recognised by the Treaty of Mignano in which the new pope, Innocent II, reluctantly reaffirmed Roger's investiture as king of Sicily, duke of Apulia and prince of Capua.

Roger's mainland campaigns foisted severe measures on the rebel barons and towns with confiscations of lands, the imposition of fines, summary executions and imprisonments. Of those put to flight or exiled, some made their way to the welcoming courts of the kingdom's rivals in Germany and Constantinople to bide their time while they and others were substituted with more loyal and trusted supporters. The kings' reliance on the military services that these vassals were obliged to provide was essential to the defence of the mainland from the Germans and Byzantines, who would form a menacing alliance in 1147. Internally, support was needed to maintain stability in the face of potentially seditious nobles and municipalities for whom the disorder of invasion served as an opportunistic prerequisite to realise aspirations for greater autonomy and local power.

'Soft-power' and the royal impression of absolute authority

As we have seen, there was a certain practical wisdom in maintaining structural frameworks of Islamic origin within which the conquered peoples might be ruled. The same argument, however, cannot be applied to the conscious decision to embrace new structures of south Mediterranean origin, post-1130. In this respect, and as far as the *appearance* of royal power was concerned, there is little to suggest that the Normans absorbed direct influences 'from below', but instead they imported them mainly 'from above and beyond'. That is to say, they did not draw inspiration from the conquered Kalbid or post-Kalbid regimes. Instead, the kings turned to southern and eastern Mediterranean models of governance where, in the great empires of the Byzantines and the Fatimids, they found an array of instruments to convey convincing impressions of absolute authority.[2]

In an article on the Arabs and Byzantium, Francesco Gabrieli made the perceptive remark that the Umayyad caliphs of the seventh and eighth centuries and the Norman rulers of the eleventh and twelfth centuries shared a number of similar outlooks with regard to Constantinople.[3] For the most part, both considered the Byzantines as the great enemy whom they believed they would one day overcome and succeed. Yet, both dynasties, at an early stage, willingly absorbed Greek elements and influences into their own systems of government. In the case of the Normans, this resulted in the employment of key personnel in civil and military roles and the use of Greek as the main royal and diplomatic language under Roger II. The creation of the kingdom allowed Byzantine notions of authority to accelerate and flourish by combining theocratic ideas of sacral kingship and absolutist imperial rule, such that the edifice of law and government quickly came to be built on a powerful and arcane bureaucratic system supported by solemn ceremony and elaborate etiquette.

The consolidation of the kingdom coincided with the construction of a lavishly decorated royal palace at Palermo, built in the enclosed Ḥalqa district of the city over ruins from classical antiquity and possibly the old Byzantine governor's residence too. As Roger's biographer, Alexander of Telese, observed, this was part of a process presented as the restoration of some ancient kingship.[4] Such a fanciful notion may help to account for the choice of location, instead of renovating the Fatimid Khāliṣa. Indeed, there were a number of important differences between the two: the Khāliṣa, almost 200 years old by 1130 and perhaps damaged in the Norman siege, had been built in time of strife and had strongly defensive aspects to it, including a garrison within its walls. It was located close to the port, as at Mahdiyya, whereas Roger's palace occupied higher ground at the opposite end of the city, closest to what would become a royal hunting park. Like the Khāliṣa, the new royal palace was to house the ruler's fiscal administration, but it was conceived and constructed in a time of peace at Palermo, serving also as a secular place of reception, relaxation and as a private residence, rather than a fortified bastion. It was doubtless the tallest building in the city, overlooking almost all of it. However, as a palace complex, the area it covered was tiny by the standards of medieval Muslim equivalents.

The new kingdom also witnessed the reconstruction of a fiscal administration (the *dīwān*) and with it the adoption of new practices and protocols. By the late 1130s, these had developed into highly nuanced expressions of authority. It was precisely such empowering apparatus that the Normans lacked in their violent transition from mercenaries to counts, dukes and then kings, but urgently needed post-1130. The offices of the royal *dīwān* were located within the palace itself and were staffed by Arabic-speaking eunuchs who were nominally Christian but adhered to Islam. These offices and their officials drew on very specific administrative and diplomatic practices that were indebted to those of Fatimid Egypt.[5] This observation allows a fundamentally important connection to be made between the emerging concepts of Sicilian kingship, power, administration and the art of governance. And, while royal art and architecture of the palaces post-1130 projected a sense of this power only locally, Norman Sicilian authority could be propagated over a much wider area and to a wider audience via the media of visual material culture which included royal coinage, seals, mottoes and documents, courtesy of the royal mints (*zikka*, cf. modern Italian *zecca*) and the *dīwān* (cf. Italian *dogane*). Extant remains of their outputs, alongside those of the royal silk workshop, provide a vital corpus of quantifiable, material evidence. However, in order to draw clearer lines of differentiation between the construction of royal authority under Roger and the development of the kingdom's art, this chapter deals largely with the former and the theoretical workings of the new administration; Chapter 12 engages with royal art and living spaces and Chapter 13 combines questions of authority over the Muslim population and the practicalities of later royal administration. In this way, degrees of separation can be made between the basis of royal authority and its Arab-Islamic elements, the way the kings chose to present themselves and the Islamic aspects within the art and architecture of royal palaces.

By comparison with the Latin West, most medieval Muslim rulers governed through a relatively centralised infrastructure. None the less, even in Islamic lands, there existed few clearly defined institutions with prescribed and efficient functions, staffed by professionals in any modern sense. In the medieval world generally, the focus of power and legitimacy came to be concentrated on the figure of the ruler whose charisma was essential to maintain political support and whose sense of authority was vital to ensure the integrity of his realm. In this respect, Roger had certain advantages over his sons: he had spent longer periods on the mainland where his presence was itself a form of command, and where he had personally met many of the kin group leaders of consequence. Although his kingship had features of a fearsome personality cult, it was not one in which he made repeatedly conspicuous appearances after the 1130s. Instead, Roger became withdrawn and hidden from view, increasingly so with age, and it was the opinion of al-Maqrīzī that such shelter from his subjects had been the idea of George of Antioch. Forming part of this physical concealment was the Via Coperta, a 400-metre long covered portico, which allowed private access to Palermo cathedral from the royal palace. Such a removed approach to kingship had precedents in the Islamic world and was also reflected in the language of royal Arabic Sicilian charters. In the same way as the Fatimid imām-caliphs were referred to indirectly as 'the shadow' (*al-ẓill*), so the Sicilian kings were referred to in oblique terms as 'the presence' (*al-ḥaḍra*), contributing to a certain mystique of the obscure and arcane for whom direct reference might have seemed disrespectful. It was befitting that frank, personal access to the royal presence should also be limited.

If the newly founded Sicilian Christian regime was seeking to convey its power to the Arab-Islamic world, it was in competition with a number of other authorities, particularly after the break up of Islamic Spain from the start of the twelfth century which had given rise to a number of petty princes in the Mediterranean, many of whom described themselves with extravagant titles.

With a number of 'cats puffed up to be lions' as the poet Ibn Rashīq put it when referring to the proliferation of the titles and epithets that accompanied the Andalusi *ṭā'ifa* rulers, the Sicilian kings were latecomers to an already established tradition, and also one in which there were already many regimes of questionable legitimacy around the southern Mediterranean – not least the Fatimids themselves.[6]

Arabic titles, formulae and the royal embroidery workshop

The use of titles collected from all extant media, but primarily deriving from coinage and charters, provides evidence of a gradual transition and development, which again coincided with the evolution of Norman rule. In this case, the transition was from Arabic transliterations of Latin titles (such as 'count' and 'duke'), to the use of Arabic equivalents of Latin and Greek titles, and then, after the creation of the kingdom, to the adoption of elaborate, precise and systematised Arabic titles derived from Islamic chancery sources.[7] While these titles and formulae had been a standard feature of Muslim regimes, the Sicilian versions repeated, or closely echoed, appellations used in Fatimid Egypt, particularly those of high-ranking officials and notables.

The diplomatically sensitive, Arabic descriptors of the Sicilian kings presented each as the temporal possessor (*al-malik*) of certain regions, thereby treading carefully so as to avoid the particular preserve of the Fatimid imām-caliphs who made their claims to legitimate leadership and universality by virtue of their inherited spiritual authority. In addition, the dynastic titles of the Norman kings were composed from passive grammatical constructions in contrast to the Fatimid rulers, whose honorific names, such as al-Ḥākim, al-Ḥāfiẓ al-Ẓāfir and al-Qā'im, were formed from active participles, which implied a more direct type of agency. Royal Norman titles were based around the Arabic consonantal root of *'-z-z*, connoting concepts of power, strength, honour and glory, even to the extent that this was echoed in the names of the palaces such as the Zisa (from Arabic *al-'Azīza*). Titles proclaimed each ruler as 'the glorified king': Roger II was 'powerful through God'; William I was 'the guide according to the command of God'; William II was 'the desirous of power through God'; and even Tancred had been 'assisted to victory by God'.[8] The reversal of this trend coincided with the accession of Henry VI of Germany, who returned to Arabic transliterations of Latin titles with Roman imperial precedents: in Henry's case, that of *Caesar Augustus*.[9]

A further, refined feature of Sicilian Arabic titulature was the use of two religiously significant and diplomatically distinctive phrases which referred to the multilateral relationships that held between the Sicilian kings, the papacy, the Fatimid imām-caliphs and the religious communities of the kingdom. In Arabic, the Sicilian rulers were described as 'the defender of the pope (*imām*) of Rome', a phrase which applied also to the Doge of Venice, and was also one used by the royal cartographer, al-Idrīsī, of his patron Roger. As early as 1109, Adelaide had been called, in Arabic, 'the helper of the Christian faith' – a description which prefigured that applied to both William I and William II, each of whom was called 'the helper of the Christian faith community' (*al-nāṣir li-l-milla al-naṣrāniyya*). One advantage of this 'off-the-peg' choice of Islamic chancery phrasing was its mutual acceptability to both Muslim and Christian regimes, since it implicitly recognised degrees of diplomatic and ideological separation between the successors to the Kalbids and the Egyptian rulers themselves. From a Fatimid perspective, the Norman kings were invested with their authority by the papacy and thus were necessarily subordinate to the imām-caliphs who had no further need for a validating agency besides God. The Norman kings, like the Byzantine emperors, chose to depict themselves in art as rulers crowned directly by Christ. But, to the Fatimids, whether crowned by Christ or vassals of the pope at Rome, these polytheistic concerns of infidel kings necessarily registered the error of their inferior beliefs. No claim to sacral kingship could ever encroach on the Fatimids' worldly or spiritual claims to power. Given the delicate task of adopting acceptable models of royal Arabic Sicilian titulature, it can be inferred that these epithets were chosen *for* the kings by one or more of their officials who had an intimate knowledge of Arabic diplomatics, and who most likely had made their selection from a cache engineered by officials with a working knowledge of Fatimid chancery practices.[10]

The Arabic facet thus comprised an essential part of Sicilian kingship and assumed a characteristic role in the wider articulation of Norman statecraft. Arabic titles also described a special relationship that the kings claimed to have with God. In this respect, they were no different from the great rulers of the southern and eastern Mediterranean. However, certain moot questions, for instance over degrees of divine agency, were presented in a different light for the benefit of different audiences. Outside the context of Arab-Islamic rulership, the visual presentation of the kings was expressed in the famous mosaic depictions in George of Antioch's church of Santa Maria dell'Ammiraglio (the Martorana), and later, in William II's foundation at Monreale. In both cases, the king, in full imperial garb, is crowned directly by Christ himself, borrowing from a Byzantine artistic and ideological precedent. However, in the same way that the kings avoided precise parallels with the Fatimids, in the Martorana mosaic Roger is referred to in Greek as a *rīx* (king) not a *basileus* (emperor), thereby evading a direct comparison with the Byzantine ruler himself.

With Roger increasingly appearing as a divinely sanctioned embodiment of the state, disobedience to the king's law and order was tantamount to acting contrary to God's own will so as to merit capital punishment. Justice, piety, peace and the defeat of the kingdom's enemies were said to have been God's gift to the kings as earthly vicars, hence the assertion in the royal Assizes that 'the office of kingship claims for itself a certain privilege of priesthood'.[11] At a politico-religious level, the kings' open declaration for the defence of Christians revealed that they could not have considered themselves impartial rulers over separate, but equal, peoples. Rather, it was widely taken for granted that they would favour the interests of their own particular faith. This notion of Christian preference and privilege was explicitly repeated in Roger's professional, royal signatures in Greek to the effect that he was 'in Christ the Lord, a pious, powerful king and helper of the Christians'.

The Sicilian kings had their own *ṭirāz* or silk workshop, the maintenance of which was a royal prerogative and an expensive undertaking.[12] The use of richly embroidered robes of honour (*khil'a*) and other accoutrements was widespread in Islamic regimes, especially in Egypt, where close links were forged between the citing of a ruler's name (with appropriate formulae on coinage, charters or in sermons) and visible signs of his authority. The same applied to the investiture of high-ranking officials in ways which all could observe, recognise and understand. In the Islamic period in Sicily, the governors had been honoured in this way and, later, in the Norman colonies of Ifrīqiya too. Thus, the *ṭirāz* was an important and closely monitored institution which came under similar high-level supervision to the mints and administrative offices. In Norman Sicily, the silk workshops – like the royal *dīwān* – were physically close to the centres of power as shown by Ibn Jubayr's visit to the royal palace of William II in 1184 when he met one of the royal embroiderers, Yaḥyā bin Fityān al-Ṭarrāz ('John the embroiderer from the clan of eunuchs').[13] The onomastic link to a professional skill is an important one since it boosts the likelihood that *qā'id* Mataracius (from the Arabic, *muṭarriz* 'embroiderer'), who was the head of the *duana baronum* on the mainland between 1174 and 1176, may have at some point overseen, or been connected with, the *ṭirāz*.

Silk-embroidered drapes were also used for internal decoration, as shown by Philagathos of Cerami's famous description of the Cappella Palatina in 1143 where 'a great many curtains are hung, the fabric of which is threads of silk, woven with gold and various dyes, that the Phoenicians [i.e. Ifrīqiyans?] have embroidered with wonderful skill and elaborate artistry'.[14] From its production of a royal mantle made for Roger II, we can infer that the royal silk workshop was operational by 1133–4, and so it is possible that these drapes were also made in-house.[15] Where the actual embroiderers themselves came from is another matter. However, there were long traditions of silk working in Sicily, and as the Cairo Geniza letters bear witness, Islamic Sicily had long been an important centre in the Mediterranean for silk production, manufacture and export.[16] This is also supported by Ibn Ḥawqal's observation of a silk workers' market in Palermo. However, it remains less clear whether the concept of a *ṭirāz* as an institution had managed to survive the civil war period in Sicily. And if it had not, was it therefore a reanimation of an old, Fatimid–Kalbid practice, or was it another import inspired by contemporary practices in Fatimid Egypt or Zirid Ifrīqiya? The lavish use of silk in Sicily of the 1100s – which was perfectly unexceptional in Arab-Islamic palaces of the Muslim rulers – was a source of wonder to observers such as Alexander of Telese, struck by its extensive use at Roger's coronation.[17] The idea, inspired by a Greek source, that the widespread royal use of silk textiles in Sicily must post-date the Normans' capture of female silk weavers in the sack of Corfù and Thebes in 1147 is certainly untenable. Scattered throughout twelfth-century records relating to Sicily and Calabria are references to mulberry trees and people who bore either the name *al-ṭarrāzī* ('embroiderer') or *al-ḥarīrī* ('silk worker or producer'). The enduring nature of high-quality textile production and manufacture with roots in Arab-Islamic traditions is shown in other evidence, such as the survival into later medieval Sicilian dialect of terms such as *tarrasiator*, 'embroiderer', attested among the Muslims at Lucera and also in mid-fifteenth-century Naples.[18] Relatively little silk textile work of certain twelfth-century Sicilian provenance has survived. However, by far the most famous existing output of the Sicilian *ṭirāz* is Roger's embroidered mantle, later worn by Frederick II at his coronation to conjure up memories of past Rogerian glory. Another fine, surviving example of Sicilian silk textile work is a full-length taffeta robe made for William II, complete with cuff bands embroidered in Latin and Arabic.[19]

Muslims and the royal Arabic administration

Legislative and administrative reform could only occur when, as the chronicler Romuald of Salerno put it, 'peace and good order had been established in the kingdom': that is to say post-1139. The subsequent period until Roger's death in 1154 is usually taken to represent the golden age of the Norman kingdom. With internal order restored, Roger was said to have 'promulgated laws which he had newly drafted', and a body of edicts, laws, admonitions and sentences known collectively as 'the Assizes' emerged thereafter as part of a wider raft of state-building and reform.[20] The legislation is known to us from two manuscripts, one from the late twelfth century, the other from the early thirteenth century. However, it can be safely inferred from references to legal cases that most of the Assizes were in place during the reign of Roger. The consensus of modern opinion holds that they were most likely a product of the 1140s, but should not be associated, as once thought, with an assembly of nobles and bishops that took place in 1140 at Ariano in Apulia that resulted in what Falco of Benevento called a 'terrible edict' whereby coinage was effectively devalued at Roger's request. Written in Latin and later translated into Greek (but not Arabic), the Assizes were original only in part since most were extracted from precepts of Justinian's law code, but also included minor elements of Lombard, south Italian Byzantine and canon law. Thus, Roger was not simply assuming for himself the role of an interpreter of existing law, but with the synthesis of different laws, he was able to fashion a new instrument for the state to govern its peoples. The Assizes consisted of a scattered array of edicts, admonitions, injunctions and offences, which could not, per se, form anything but the most rudimentary basis for the growth of more complicated jurisprudence. Indeed, by comparison with Islamic law, the Assizes were crude and simplistic, yet in terms of the evolution of medieval law in the Latin West, they represent an important stage of development and can be understood in context with the great law-givers of the twelfth and thirteenth centuries. They were also a precursor to the famous legislation of the *Liber Augustalis* known as the 'Constitutions of Melfi', promulgated by the Sicilian king and the German emperor, Frederick II, in 1230.

As far as the Sicilian Muslims were concerned, two of the Assizes were of paramount importance. The first concerned the interpretation of laws in the kingdom and stated: 'Because of the variety of different people subject to our rule, the usages, customs and laws which have existed among them up to now are not abrogated unless what is observed in them is clearly in contradiction to our edicts here'.[21] In effect, since Islamic law was already in place before the Norman conquest, and had continued thereafter under the terms of capitulation, this Assize confirmed the theoretical basis of indirect rule for the Muslim community under Islamic *sharīʿa* law, with their own *qāḍī*s and courts. In practice, since most disputes were likely to occur locally or otherwise within the Islamic community, this legislation allowed the Muslims a sheltered degree of autonomy. It also afforded protection of the community from interference and the potential for moral pollution and error that infidel law might bring. This arrangement, therefore, formalised the superimposition of the king's authority over the Muslims in Sicily, Calabria and later in the decade, in Ifrīqiya too. Secondly, Christian legal superiority over Jews and Muslims was confirmed by the prohibition:

> No Jew or pagan shall dare either to buy or sell Christian servants, or to possess them by any title [whatsoever], or to hold them as a pledge. If he should presume to do this, all his property will be confiscated, and he shall become the servant of the Court. If he should by some wicked trick or persuasion have the servant circumcised or make him deny his faith, then he shall be punished by capital penalty.[22]

A third Assize was of particular relevance for ex-Muslims, since it regarded the question of apostasy, which here referred to the abandonment of Christianity. Contravention of the Assize was severely punished:

> We curse thoroughly those who apostatise from the Catholic faith. We pursue them with vengeance. We despoil them of all their goods. We withdraw the protection of our laws from those who break a promise or vow, we abolish their right of inheritance and cancel their every legitimate right.[23]

Therefore, Muslims who had converted to Christianity, were in the process of converting, or had converted then lapsed, or those who had merely pretended to convert, were particularly vulnerable to accusations of apostasy.

Since effective medieval rulership was not always contingent on efficient government, the practical benefits of issuing written documentation from the perspective of book-keeping or the accumulation of records were only one of several considerations for a regime whose legitimacy was repeatedly called into question and which had little surviving local tradition of rulership on which to draw. Royal expressions and communication served to fulfil several functions other than simply to convey information. The document was itself an instrument of governance, and the ways in which information was transmitted, the external form of the medium and the language in which it was composed were also important. Indeed, the diplomatic language(s) of the message itself played a role in royal art and power in the visual form of the letters in which it was written. Here, the meaning of the message was carried by the use of different scripts, with the translation not necessarily being of prime importance.

In Sicilian Arabic diplomatics especially, devices such as the accurate co-ordination of multiple dating systems, the use of specific calligraphy, the correct articulation of chancery formulae, titles, mottoes, seals and signatures, as well as document format and layout all served to verify and authenticate charters. But acceptance of a document's legitimacy also presupposed acceptance of the legitimacy of the issuing administrative body of chancery offices whose authority was, in the case of the Normans, derived from the crown, in whose name, and on whose divinely sanctioned orders, they had been instructed to act. Thus, royal diplomata formed part of an elaborate, multi-layered construction of authority which transmitted and recorded the content of royal commands to royal subjects. The manifold way in which this was achieved conspicuously developed the Arab-Islamic facet of the kingship as channelled primarily through the new royal *dīwān*. Here the use of Arabic in royal charters (and also in royal inscriptions) enjoyed a revival as one of three royal languages after a long period (1111–32) during which it does not appear to have been used at all.[24] The distinctive type of royal Arabic *dīwānī* calligraphy in use thereafter mirrored that used by professional scribes trained in Egyptian or Levantine chanceries through which it is possible that scribes employed in Sicily had passed.[25] The rounded Arabic chancery script was also the most likely source for the royal style of Sicilian Arabic epigraphy.[26] However, very little can be inferred about the scribes who penned the documents. Contrary to their general inscrutability, a certain Yūsuf is known to have been one of William II's most favoured scribes, and had probably received an estate in western Sicily for his skills and services. As in the case of at least one other royal scribe, he applied diacritical marks to his Sicilian *dīwānī* script in a 'Maghribi' style, in the sense that he placed a dot below, not above, the letter *fā'*. Although the fiscal administration's record books were kept in Arabic, the number of charters on which Arabic appeared was relatively limited, and in Roger's reign, Greek remained the most frequently used language in royal diplomata.

By the mid-1140s, the *dīwān* had compiled Arabic descriptions of boundaries around towns, estates and provinces which were kept in record-books called *daftars*. Concessions of lands and men, their terms and conditions of tenure and the names of feudatories to whom they were granted, can be inferred to have been kept in separate *daftars*. These have not survived for Sicily, but it is probable that they resembled the *Catalogus Baronum* ('The List of Barons'). This was first drafted *c.* 1150 to record military services owed by nobles on the mainland, and to register the services and conditions of tenure a landlord owed to the crown in return for holding a particular benefice. Since these are presumed to have been undertaken for a fee, a link may be made between the raising of revenues via administrative reform and the funding of military operations. As Arabic influence and Muslim personnel in the mainland administration were minimal, a discussion of mainland practice here would be out of place. Suffice to note that when the *Catalogus Baronum* was revised *c.* 1168, it was done so with the key participation of Richard, a crypto-Muslim eunuch, royal chamberlain and first *magister* or head official of the *duana baronum* based at Salerno.[27]

As we have seen, lay and ecclesiastical lords were largely responsible for the upkeep of their own records of lands, men and the taxes collected from them, a task which was conducted with varying degrees of administrative competence. The royal *dīwān*, on the other hand, had its own records of the population who lived in the towns and estates of Sicily and Calabria which could be gathered or supplemented from a number of sources: from lists of men (*jarā'id al-rijāl*) that had previously been drawn up; from the private records of feudatories; or from surveys conducted by officials of the *dīwān* in conjunction with an *'āmil* or provincial administrator. It is clear from inquests held by the *dīwān* that information about land boundaries and the population living within them derived from, and was corroborated by, the oral testimony of trusted elders (called *boni homines*, *gerontoi* or *shaykhs*). Across most of Sicily, the locals who preserved the historical memory of the boundaries were Arabic-speaking and Muslim.

The mid-1140s were an important period of reform for the royal fiscal administration. Between October 1144 and June 1145, an estimated minimum of 120 confirmations were reissued by the *dīwān* to lords who had previously been conceded privileges of lands and men. Ecclesiastical and lay lords were called to Palermo and required to surrender their documents for inspection by the administration's officers, after which a renewed (or revised) grant might be written out for them.[28] Thirty-three surviving confirmations cover areas in Sicily and Calabria. The vast majority were written in Greek, or in Greek and Arabic. Only five were composed in Latin.

Instrumental to the issuing of the grant renewals were two offices: the *Dīwān al-ma'mūr*, which literally translates as 'the busy office', and was known in Greek as the *sékreton* and in Latin it was called the *duana de secretis*. This was in operation by 1136. The other was the *Dīwān al-taḥqīq al-ma'mūr* – literally, 'the busy office of verification', operational by 1149 and probably earlier. The latter office partially echoes the name of the Fatimid 'office of verification' or *Dīwān al-taḥqīq*, created during 1107–8 as part of an overhaul and reform of fiefs in Egypt, which had included the annulling and renewing of previous grants as well as undertaking revised cadastral surveys.[29] In Sicily, snatches of information from charter evidence suggest a degree of separation between these two offices in terms of their function: the *Dīwān al-ma'mūr* generally oversaw the fiscal administration and its management of crown lands and men (and might also refer in an abstract sense to the whole Arabic sector of the administration). On the other hand, the executive office of the *Dīwān al-taḥqīq al-ma'mūr* supervised, composed and verified confirmations of royal grants of lands and/or men. However, the practical distinctions between these offices might easily be overstated since both undertook interrelated types of activity, and it is reasonably clear that the officers of both worked together closely and made use of the same Arabic record books which contained the names of landholders, the descriptions of the boundaries of estates and lists of men who lived on them. Even at the height of the renewals in the mid-1140s, these offices were less busy or well-populated than their names suggest, and the number of scribes working in them was small by comparison with Arab-Islamic chanceries of major Muslim dynasties.

The renewals which issued from the royal *dīwān* indicate that they had a number of diplomatic ancestors, some more distant than others. On the one hand, they were confirmations of Arabic and Greek grants made by Roger I in the mid-1090s, and these were derived from pre-existing local data. Therefore, at a certain level, practices from the administration of the late Kalbid/Islamic civil war period can be spoken of in terms of continuity. However, the inspiration for both these reforms, the names of the new offices and the format of the charters issued can be shown to have been imported directly from Fatimid Egypt with which diplomatic contacts between Palermo (under Roger) and Cairo (under al-Ḥāfiẓ) were genial and co-operative. Indeed, they are strikingly dissimilar to the troubled relations with the great empires of the Germans and Byzantines whose interests crossed those of Sicily.

Pretence, competence and empowerment in the Arabic administration

It is highly likely that the crown required a fee to be paid for the confirmations. If similar, but later, renewals made by Richard I of England are a valid parallel, then the charges may have been substantial and were presumably resented.[30] Thus, it is likely that the crown stood to benefit materially from this burst of centralised administrative activity during 1144–5, and these renewals can be located in the context of revenue-raising to fund Roger's military manoeuvres along the kingdom's northern borders, and especially for his naval campaigns in the eastern and southern Mediterranean.

The text of the confirmations defined – and therefore limited – the rights of the recipient over the lands and/or men registered by name in the document in a very explicit way, since it was stipulated (as it had been in the 1090s) that anyone whose name did not appear on the list, automatically reverted to the crown. In the event of a dispute between the crown and a beneficiary over rights to the men conceded to the latter, an inquest could be held in which officers of the *dīwān* might (at least in theory) conduct a survey of the men living on the lands, and check them against the list in the confirmation. Any disparity therefore favoured the crown.

As for the Muslims, the absence of any reference to mosques, *madrasas*, Sufi lodges, *ribāṭs* or any Muslim 'lord' as having had to present their privileges implies that they had not been conceded landed possessions in the post-conquest period, and suggests that their benefices may have been appropriated by Roger I and Robert Guiscard and partially redistributed. If so, then key Muslim institutions had been quietly dispossessed of their primary sources of revenue on which they depended and which, in some cases, had probably been considered as perpetual and inalienable grants when they were first made in the Islamic period. In part, document survival has played a role in distorting such observations because an unknown number of grants are likely to have been lost entirely. In some cases, missing documents (*deperdita*) can be inferred to have existed from references later made to them. Documents lost without trace are more common for lay lords than for record-collecting institutions such as churches and monasteries, whose larger and more diverse possessions resulted in more enduring and complex forms of book-keeping and the compilation of later chartularies.

At first glance, and given the generational gap between the original donations and the confirmations, it has been argued that, motivated by 'the king's dutiful concern for better order', 'there can be no doubt about the meaning of this evidence [that is, the confirmations from 1144–5] for better office organisation'.[31] However, closer examination of the text of the confirmations would seem to argue against this idea of improved bureaucratic efficiency since not all the renewals were as useful to their beneficiaries as they might reasonably have expected them to be. In some cases, they cited verbatim the same people who had appeared on the lists of the 1090s (or simply preceded the name with 'the children of'). Certainly, 'the old woman at the house of the tailor', who was registered in the grant to the church of Catania in 1095, was fifty years older when she appeared on the renewal of 1145. It showed too that lords' records of grants had not been kept up to date and implies that the management of a displaced population was still chaotic and patchy, and that levels of administrative competence were often quite low. That said, there is little doubt that the administrative capabilities of the kingdom had progressed greatly from the confusion and ad hockery of the 1090s and, as a generation had elapsed since the initial grants, there was sufficient reason in the 1140s to justify re-establishing the link between comital grants which were now conceived to have been made from crown lands.

The Catania renewal was not alone in exposing the pretence to knowledge that the administration did not actually possess. A long list of men reissued in 1145 to Roger's royal church at Cefalù is also revealing. The monks had presented themselves at the *dīwān* in Palermo with, among other documents, a list of men written in Latin in 1136. In theory, this should have been checked against an internal *dīwānī* record, then reissued. However, a study of the Arabic and Greek confirmation shows that the administration possessed no such record on their books, but had merely copied out, in Arabic and Greek, the Latin list which the monks had brought along themselves.[32]

Incompetence rather than pretence was at issue when the Greek-rite monks of the San Nicolò lo Gurguro (also called al-Hurhur or Chúrchuro) requested and, in December 1149, received, a copy of a small royal grant of lands and men they had been conceded.[33] Seeing that the Arabic copy did not bear a royal seal (which it did not necessarily need to have), the monks requested another copy. Almost four and a half years later, a second copy was written out for them. This did bear a royal seal, but it was lacking in a more important respect: it confirmed another, completely different, set of boundaries from the first copy. Although there are signs that the *dīwān* might at least have become aware of an irregularity in this case when the correct boundaries were written out as part of the Monreale concession in 1182, the monks of San Nicolò apparently did not notice the glaring discrepancy between their two documents. The tract of land to which they were entitled continued to be a matter of intermittent dispute until the modern period.

In some cases, there was a difference between the original grant and its confirmation to a second generation of beneficiaries. Between 1093 and 1095, a Norman knight called Roger Forestal (presumably a follower of the Hauteville brothers) had been given lands and men by Count Roger I in western Sicily, deep in the Muslim heartlands. In 1145, his son, Walter Forestal, presented his privilege for inspection and renewal at Palermo, and received confirmation of rights over those men in his possession on the unwalled estate of Jāliṣū, but not those in the town of Corleone.

The advantages that the renewals gave both crown and administration were thus considerable since the king could use bureaucratic and legal mechanisms to dispossess holders of privileges. In so doing, the administration and its officers not only empowered themselves in the name of the king and at the expense of the king's feudatories, but also the use of visually impressive documentary records (whose Arabic and Greek would have mainly been illegible to their Latin recipients) also served another important purpose: to reaffirm Roger's rights and privileges as king to dispose of his lands and men in the way in which he commanded via his officials, rather than allow the beneficiaries to become accustomed to automatic inheritance by their successors and sons.

Notes

1 Helene Wieruszowski, 'Roger II of Sicily, Rex-Tyrannus, in twelfth-century political thought', *Speculum*, 38/1 (1963): 46–78.

2 See the classic article by Antonio Marongiu, 'A model state in the Middle Ages: the Norman and Swabian kingdom of Sicily', *Comparative Studies in Society and History*, 6/3 (1964): 307–20.

3 Francesco Gabrieli, 'Greeks and Arabs in the central Mediterranean area', *Dumbarton Oaks Papers*, 18 (1964): 57–65.

4 For the notion that Roger was restoring some ancient kingship, see Alexander of Telese, *Ystoria Rogerii*, II:2, p. 24: 'it was certain that there had once been in that city a seat of kingship to rule all Sicily, and which now appeared to have lapsed for a long time, it was absolutely right and just that the crown be put on Roger's head and that realm restored – not only there, but also that it should be extended to the other regions in which he was now seen to be lord.'

5 Sicilian–Fatimid connections are found in Jeremy Johns, 'The Norman kings of Sicily and the Fatimid caliphate', *Anglo-Norman Studies*, M. Chibnall (ed.), 15 (1993): 133–59.

6 Referring to the Abbadid *ṭā'ifa* of Seville in the 1070s, Ibn Rashīq was twice quoted by Ibn Khaldūn: 'What makes me feel humble in Spain/Is the use of the names Muʿtaṣim and Muʿtaḍid there./Royal surnames not in their proper place:/Like a cat that by blowing itself up imitates the lion.' *Ibn Khaldūn, The Muqaddimah. An Introduction to History*, trans. Franz Rosenthal, 3 vols (Princeton. 1958), I:3/1 and I:3/30, pp. 316 and 470.

7 Jeremy Johns, 'I titoli arabi dei sovrani normanni di Sicilia', *Bollettino di Numismatica*, 6–7 (1986): 11–54.

8 Further discussion on this and 'standard' translations can be found in Johns, *Arabic Administration*, pp. 268–74. Although these could be translated with minor variants, I have taken Johns's renditions as a type of standard.

9 Jeremy Johns, 'I titoli arabi', p. 30. See also the discussion in Karla Mallette, 'Trans-

lating Sicily', in *Medieval Encounters*, 9/1 (2003): 140–62 (p. 150).

10 Johns, *Arabic Administration*, pp. 268–74 (p. 274).

11 Translations of Roger's Assizes in this section are taken from those of Graham A. Loud and can be found at: www.leeds.ac.uk/history/weblearning/MedievalHistory-TextCentre/medievalTexts.htm (accessed on 13 June 2008). Henceforth, *Roger's Assizes*.

12 On the royal *ṭirāz* in Sicily, see the dated, but seminal, article by Ugo Monneret de Villard, 'La tessitura palermitana sotti i Normanni e i suoi rapporti con l'arte bizantina', in *Miscellanea Giovanni mercati*, III, Città del Vaticano (*Studi e Testi*, 123), 1946, pp. 464–89; also Johns, *Arabic Administration*, pp. 213, 243–4, 269. For a wider perspective in south Italy, see Filippo Burgarella, 'The Byzantine background to the silk industry in southern Italy' and David Jacoby, 'Silk and silk textiles in Arab and Norman Sicily: the economic context', in *Nobiles Officinae*, II:373–82 and 383–9.

13 Ibn Jubayr, *BAS*² Ar. I:87; Eng. trans. Broadhurst, p. 341. For a florid description of silk-working in the palaces, see *Falcandus, Letter to Peter*, p. 259.

14 A parallel Greek-English text by Jeremy Johns of relevant passages of Philagathos can be found in Ernst. J. Grube and Jeremy Johns, *The Painted Ceilings of the Cappella Palatina* (Genoa and New York, 2005), pp. 13–14.

15 For a recent assessment (with bibliography) of Roger II's silk mantle, see Rotraud Bauer, 'The mantle of Roger II and the Siculo-Norman vestments from the royal court workshop in Palermo' and William Tronzo, 'King Roger's mantle, part and whole', in *Nobiles Officinae*, II:403–7 and II:443–6 respectively.

16 Moshe Gil, 'References to silk in Geniza documents of the eleventh century AD', *Journal of Near Eastern Studies*, 61/1 (2002): 31–8.

17 On the use of silk garments by the kings attendants in 1130, see Alexander of Telese, II:5–6, p. 26. The impressive maximum dimensions of Roger's mantle, which had the form of an elliptical semi-circle, were 3 m 45 cm × 1 m 46 cm.

18 Caracausi, *Arabismi*, p. 374 shows continuity and diffusion of terms for this important profession in south Italy.

19 For further images of Sicilian textiles with notes and bibliographic references, see Grube and Johns, *Ceilings of the Cappella Palatina*, pp.260–5. The royal mantle, taffeta robe and gloves are now housed in the Kunsthistorisches Museum in Vienna.

20 For a rounded introduction to the Assizes, see Kenneth Pennington, 'The birth of the Ius commune: King Roger II's legislation', *Rivista internazionale del diritto comune*, 17 (2006) at: faculty.cua.edu/Pennington/Law508/NormansPalermoRIDC.htm (accessed on 6 April 2008). See also the discussion in Houben, *Roger II*, pp. 135–47, and Donald Matthew, *The Norman Kingdom of Sicily* (Cambridge, 1992), pp. 184–8.

21 *Roger's Assizes*, 'About the interpretation of laws' (no. 1).

22 *Roger's Assizes*, Untitled (no. 12).

23 *Roger's Assizes*, 'About those apostatising' (no. 13).

24 Johns, *Arabic Administration*, pp. 63, 79–80, 111–14 seems justified in associating the return of Arabic as a royal language with the creation of the kingdom in 1130. However, the first known Arabic document dates from 1132. For the Arabic charters of the royal administration, Johns's monograph supersedes the older works of John Wansborough, 'Diplomatica siciliana', *Bulletin of the School of Oriental and African Studies (BSOAS)*, 30 (1984): 305–13, and Albrecht Noth, 'I documenti arabi di

Ruggero II', in *Diplomi e Cancelleria di Ruggero II*, Carlrichard Brühl (ed.) (Palermo, 1983), pp. 189–222.

25 On *dīwānī* Arabic scripts, see Johns, *Arabic Administration*, pp. 275–7.

26 On royal epigraphy, see Michele Amari (ed.), *Le epigrafi arabiche di Sicilia* (Palermo, 1971) and Jeremy Johns, 'The Arabic inscriptions of the Norman kings of Sicily: a reinterpretation', in *Nobiles Officinae*, II:324–37.

27 See Evelyn Jamison, *Catalogus Baronum*, FSI 101 (Rome, 1972) and Errico Cuozzo, *Catalogus Baronum. Commentario*, FSI 101 (Rome, 1984). For administrative structures on the mainland under William II, see Hiroshi Takayama, *Administration of the Norman Kingdom* (Leiden, 1993), especially pp. 143–62; also, Horst Enzensberger, 'Chanceries, charters and administration in Norman Italy', in Loud and Metcalfe, *Society of Norman Italy*, pp. 117–50.

28 For the estimate and for a detailed discussion see Johns, *Arabic Administration*, pp. 115–143.

29 On the origins and functions of the *dīwān*'s offices, see Johns, *Arabic Administration*, pp. 193–203.

30 For parallels and precedents of renewals, see Carlrichard Brühl, 'La Cancelleria latina di Ruggero II', in *Diplomi e Cancelleria*, pp. 44–6.

31 Matthew, *Norman Kingdom of Sicily*, p. 211.

32 Metcalfe, *Muslims and Christians*, pp. 146–7.

33 For editions of the Chúrchuro documents and questions of administrative efficiency, see Jeremy Johns and Alex Metcalfe, 'The Mystery at Chúrchuro: conspiracy or incompetence in twelfth-century Sicily?', *BSOAS*, 62 (1999): 226–59.

8

The Normans in Africa

Norman Sicily and Zirid Ifrīqiya in the 1140s

In Sicily, the 1140s was a period of internal peace and prosperity for the rapidly maturing kingdom, which was successfully developing and refining its instruments of government. With strategic expansion north into the mountains of the Abruzzo, and south into Ifrīqiya culminating in the capture of Mahdiyya, the kingdom under Roger and George reached the peak of its power, population size and physical extent in a changing Mediterranean. To the east, in the crusader states, the fall of Edessa at the end of 1144 saw the launch of the Second Crusade. Sicily was not directly involved in the crusade, but its progress was undermined by their naval attacks on the Byzantines after the breakdown of negotiations between Roger and Manuel Comnenus. Nor was the central Mediterranean region untouched by conceptual shifts over the nature of religiously inspired hostility, in part stimulated by the preaching of Bernard of Clairvaux, as the physical focus on the Holy Land and the capture and defence of Jerusalem broadened to include personal disposition towards faith and the potentially heretical attitudes of those of other beliefs.

In the western Maghrib, attitudes were also changing. The Almohads – militantly zealous Maṣmūda Berber tribesmen from the High Atlas mountains – consolidated their rule under ʿAbd al-Mu'min at the expense of the Almoravids. From the African mainland they expanded northwards into the Iberian peninsula first taking Cádiz, Jeréz and Seville, while, from the north, Christian forces made significant and lasting gains with the capture of Lisbon in 1147. The Almohads, with their capital established at Marrakesh, advanced swiftly eastwards across the central Maghrib throughout 1152 towards the city-states of Ifrīqiya which had been weakened by more than a century of repeated economic and political crises, exacerbated by Norman incursions against them. It was against this background of unpredictable change and conflict that the kingdom of Sicily again sought to extend its sway into the south Mediterranean with the gradual conquest of towns in Ifrīqiya itself.

Given the events being played out across the Mediterranean at this time, attention paid to the so-called 'Normans in Africa' has been understandably limited. Events elsewhere were of greater immediate importance, and even within the Sicilian kingdom more attention was given at the time to relations with the papacy and the continuing external threat from the Byzantines and Germans. Indeed, Norman expansion into north Africa raised concerns at courts in Germany and Constantinople since these were territories that had once been imperial provinces of Roman and then Byzantine Africa prior to the Muslim conquests. Sicilian attention was also sharply focused on developments within its own borders, especially on the dangerous tensions which emerged after the deaths of George of Antioch in 1151 and Roger II in 1154, followed by threats of invasion and major baronial uprisings during 1155–6. None the less, there remains a tendency to understate the significance of the Normans in Africa, whose ultimate failure resulted in a clear separation of forces in Sicily and Ifrīqiya. In effect, this consolidated the political boundary between Muslim north Africa and Christian Italy which, although later contested by Angevins, Catalans, Ḥafṣids, Marīnids, Spaniards, Ottomans and privateers, would, by and large, hold firm. The collapse of Norman rule in Ifrīqiya also marked the end of a brief rally of Christianity after five centuries of continual decline, whereas Islam was reinvigorated with the lasting impression of a more radical dimension in the areas now covered by eastern Algeria, Tunisia and western Libya. The complex case studies of, and primary sources for, the Ifrīqiyan Muslims under Norman rule also make for incisive comparisons with the Sicilian Muslims under the same rulers.[1]

Centrifugal political forces within Muslim north Africa had tended to push certain groups to its margins, into mountains, oases refuges or in the case of Djerba (Arabic: Jārba) onto a peripheral island hideaway. In the minds of contemporary Arab-Muslim chroniclers and geographers, Djerba was a byword for unruliness and piracy, confirmed by its population of Kharijite Ibāḍīs who, according to al-Idrīsī, spoke only Berber. Agriculturally poor due to its lack of water resources, and connected to the mainland by a causeway originally built in the Roman period, Djerba had been a safe haven for outlaws and refugees, and was also home to a significant Jewish community that had been there since the sack of Jerusalem in AD 70. The threat posed by the Djerbans to trans-Mediterranean shipping was the most likely cause of the fierce attack which Roger launched against them in 1135, even though the island was still nominally under the authority of the Zirid *amīr*, al-Ḥasan b. 'Alī (r. 1121–48, d. 1167).[2] Later, in 1153, when the island revolted it was again subject to Sicilian attack. A treaty was announced; the *jizya* was to be paid as material proof of Djerba's submission; its people were said to have been made Roger's personal chattels; and an administrative officer (*'āmil*) was externally appointed. As we shall see, the severity of the treatment of the rebel Djerbans was exceptional and exemplary. In the 1135 attack, such a forceful and diplomatically sensitive intervention raised concerns in Cairo, not least because the Fatimids' desire to assume and maintain commanding positions in the central and eastern Mediterranean as well as the Red Sea was linked to preserving a state of affairs from which they might ultimately benefit. For the central Mediterranean, nurturing political stability in and around Ifrīqiya was essential. Concerns to maintain order were expressed in rare surviving correspondence between Roger and the imām-caliph al-Ḥāfiẓ which can be dated to the winter of 1137.[3] Besides the shared mutual interests in the central Mediterranean, the Cairo–Palermo letters also reveal a sustained level of warm but cautious diplomatic contacts as well as the extent to which the Arab–Sicilian bureau was now capable of effective engagement – in Arabic – with the sophisticated diplomatic machinery of chanceries in the Islamic world.

From the time of the first treaty concluded between Roger I and Tamīm, the Normans had continued to recognise the importance of Ifrīqiya to Sicily. By the 1130s, dependency on Sicilian military, economic and logistical assistance, mainly in the form of ensuring a supply of Sicilian grain in return for gold, had become so essential for Ifrīqiyan regimes that the region was effectively becoming transformed into a Sicilian protectorate. As such, this led to increasingly direct forms of intervention in the former Fatimid territories. Thus, in 1135, Roger sent ships to the Zirids to protect Mahdiyya against the raids launched against it by the Banū Ḥammād, who were responding to appeals from the Mahdiyyans who, in turn, were uneasy with political deals that the Zirid *amīr* al-Ḥasan had been obliged to cut with Roger.[4] For their part, the Fatimids detained a Zirid ship at Alexandria in 1141 and conspicuously allowed a Banū Ḥammād ship to proceed.

For the year 1142–3, the Arabic chroniclers recorded a series of famines in Ifrīqiya which led to the decimation of the rural population and the emigration of many to Sicily; Ibn al-Athīr added that 'they suffered greatly for this', the precise implications of which are unclear.[5] None the less, al-Ḥasan of Mahdiyya, under unbearable political strain caused by the food shortages, agreed to submit himself to Roger and rule on his behalf. Destructive Sicilian expeditions were subsequently undertaken against Djidjelli (Jījil) in 1143, the small port of Brask (modern Sīdī Brahīm) in 1144–5, where the men were killed and the women enslaved and Kerkenna in 1145–6, which was also depopulated as a result.[6] Al-Ḥasan's plea to Roger to observe the treaties that held between them was rebutted and, after a failed attempt two years previously, the prized town of Trípoli fell in June 1146 to the Sicilian fleet under George of Antioch.[7]

The fall of Trípoli and the coup at Gabès

Trípoli (Ṭarābulus), located in what is now Libya, dominated the most westerly areas of Ifrīqiya and had been under the control of the Banū Khazrūn. After its fall, which was assisted by strife between factions within the town, the Sicilians established a garrison, fortified its walls and dug a moat over a six-month period.[8] After a treaty was agreed and hostages taken, power was devolved into the hands of Arab tribal rulers and the town was put under a governor (*wālī*), Abū Yaḥyā from the Banū Maṭruḥ, who received a robe of office from Palermo and a diploma to confirm his investiture. Alongside the *wālī*, a respected religious authority from among the Berbers was appointed chief magistrate (*qāḍī*) by the Normans. In the aftermath of the conquest, the town was reported by Ibn al-Athīr to have regained its political stability and thrived from its subsequent economic rejuvenation, the population boosted by settlers encouraged to colonise it from Sicily. It is unclear who these migrants were, but some form of mandate was issued which applied to 'people of Sicily' as well as Christians (*al-Rūm*), suggesting that Christians may have lived there on privileged terms. However, the possibility that Roger was resettling some earlier Ifrīqiyan refugees cannot be discounted either. The conquest of Trípoli set important precedents because of its apparently 'benign' political control in which local strongmen were appointed directly from Palermo and allowed to conduct affairs with minimal interference from Sicily or its garrison commander, so long as they paid their taxes to the Norman *dīwān*. These elements of capitulation by treaty and trust are also corroborated by an independent Latin source.[9]

The political flashpoint of the 1140s which brought most of Ifrīqiya to recognise the authority of Norman Sicily occurred further north at Gabès (Qābis). By the end of the eleventh century, the city was under the control of the Banū Jāmi', who had been brought to power with the help of factions that claimed links with the Banū Hilāl, and who had overthrown Zirid rule in the form of 'Umar b. al-Mu'izz, Tamīm's brother. Its governor from the early 1120s, Rushayd ibn Kāmil, had coins minted in his own name, affirming the degree of independence that he enjoyed. In 1146–7, Rushayd died and, of his two sons, Mu'ammar and Muḥammad, the former was quickly ousted by one of Rushayd's 'clients' (*mawlā*) named Yūsuf. While Mu'ammar appealed to the Zirid *amīr* al-Ḥasan, Yūsuf offered Gabès to Roger in return for which he received robes from Palermo as confirmation of his status. As Ibn al-Athīr reflected, such a non-interventionist arrangement mirrored that which was already in place between Palermo and the Banū Maṭrūḥ of Trípoli. The following year, 1147–8, a coalition force of Zirids under al-Ḥasan, Arab tribesmen from the Banū Qurra and local townsfolk overthrew Yūsuf, who was then tortured to death. There was a strong suggestion in the sources that some of the ire was also part of a personal vendetta.

His brother, ʿIsā, then at Palermo, appealed to the Sicilians with the offer of putting Rushayd's infant son, Muḥammad, in control of the town. For his negotiations with the infidels in Palermo, where he had also fallen out with Ḥasan's envoy, Yūsuf's brother was brought to Mahdiyya and subjected to an ignominious parade (*tashhīr*), wearing a pointed hat with bells on it while being strapped over a camel. The authorities did not halt the crowd when they began stoning him to death.[10] Consequently, Muʿammar was appointed as Zirid governor at Gabès. Roger now had the political pretext he needed for an intervention against Ḥasan over his choice of governor. With the Sicilian fleet already at sea, George of Antioch prepared for the final push in the summer of 1148.

When George arrived in Mahdiyya he requested that al-Ḥasan provide an army to help install Muḥammad at Gabès. Al-Ḥasan was thus manoeuvred into an impossible position: he had made pledges with Roger that now stood to be broken as a result of which he would be ousted himself. On the other hand, the Muslim sources were equally clear in pointing out that he was faced with an option that was both legally and religiously unacceptable: he was assisting infidels to lord over a Muslim community, and one which had already shown its gruesome disapproval at the prospect of submission to non-Muslim rule.[11] Thus, the last Zirid *amīr* of Ifrīqiya, al-Ḥasan, stepped down from power, and, with a pro-Sicilian governor installed at Gabès, Mahdiyya, which had been evacuated, was taken without bloodshed by George of Antioch in July 1148. The invaders reportedly seized an immense amount of booty in the palace complexes. The treasures of Ifrīqiya were presumably ferried back to Palermo. The culmination of the Ifrīqiyan campaigns may also shed light on the timing of the Normans' attack on Thebes and Corfù in the Byzantine eastern Mediterranean during the previous year which seriously undermined the Second Crusade. On the one hand, the Normans needed to keep their ships at sea, but could not risk sending them west towards Almohad waters; they may also have been reticent about prematurely stoking up opposition in Ifrīqiya by holding the fleet off the coast before the attack on Mahdiyya could be engineered. The eastern Mediterranean raids ensured that the fleet was ready and active while also helping to raise extra funds for the final push against Ifrīqiya.

It is doubtful whether the Ifrīqiyan campaigns should themselves be viewed as a type of crusader activity, especially when there were such obvious economic advantages to be gained from dominating the south-central Mediterranean trade routes. Thus, their desire to extend military and political influence in the same strategic direction led the Normans to be willingly sucked into a fractious Ifrīqiya, whose implosion they had helped to cause. However, alongside this might also be placed the personal ambition of the Sicilian leadership. In the case of Roger, motives were less tangible, but a desire to further his imperial pretensions is perfectly credible in the context of the 1140s. Ibn al-Athīr, who was often quick to link economic motives to conquest campaigns, recorded that in the year 1147–8 there was another particularly severe famine across Ifrīqiya, followed by an outbreak of disease which devastated the countryside and forced large numbers of those who could afford it to travel overseas, to leave for Sicily. Opportunism, the chronicler explained, thus prompted Roger to take full advantage of the desperate situation and launch an attack against a weakened Mahdiyya. In George's case, taking revenge on the Zirids as his former employers, from whom he had fled for his life forty years earlier, provides an equally strong reason for action.

Much is made of George of Antioch's political awareness and tactical wisdom in his dealings with the Islamic world. However, on this occasion, his treatment of the Zirids created in the figure of al-Ḥasan, an important, disaffected enemy. Freed from further political or religious compromise, he eventually made his way to Marrakesh, where he put the case for a counterattack to the Almohad caliph, ʿAbd al-Mu'min. The vestiges of Zirid power in Ifrīqiya would soon be forgotten, but their dislike for the Normans was not, and the rise of a domineering Zirid *wazīr* in Cairo after the death of al-Ḥāfiẓ may also account for deteriorating relations between Cairo and Palermo during the mid-1150s, which culminated in a Sicilian attack on the Egyptian port of Tinnīs by William I in 1155.[12]

After the fall of Mahdiyya, Sicilian attention was again distracted towards the eastern Mediterranean. In Ifrīqiya, rather than establishing Christian lordships based on the model of the south Italian mainland and in parts of Sicily, the Normans adopted more subtle and inconspicuous strategies. Sousse, for example, which was governed by a type of council or *shūrā*, had surrendered quickly and was placed in the hands of a certain Jabbāra b. Kāmil al-Fādighī, who was linked to the Zirid governor, while the forceful conquest of Sfax resulted in the town being handed over to a local, ʿUmar ibn Abī l-Ḥasan al-Furriyānī, in lieu of a governor previously appointed from Mahdiyya. ʿUmar's aged father Abū l-Ḥasan had been a prominent jurist in Sfax, and declined the position in favour of his son, but agreed to be taken himself as a hostage to Palermo. Yet again, rule from Sicily was conducted at a distance, and it was also heavily reliant on the co-operation of local strongmen whom they had empowered.

The short-term effects of the Norman conquest were ambivalent. On the one hand, their greater involvement with Ifrīqiya brought vital and immediate economic benefit to areas repeatedly weakened and reduced by famine. In addition, each city-state enjoyed greater commercial and, hence, political independence from Mahdiyya, while short-term stimulation of trade was spurred by a new-found optimism and an increased number of merchants operating in their ports and marketplaces. On the other hand, the testimony of al-Idrīsī, a contemporary source who had been observing events from Palermo, emphasised the enormous devastation which the Norman attacks had wrought on the population, blaming this, rather than any longer-term malaise, for the subsequent debility of the Ifrīqiyan towns. Hence, according to Idrīsī, Jījil and Marsā l-Zaytūna had been sacked completely, Sfax was a shadow of its former self in terms of its population and wealth, Būna was said to have been in a wretched condition; the male inhabitants of Trípoli had been massacred and later, he may have personally seen the prisoners from Djerba who were carried off to Palermo itself.[13]

When other major towns capitulated, including Tunis, almost all the key cities in Ifrīqiya now recognised the authority of Roger to whom they would pay tribute. This situation was confirmed by the issuing of a general treaty in which Ibn al-Athīr reported that, 'treaty documents and pledges of fine promises (*al-mawā'īd al-ḥusna*) arrived from Roger addressed to the entire population of Ifrīqiya'. In September 1148, an 'Archbishop of Africa' was announced by Pope Eugenius III and confirmed two years later. Embryonic as this see was, it none the less signalled a clear intention. Indeed, had Sicilian rule in Ifrīqiya endured, it is reasonable to presume that the archbishopric at Mahdiyya would have expanded with grants to support it, leading to the creation of other foundations around which privileged Christian settlement could have flourished.

Almohad expansion and Philip of Mahdiyya at Būna

The Sicilians' indirect approach to government in Ifrīqiya was designed to minimise the chances of local rebellion, but a major threat loomed from the west with the rapid conquest of the central Maghrib and main coastal towns by a large and unified Almohad army under the *amīr al-mu'minīn* (the Commander of the Faithful), 'Abd al-Mu'min. By the end of summer 1152, the Ḥammādid stronghold at Bougie (Bijāya) had fallen. In April of the following year, a local army was defeated by 'Abd al-Mu'min at Setif (Saṭīf), leaving the Ḥammādid dynasty crippled and the towns of Norman Ifrīqiya exposed to Almohad attack.[14] However, after his initial successes, 'Abd al-Mu'min turned his attention back to the political and administrative reorganisation of the western Maghrib while preparing a large fleet and army. This break in the advance allowed the Normans to launch a strategic attack on the town of Būna (Bône, modern 'Annāba in eastern Algeria) in autumn 1153 with the idea of installing a pro-Sicilian governor who, with the support of the local populace and military back-up from Sicily, might be willing and able to withstand future Almohad advances. It was essential, therefore, to maintain the goodwill of the conquered town. So, when forces arrived from Sicily under the command of Philip 'of Mahdiyya', both Arabic and Latin sources said that destruction and booty-taking was kept to a minimum. At Būna, a local Ḥammādid governor was put in charge of the compliant town. However, on his return to Palermo, Philip was arrested and accused of apostasy.

Philip was one of many eunuchs in royal service and had been favoured by Roger from a young age. Along with his fellow eunuchs in the palaces, they claimed to be Christian converts, but were widely known to conceal their faith by inwardly adhering to Islam. Philip's trial and execution in late 1153, with all their historiographical nuances, are worthy of close attention, particularly because of the ways in which they highlight important links between Sicilian expansion in Ifrīqiya, Muslim–Christian relations on the island and looming political crises in the royal palaces at Palermo. These would set the tone at court for the rest of the Norman period. The Arabic accounts are found in Ibn al-Athīr and later in Ibn Khaldūn, who gave an abbreviated version; a long marginal note exists in the Latin *Chronicon* of Romuald of Salerno.[15]

Romuald made a very specific claim about Roger, namely that 'towards the end of his life, allowing secular matters to be neglected and delayed, he laboured in every conceivable way to convert Jews and Muslims to the faith of Christ'.[16] This raises a number of thorny historical problems, not least of which is whether Philip's execution was precisely a consequence of this alleged zeal. The statement might also be read as a pious medieval topos, and there is no recorded evidence for the rewards said to have been given to converts, such as estates granted from the royal demesnes. That said, during the raids on Thebes and Corfù in 1147, Jews had been rounded up and brought back to Sicily, an action for which there is no obvious motive other than perhaps their conversion. Problems of interpretation are compounded by Romuald's account of Philip which was interpolated into the margin of the manuscript at an anachronistic and inappropriate juncture in the text. The note is, in fact, a long, self-contained passage packed with theatrical drama and direct speech, quite unlike the rest of Romuald's work and dissimilar in style to that of other Latin chroniclers who wrote about Sicily.

The specific subject of the note was Philip's trial, over which Roger himself presided. Accusations of religious impropriety were presented to the royal court: Philip was said to have preferred Muslim practices to Christian ones, he looked like a Christian but was secretly a Muslim, he gave oil for mosque lanterns, he had sent gifts to Muḥammad's tomb, and had generally acted against Christians and the Christian faith. His close ties to Roger and his importance as a military commander were also recorded. In spite of the pleas of the accused, and Roger's defensive and tearful outburst, Philip was condemned at the hands of the gathered counts, justiciars, barons and judges of the kingdom, who were made to act on Roger's unwilling but dutiful steer towards a guilty verdict.[17] Philip was then dragged around by horses and burned alive in a lime kiln outside the palace – a holocaust to purify and destroy all trace of body and soul, and to prevent access to paradise. It was an execution that was perhaps all the more disturbing for a Muslim audience familiar with the imagery of hell as an oven, and who knew from the *ḥadīth* that punishment by fire was prohibited to all but God.

In Ibn al-Athīr's report of the Sicilian expedition against Būna, he claimed that Philip's downfall was instead precipitated by the leniency he had shown toward the town's inhabitants; a strategy exactly in line with royal thinking. He also provides a date for the execution: Ramaḍān 548 AH or between 20 November and 19 December 1153, just months before Roger's own death on 26 February 1154. Ibn al-Athīr's account – quite probably based on information in the lost history of the close Zirid source, Ibn Shaddād – also mentioned that it was not just Philip who was accused of apostasy, but also the palace eunuchs around him. The Latin version claimed that they too received a capital punishment. The Arabic account also drew attention to Philip's dissemblance as a pseudo-Christian and crypto-Muslim, that he did not fast (that is, during Lent), was tried before the kingdom's magnates and was burned alive. So similar are certain fine, incidental details in both the Latin and Arabic accounts that the veracity of the episode is significantly boosted and demands to be treated seriously. With the benefit of hindsight, Ibn al-Athīr drew the episode to a close on a chilling note: 'this was the first weakening blow that fell upon the Muslims of Sicily'.

The implications and aftermath of Philip's trial

The religious overtones of the trial and execution reflected the growing Muslim–Christian tensions in Sicily and Ifrīqiya, and specifically in the royal palaces. After the death of George of Antioch, this had been fuelled by the rise of the Latin aristocracy who felt alienated from power which had come to be concentrated in the hands of George's successor as *amīr* of *amīr*s, Maio of Bari, a Latin of non-noble origins who had worked closely with crypto-Muslim eunuchs in the royal administration. Tensions can only have been exacerbated by the critical situation unfolding across the contested frontiers of the Mediterranean. As such, Romuald's marginal note might also be interpreted in the light of pressures building between the king and his officials against the rising force of the Latin nobility since the conquest of towns in Ifrīqiya had not led to the creation of new lordships or expansion of older ones. Rather, it had resulted in the preservation of local Muslim elites. They were appointed directly by the king and their point of contact with Palermo was via the king's officers and crypto-Muslim eunuchs who ran the palaces and enjoyed increasing powers in the royal *dīwān*. This resentment would be felt all the more keenly when Ifrīqiya revolted from 1156 and was not defended.

In his dying days, Roger's political and religious predicament was clear and royal justice risked exposure as inconsistent: apostasy from Christianity ran contrary to his own Assizes, yet it was acceptable in his own palaces. However, his sacrifice of Philip served less as an act of religious piety than as a concession to the Latin baronage, who had successfully anticipated the political shape and direction of the future kingdom. Unwilling to appear openly seditious when the once-great king was still alive, they instead forced his hand in their own favour at a crucial juncture in the kingdom's development by gaining ground at the expense of the palace servant-officers.

The trial revealed that the faith communities of the kingdom were not only perceived as distinct, but were hierarchically arranged. Indeed, in this respect, the configuration of the monotheistic faiths within the kingdom mirrored an Islamic understanding of them: conversion to the prestigious faith of the ruler was open, even desirable, but backsliding was a crime against God, and transgressors could expect no mercy. In a kingdom undergoing enormous socio-religious flux, where both old and new communities were thinking hard about their identities, orientation and position within it, strategies that aimed at clarifying the degrees of separation would not only lead to even greater attrition of the Muslim communities via assimilation, conversion and emigration on the one hand, but would also create a core that was increasingly hostile and resistant to such pressures, on the other hand.

There was an important contrast in the remote government of Ifrīqiya compared with the arrangements under which the Sicilian Muslims lived. The latter were under direct rule from the royal *dīwān* in which Muslim community leaders occupied an ambivalent position in that they held sway in their own communities, but were neither invested by the *dīwān* nor could they be removed by the *dīwān*. Most of Ifrīqiya, however, was ruled indirectly and by royal appointment.[18] In this respect, there were some important underlying similarities and differences between the ways in which the Normans had gained and developed control over the Sicilian and Ifrīqiyan Muslims. In both early Norman Sicily and mid-twelfth-century Ifrīqiya, the initial limits of possibility had been narrow. In neither case was it practical to impose rule too harshly, too soon. In post-conquest Sicily, terms of capitulation had been concluded over a thirty-year period and were subject to degrees of regional variation: some local strongmen were deposed; some were replaced at later stages; others passed on their political influence to later generations. The foundation of the kingdom and formation of a royal administration superimposed and formalised a higher structure of authority over the Muslim community, thereby increasing the ambivalent status beneath it of some of their community leaders, who lacked official recognition. In Ifrīqiya, terms of capitulation had been concluded swiftly but, as Norman rule lasted less than a generation, the new structures of government had no time to develop or to be put to the test. However, seeds of change had already been sown in Ifrīqiya: in particular, the presence of Sicilian officials in the capital and rebellious areas; immigration from Sicily had been encouraged;

and Christian merchants were quick to appear in Ifrīqiyan ports, perhaps especially the Genoese who had been conceded lucrative trading concessions in the kingdom in 1156–7.[19] Finally, although lordships had not been created, the announcement of an archbishopric of Africa had long-term implications.

Legally, the Sicilian Muslims were subject to the judgements of their own *qāḍīs*, who were resident within an infidel land and were ultimately subject to royal authority and justice. Juridical considerations were compounded by the complicity of the old surrender treaties, which made the argument that they (still) lived in an overtly Christian kingdom only under duress more difficult to substantiate. In Ifrīqiya, there was even greater ambivalence, not least because the *qāḍīs* were not resident in infidel lands in quite the same, long-standing way as they were in the kingdom of Sicily proper. Furthermore, the variations in the treatment of different towns implies that there was a wider scope for legal interpretation. For example, in the case of Trípoli, we are told that the Christians could not interfere in any legal case of the Muslims. This does not necessarily imply that the Muslim *qāḍī* had absolute powers of jurisdiction in that city, since his powers may have applied only in cases which arose within the Muslim community and therefore did not exclude the possibility that serious crimes or inter-faith cases could be passed up to a royal court. If so, then their legal position was theoretically comparable to that of the royal Sicilian *dhimmīs*: autonomous within their own community, yet ultimately subordinate to the crown.

Fiscally, the Sicilian Muslims were administered directly by officers of the *dīwān*, who co-ordinated collection of the *jizya* with local shaykhs and/or community leaders. By contrast, tribute payable to the crown was, in most of the Ifrīqiyan towns, collected by the local, but royally appointed, governor; and then they were passed to the *dīwān* in Palermo. However, the arrangements were complex and not uniform. For example, the Muslims' payment of the *jizya* was specifically attested at Trípoli, Mahdiyya and Djerba but not elsewhere in Ifrīqiya. If we are to trust that the sources have presented sufficiently full evidence in these cases, a likely explanation for the lack of consistency in referring to the *jizya* is that Trípoli had been the first city to fall under Christian rule, while in Mahdiyya and Djerba, externally appointed governors had been imposed. Thus, avoidance of the term elsewhere may not have been guided by legal questions, but rather reflected a political desire on the part of the Sicilians to avoid provoking the local population into rising up against them or against the agents they had empowered and through whom they ruled. If accepted, then we may see in it a policy deriving from the practical expediency of a light touch, rather than a well-meaning benignity. Sicilian awareness of issues that were sensitive for the conquered Muslims, such as residency in regions under non-Muslim rule and resistance or obedience to authority of questionable legitimacy, may also account for the fact that the term *jizya* was rarely attested. Indeed, it is not found by name in any royal document from the Norman period.

Problems of how to describe and articulate the uncertain relationship between the Sicilian crown and the city-states of Ifrīqiya may be seen in the initially enthusiastic, but then somewhat more hesitant, adoption by Roger II and William I of the royal title of *Malik Ifrīqiya* or 'King of Africa'.[20] The term *malik* is attested on two royal dinars minted in Mahdiyya when it was under Sicilian rule. The first is dated to between May 1148 and May 1149, and the second between March 1154 and March 1155. Although they style Roger II and his son William I as '*al-malik*', implicitly referring to Ifrīqiya, they do not explicitly use that term. In addition, three private documents exist, two as late as 1157 and 1158, in which William was called either 'Master of Africa' or 'King of Africa'. An inscribed sword expressed a similar sentiment. Further important evidence comes from an inscription from May 1149, which was commissioned by a royal cleric called Grizandus and commemorated the translation of his mother's body to a specially built chapel in Palermo.[21] Three points are of particular note. First, is the status of Grizandus as a royal priest of the Greek and Latin rite, which is known to us from a second commemoration from 1153. Secondly, is that the unusual memorial plaque was written in four scripts (Latin, Greek, Arabic and Judeo-Arabic) (see fig. 10 on p. 232). Finally, the date of the commemoration in May 1149 came less than a year after the fall of Mahdiyya in June 1148. The deployment of Roger's titles, including two references to him as 'King of Africa' in the inscription in multiple languages, can thus be considered as at least semi-official. Other formulae employed also closely echoed contemporary royal usages.

The royal title appears to be evidence for Norman imperial pretensions to rule over Ifrīqiya, but if so, why was it not more widely adopted? Greater diplomatic sensitivity and discretion may have been favoured under Roger, in particular to caution against provoking the Ifrīqiyan Muslims to the extent that they might be inclined to switch their allegiance to the much-feared Almohads. More specifically, the answer may lie in Palermo–Cairo diplomatic relations, which were warm during the contemporaneous reigns of Roger II and al-Ḥāfiẓ, but which deteriorated after the death of the latter, and/or with the death of Roger's special envoy to the Islamic world, George, in 1151. The thesis proposed by Jeremy Johns is that a subsequent failure in personal diplomacy over a region of such political and economic sensitivity to both the Fatimids and the Sicilians persuaded Roger to drop the triumphalist claim to have possessed lands over which the caliph still had vested commercial and political interests.

The revolts in Ifrīqiya, Sicily and the Italian mainland

At Palermo, the very way in which the campaigns had been conducted became a political issue with strong religious overtones. In Ifrīqiya, too, the conquest raised questions of religious principle and propriety. Thus, given the 'hands-off' approach of Norman rule generally in Ifrīqiya and the revitalisation of trade in its cities, the causes of revolts which began in 1156 are not satisfactorily explicable in either political or economic terms alone. Nor, for that matter, can the rise and initial eastward expansion of the Almohads suffice either, although this was clearly a concern for the Normans, who had requested that the Almohads be cursed at Trípoli – a demand which was refused. Ifrīqiyan appeals were made to the Almohads, but the city-states *began* their revolts without direct assistance and, although they were doubtless emboldened by news of the Muslim advance, not all acquiesced with open enthusiasm when the Almohad armies arrived in 1159–60.

The initial epicentre of the revolts was at Sfax (under the command of 'Umar al-Furriyānī), where Ibn Khaldūn reported that the Christians – presumably a mix of indigenous and recent settlers, as well as merchants – had inflicted unspecified 'loss and harm' on the locals. Quite possibly this is a reference to commercial rivalries from which the rapidly expanding, and probably privileged, Christian community was benefiting. Alternatively, it may refer to opposition to a more systematic and regular collection of taxes and dues by a non-native, infidel regime. In the figure of 'Umar al-Furriyānī, some have seen a budding Ifrīqiyan version of the 'commander of the faithful', designated by his pious father in a not dissimilar manner to that of the Almohad Mahdī, Ibn Tūmart and his successor, 'Abd al-Mu'min.[22] However, such an interpretation may appear too nuanced given the blunt opportunistic motives behind the revolt. This can be seen most clearly when the timing of the initial uprising is viewed against the background of the rebellions and war in Sicily and on the south Italian mainland between 1155 and 1157, which threatened the very existence of William I's new kingship. Significantly, the date given by Ibn al-Athīr for 'Umar's revolt in Sfax against 'all the Franks and the local Christians' was the beginning of 551 AH which ran from 25 February 1156.[23]

During the previous year, the internal stability of the kingdom was seriously threatened by the dual intervention of German and Byzantine forces on the mainland, coupled with baronial revolts both there and on the island.[24] The German emperor, Frederick Barbarossa, had crossed the Alps and advanced southward, reaching Rome, where he was crowned in June of the same year. One of the most important and persistently rebellious lords on the mainland, the king's cousin, Robert of Bassunvilla, recently made count of Loritello, rose in revolt and the northern parts of the kingdom, such as Capua – where Roger had reasserted his authority in the 1130s, and Abruzzo into which he had expanded in the 1140s – followed suit, with many of the rebel nobles coming from long-established families in the south. The threat to the integrity of the kingdom was compounded by the opposition of Pope Adrian IV and the arrival of a Byzantine army in south Apulia in the autumn of 1155. Worse still, from September until December, William had fallen seriously ill, sparking dangerous rumours of his death. The insurrection quickly spread across Apulia where the key towns of Bari, Trani, Bríndisi and Táranto fell. At Bari, the royal citadel was destroyed, while rebellion broke out on the island of Sicily itself. William was forced to quash the revolt on the island first by directing his army against the 'Lombard' town of Butera, which had been the stronghold of his rebellious cousin and Master Constable of Apulia, count Simon of Policastro, before turning his attention to the mainland during the spring of 1156. Having retaken Bríndisi and Bari, the opposition forces soon split, retreated or were defeated with relative ease; Bari itself was partially destroyed in retribution for its treachery; Campania was pacified, and Robert of Bassunvilla exiled for the time being.

The resolution of the revolts resulted in the Treaty of Benevento in June 1156, signed in the town where Pope Adrian had been besieged. The treaty expressed papal recognition of William's royal status in Sicily and the mainland, and confirmed his powers as legate on the island.[25] William remained in the area and was attested at Salerno the following month. Although relations with the papacy had ameliorated since 1139, and warmed with the meeting of Eugenius and Roger at Ceprano in 1150, they had deteriorated thereafter when William was crowned as joint ruler in April 1151, without papal consent.

In 1156, however, the Treaty of Benevento marked an important milestone in the development of the kingdom, and it offered a solution to most of the main problems which had tainted papal–Sicilian relations. In particular, it included a clarification of the royal right to restrict the powers of papal legates, by allowing them on to the island only with his permission. Although papal legates might operate on the mainland, another contentious point that stemmed from the concession originally made in 1098 by Urban II was clarified and agreed – namely, that the king had the power to reject the appointment of particular bishops, thereby giving him a high level of continued control over the Church in the kingdom. As John of Salisbury noted, the Muslims had provided a convenient leverage in the negotiations, since Roger had been able to argue that he maintained his rights because he had recovered the island from them for the Church of God.[26]

It was against this wider background of conflict and complex diplomacy, during which the king's attention was firmly fixed on problems within the kingdom itself, that the revolt in Sfax was launched. According to Ibn al-Athīr, it was instigated at the request of 'Umar's father, held under arrest in Palermo. By so doing, he resigned himself to execution. At Sfax, in a public act of political theatre, a funeral procession was held to commemorate his presumed execution in Palermo.[27] Given the timing of 'Umar's revolt at Sfax, it is quite clear that his venerable father had been well placed at Palermo to know that the Normans were unlikely to commit large forces for long campaigns in Ifrīqiya so long as William was engaged with restoring order in the kingdom. It is not wholly unreasonable to imagine that, perhaps as early as Easter 1156, Ifrīqiya had been written off as a loss by William and his *amīr* of *amīrs*, Maio. If so, then any subsequent attempt at intervention was little more than an exercise in damage limitation.

Following the successful precedent of Sfax, the governors of both Trípoli and Gabès led their citizens in revolt against Sicilian control. Būna fell, and, although Sousse did not revolt, it would later submit to Almohad rule. However, the initial attempt at revolt in Mahdiyya – again with the support of Sfax – failed. The peculiar geography of the old Fatimid and Zirid capital Mahdiyya presents an illuminating example of how the Normans and their Christian followers viewed their own presence there. The site was effectively split into two: on the headland of Mahdiyya proper were the palaces, administration and port; on the mainland was the suburb of Zawīla. It seems probable that the Norman capital of Mahdiyya became a Christian enclave with its own churches, while Zawīla was administered as if it were a Muslim town under Sicilian Christian rule. Thus, in the unsuccessful revolt of 1157–8, the Zawīlans besieged those in Mahdiyya from the land, and ships from Sfax besieged it from the sea. Massacred by Sicilian reinforcements as a punishment for their failed rebellion, it was the Zawīlans' subsequent appeal to the Almohad leader 'Abd al-Mu'min that was said to have spurred him to launch his invasion in 1159, culminating in the long siege of Mahdiyya which began at the end of July the same year. The Sicilian fleet under the command of a leading palace eunuch, *qā'id* Peter, failed to relieve the town. On 21 January 1160, Mahdiyya fell and Norman Africa had been lost: al-Ḥasan was restored as its joint ruler.[28]

Brief accounts of the Sicilian attempt to recapture Mahdiyya from the sea are mentioned in Latin and Arabic sources, and they reveal shared points of agreement as well as significant areas of confusion and dispute. The Norman fleet under Peter had been recalled from the Iberian coast and was an impressive outfit – if it really had consisted of 150 or 160 galleys, according to the estimates of Ibn Khaldūn and Falcandus, respectively.[29] Falcandus, however, claimed that Peter did not engage the Almohads, whereas the other accounts suggested that the engagement had been unsuccessful, and that Peter had withdrawn. However, implicit in both Latin and Arabic versions is that some form of diplomatic contact had occurred: Falcandus stated that 'Abd al-Mu'min had treacherously received letters from the palace eunuchs in Palermo; Ibn al-Athīr cited a threat issued by William I to kill Muslims in Sicily if the Mahdiyyan Christians were not allowed to leave unharmed. It is not improbable, therefore, that Peter as admiral was the lynchpin to the personal conduct of royal diplomacy 'on the ground' at the time. In any event, blame for the loss of Africa was firmly laid by the nobility on Peter, the palace eunuchs and the head of the administration, Maio, with serious consequences which, combined with other grievances, would unwind throughout the course of 1160–1, resulting in Maio's murder followed by a major baronial revolt, the sacking of the royal palace and large-scale massacres of palace eunuchs and of Muslims across the island.

For both Muslim and Christian sources, religion, authority and allegiance were most certainly issues even prior to the Almohads' conquest, as shown by the display of popular resentment at Gabès, Ḥasan's dilemma, Philip's trial and the partition of Mahdiyya. Religious motifs also feature prominently in the historical narratives with the sacrifice of the pious and dutiful Abū l-Ḥasan al-Furriyānī, which allowed his son to pursue holy war against infidel rule in Sfax and beyond. Indeed, when the revolts began, they assumed an increasingly religious nature. At both Sfax and Trípoli, the Christian population was massacred; at Tunis, the Almohad army under 'Abd al-Mu'min offered them the chance to convert or be killed. After negotiations, the Christians of Mahdiyya were permitted to leave, and it is likely that this period saw a general movement of Christians from Ifrīqiya to Sicily, such that if the Normans in Africa had prompted a temporary revival of Christianity there, the fall of Mahdiyya marked its failure from which it would not recover until European colonisation of the late nineteenth century. Norman rule in Ifrīqiya also saw the clear but illegal use of entire faith communities as collateral. On the one hand, the Christians and Jews of Mahdiyya had faced conversion or death under the Almohads, on the other hand, William I had threatened to remove royal protection from the Sicilian Muslims by killing them and taking their women and possessions in the event of a massacre at Mahdiyya.

Responses to infidel rule: the Mālikī jurists and the Almohads

Although opportunistic motives can be detected behind the initial instigation of the revolt at Sfax and its propagation under the leadership of 'Umar al-Furriyānī, the Ifrīqiyan revolts were accompanied by important legal considerations about the question of Muslims' conduct should they find themselves living under the authority of non-believers. We have no collection of Muslim legal opinions (*fatwās*) from Norman Sicily itself, but we are furnished with the opinions of jurists from the Mālikī law school as found in al-Wansharīsī's (d. 1508) *al-Mi'yār al-mu'rib*, a vast corpus of around 6,000 *fatwās* collected from the medieval western and central Mediterranean, from al-Andalus to Ifrīqiya.[30] From these it is possible to establish a broad theoretical context for legal opinions and a range of contemporary responses to infidel rule, especially over the contentious issues of whether one should resist, submit or retreat in the face of infidel opposition; conduct trade with the infidels or in their areas; be resident (willingly or otherwise) in non-Muslim lands, or accept as valid the rulings of *qāḍīs* appointed by a non-Muslim authority.

In answer to these questions, jurists could draw on several well-known precedents from the time of Muḥammad himself, for instance, his *hijra* or 'migration' from Mecca to Medina in 622, which could be understood as a temporary retreat in the face of irresistible opposition. Interpretations of such episodes formed the basis of legitimising similar types of reaction, including *taqiyya* or dissimulation of the faith as practised by the palace eunuchs in Palermo, who merely pretended to be Christian. In the Qur'ān and *ḥadīth*, the particulars of each case were seldom clear-cut. For instance, in very specific circumstances, Muḥammad was reported to have considered himself rid of any Muslim who sojourned among the polytheists. Elsewhere, numerous verses corroborate the notion that supporters in Mecca were encouraged to join the fledgling Islamic state in Medina. However, in the medieval Islamic world, such was the complex and interwoven relationship between legal theory, reason for action and retrospective justification for a particular action, that an over-reliance on evidence from *fatwās* to account for particular motives comes with a number of caveats, not least that this methodology might result in teleological confusion of cause and effect.

The predominant view of jurists from the Mālikī school, particularly with reference to al-Andalus and, later, to its *mudéjar* (*ahl al-dajan*) population of Muslims under Christian rule, was to register strong opposition to the idea, in theory, of living beyond the bounds of the *dār al-Islām* (literally, 'the house of Islam', referring to areas in which Islamic law can be enforced). Thus, Ibn Ḥazm (d. 1064) argued that travel into infidel zones (the *dār al-ḥarb* or literally, 'the house of war') should only be undertaken to fight infidels or to deliver diplomatic correspondence; al-Qurṭubī (d. 1071) also argued that Muslims should not travel or stay in regions where Islamic law was not, or could not be, applied. Ibn Rushd (d. 1126) and Ibn al-ʿArabī (d. 1148), *inter alia*, argued from similar perspectives. However, no less important than the establishment of a theoretical ideal was its temperance by a range of practical considerations, including special dispensations in cases where it was arguably valid to act contrary to a moral imperative. Exceptions included staying in infidel regions with the intention of spreading Islam or intending to prosecute *jihād*. Alternatively, the law covered cases of involuntary residence, for example, of Muslim captives, or the willing (but temporary) stays that travellers or merchants might make. Such problematic cases were debatable and contentious. But both Sicily and Ifrīqiya under the Normans were precisely debatable and contentious.

In this respect, the reported opinions of the leading Mālikī jurist, the imām al-Māzarī (1061–1141) are of particular importance because he was asked specifically about the situation of Muslims in Sicily – a place he may have known personally.[31] Although his family were most probably from Mazara, he was said to have studied in Sfax under al-Lakhmī, who died in 1085. Thus, had al-Māzarī lived in Sicily, he had done so only in his youth. None the less, in Ifrīqiya he had come to be regarded as a major religious authority, notable for his practical lenience and application of the maxim of opting for the lesser of two evils when presented with such an unfortunate choice. First, al-Māzarī argued that although there were theoretical grounds for dismissing as invalid the legal acts and judgements of *qāḍī*s in Norman Sicily, they might otherwise be upheld as long as their residence in infidel territory was matched by their intention of retaking it for Islam, or of guiding the infidel away from error. Secondly, he maintained as valid the verdicts of judges appointed by infidels provided that they were just and sound from the perspective of legal competence, even if they were made in a community which was separated from the *dār al-Islām*. Such arguments from practical expediency were consistent with, and stemmed from, the consciously conservative and normative thinking of the Mālikī school, which had been shaped by its opposition in Ifrīqiya, Sicily and al-Andalus to the revolutionary doctrines of the Fatimids. It also echoed the view of another major Ifrīqiyan jurist, al-Qābisī (d. 1012), who had put similar arguments when questioned about whether Islamic law pertaining to commercial contracts and inheritance might be properly applied in sub-Saharan Africa. Thus, it has been convincingly suggested that Islamic jurisprudence 'played a major role in the creation of Roger's African empire, largely resolving the initial dilemma of the Muslim population to submit or resist'.[32] However, the arrival of the Almohads may also have introduced a much harder religious line: if their opposition to the 'corrupt' Muslim rule of the Almoravids and Andalusi *ṭā'ifa* statelets was confrontational and uncompromising, how much more unyielding were their attitudes towards infidel Christian rule in Ifrīqiya, or their reluctance to be ruled either from Sicily or like the Muslims in Sicily? From the 1160s, many Sicilian Muslims presumably asked similar questions about resistance or continued submission, especially as their circumstances worsened.

As we have seen, on the island of Sicily itself, the *qāḍī*s of Palermo are known to us as members of the Banū Rajā'. However, nothing further is known about Roger's *maẓālim* courts and, outside Palermo, the extent to which Islamic juridical infrastructure might have survived intact under the Normans remains unclear. Among names suggesting professions found in the registers of men conceded to the church at Cefalù, is found a certain Ḥasan *al-qāḍī* along with his three sons.[33] Two further sons of *qāḍī*s are attested from 1183 living on crown lands in western Sicily, while Ibn Jubayr shortly afterwards mentioned in passing a high-ranking judicial expert (*ṣāḥib al-aḥkām*) of Trápani.[34] On a practical level, it must be presumed that most petitions or disputes that occurred within the

Muslim community would, or could, be dealt with locally and without recourse to any higher authority. So, for most Muslims, the question of life under royal, infidel justice remained a purely theoretical issue, particularly in the huge royal enclaves of Muslims in western Sicily which were administered by the *dīwān* under royal jurisdiction, but which were, by and large, self-regulating in terms of law and order. Of those with some knowledge of Islamic law among the lists of Muslims granted to lords between 1090 and 1183 are to be found half a dozen *faqīhs* or men claiming expertise in the practical application of legal ethics. At Palermo, a member of the Banū Rajā' who acted as Palermo's *qāḍīs* was referred to as *al-shaykh al-faqīh al-qāḍī* in a deed of sale from 1161.[35] Indeed, Islamic law was attested as having been used in another Arabic deed of sale relating to a Palermitan house in 1190. As the agreement was concluded between Christian and Muslim parties, it is possible that Islamic law, explicit and sophisticated in questions of contract, was the medium with which both were most familiar.

Questions of jurisprudence aside, the expansion into Ifrīqiya under Roger and George of Antioch had not only ended in spectacular failure, but it was also one for which their successors, William I and his chief minister, Maio, would pay a heavy price. Furthermore, it would become a significant factor in the rapidly changing complexion of Muslim–Christian relations on the island, and in stabilising the Ifrīqiya–Sicily frontier as a politico-religious one.

Notes

1 The sources for this region and period are mainly Arabic, although some illumination comes from Latin authors such as Falcandus and Romuald of Salerno. Since the Kalbids did not become independent of Fatimid Cairo, they do not appear to have developed their own dynastic historiographical tradition like the Zirids, on whose sources we are forced to rely for tangential references to Sicily. Indeed, had it not been for a contemporary Zirid source, even that knowledge would be considerably poorer (particularly for the period post-1123 at which point Abū l-Ṣalt Umayya's chronicle of the Zirids of al-Mahdiyya ends) since it was a Zirid prince and grandson of Tamīm, 'Abd al-'Azīz Ibn Shaddād (not to be confused with the chronicler of the Crusader period Bahā' al-Dīn ibn Shaddād), whose lost 'History of the Maghrib and Qayrawān', which comprised both original and copied material, can be shown to have formed the basis of the later accounts of Ibn al-Athīr (d. 1233), the early fourteenth-century sources (Ibn 'Idhārī, (fl. 1300) al-Tijānī (fl. 1308), Abū l-Fidā' (d. 1331) al-Nuwayrī (d. 1333) and finally Ibn Khaldūn (d. 1406). Ibn Shaddād is believed to have left Mahdiyya after its fall in 1148, passed through the royal palaces at Palermo during 1156–7; transferred to Damascus, but had returned to Mahdiyya by 1160. For more on the transmission of these sources, see Michael Brett's unpublished doctoral thesis 'Fitnat al-Qayrawān: a study of a traditional Arab historiography', University of London (SOAS), 1969, I:387–425, and Johns, *Arabic Administration*, pp. 84–90.

2 On the events in Ifrīqiya see Ibn al-Athīr *BAS*[2] Ar. I:321–45; *BAS*[2] It. I:452–91. For

English translations, see the following two volumes: *The Chronicle of Ibn al-Athīr for The Crusading Period from* al-Kāmil fī'l-ta'rīkh, *Part 1. The Years 491–541/1097–1146: The Coming of the Franks and the Muslim Response*, trans. D. S. Richards (Aldershot, 2006) and *The Chronicle of Ibn al-Athīr for The Crusading Period from* al-Kāmil fī'l-ta'rīkh, *Part 2, The Years 541–589/1146–1193: The Age of Nur al-Din and Saladin*, trans. by D. S. Richards (Aldershot, 2007). Henceforth, Ibn al-Athīr, Eng. I or II. For a dependable survey of the Ifrīqiyan contexts, see Hady Roger Idris, *La Berbérie orientale sous les Zīrides X^{e}–XIIe siècles*, 2 vols (Paris, 1962), I:317–400.

3 Johns, *Arabic Administration*, pp. 258–65.

4 Ibn al-Athīr, *BAS*^{2} Ar. I:327; Eng. I:320–1.

5 On the Ifrīqiyan famine of 1142–3 and its repercussions for relations between Sicily and Ifrīqiya in the run-up to the Gabès crisis, see Ibn al-Athīr, *BAS*^{2} Ar. I:332; *BAS*^{2} It. I:469; Eng. II:16–20.

6 Ibn al-Athīr, *BAS*^{2} Ar. I:327–8; Eng. I:366–7.

7 For the two Norman assaults on Trípoli, see Ibn al-Athīr, *BAS*^{2} Ar.I:327 and I:329; Eng. I:366 and 380.

8 Ibn al-Athīr, *BAS*^{2} Ar. I:329–30; Eng. I:380. On the question of repopulation of Ifrīqiya from Sicily, see Idris, *La Berbérie*, I:350–2.

9 See *Chronicon Ignoti Monachi Cistercisensis S. Mariae de Ferraria*, A. Gaudenzi (ed.) (Naples, 1888), p. 27.

10 Ibn al-Athīr, *BAS*^{2} Ar. I:331–2; Eng. II:14. On the practice of legitimised humiliation, see Christian Lange, 'Legal and cultural aspects of ignominious parading (*Tashhīr*) in Islam', in *Islamic Law and Society*, 14/1 (2007): 81–108.

11 On the Gabès affair, see Michael Brett, 'The Normans in Ifriqiya', in *Ibn Khaldūn and the Medieval Maghrib* (Aldershot, 1999), XIII, pp. 1–26. This Variorum Reprints version is revised and more widely available than the original published as 'Muslim justice under infidel rule: the Normans in Ifrīqiya 517–555 H/1123–1160 AD', in *Cahiers de Tunisie*, 43/155–6 (1991): 325–68. For the fall of Mahdiyya, see Ibn al-Athīr, *BAS*^{2} Ar. I:332–6; Eng. II:18–20.

12 For this argument, see Jeremy Johns, 'Malik Ifrīqiya', *Libyan Studies*, 18 (1987): 89–101, especially pp. 97–9.

13 For Idrīsī on the effects of Roger's Sicily in Ifrīqiya, see *BAS*^{2} Ar. I:72–4; *BAS*^{2} It. I:130–3.

14 Ibn al-Athīr, *BAS*^{2} Ar. I:337; Eng. II:42–3 for the Almohad advance and fall of Bougie, and Eng. II:62 on the battle at Saṭīf in 1153.

15 Ibn al-Athīr, *BAS*^{2} Ar. I:338; *BAS*^{2} It. I:479–80. Full English translations of Philip's trial can now be found in *Ibn al-Athīr*, Eng. II:63–4; Johns, *Arabic Administration*, pp. 215–17 and Houben, *Roger II*, pp. 110–12.

16 *Romuald*, Lat. p. 236; Eng. p. 220. On Roger's alleged death bed piety, see Donald Matthew, 'The Chronicle of Romuald of Salerno', in *The Writing of History in the Middle Ages: Essays Presented to Richard William Southern*, R. H. C. Davies and J. Michael Wallace-Hadrill (eds) (Oxford, 1981), pp. 239–74.

17 Philip's trial contains a passing reference to the Assizes when Roger is made to exclaim that, had Philip merely been guilty of embezzlement (which was a capital offence), he could have used his right of royal pardon. Apostates lost all their rights to legal protection, but the implication is that they did not automatically warrant the death penalty.

18 For further comparisons between governance over the Sicilian and Ifrīqiyan Muslims, see Johns, *Arabic Administration*, pp. 289–92, and Brett, 'Normans in Ifriqiya', pp. 11–19.
19 David Abulafia, 'The Norman kingdom of Africa and the Norman expedition to Majorca and the Muslim Mediterranean', in *Anglo-Norman Studies*, R. Allen Brown (ed.), 7 (1985): 26–49 (pp. 35–6) and 'Attività commerciale genovese nell'Africa normanna', *Atti del Congresso internazionale di studi sulla Sicilia normanna* (Palermo, 1973), pp. 395–402.
20 Johns, 'Malik Ifrīqiya', pp. 89–101.
21 For discussion of the Grizandus inscription, see Johns, 'Malik Ifrīqiya', pp. 90–1; more recently, Johns, 'Three funerary memorials to Anna and Drogo, parents of the royal priest Grizandus', in *Nobiles Officinae: perle, filigrane e trame di seta dal Palazzo Reale di Palermo*, Maria Andaloro (ed.) (Catania, 2006), I:775–8.
22 For this argument, see Brett, 'Normans in Ifriqiya', pp. 13–14.
23 On the Ifrīqiyan revolts against Norman rule, see Ibn al-Athīr, *BAS*[2] Ar. I:339–40; Eng. II:76–7.
24 For Romuald's account of the events of 1155–6, see *Romuald*, Lat. pp. 237–40; Eng. pp. 222–5.
25 An English translation of the Benevento treaty can be found in Loud and Wiedemann, *Falcandus*, pp. 248–52.
26 John of Salisbury, *Historia Pontificalis*, Marjorie Chibnall (ed.) (Oxford, 1986), p. 69.
27 For the revolts at Djerba and Kerkenna; the mock funeral at Sfax, and the repression of the Zawīla revolt, see Ibn al-Athīr, *BAS*[2] Ar. I:339–40; Eng. II:76–7.
28 On the fall of Norman Mahdiyya to the Almohads, and on William I's threat to harm the Sicilian Muslims, see Ibn al-Athīr, *BAS*[2] Ar. I:344–5; Eng. II:105–6.
29 On the loss of 'Africa' in Latin sources, see *Falcandus*, Lat. pp. 24–8; Eng. pp. 78–81; *Romuald*, Lat. pp. 241–2; Eng. p. 225.
30 Abū l-ʿAbbās Aḥmad b. Yaḥyā al-Wansharīsī, *Kitāb al-Miʿyār al-muʿrib wa-l-jāmiʿ al-mughrib ʿan fatāwī ahl Ifrīqiya wa-l-Andalus wa-l-Maghrib*, M. Ḥajjī (ed.), 13 vols (Rabat, 1981–3), II: 133–4. The Arabic text of al-Māzarī's *fatwā* is reproduced with a French translation and commentary in Abdel-Magid Turki, 'Consultation juridique d'al-Imām al-Māzarī sur le cas des Musulmans vivant en Sicile sous l'authorité des Normands', in *Mélanges de l'Université Saint-Joseph. Sur les débuts de la pensée spéculative en Andalus*, D. Urvoy (ed.) (Beirut, 1984), pp. 691–704. For a wider context, see Kathryn A. Miller, 'Muslim minorities and the obligation to emigrate to Islamic territory: two fatwās from fifteenth-century Granada', *Islamic Law and Society*, 7/2 (2000): 256–88; also the monograph by David S. Powers, *Law, Society and Culture in the Maghrib, 1300–1500* (Cambridge, 2002).
31 For a brief biography, see Ch. Pellat, *al-Māzarī*, in *EI*[2], VI: 942.
32 For the legal implications of the Norman occupation, see Brett, 'Normans in Ifriqiya', *passim*.
33 Cusa, *Diplomi*, pp. 475–6.
34 The title *ṣāḥib al-aḥkām* may have been the description that Ibn Jubayr thought most appropriate, although it is not clear whether he had borrowed it from an Andalusi context. See *BAS*[2] Ar. I:97; Eng. trans. Broadhurst, p. 353.
35 For the deeds of sale, see Cusa, *Diplomi*, pp. 101–6 and 44–6. For brief comment and summary, Johns, *Arabic Administration*, pp. 318, 295 and 323.

9

The Muslim massacres of the 1160s

Sicilian domestic and external affairs

By 1158, the kingdom had treaties and truces in place with Venice, Genoa, the papacy and the Byzantines. The following year, the double papal election of Alexander III (1159–81) and Victor IV (1159–64) forged closer ties between Alexander and Palermo, not least because Victor, although less widely favoured as a candidate, had the support of the German emperor. The threat to Sicily from beyond the Alps was undiminished, but the treaty agreed with Genoa reduced the potential for future Genoese alliances with the Germans, who lacked naval power in the Mediterranean. At the same time, the treaty gave advantages to north Italian merchants in Sicilian ports by strengthening their longer-term hold over trade routes in the south Mediterranean. The arrangement provided short-term economic benefits to the crown through the commerce it generated, much of which involved the sale of goods and foodstuffs produced on royal lands.

By 1160, the Sicilian colonies in Ifrīqiya had shaken off control from Palermo. The blame for this Muslim revolt in the kingdom's new colonies had been pinned squarely on the royal eunuch admirals and the crypto-Muslims Philip and Peter, and on the king's *amīr* of *amīrs*, Maio of Bari, for their alleged lenience, incompetence and for their reluctance to become embroiled in retaking the Muslim colonies. Arguably, the material, strategic and political loss of Ifrīqiya to the kingdom were not the only issues at stake. The violent re-establishment of Muslim control over Ifrīqiya had inflicted a humiliating, psychological blow on the Sicilian Christians.[1] Incalculable as this was, it helps to explain why political discontent in the kingdom was, after the loss of Ifrīqiya, more likely than before to manifest itself in religiously inspired violence between different faith communities, particularly as the king's powerful Palermitan state officials had now become the lightning rods for discontent in the eyes of the kingdom's Latin nobility. When viewed as such, the points in the political matrix that brought the forces of disaffection into conflict with William I and his influential bureaucrats become clearer and help to explain why the turbulent events of 1160–2 translated into massacres of the island's Muslims, whose political and defensive weakness was exposed and exploited when urban mobs and north Italian 'Lombard' settlers indiscriminately set upon them. The starting point in most explanations of the events that unfurled in this period is an indirect one; namely, evaluating the role of the head of William's administration, Maio, whose unpopularity led to his murder in 1160.

The rise and fall of the *amīr* of *amīrs*, Maio of Bari

Maio 'of Bari' was first attested in October 1144 as a royal *scriniarius*, perhaps a type of archivist.[2] However, to suggest that he was merely some functionary underplays his importance because this was precisely the year in which the confirmations of royal grants to landholders began. It is clear not only that Maio's career was intimately connected with the royal *dīwān*, but also that he was a product of that very system of bureaucratic government. Besides which, he had made political connections of consequence within the palace and administration which marked him out for high office during the lifetimes of George and Roger himself. Hence, his rise to vice-chancellor in 1149 had been followed by his succession to Robert of Selby as chancellor three years later. Maio's grip on executive power in the royal *dīwān* is shown in two Arabic writs from May 1152 in which crown lands were conceded to the Greek-rite monastery of San Giorgio di Triocalà near Caltabellotta.[3] These had become the object of a dispute, and an inquest was held. Crucially, neither of these writs was directed by royal command as precedent demanded. Thus, even prior to Roger II's death, Maio can be seen conducting royal business on his own account, supporting the opinions of Falcandus and Romuald that he had become dictatorial in matters of state and was effectively running the kingdom. For his part, Roger had apparently even lost his nominal involvement in the execution of state affairs. Although the claim of Falcandus that Maio intended to assassinate the new king seems either a malicious exaggeration or a figurative flourish, there can be little doubt that Maio aspired to the same power and dominance that the charismatic George of Antioch had acquired. Indeed, in the months after the death of Roger II in 1154, Maio assumed George's former title of *amīr* of *amīrs* and was also referred to as the king's *familiarissimus* in the Treaty of Benevento, of which he had been instrumental in the drafting.[4]

Maio's own background suggests a strong Latin influence, in spite of the prevalence of Greek names in his immediate family and their connections with Bari where his father, Leo de Rayza, was a royal judge and his sister Eustochia was the abbess of Santa Scholastica.[5] He is known to have patronised a Latin translation of a Greek biographical work on the ancient philosophers, and his autograph signature and commentary on the Lord's Prayer were written in Latin. He may even have written in Latin an inaccurate archivist's note on the *verso* of the Forestal renewal in 1145 suggesting that the author could not read the unpointed calligraphy of the Arabic on the *recto* – an idea supported by his own (Latin) autograph signature on the incorrect set of boundaries that the *dīwān* had confirmed to the church of Chúrchuro in 1154.

Maio's rise after the deaths of George and Roger was contemporary with stronger representation of Latin contingents, especially Latin-rite prelates at court. He was initially tolerated, even supported, by the Latin nobility, perhaps hoping that his pre-eminence would decentralise and reallocate power in their favour while subverting the sway of royal servants. Indeed, it is not implausible that Maio had helped to engineer the downfall of Philip of Mahdiyya over the issue of the early Ifrīqiyan campaigns. In any event, he had not prevented Philip's execution and his rise to prominence continued unabated thereafter. Maio, however, was in a difficult position: he was one of the later architects of the Sicilian fiscal administration which was a source of his own authority and influence. He thus proved unwilling and unable to redistribute power within or beyond the palaces. Instead, under his direction, the issuing of royal charters was merely limited relative to preceding and subsequent reigns, Greek declined in status as a royal language, and Greeks had a lower profile in official capacities within the *dīwān*. But in the eyes of the Latin nobles, Maio's political compromises did little to sap the essence of royal government in Sicily and Calabria. Rather, as *amīr* of *amīr*s after Roger's death, he had successfully come to epitomise the hated Arab–Norman bureaucratic system.

When the lay aristocracy turned on him, they first sought to undermine his social standing. Their smear that he had a mercantile background as the son of an olive-oil vendor is possible: if it is, then we can assume that his father had some serious, vested interest in this burgeoning Apulian commerce. Falcandus' accusations of sexual impropriety with decent women of noble standing might be interpreted figuratively as Maio's desire to marry into baronial families, revealing his political proximity to them. Indeed, he had arranged for Matthew Bonellus, a noble from an old Norman family, to be his son-in-law. Maio also sought to strengthen his position by promoting members of his own family. Among the books kept in the royal palace was one devoted to his genealogy, which reveals his enthusiasm for tracing his lineage, perhaps confirming a degree of dynastic pretension.[6] The baronage's slur that Maio was of 'low birth' and, therefore, unsuitable for holding the reins of authority over them, was a persuasive rallying cry for such a group. The concentration of power in the hands of a bureaucrat who was neither noble nor knightly, but supported by mere notaries and castrated Muslims, served as the ideal focus channelling their growing sense of resentment and injustice.

On 10 November 1160, a Palermitan gang, acting at the behest of Matthew Bonellus, stabbed Maio to death in the street not far from his home and near the Sant'Agata gate.[7] In the immediate aftermath of his murder, so unpopular and dangerous was the post of *amīr* of *amīrs* considered to be, that no one serious dared to assume the same title. The following day, the archdeacon of Catania, Henry Aristippus, briefly took over as *familiaris*, avoiding the title *amīr* of *amīrs*, but he soon lost the king's confidence and was arrested thereafter. Maio's brother Stephen was also arrested, and one of the palace eunuchs, Andrew, was tortured. The palace eunuchs were said to have feared the nobles' revenge and growing power and, indeed, the Sicilian Muslims in general had cause for serious concern given the shifting balance of power on the island.

Both Falcandus and Romuald pointed to simmering tensions in the wider kingdom and beyond, the latter giving a brief list of mainland nobles opposed to Maio. Many of these, like Bonellus, came from established families of the kingdom who could trace their privileges back to Roger's time.[8] After Maio's murder, Bonellus fled to Cáccamo, site of one of the largest fortresses in Sicily, but returned to Palermo and, with popular support, was restored to favour. The king had then pressed Bonellus for a substantial inheritance payment, which was said to have prompted him to instigate the rebellion of April 1161. Of others among the barons who had rebelled previously in 1155–6, most notable was Robert, the count of Loritello, an exiled rebel who had found favour at courts in both Germany and Constantinople, and who had been a ringleader of the uprising on the mainland in 1155–6.

The two leaders of the group that would begin the rebellion with the sacking of the royal palace were Simon, formerly prince of Táranto, and Tancred of Lecce. Simon was the illegitimate son of Roger II, who, shortly after the accession of William I, had been dispossessed of Táranto. Greek and Latin sources both recorded his attempt to broker a deal with Manuel Comnenus to usurp the Sicilian throne, and, according to Romuald, he may have been offered the emperor's daughter in marriage. However, the peace treaty signed in 1158 between the Sicilians and the Byzantines had held firm, leaving Simon to harbour his resentment until his chance came to join the rebels in 1161. He was joined by Tancred, who was also illegitimate and was the eldest son of Roger, duke of Apulia (d. 1149). This made Tancred not only William I's nephew, but also the grandson of Roger II himself. Exiled for his part in the rebellion, Tancred would return to become the count of Lecce from 1169 and – eventually – the king after the death of William II. Another leading protagonist in the ensuing massacres of Muslims was Roger 'Sclavus', the illegitimate son of Simon, the count of Policastro, whose arrest had fuelled the rebellions of 1155–6.[9]

The sack of the palace, coup attempt and massacre of Muslims

According to the narrative of Falcandus, a conspiracy was hatched between the nobles to take the king prisoner and raise his nine-year-old son, Roger, the duke of Apulia to the throne instead. On 9 March 1161, a planned prison breakout within the palace led to the king's capture, while the palace was looted under the direction of Simon – who knew its layout well from his childhood – accompanied by Tancred.[10] The sack of the palace was not merely a wanton act of destruction. Rather, the noble conspirators broke into the offices of the *dīwān* and either burned or stole the record books (*daftars*) in which were written, in Arabic, the boundaries of estates and the names of the people who lived on them, as well as the names of the feudatories to whom royal grants and privileges had been made. It is hard to estimate how great a loss this was to the fiscal administration. Certainly, we know from the verbatim text of grants made before and after 1161 that not *all* the records books could have been destroyed, and that later Matthew 'of Salerno' (also known as Matthew Ajello or 'the notary') was released from prison and charged with the task of recompiling the information in them.[11] However, the deliberate elimination of the reviled instruments of central government soon spread to their authors – the palace eunuchs – who were cut down within the palace where they worked and where some had been brought up alongside Count Simon himself. The massacre quickly reached beyond the walls of the palace, and the eunuchs were slaughtered in and around the Kemonia district where they had their houses. Soldiers from the Sea Castle joined the fray and the massacre of the Muslim eunuchs extended to the killing of any Muslim who was unfortunate enough to have been in the streets. The violence then engulfed a large section of the city. The account of the riot is based heavily on the details cited in Falcandus who reported:

> afterwards, when they [the Muslims] realised the extent of the rioting, and thought that they were not strong enough to resist since the previous year the *amīr* of *amīrs* [Maio] had forced them to hand in their weapons to the court. The Muslims left the homes which most of them had in the centre of the city and withdrew to the suburb which lies across the Papyrus Lake. The Christians attacked them there, and for some time there was indecisive fighting. They could repulse our people from the entrances and narrow passageways.[12]

For his part, Romuald made only the clipped remark that 'heavy fighting had broken out between the Muslims and Christians of the city; many of the Muslims were robbed'.

Falcandus and Romuald are the only explicit sources for these events in Palermo itself and, although they commented in brief, they leave little doubt as to the seriousness and extent of the massacres. Indeed, even a sceptical and hardened observer like Falcandus, whose sympathy for the Muslims and palace eunuchs was limited, appeared to have been moved by the indiscriminate nature of the attacks in spite of his 'them and us' reference to the Muslims and the Christian mob. What had begun as a political coup now manifested itself in a religious pogrom which had been facilitated by popular hostility, inflamed and encouraged by the noble leaders of the revolt.

Keeping law and order in the cities: gangs and mob violence

Mob violence in the cities, particularly in Palermo, played an important role in the riots of both the 1150s and the 1160s, yet we know very little about its dynamics except that which can be inferred from the narrative sources. For centuries, serious outbreaks of urban violence had been important features in the great cities of the Byzantine and Islamic empires, and had been a destabilising factor in Islamic Sicily too – a symptom, not a cause, of its problems. Certainly, urban violence in later Norman Sicily was a more frequent occurrence than it was in contemporary northern Europe, and aggressive rivalry between city quarters was to develop only later in north Italian cities. Indeed, in the cities on the island of Sicily after its conquest until the 1150s, urban violence was barely attested either.

The division into quarters of cities such as Palermo and Messina, in part reflected differences in the ethnicity or geographical origins of the residents, and differences in religion with Christian, Muslim and Jewish districts. In times of sharp demographic shift or political instability, this left the city vulnerable to the orchestration of gang violence conducted between its different sectors.[13] In the Norman period, such zones were to some degree self-regulating and capable of maintaining their own defence. In Muslim Palermo, the Christian population had been quickly reduced to a small minority which did not feature in uprisings, and the garrisoned soldiers had usually acted to quell disorder rather than join in it.

In large Muslim cities, the roles played by the *shurṭa*, a type of medieval police force, as well as by guild-like organisations within the towns, were important elements which could control (and initiate) violence – as, indeed, was the patronage of such groups by ambitious individuals who could play out their rivalries on the streets. In Islamic and Norman Sicily, evidence for such dynamics is sparse. There is, for instance, no recorded example of a named market inspector (*muḥtasib*), or an equivalent of this pivotal and powerful appointee who not only oversaw the markets, but also dealt with day-to-day disputes, answered to the *qāḍī* and co-ordinated with the *shurṭa*. That said, a remarkable anecdote recorded in Ibn Khallikān's biographical dictionary, the *Wafayāt al-a'yān*, relates how a mendicant, vagrant alchemist/poet known as Ibn al-Mu'addib travelled from his native Ifrīqiya to Sicily in search of the philosopher's stone.[14] After his interception by the Byzantines, he was eventually released as part of the truce concluded between them and the Kalbid *amīr* Yūsuf 'Thiqat al-Dawla' (r. 990–8). Ibn al-Mu'addib then eulogised the *amīr* in verse, but soon fell out with him over a question of patronage. Having stayed at the house of an alchemist friend, Ibn al-Mu'addib was arrested by the *ṣāḥib al-shurṭa* ('chief of police') in Palermo for publically and drunkenly slandering the *amīr* but, through his wit, secured a payment of 100 *tarìs* before being thrown out of the city. Clearly, this story itself bears all the hallmarks of a literary fiction that should not be taken at face value, but the incidental reference to a *ṣāḥib al-shurṭa* provides evidence for this title in early medieval Sicily. This reference is not entirely isolated. Frequent occurrences of the loan translations *magistri surtae*, *surterius* and *capixurta* are known from later medieval charters.[15] Derivatives of the same root have survived in modern Sicilian dialect and also as a surname. Attested from 1172 was a locality which had taken its name from the barracks or lodge of the *shurṭa*.[16] Clearly, the same Arabic term had continued to be used throughout, and beyond, the Norman period. Indeed, officers of the *shurṭa* appear engaged in the maintenance of urban order such as running night-time vigils and patrols, thus implying that the concept of a medieval 'police' force as well as the terms used to describe it had been carried forward from the Islamic period into later periods. The appearance of the *shurṭa* in the isolated ex-Sicilian Muslim colony of Lucera in 1278 can be inferred to have had precedents on the island and were, therefore, unlikely to have been imported from Spain with the Aragonese.[17]

The common, indeed standard, modern Italian noun, *ragazzo*, meaning a 'boy' or 'lad' is widely accepted to derive from the medieval Arabic slang term *raqqāṣ* which refers literally to 'a dancer', but colloquially to 'a runner' and hence also to 'an odd-job man'. However, more specifically, and frequently attested in the Cairo Geniza documents, the *raqqāṣīn* were closely associated with the police for whom they ran errands, particularly to execute summons and arrests. A feasible explanation for the origins of the modern Italian *ragazzo* is that the *raqqāṣīn* operated in late Islamic Sicily, although the precise lines of lexical transmission are obfuscated by cognates in medieval Catalan and the thirteenth-century surname *Raguacius*. When the terms first appeared in Sicily in their Latinate forms (*regracius*, *ragacius* and *ragaççu*) in the 1300s, they are mentioned in the context of 'those who perform public tasks in public places' and of (non-arms bearing) 'servants of counts, barons, soldiers and others'.[18]

Similar arguments of retrospective inference apply to the 'inspectors' (*nuzzārīn*) of Muslim Palermo, who were generally known to have acted in league with customs officials and the 'secret police', giving rise to the later Sicilian term, *nadaru*, an official who checked weights and measures. However, the earliest attested forms of the term in Sicily occur late and tend to refer to the surveying of land rather than the controlling of measures. Thus, in 1317, we find two men named Nicholas said to have been 'the *nadarie* of the aforesaid lands of Corleone'. In any case, it is unlikely that the Norman *shurṭa*, and their *raqqāṣīn* and *nuzzārīn* had been adopted from the Muslims without modification for, in an Islamic city, the defining chain of authority that connected the 'police' chiefs to the *qāḍī* via the *muḥtasib* was almost certainly modified since the Normans adopted the institution they found on their arrival, but then de-Islamicised it by putting it under their own control.

The Sicilian *futuwwa* have left barely a trace of their existence, yet it is well known that these hierarchically organised, young men's associations played important roles in the daily life, trade and organisation of the cities and were often in operation in specific quarters relating to particular professions. Some of the *futuwwa* also played important roles in the defence of those quarters, and their *shaykhs* enjoyed powerful patronage, especially under the Fatimids. Evidence for the *futuwwa* in Sicily is not entirely negative, since among the people of Corleone in 1178 were three named sons of a certain Abū Sarāwīl (literally, 'father of the trousers') whose unusual name implies that he may have been the head of a *futuwwa* or some guild-like institution which were well known for their induction ceremonies requiring the initiates to don the *shaykh*'s trousers.[19] If the evidence is barely enough to infer their existence, we can say nothing of their impact, nor the extent to which such structures continued (if at all) under the Normans; for example, whether they quickly lost their Muslim patrons and increasingly took on the dynamics of trade guilds in a more European sense.

The Sicilian Muslims: royally threatened and disarmed

In terms of the mob violence directed towards the Muslims in the 1160s, it is of particular significance that, in the year prior to their massacre, the Palermitan Muslims had handed in their arms on the orders of Maio. It is not clear why this might have been done. Given their generally quiescent disposition towards the crown, it seems unlikely that they posed a genuine threat to the kingdom's security. On the contrary, the main internal threat came from the baronage on the mainland or from the 'Lombard' towns in eastern Sicily, while the shattered Ifrīqiyan towns, even with the support of the Almohads, were unlikely to have been able to conquer and hold Sicily from Ifrīqiya. Nor is it clear how this disarming might have been done without the co-operation of their local Muslim community leader(s). Presumably, the removal of weapons referred to the key defenders of the community, rather than everyone within the community. Equally unclear is whether it had become illegal for Muslims to hold arms, and thus the disarming was presented in the context of an amnesty agreement. In any event, it is likely that it had taken place before the fall of Mahdiyya as part of William's threat to the Almohads to kill or despoil the Sicilian Muslims, leaving them open to recriminations or, in the event of general disorder, to the likelihood that hostile factions might enrich themselves materially at their expense and with impunity. It is also of note that the Muslims were not simply attacked but were also displaced within the city, so that the Muslim areas became more concentrated in the Seralcadi district (*shāriʿ al-qāḍī*, 'street of the *qāḍī*') in the northern parts of the town, roughly corresponding to the Capo area of modern Palermo.[20] A 'top-down' model works well as an explanation for the orchestration of this mob violence in Sicily, but there were also opportunist, economic motives for the attacks, for example when the Muslims' homes were looted. In the countryside, lands were usurped, prompting many to flee who would not return, thus further segregating and alienating an increasingly bitter and hostile Muslim population.

The abrupt way in which a 'rent-a-mob' could materialise at times of disorder in Palermo or Messina in the latter half of the 1100s, and then significantly affect the outcome of a particular episode is striking. During the revolts of 1155–6, 'tremendous disturbances' were said to have occurred at Palermo.[21] Although virtually nothing is known of these events, a similar pattern emerged each time there was a breakdown in law and order. After his murder in 1160, Maio's body was allegedly abused by a crowd; many people had appeared outside the royal palace as it was being sacked, and valuables from the treasury were thrown down to them; the infant duke Roger was paraded in the city to popular acclaim; and victory to the rebels seemed assured until the mob turned and besieged the palace, during which Roger was killed by a stray arrow. After this, when the rebels had retreated to Cáccamo, Roger Sclavus and Tancred took Butera and raised support in the Lombard towns. Later in the decade, the parading of the Muslim keeper of the Sea Castle prison, Robert of Calatabiano, through the streets of Palermo prior to his public flogging, had to be cancelled due to the crowds in the narrow streets who were ready to pelt him with stones. Presumably, hostility levels depended largely on the particular district. In 1168, a serious, popular riot broke out at Messina against the French faction. At Palermo, the royal musical band of Muslim eunuchs from the palace literally drummed up support around the city to bring the populace onto the streets and harry the then chancellor, Stephen of Perche, into the bell-tower of the cathedral – the clearest possible indicator that events on the streets were orchestrated 'from above'.

The spread of anti-Muslim violence across Sicily

The violent activities of Roger Sclavus in the east of the island had serious repercussions for the Sicilian Muslims. Their massacre was recorded by both Falcandus and Romuald:

> They ['the Lombards'] made unprovoked attacks on nearby places, and massacred both those who lived alongside the Christians in various towns as well as those who owned their own estates, forming distinct communities. They made no distinction between sex and age. The number of those of that community who died is not easy

> to reckon, and the few who experienced a better fate – either by escaping by secret flight or by assuming the guise of Christians – fled to the less dangerous Muslim towns in the southern part of Sicily. To the present day they hate the 'Lombard' people so much that they have not only refused to live in that part of Sicily again, but even avoid going there at all. Roger Sclavus also disturbed the nearby territory of Syracuse and Catania with frequent attacks.[22]

Romuald confirmed an important link between these episodes and incursions into, if not the usurping of, crown lands, claiming that 'Roger Sclavus, along with the "Lombards" started to stir up sedition in Sicily, invading the land of the royal demesne and killing Muslims wherever he could find them'.[23] One important consequence of this was to push the Muslims even further into western Sicily, where their numbers were greater and where there was more chance of royal protection, since most of this region was part of the royal demesne. Corroborating, but not compelling, evidence for Muslim movement into the crown lands of the Val di Mazara comes from the lists of families conceded to the church of Monreale from the 1170s. They include families from Castrogiovanni, Rometta, Demenna, Ragusa, Mineo, Termini and Palermo itself.[24]

For his part, Matthew Bonellus failed in his attempt to take Palermo, resulting in his arrest and, unrepentant, his torture in prison where he died shortly afterwards. Serious rioting also broke out in the Lombard town of Piazza Armerina between Muslims and Christians in the king's own army while on campaign. The Christian factions were said to have continued their slaughter in spite of the efforts and threats from the king and his officers.[25] Again, the key rebel stronghold to which Sclavus had retreated was the town of Butera which, in the king's counter-offensive, was attacked and destroyed. Sclavus and his supporters were able to negotiate themselves into exile. Butera was razed to the ground, allowing William to cross again onto the mainland to pacify Calabria and Apulia, after which he imposed an unpopular penal tax (the *redemptio*) on the rebel towns.[26]

Prior to his death on 15 May 1166, William had fallen ill with sickness and diarrhoea while he was staying at the Favara palace during Lent, presumably to eat the fish from its twin lakes of salt and fresh water.[27] Falcandus' remark that the only people in the kingdom who mourned his death were Muslim women, perhaps gives a misleading impression of his popularity with the Muslims, particularly as Falcandus was writing with the benefit of hindsight at a time when the Muslims had become even more ill-protected.[28] It is also likely that Falcandus was referring to the practice of employing professional mourners which was common in the Islamic world – and even in the crusader states by Latin rulers – hence his disingenuous remark that the weeping was not feigned. On the other hand, although William had fought off two rebellions, many Muslims may have realised by now that their best chances of survival rested in their unflagging support for the king and his crypto-Muslim administrators – who had a shared experience at the hands of the king's opponents.

Notes

1 For a different perspective, see Houben, *Roger II*, p. 170: 'the loss in the next few years of the bases that Roger had established on the north African coast which fell to the attacks of the Almohads, was not particularly significant'.

2 On Maio's early career, see *Romuald*, Lat. p. 235; Eng. p. 221. An archivist's note on the verso of an Arabic confirmation of villeins to a certain Walter Forestal dating from 1145 resembles Maio's hand. The note observes 'quod tenuit Adam (*sic*) Ferstal'. His autograph signature on a renewed Arabic copy from 1154 of a previous grant that confirmed the incorrect set of boundaries supports the idea that he did not read Arabic well in spite of his importance in the *dīwān*. On Maio's career, see Johns, *Arabic Administration*, pp. 197–8.

3 The Medinaceli documents are not yet fully edited. For a brief discussion, see Johns, *Arabic Administration*, pp. 197–8 and 309.

4 On Maio's role in government, see *Falcandus*, Lat. pp. 7 ff; Eng. pp. 60ff; *Romuald*, Lat. pp. 234–5; Eng. p. 221. For Maio's involvement at Benevento, see *Falcandus*, Eng. p. 249. Although Maio was mentioned only fleetingly in Arabic sources, they concur that he was the *wazīr* William I had appointed against whom there was a baronial revolt. Ibn al-Athīr, *BAS*[2] Ar. I:338; *BAS*[2] It. I:480.

5 Both Maio's brother and son were called Stephen, and both were attested as *amīrs*. *Falcandus*, Lat. p. 45; Eng. p. 99.

6 Evidence for Maio's interest in tracing his lineage comes from an unpublished paper fragment (dated to 1161, shortly after the palace sack?) found in the Cappella Palatina on which an inventory of books had been scribbled ungrammatically in Sicilian Arabic. Among them was a 'book of the ancestors of Māyū by Juwān (John) al-A[ndulsi?]', which appears to corroborate claims elsewhere: see *Falcandus*, Lat. p. 8; Eng. pp. 60–1.

7 For Maio's murder, see *Falcandus*, Lat. pp. 42–3; Eng. pp. 96–7; *Romuald*, Lat. pp. 245–6; Eng. p. 229.

8 For the anti-Maio conspirators, see *Romuald*, Lat. p. 244; Eng. p. 228.

9 It is not clear why Roger was called 'Sclavus' by Falcandus, but he may have acquired the appellation by 1180 when he can be cautiously identified with Roger 'Sclavone', the last Byzantine *dux* of Dalmatia and Croatia. See Jadran Ferluga, *Byzantium on the Balkans: Studies on the Byzantine Administration. and the Southern Slavs from the VIIth to the XIIIth Centuries* (Amsterdam, 1976), pp. 209 and 420. If accepted, this has implications for the intricate dating argument regarding the composition of Falcandus' *History*. For a summary of other aspects of that argument, see Loud and Wiedemann, *Falcandus*, pp. 28–42.

10 For the wider events of the insurrection, see *Falcandus*, Lat. pp. 44–77; Eng. pp. 99–128 and *Romuald*, Lat. pp. 245–9; Eng. pp. 229–32.

11 On the destruction of the *daftars*, *Falcandus*, Lat. p. 69; Eng. pp. 120–1. Their physical destruction seems more plausible than Falcandus' claim that the eunuchs were massacred at precisely the time when they were going about collecting taxes,

which can be read figuratively: destroying such irreplaceable revenue-raising mechanisms was a grave error.

12 The descriptions of the anti-Muslim massacre are given in *Falcandus*, Lat. pp. 56–7; Eng. p. 110 and *Romuald*, Lat. pp. 246–7; Eng. p. 230.

13 For a brief twelfth-century description of the city, see Falcandus, *Letter to Peter*, Lat. pp. 180–3; Eng. pp. 260–1.

14 *Ṭalab al-kīmiyā' wa-l-aḥjār*. Ibn Khallikān, *BAS*[2] Ar. II:763–4; *BAS*[2] It. II:527–8; Eng. transl. de Slane, S. Moinul Haq (ed.); reprinted in 7 vols (New Delhi, 1996), VI:237–8. His full name was given as 'Abd Allāh ibn Ibrāhīm ibn al-Muthānnā al-Ṭūsī, whose family was said to have come from Mahdiyya, but he came from Qayrawān. There is otherwise little evidence for alchemy in Islamic Sicily, although the loan word *lanbicum* 'alembic', or similar such vase, is attested in the mid-fifteenth century by which time it was quite widely diffused. See Girolamo Caracausi, *Arabismi medievali di Sicilia* (Palermo, 1983), pp. 266–7.

15 Caracausi, *Arabismi*, pp. 353–5.

16 εἰς τὴν σουρτίεν, Cusa, *Diplomi*, p. 663.

17 Nallino's note in *SMS*[2] III:916, n. 2 builds on Amari's commentless observation of the *sāḥib al-shurṭā* in the Islamic period, *SMS*[2] II:12–13. The Luceran *shurṭā* appears to have comprised both men and women.

18 Caracausi, *Arabismi*, pp. 302–4 (*nadaru*); pp. 311–12 (*ragazzo*); Goitein, *Mediterranean Society*, II:370–1.

19 Starting points for this include: W. Björkman on *sirwāl* in *EI*[2] IX:676; H. Algar and A. Raymond on *shadd* in *EI*[2] IX:166; C. Cahen and F. Taeschner on *futuwwa*: II:961; M. Marín on *shurṭā* in *EI*[2] IX:510.

20 For the topography of medieval Palermo, see the discussion in chapter 3 and endnote 15 for further references.

21 On the effects of the 1155–6 revolt at Palermo, see *Falcandus*, Lat. p. 19; Eng. p. 72.

22 For the Lombard attacks on the Muslims: *Falcandus*, Lat. p. 70; Eng. p. 122, with minor adjustments.

23 *Romuald*, Lat. p. 248; Eng. pp. 231–2.

24 For the lists of 'villeins' conceded to Monreale, see Cusa, *Diplomi*, pp. 134–79 and pp. 245–86. For the specific area around Corleone, see also Franco D'Angelo, 'Corleone dai musulmani del XII ai lombardi del XIII secolo', *Archivio Storico Siciliano*, 20 (1994): 17–26.

25 On the inter-faith violence between regiments of the royal army, see *Falcandus*, Lat. p. 73; Eng. p. 124.

26 *Falcandus*, Lat. p. 78; Eng. p. 129, for the 'redemption' fine on the rebel towns.

27 On the Favara lakes and William's death, see *Romuald*, Lat. pp. 252–3; Eng. p. 237.

28 *Falcandus*, Lat. p. 89; Eng. p. 138, for Muslim women mourning William I's death.

10

Eunuchs, familiars, collaborators and conspirators

The use of eunuchs in the south Mediterranean

The employment of highly trained eunuch functionaries on a grand scale had a long history in the ancient and medieval Mediterranean. Indeed, they were a standard feature of Byzantine and Arab-Muslim regimes. Moreover, from the ninth century, it was not unusual to find ruler, court and administration dominated by powerful cliques of bureaucrats (both eunuchs and kin groups), to the extent that the ruler was often reduced to assuming the role of a figurehead.[1]

In Sicily, it was the formal creation of the kingdom, followed by the invention of a centralised and sophisticated administration that had given rise to a class of royal administrators whose devotion and loyalty to the crown served the interests of both masters and servants. However, the palace eunuchs at Palermo and Messina were not merely administrative functionaries who acted on the bidding of the king's officials – many of them *were* the king's officials. Unlike the Latin magnates of the kingdom, the high-ranking eunuchs lived in close physical proximity to the royal palace and maintained a permanent presence within them, in part, because the *dīwān* offices were located inside the main palace itself.[2] In addition, there were many lower level, ancillary staff who were also eunuchs and who were likely to have had access to all areas of the palaces, including the women's quarters. Hence, the palace eunuchs held sway at a range of levels in the very nerve centre of the kingdom and their senior staff quickly came to be key political players. Along with the burgeoning royal household, as the size and complexity of the royal administration and organisational needs of the kingdom grew, so too did the power, influence and indispensability of the eunuchs. In the regimes of the Fatimids and Abbasids, it was not uncommon to find a purge of eunuchs, scribes and officials after the fall of a chief administrator. In Sicily, where the system had developed under George of Antioch and Maio of Bari, similar dynamics are perhaps seen with the deaths of Philip of Maydiyya and other palace eunuchs in 1153, and the massacre of eunuchs in 1161.

Precisely who was and who was not a eunuch is not always obvious in the narrative and charter sources, and even less so from some of the modern translations of these sources. In the *Riḥla* (travelogue) of Ibn Jubayr, the Andalusi pilgrim and administrator who passed through the kingdom in 1184–5 visiting royal palaces in both Messina and Palermo, the eunuchs were most usually referred to as *fityān*, literally translatable as 'lads'. This deceptive understatement has been rendered in Roland Broadhurst's English translation of Ibn Jubayr as 'pages'. Although the term had a number of different connotations in medieval Arabic, in the context of palaces and chancery offices, *fityān* had the particular meaning of 'eunuch slaves'. Latin sources, most importantly that of Falcandus, referred to them generically as the 'palace servants', 'palace eunuchs' or by the titles of the offices held by the more important ones. As individuals, they were normally called by the Christian (predominantly Latinate or Frankish) names they had been required to adopt on their conversion to Christianity, preceded by the Sicilian Arabic honorific term, *qā'id* (literally 'leader'). In Latin and Greek, this was usually transliterated as *gaitus* or κάϊτος. In societies where great value was placed on the attributes that a name implied, no Sicilian eunuch was attested with a disparaging slave name, as is sometimes found at Arab-Muslim courts. Rather, their Christian names and honorifics accorded them status and theoretically gave them admission into 'Frankish' Christian circles – an identity which none, or very few, of them chose to claim except in the most superficial way.

Most of the eunuchs seem to have been bought from slave markets or acquired as booty from Muslim lands. Thus, Ibn Khaldūn reported that *qā'id* Peter, a dominant force at court especially under the queen-regent in the 1160s, was a Berber from Djerba. We have already encountered the unfortunate case of Philip 'of Mahdiyya'. It is not clear why Philip had acquired this name tag, but as he was reported to have been brought up from boyhood by Roger personally in the royal household, then we might expect an age gap between them in the region of at least fifteen years. If this is accepted then Philip would perhaps have been twenty years old when Roger was crowned in 1130. So, perhaps like the Roman general Scipio Africanus, he had gained his nickname in campaigns fought in Africa and had been involved with George of Antioch's capture and submission of Mahdiyya in 1148.[3] An alternative chronology, which is equally troublesome to substantiate, would be that he had been brought to Sicily from Ifrīqiya with George in 1108, in which case, he would have been about the same age as Roger himself. In support of this view of an older Philip, is a tentative identification of him with a 'Philip of Africa', a signatory of a deed of sale in Greek in 1129.[4] However, beyond incidental snippets from narrative sources, we can infer little else about the eunuchs' geographical or ethnic origins. It is significant that another powerful servant who was brought up from boyhood in the palaces, Matthew, was sometimes known by the appellation 'of Salerno'. Matthew was not a eunuch, and he may not have been from Salerno either, in spite of strong connections he later cultivated.[5] Perhaps in both cases, these pseudonym epithets helped to conjure up a misleading sense of geographical diversity and representation from across the kingdom precisely because such royal officials had adopted their roots and had rarely been beyond the walls of the palace when they first assumed power.

Ibn Jubayr's ease of communication with the eunuchs, in addition to their connections with the Islamic world and the royal Arabic *dīwān*, strongly indicates that they were all at least Arabic-speaking. The lingua franca around the royal complexes was Arabic for most of the people who lived and worked there, but from the eunuchs' implied communication with non-Arabic speakers within the palaces, it seems highly probable that they had learned some form of French or local Italo-Romance dialect. Apart from the uncertain link between 'Philip of Africa' and Philip of Mahdiyya via a Greek signature, there is no evidence to suggest that the eunuchs worked or communicated in Greek in spite of its prominence as a royal language under Roger II. When translations or interpretations to and from Greek were required, these were most likely to have been made by bilingual, non-eunuch, Christian notaries and officers of the crown.

Religious ambivalence among the Sicilian Muslims

The religious outlook of the palace eunuchs was famously ambivalent. On the one hand, they were all nominally Christian and were said to have been visually indistinguishable from Christians, perhaps only in their lack of a thick beard which appears to have been otherwise de rigueur for adult males. However, it was common knowledge that the eunuchs had continued to practise Islam in secret. Remarkably, the evidence for this deception comes from a variety of independent sources and is so widespread as to put it beyond serious doubt. For instance, Falcandus claimed of *qā'id* Peter that, 'like all the palace eunuchs, this man was a Christian only in name and appearance, but a Muslim by conviction'.[6] An uncannily close echo to these words are found in the anonymous marginal note added to Romuald's *Chronicon*, which said of Philip of Mahdiyya that he 'kept up the appearance of being a Christian, [but] in mind and deed he was completely Saracen'.[7] The evidence from Latin sources is corroborated by the independent Arabic account of Ibn Jubayr, who noted in some detail their surreptitious practices.[8] Concealing one's true faith was also a strategy used by converts outside the palaces. This, as Ibn Jubayr recalled, was the means by which converts could be accepted into the Christian community and profit from the socio-economic advantage of joining the dominant, prestige religion of the kingdom, while not being entirely alienated from their former communities. To justify this behaviour he quoted a phrase from the Qur'ān that the wrath of God will be upon those who disbelieve, 'save him who is forced thereto and whose heart is still content with the faith'.[9] In Islamic law, such a permissible dissimulation of the faith when under duress is known as *taqiyya*.[10] The idea of enforced concealment of belief was a particularly important concept in Ismāʿīlī forms of Islam which had emerged from underground, revolutionary origins to create an alternative line of 'hidden' imāms from the eighth century. Under the Fatimid imām-caliphs, such notions developed into an elaborate and arcane ideology that emphasised a balanced distinction between the inner, concealed, esoteric values of Islam (*bāṭin*) as revealed and articulated by the imām-caliph to his close circle of adherents, in contrast to the external and the obvious (*ẓāhir*), such as obedience to the law and the execution of prescribed obligations and duties. *Taqiyya* allowed the internalisation of belief where unfavourable circumstances necessitated and, following the fall of the Fatimids in Egypt, it also provided a strategy whereby Ismaʿīlī ideas could survive or be reinvented in the guise of Sunnī orthodoxy under the cloak of Sufi mysticism. In a non-ruling community under socio-political pressure and in a state of religious flux, such as that of the Sicilian Muslims, the phenomenon of dissimulation explains and describes the common condition of those who only outwardly appeared to be Christian.

The *ʿalāma* evidence: messages of hope and resistance

Some of the palace eunuchs who were involved with issuing royal Arabic diplomata occasionally left a motto towards the foot of a document. These 'signatures' (in Arabic *ʿalāmāt*; singular, *ʿalāma*) typically consisted of a phrase of up to half a dozen conjoined words written as a monogram in which the reed pen usually maintained contact with the parchment throughout. Only recently have the hidden messages behind these tortuous designs been deciphered in a palaeographic tour de force.[11] Several of the readings were found to have close Quranic echoes, such as that of *qāʾid* Richard's that 'nothing is hidden from God', which implies that he was indeed feigning his religion to all but God.[12] Richard, a long-lived survivor of the Norman administration whose high-flying career at court is well attested, is particularly important since he was considered by many scholars until recently to be a genuine convert. Indeed, the bishop of Patti, who once referred to him as 'a brother of our church', presumed as much too.[13] Another example comes from the pen of the (otherwise unknown) eunuch scribe ʿAmmār, and offers an even more explicit statement of Muslim defiance, reading: 'God and the Muslims are sufficient for me'. Apart from implicitly circumventing an important aspect of Norman Sicilian ideology – the kings may have been the vicars of Christ, but Muslims required only the agency of God – to the cognoscenti, these cryptic messages, embedded into royal diplomata, signalled hope and resistance from within, and proved to informed audiences, present and future, that Muslims were active at the highest level in the royal administration.

Operating in the tense atmosphere of the palaces, the top-ranking eunuchs were charged with some of the most diplomatically sensitive and politically dangerous tasks that the kingdom could offer. That some of them found their positions challenged the moment they left the confines of the palace walls is testament to the almost impossible balancing acts they were required to perform in order to guarantee their own survival within them. As an institution, they were vital to the palace and crown, but as individuals their vulnerability was all too apparent. Unsurprisingly then, they tended to act together as a tightly knit group, to the extent of developing a matrix of pseudo-familial relations, forming bonds through patronage or close mentoring that might appear as a form of 'adoption' or clientage. Thus, *qā'id* Peter is attested as having a 'son'; the embroiderer Yaḥyā (the Arabic equivalent of 'John'), whom Ibn Jubayr met, had the name Ibn Fityān, meaning 'of the clan of eunuchs'. It may not be coincidental that there are no attested examples of damaging feuds between eunuchs. Indeed, if considered as a species of kin group, the palace eunuchs were the most successful and long-lived of any at the epicentre of power outside the immediate royal family.

Other than defending their own sense of faith, the palace eunuchs played behind-the-scenes roles in the wider Sicilian Muslim community, even if it is unclear how far their influence extended beyond the Muslim heartlands of Palermo and the towns of western Sicily. If there were grand occasions outside the palace, such as royal processions, they were likely to have paraded in their finery and in close physical proximity to the king. Unlike eunuchs in the Islamic world, who were considered as necessarily less capable of spiritually impure acts (by virtue of which they were sometimes chosen to play religious roles, for example as transmitters of *ḥadīth* or as guardians of holy places), the nominally Christian eunuchs of Sicily were not conspicuous in Islamic religious life on the island.

We can infer that they maintained significant contacts with the world outside the palaces, both locally and further afield, since they were sent around Sicily in their capacity as royal officials collecting taxes, convening inquests and supervising the management of *dīwānī* business. As such, they would have had important co-ordinating roles with the leaders of the Muslim community as well as with the *'āmils* or provincial administrators who were the crown's primary link with the local Muslim *shaykhs* in the towns, villages and estates on crown lands. On one occasion, we see *qā'id* Peter involved (it is not clear how) with overseeing the construction of a royal building in Términi Imerese, which is confirmed by the surviving fragment of a trilingual inscription in keeping with Rogerian style.[14] As literate officials of the *dīwān* who drafted royal diplomata in

Arabic, the palace eunuchs were ideally placed to establish and maintain long-distance communications with the Islamic world, transforming the palace in Palermo into a hub for the receipt and distribution of news, views and sensitive information, fulfilling functions not unlike those of an ancient oracle site for distinguished visitors. Inevitably, the eunuchs were repeatedly accused of treachery and of being in communication with the Almohads. These were not empty accusations; rather, one would precisely expect diplomatic relations to have involved the higher-ranking eunuchs. Contacts appear to have extended down the pilgrimage routes too, as shown by Philip of Mahdiyya's gifts of oil for the mosque lamps of Medina, where he was said to have established a good rapport with the imām.[15]

An unusual link to the wider populace is shown by the royal musical band who were able to rouse a mob into action in the streets of Palermo during a disturbance in 1168.[16] The eunuchs were also said by Ibn Jubayr to have done many good deeds for the Muslims, specifically the ransoming of Muslim prisoners, an act which implies that they had contacts with the Muslim community, presumably in Sicily, and that they had financial means. Even Falcandus noted *qā'id* Peter's sense of liberality, stating that Peter preferred to give than to receive, and it is likely that eunuchs had used the issuing of documents as a means of generating income, in effect, by making a charge for services rendered. As a manumitted eunuch, Peter's wealth may have been exceptional, but he is known to have possessed (owned?) at least one impressive Palermitan property and had amassed great personal riches in his lifetime. Other indications are that this may not have been untypical for one of the higher ranking eunuchs. Both *qā'ids* Peter and Martin, probably like many of the other eunuchs, lived in the walled district of Kemonia in Palermo, a stone's throw from the royal palace. *Qā'id* Richard was attested as being a landholder in that same area. Towards the end of his professional life, the long-serving Richard was granted the priory of Santa Sofia at Vícari and an estate, both of which were in need of repair and investment, on the understanding that any revenue generated from these would remain in his hands.

The development of the *familiares regis* system in the 1160s

After the violent removal of Maio, the position of chief minister with the title of *amīr* of *amīrs*, which had existed since 1124, became increasingly untenable given the inherent dangers associated with it. The academically minded administrator, Henry Aristippus, had momentarily held the post in the immediate aftermath of Maio's death, but was soon substituted by three of the king's inner circle – the *familiares regis*. Unlike the *familiares* of northern European kingdoms, the Sicilian version was a more structured institution whose members can often be seen holding specific offices or engaging in reasonably well-defined tasks.[17] The post-Maio decade of the 1160s witnessed the development of the Sicilian *familiares* system, whose numbers expanded and contracted depending on political circumstances. One important effect of this was that, by the end of the decade, a greater degree of political stability had been introduced. However, this evolved only during and after yet further political conflict, which now tended to be played out between competing factions in and around the palaces of the capital, instead of taking place in the form of open revolt as had happened in 1155–6 and 1161–2.

Even before the death of Maio, the political dynamics at court among ecclesiastical and lay lords, alongside the administrative classes of notaries and eunuchs, had produced a number of overlapping and fiercely competitive circles. Such was the complexity of the interactions between these groups and the individuals within them, that the dividing lines were both indistinct and subject to change. An additional complication, as far as the political machinations of the 1160s were concerned, is that we must view many of them as refracted through the distorting prism of Falcandus' *History*. The most clearly discernible antagonism erupted between those with power centres on the mainland, and those whose interests were based on the island. In part, this reflected a difference between government and society of the Italian peninsula where more lay lords were enfeoffed and derived their income from the lands they had been conceded, compared with the island of Sicily where more lands were in the royal demesne (and therefore managed by the palace eunuchs and *dīwān*) or had been conceded to churches, whose prelates like Richard Palmer, the bishop-elect of Syracuse, or Gentile, the bishop of Agrigento were often attested at court in Palermo. The tensions could thus be characterised as a conflict between the centre and the peripheries. But even within the Sicily-based factions there were visible splits and subdivisions of shared or opposing interest groups who, when faced with a threat from without, might form short-lived alliances: the Latin notaries under Matthew of Salerno, for example, were often in league with some of the prelates and the eunuchs. In turn, these were broadly in opposition with the 'Latin' knights and mainland and insular lay lords. The Latin-Christian baronage and the Muslim eunuchs were by no means clashing simply over questions of religious difference either, but such tensions were never far from the surface, and the eunuchs' perceived political corruption, religious duplicity and even their lack of manliness were turned against them as reasons for their imagined unsuitability for power. Three episodes from the 1160s illustrate the political struggles and evolution under William I and II which pitted the palace eunuchs and their allies against elements from within the kingdom's Latin nobility and their supporters.

The roles of *qā'id* Martin and *qā'id* Peter

As the eunuchs were theoretically Christian, we see on at least one important occasion one of William I's most trusted, *qā'id* Martin, presiding over a Christian court in Palermo at a particularly delicate and dangerous period following the baronial rebellion of 1161 and the massacre of eunuchs and Muslims.[18] Having put down the rebels on the island, William marched out to do the same on the mainland during 1162. In the meantime, *qā'id* Martin was charged with the task of bringing to justice the Latin rebels in Palermo. If our main source for the details of these events, the partisan Falcandus, is to be credited, then *qā'id* Martin presided over his own court which sat in special session. Martin, whose brother had been killed in the conspirators' looting of the palace, was reported to have abused his judicial power by making enthusiastic use of *monomachia* or single combat to turn rival Christians against one another. To Muslims, this Frankish practice was a well-known source of horror and reminiscent of blood-letting vendettas that Islamic law had sought to curb from its inception. Usāma ibn Munqidh's famous description of a duel to the death in the Latin East provides the classic example of medieval Muslim attitudes to such 'infidel' Frankish justice and mores.[19] Martin's choice of using his position to turn the Christians against themselves is thus not inconsistent with his being crypto-Muslim. However, that a pseudo-Christian palace eunuch should have been trusted with the executive responsibility of royal justice in the absence of the king shows the extent to which the kings were not only dependent on their abilities, but also had greater faith in them than they did in many of their Christian lords.

Although attested earlier than Martin, and leaving the political scene before him, *qā'id* Peter was central to the events around the palace during the turbulent period 1162–6. The identification of Peter, linked via different versions of his name attested in Greek, Latin and Arabic (Perroun, Petrus and Barrūn), is problematic but it can be established with a reasonable degree of safety that he was acting as a *dīwānī* officer as early as 1141 and continued to hold high office and military posts until his enforced departure from the island in 1166.[20] After the death of Maio in November 1160 and the failed coup attempt by rebel barons against the king in March of the following year, Peter was also entrusted with the unenviably dangerous prosecution of the remaining rebels, while justiciars under his sway on the mainland collected the despised redemption tax. This was levied on the former rebels until the regency of Margaret, who abolished it shortly after William I's death. Peter had also taken over from the Master Chamberlain of the palace, a fellow eunuch called Jawhar who, according to Falcandus, had escaped with the royal seals in 1162 to join the rebel factions after apparent physical maltreatment at the hands of the king. When captured, Jawhar was publicly put to death by drowning.[21] By the time of the French contingents' dominance at court between 1166 and 1168 under the queen-regent, Margaret, the royal seals had been entrusted to Peter of Blois as royal *sigillarius*. After Jawhar's death, Peter was included among a triumvirate of *familiares* alongside Richard Palmer (of English origin) and Matthew 'of Salerno'. A multilingual administrator, Matthew had spent most of his life since childhood in the royal palace complexes, like Philip of Mahdiyya and Count Simon among others. He had been imprisoned following his alleged involvement in the murder of Maio, but was released soon after in order to organise the reconstruction of the fiscal administration's record books which had gone missing during the sack of the palace. Under William II, Matthew would continue as a *familiaris* and come to be promoted to vice-chancellor (1169–89). He was quite likely the bearded, long-robed, Arabic-speaking official who graciously met Ibn Jubayr in 1184, quizzing him about events in Constantinople. Eventually, he became chancellor under Tancred until his death in May 1193 and is often portrayed as a bearded, long-robed figure in Peter of Eboli's sketches.[22] The third *familiaris* alongside *qā'id* Peter and Matthew was Richard Palmer, the bishop-elect of Syracuse, and another wily, long-lived political player. On William's instruction, Peter was manumitted shortly after the king's death in May 1166. Under Margaret, William I's wife and mother of their infant son William II, Peter was raised above the status of his other two colleagues, Matthew of Salerno and Richard Palmer, to become the most influential holder of executive power in the kingdom until his defection to the Almohads in the summer of 1166.

The Muslims under the queen-regent, Margaret

The queen-regent, Margaret, was the daughter of another veteran of the *Reconquista*, García Ramirez (d. 1150), the king of Navarre in the north-east of the Iberian peninsula. At the start of her five-year regency, the palace was dominated by what might be termed a 'Sicilian' faction: in this case, a triumvirate of *familiares* comprising *qā'id* Peter, Richard Palmer and Matthew, who held sway over the powerful faction of the notaries. Although this group's interests lay on the island rather than on the mainland, it may be misleading to overemphasise their 'Sicilian-ness', as they acted out of shared political interests as much as any innate or coherent sense of regional identity. According to Falcandus, Peter was not only cherished by Margaret, but was also popular with his knights with whom he rode out. However, he remained a figure of hate for many lay lords, in particular the governor of the mainland Gilbert, count of Gravina, a cousin of Margaret's whose ambitions extended to controlling the entire kingdom.

In a set-piece scene presented in Falcandus' *History*, Gilbert openly argued with Margaret over the question of Peter's power in the kingdom, reducing the queen to tears and accusing her of having put a 'castrated slave' in charge of the kingdom. A revealing strand to Gilbert's complaint appears to be an objection to the increased feminisation of the kingship and ruling classes, with a queen who ruled through 'an effeminate slave',[23] and (with Falcandian hindsight) a king whose only son would fail to produce an heir to the throne. Also of note in this respect is Falcandus' derisory comment that the queen-regent's unpopular brother Rodrigo/Henry had a 'most thin beard'.[24] The criticism was not only of his youth but also of his manliness: both of which confirm the perception that he was unfit for high office. A similar line of argument for the failure of the kingdom from its robust origins was directed against the Hautevilles themselves in the twentieth century by Ferdinand Chalandon who, in a quite literal sense, spoke of ever more orientalised and impotent rulers increasingly unable to reproduce themselves.[25] Thus, while Roger I had brought into the world a total of eighteen children (legitimate and illegitimate); Roger II had produced eight children; William I had four; and William II none. This accords well with the misleading, but enduring, historical illusion conjured by Falcandus' medieval metaphor at the beginning of his *History*, namely, that Roger's era was decidedly not one of effeminate decadence nor government by tyrannical proxy like that of his sons: on the contrary, Roger's enjoyment of sex was so unrestrained that he had even lost his mind.[26]

Perhaps fearing a purge of eunuchs on the same scale as that seen at the end of Roger's reign which he would have personally witnessed, Peter and his entourage fled to the Almohads. By all accounts, he took with him a large amount of transferable wealth.[27] There, abandoning his Christian name (and any reference to his Djerban origins), he adopted, or readopted, the name Aḥmad, adding to it the *nisba*, al-Ṣiqillī, 'the Sicilian'. Such a defection to the enemies of the state was hardly without precedent, and Peter/Aḥmad was merely following a well-trodden course of action taken by many political exiles from the kingdom. Although he did not launch attacks against his former employers, it was under his captaincy that the Almohad fleet of ʿAbd al-Mu'min's son, Yūsuf I (r. 1163–85) reached its height, as noted by Ibn Khaldūn.[28] Peter was still alive by the time the Sicilians concluded a truce with the Almohads in 1180 when he was presumably in his sixties.

It is noticeable how, in Sicily, the eunuchs repeatedly attracted harsh criticisms as admirals of the fleet, even when they were successful. In contrast, failed expeditions, such as had been led by Christódoulos, George of Antioch or, later, Margaritus did not result in personal attacks on them. The tensions behind the Gilbert–Peter episodes at court might also help to explain the unexpected overcompensation and display of machismo by Richard of Molise with his challenge to Gilbert of a duel following Peter's departure. In the event, any threat Gilbert posed was diffused when he was dispatched to the mainland to counter the invasion threat from Frederick Barbarossa's German army which, in May 1167, overcame papal forces in a major engagement.[29] By July, disease had broken out among Barbarossa's army at Rome while the pope, Alexander III, was evacuated with the help of Sicilian support to the safety of Benevento where he remained, unable to return, until early 1171.

The Muslim convert, Robert of Calatabiano

The factions at work within the palaces are no more clearly seen than during Margaret's regency period when *qā'id* Martin was managing the royal *dīwān* and when *qā'id* Richard was Master Chamberlain of the royal palace. They were joined by two other *familares*: Richard Palmer and Richard of Mandra, the Master Constable and count of Molise. Margaret chose to surround herself with her blood-relatives led by Stephen, son of the count of Perche, who had arrived in Sicily by autumn 1166 with a contingent of thirty-seven from northern France. The youthful Stephen was quickly appointed chancellor and, a year later, archbishop of Palermo. Although Stephen enjoyed the benefit of the queen's approval, his entourage had all the considerable disadvantages from which privileged 'outsiders' to the kingdom suffered: great, executive powers were put into their hands, but they did not know the system of government nor that of the society. Political hostility to Stephen began when he attempted to undermine his opponents among the palace notaries by successfully reforming their practice of charging unregulated fees for the issuing of documents. The extent to which the palace eunuchs, as opposed to the Latin notaries, were directly affected by this, or rallied in support of administrative colleagues, is unclear. However, Stephen's subsequent efforts to prosecute 'backsliders' to Islam, who were not considered to be sufficiently Christian, brought the French contingent directly into conflict with the eunuchs and their Muslim supporters.

Accusations of apostasy against religious converts were not only potentially ruinous to transgressors, but they were also a key tool by which the legal system could be applied to create and maintain clear distinctions between the main religious groups of the kingdom. It is likely that, as an outsider on his way to the Holy Land, Stephen was, if not uncomfortable with, then at least disturbed by, the proximity and intermingling of Muslims and Christians in cities such as Palermo. On the other hand, the counts of Perche, like Margaret herself, had important connections in the Iberian peninsula and, according to Falcandus, had benefited materially during the Christian *Reconquista* by gaining possession of lands at the Muslims' expense.[30] An additional concern for the Sicilian Muslims was the extensive support Stephen had from the feared and favoured north Italian 'Lombard' communities, even when all other support had drained away from him.[31]

Stephen's crackdown on false Christians, that is to say, former Muslims, who had allegedly reverted to Islam, was documented by Falcandus and epitomised by the arrest, torture, flogging and death in prison shortly afterwards of Robert 'of Calatabiano'.[32] He was the keeper of the Sea Castle prison which, after the outbreaks during the uprisings of 1161–2 from the old prison in the royal palace, had supplanted it as the principal royal jail in Palermo. Robert was said by Falcandus to have been 'particularly friendly to the eunuchs'. That he had ingratiated himself with them and sought their protection, strongly implies that he was not one of them himself, although he appears to have been a nominal convert from Islam.[33] As such, he represents an important category of royal employees who were not eunuchs, but who seemed to be free or freedmen and who were either converts or crypto-Muslims. As someone who oversaw punishments in prison and had the ear of the palace eunuchs, Robert was loathed by the nobles and became a target for their revenge, not least because he had been involved in punishments and prosecutions made after the uprisings against William I and the massacres of Muslims which had accompanied the revolts. The most serious accusations against Robert were that of raping a Christian virgin, and of restoring a Muslim shrine in the Sea Castle.

A letter Stephen composed to Pope Alexander III asking for advice in the final months of 1167 on cases where Muslims had raped Christian women, abused boys or killed them indicates that he may not have been motivated by political concerns alone, but also by piety and a genuine concern for the moral threat posed by apostasy.[34] The pope's reply makes greater sense when the rape of Christians is taken figuratively and understood as referring to incidences of inter-faith marriage or attempts at similar such intermingling. His suggestion was a sliding scale of punishments that correspond to the gravity of the offence. Exacting fines or a whipping were appropriate for lesser excesses (for example, 'rape'), while royal justice might be applied to more serious cases (for example, the killing of Christians by Muslims) in which death or amputation were recommended as punishments. Robert's flogging implies that more serious charges, such as apostasy, could not be made to stick. Rather, he could be found guilty only on some lesser charge. However, his death in prison shortly afterwards serves as a reminder that legal protocols were theoretical, and the letter to the pope seems to have served primarily to express the Christian concerns and credentials of king and chancellor. Stephen, however, was arguing in favour of a greater degree of segregation between the Sicilian Muslim and Christian communities, a policy which worked against the subtle processes of religious transition via gradual assimilation and acculturation. The importance of this strategy, which also threatened indigenous Arabic-speaking Christians who might not be deemed Christian enough, presumably found greater favour with the north Italians or newcomers like Stephen, unhappy with the island's customary peculiarities.

It was the treatment of Robert that brought together *qā'id* Richard and the leader of the Sicilian Muslims, Abū l-Qāsim ibn Ḥammūd, in their opposition to Stephen. Richard and Abū l-Qāsim were probably well known to one another from the positions and roles they had played in the fiscal administration. The popular resistance among the Muslims that they were said to have raised against Stephen would be an important factor in his eventual expulsion from Palermo. However, that opposition may not have been unanimous, since we are told that Abū l-Qāsim was himself opposed by the island's wealthiest Muslim, a certain 'Sedictus', of whom we shall hear more in the next chapter.[35] The events which followed are covered in some detail by Falcandus, but have only indirect relevance to the Muslims of the island and need not be covered here in full.[36] After Stephen's initial success against his detractors, an alleged plot to assassinate him by the palace faction, comprising *qā'id* Richard, Matthew and Gentile, the bishop of Agrigento, resulted in their arrest. Further evidence of the French contingents' ignorance of Sicilian customs and the wide unpopularity this caused was shown by the attempt of a certain John of Lavardin to exact taxes not just from Muslims and Greeks, but also from the 'free' Latin population living on his lands.[37] A popular revolt against the French erupted at Messina in April 1168 and was quickly repeated in Palermo, where a mob was raised which besieged Stephen in the cathedral bell tower, after which he negotiated his escape from the island, along with the remaining few from among his original retinue.[38]

The earthquake of February 1169

One of the few survivors of the French contingent, Peter of Blois – an unfettered critic of the island and its population – concluded that the massive earthquake which struck eastern Sicily was divine retribution for the expulsion of the Stephen's supporters. The earthquake, which can be dated to 4 February 1169, destroyed or seriously damaged many of the cities of eastern Sicily and Calabria, including Réggio, Catania, Syracuse, Moac and Lentini, while Messina was flooded by a tsunami.[39] The chaos it caused prompted fears of a Byzantine invasion in league with disaffected exiles who, in turn, might have sparked a rebellion within the kingdom. That this did not occur is testament to the more robust level of stability overall which the kingdom enjoyed by this period, bolstered by the reaccommodation of former exiles such as Tancred of Lecce and Robert of Loritello who had been generously allowed to return.

In the 1180s, Ibn Jubayr reported an old anecdote that when the tremors had been felt in the royal palace (presumably in Messina), the young William II told the panicking palace staff to 'each invoke the God he worships, and those who have faith shall be comforted'.[40] If this story is credible – and it had been repeated by Sicilian Muslims for over fifteen years – then it defends the contemporary Muslim view that William was aware, from a young age, that many among his staff were Muslim or only nominally Christian. Unlike his chancellor, William was apparently comfortable with the idea, and a natural disaster which could have killed him was thought by the Muslims to have brought out some underlying toleration of religious pluralism.

Following Stephen's departure, *qā'id* Richard continued to be attested in the *dīwān* and also served as one of ten *familiares*, along with three lay lords and a remainder of mainly Sicilian-based prelates. The power and influence that Peter had wielded until the mid-1160s was not reproduced thereafter. Of later notable eunuchs, *qā'id* Richard stands out as an exception – as a person of lasting consequence who was able to survive the political upheavals of the 1160s and maintain a presence at court until he was last attested in 1187. Richard was thus the great survivor among the high-profile palace eunuchs, while the royal *familiares* under William II were dominated by Latin-rite bishops and archbishops, in particular by the king's domineering personal tutor, Walter, who had been appointed archbishop of Palermo on 28 October 1169, and had formerly been the dean of Agrigento. In the absence of an *amīr* of *amīr*s and then of a chancellor, royal charters were dated by the *familiares* themselves. Walter's seniority in Palermitan political life is shown by the appearance of his name as *datarius* first among the other *familiares* on royal diplomata. Until 1188, Walter, as archbishop of Palermo was one of a triumvirate of *familiares*, which at varying times included his brother Bartholomew (1171–7, then 1184–9), and Gentile, bishop of Agrigento (1170–1), Richard Palmer, bishop-elect of Syracuse and then archbishop of Messina (1177–84) and Matthew of Salerno (until 1189), who later became chancellor under Tancred.

With the encouragement of Matthew, when William's great monastic foundation at Monreale was raised to an archbishopric in 1183, Walter's brother Bartholomew was made a *familiaris*. Thus, the triumvirate had become four, consisting of Walter and Bartholomew, on the one hand, countered with Matthew and archbishop William of Monreale, on the other hand, so splitting influence between the archbishoprics of Monreale and Palermo and their supporters. Complex and unpredictable as changes of individuals within the *familiares regis* were, they none the less managed to strike a balance between the most powerful factions in the kingdom, particularly between Latin-rite prelates and the Latin nobility. However, by the 1170s, this also shows the extent to which power had shifted into the hands of the 'Latins' at the expense of the Greeks and Muslims.

The eunuchs managed to retain their influence as chamberlains of the palace and as other officials working behind the scenes and within the *dīwān*. But, after 1169, the eunuchs were excluded from the king's *familiares*.

Notes

1 The best introduction to eunuchs in medieval Islamic lands is David Ayalon's *Eunuchs, Caliphs and Sultans: A Study in Power Relationships* (Jerusalem, 1999). For eunuchs in Norman Sicily, detailed, up-to-date discussions are to be found in Johns, *Arabic Administration*, especially pp. 212–34, 243–56.

2 *Falcandus*, Lat. p. 85; Eng. p. 135, gives the specific location of *qā'id* Martin's office in the palace. The eunuchs lived in the Kemonia district adjacent to the royal palace.

3 For the hypothesis that Philip had been brought from Mahdiyya as a child around 1108 with George of Antioch and was therefore about the same age as Roger, see Johns, *Arabic Administration*, p. 249.

4 On Philip 'of Africa's' Greek signature, see Johns, *Arabic Administration*, p. 215.

5 Clearly, Matthew came to be associated with Salerno, but not everyone agrees with this sceptical assessment of his origins. I am grateful to Graham Loud for pointing out that Matthew begged William I not to destroy the city in 1162; he founded a hospital there; his son, Nicholas, became the archbishop in 1181; and he left substantial funds to the abbey of Cava to buy property in Salerno.

6 *Falcandus*, Lat. p. 25; Eng. p. 78.

7 On Philip of Mahdiyya's trial and translations of the texts, see Chapter 8, note 14.

8 On the palace eunuchs, see Ibn Jubayr, *BAS*² Ar. I:86–8; Eng. trans. Broadhurst, pp. 341–3. See Johns, *Arabic Administration*, pp. 212–14, for a translation of relevant passages.

9 Ibn Jubayr, *BAS*² Ar. I:101; Eng. trans. Broadhurst, p. 358. See also Qur'ān, 16:106 and 3:28.

10 R. Strothmann and Moktar Djebli, *Taḳiyya*, in *EI*² X:134.

11 Johns, *Arabic Administration*, pp. 251–2. Also, J. Johns and N. Jamil, 'Signs of the times: Arabic signatures as a measure of acculturation in Norman Sicily', in *Muqarnas*, 21 (2004): 181–92 with photographs and enlarged details of *'alāmas*.

12 'That nothing is hidden from God', see Qur'ān, 3:5, 10:61, 14:38 and 27:75.

13 White, *Latin Monasticism*, pp. 278–9; for the career of *qā'id* Richard, see Johns, *Arabic Administration*, pp. 228–34.

14 Jeremy Johns, 'Trilingual inscription of Peter-Barrūn, a eunuch of Roger II', in *Nobiles Officinae: perle, filigrane e trame di seta dal Palazzo Reale di Palermo*, Maria Andaloro (ed.) (Catania, 2006), pp. 771–2.

15 *Falcandus*, Lat. p. 27; Eng. p. 80.

16 Turbaned, Muslim musicians (quite possibly from the royal band) are depicted celebrating Tancred's victory in a late twelfth-century illustration. See *Petrus de Ebulo. Liber ad honorem Augusti sive de rebus Siculis. Codex 120 II der Burgerbibliothek Bern* (Sigmaringen, 1994), p. 63. The position of the figures hints that they were marching in time.

17 For the royal *familiares*, see Takayama, *Administration of the Norman Kingdom*, pp. 95–101 and 115–27.

18 On *qā'id* Martin, see Johns, *Arabic Administration*, pp. 219–22.

19 For Muslim attitudes to Frankish justice, see *An Arab-Syrian Gentleman and Warrior in the Period of the Crusades: Memoirs of Usāmah Ibn-Munqidh*, trans. P. K. Hitti (New York, 1929. Reprinted 2000), pp. 167–8.

20 On *qā'id* Peter, see Johns, *Arabic Administration*, pp. 222–8.

21 *Falcandus*, Lat. p. 77; Eng. p. 128.

22 Matthew of Salerno is seen in the Bern manuscript of *Peter of Eboli*, pp. 54, 59, 159 and 163.

23 *Falcandus*, Lat. p. 97; Eng. p. 145.

24 On Rodrigo's characteristics that disposed him to a general unsuitability to govern, including his *barba rarissima*, short stature, dark complexion and loud-mouthed ineloquence, see *Falcandus*, Lat. p. 107; Eng. p. 155.

25 On the kings' increasing sexual and political impotence, see Ferdinand Chalandon, 'The Norman kingdom of Sicily', in *The Cambridge Medieval History*, J. R. Tanner, C. W. Prévite-Orton and Z. N. Brooke (eds) (Cambridge, 1968), V:184–98 (p. 198).

26 *Falcandus*, Lat. p. 7; Eng. p. 59. There are some indications that Falcandus was familiar with Virgil's *Aeneid*, or at least parts of it. The figurative description of Rumour (*Falcandus*, Lat. p. 72; Eng. p. 123) also seems to pick up *Aeneid*, iv.173. For other resonances of classical learning, see *Falcandus*, Eng., pp. 42–50.

27 *Falcandus*, Lat. p. 99; Eng. pp. 147–8. *Romuald*, Lat. p. 254; Eng. p. 239.

28 Ibn Khaldūn, *BAS*[2] Ar. II: 515; *BAS*[2] It. II:568.

29 Otto of St Blasien, *MGH*, *SRG*, 47:20–7.

30 *Falcandus*, Lat. p. 110; Eng. p. 160, for how the counts of Perche gained land from the Andalusi Muslims.

31 For Lombard support of the French factions, see *Falcandus*, Lat. p. 155; Eng. p. 208.

32 *Falcandus*, Lat. pp. 115–18; Eng. pp. 166–9, on the trial of Robert of Calatabiano.

33 *Falcandus*, Lat. pp. 85–6; Eng. pp. 135–6, where the reference to Robert 'Calataboianensis' as 'of Caltabellotta' in the translation is mistaken. Calatabiano is 6.5km to the south-west of Taormina.

34 For the Latin text, see *Italia Pontificia*, P. F. Kehr (ed.), 10 vols (Berlin, 1905–74), X:232, no. 231, and quoted in Johns, *Arabic Administration*, pp. 229–30, n. 68.

35 On 'Sedictus' as the island's richest Muslim, see *Falcandus*, Lat. p. 119; Eng. p. 170.

36 *Falcandus*, Lat. pp. 119–31; Eng. pp. 170–83.

37 *Falcandus*, Lat. pp. 144–5; Eng. p. 197.

38 *Falcandus*, Lat. p. 159; Eng. p. 212; *Romuald*, Lat. p. 257; Eng. p. 242. The uprising had been particularly violent at Messina where the locals put Odo Quarrel to death by strapping him over the back of an ass and stabbing him. *Falcandus*, Lat. pp. 152–3; Eng. p. 205.

39 On the 1169 earthquake, see *Falcandus*, Lat. pp. 164–5; Eng. pp. 216–18; *Romuald*, Lat. p. 258; Eng. p. 243.

40 Ibn Jubayr, *BAS*[2] Ar. I:87; Eng. trans. Broadhurst, p. 341, for the earthquake anecdote.

11

Monreale and the Muslims

William II's reign: diplomatic successes and expensive failures

Falcandus' dense and thorny narrative of Sicilian affairs ends abruptly with the earthquake of 1169. Thereafter, sources which deal with the Muslims, even tangentially, throughout most of the 1170s are limited. When they resume with the detailed eye-witness account of Ibn Jubayr, we see a Muslim community in crisis and in which serious differences of opinion had begun to emerge. Prior to the fuller and wider range of evidence supplied by charters from the late 1170s and 1180s, it is possible to infer that, for most of the 1170s, the Sicilian Muslims continued their decline under the hereditary leadership of Abū l-Qāsim, a momentous figure who formed a vital link between the palaces and the wider Muslim communities, especially that of western Sicily.

Otherwise, there were grounds for cautious optimism by the mid-1170s, at least for the long-term survival of the Hauteville dynasty and for the kingdom of Sicily which had maintained its integrity into a third generation of kings. The threat of invasion from the north was again averted when Frederick Barbarossa's army suffered defeat at the hands of Lombard League forces at the battle of Legnano in May 1176, a defeat which directly informed the delicate negotiations behind the Treaty of Venice signed the following year, sealing a fifteen-year peace between Sicily, the papacy, the German emperor and the towns of north Italy. The improving relations with the Holy Roman Empire would ultimately lead to a proposed intermarriage between ruling houses. Remote from the lives of the Sicilian Muslims that this move appeared at the time, it would have far-reaching consequences for the kingdom and its Muslim population in the thirteenth century.

If one leaves aside the resumption of costly overseas expeditions (first, the failed attacks against Ṣalāḥ al-Dīn's Egypt in 1174, which Romuald played up at the Venice negotiations as evidence of William's crusader credentials and, secondly, the attempt of assuming power at Constantinople in 1185 via a pretender claiming to be Alexios II, which came to nothing), then the kingdom *internally* enjoyed political stability for most of William II's reign. This earned him a reputation for peace and piety as well as the later, enduring epithet of 'the good'. In popular imagination to this day, he is favourably contrasted with his father, William 'the bad', remembered for his dark portrayal in Falcandus, his reliance on Maio and the eunuchs, and for his suppression of the nobility. The epithet of 'the good' also derives from the conspicuous munificence of his charity shown towards the Latin Church, and refers to another expensive and disastrous project – the foundation of the Benedictine abbey of Santa Maria Nuova located in the hills surrounding Palermo, just 6.6 kilometres from its cathedral as the crow flies, and not much further by road, passing close to the main palace, the smaller Cuba palace and Cúbula pavilion located in a royal park. It was to Monreale that the Muslims of western Sicily would be granted, along with the estates on which they lived and worked. Thus, for both local Muslims and outside visitors, William II was, at best, an ambivalent figure. At worst, he was the Muslims' betrayer since he was to dissolve the arrangement of royal protection for the Muslims of western Sicily – one of the few regions where they could still live unmolested.

The foundation of Santa Maria Nuova at Monreale

In March 1174, a royal decision was recorded to build a new monastery devoted to the Virgin Mary 'near Palermo'. The chosen locality did not yet have a name, other than that it was said to be located 'above Saint Cyriacus', a small Greek church in the vicinity. This was the 'poor church' in which the Normans who had conquered Palermo in 1072 discovered Nicodemus, the timid Greek archbishop, expelled by the Muslims.[1] The ambiguity inherent in the phrase 'above Saint Cyriacus', which occurs three times between 1174 and 1176, is an important one because it could be taken to mean that William, by building on top of a Byzantine church, was merely a restorer.[2] If so, then this might also have a bearing on the all-important motives for the foundation because it could be interpreted as the triumph of Latin Christianity on the island which, having supplanted Muslim rule, assisted the gradual transition from Greek-rite to Latin-rite churches; Monreale being the most Latin of foundations as shown by the mosaic cycles and choice of saints depicted therein.[3] However, the church of Saint Cyriacus was granted *to* Monreale in 1176, indicating that it could not have been directly beneath its very walls, but was below it in the sense that it was located further down the hillside. Yet, that Saint Cyriacus was cited in the earliest documents relating to Monreale indicates how it served as the justification for placing a major new foundation so unprecedentedly close to the archbishopric of Palermo. Only several years later, in 1183, does the site of the abbey appear with the name *Mons Regalis* and, in a royal Arabic confirmation of the same year, as *Munt Riyāl* – a rendition which, among a handful of other similar examples, is suggestive of Francophone influence in *dīwānī* Sicilian Arabic.

Precisely when and, more importantly, why Monreale was conceived is unclear. More can be said about how this monumental project developed and how the church's possessions and powers expanded. In 1174, there were no indications that the church existed in anything but embryonic form or that its future was but a grand idea in the mind of the king or his powerful and enormously experienced vice-chancellor, Matthew of Salerno. But even at an early stage, rights in matters of ecclesiastical jurisdiction were beginning to be transferred and confirmed to the new church.

The first unambiguous evidence that Monreale was intended as a major royal foundation can be found in an endowment charter dated to 15 August 1176 when, on the feast of the Assumption of the Virgin Mary, the abbey was granted the large, walled towns (*castella*) of Iato, Corleone and Calatrasi in western Sicily in addition to holdings on the mainland. On its lands, the abbey was to be exempt from any form of taxation and free of all service, and the abbot was to act as justiciar. Lords who held land within the boundaries of the grants were to retain their possessions which their sons might inherit. Otherwise, they would revert to the church which would oversee that any services to the crown were duly rendered. In 1178, again coinciding with the feast of the Assumption of the Virgin, Monreale received the *castellum* of Battallaro, and maybe also at this juncture, the large *casale* of Bū Zākī (modern Bisacquino). On 5 February 1183, Monreale was raised to an archbishopric by a papal bull of Lucius III and, over the next two years, received further grants of estates along with the families who lived and worked on them. With rights, exemptions, privileges and vast material holdings of land, men and property around the kingdom conceded to it by the mid-1180s, Monreale rapidly became the largest landholder in the kingdom after the king himself. The main grants of lands made between 1176 and 1185 gave the abbey control of over 1,200 square kilometres of fertile agricultural lands dotted with numerous towns and estates, in all representing around 4.5 per cent of the surface area of the island. On these lands the population was still overwhelmingly Muslim. Most of Monreale's holdings were contiguous and fanned out southwards from the slopes of Monte Iato towards the Valle del Bélice in central-western areas of the Val di Mazara. On the unexpected death of the king in November 1189, these same areas would be the focus of a sustained Muslim revolt leading to the irrevocable breakdown of the one state, several systems arrangement conceived in the Assizes, quickly resulting in the creation of an Islamic state within a state prior to the Muslims' defeat and deportation from the island under Frederick II from 1223.

Apart from setting many new precedents on the island, the foundation also introduced important changes to the organisation of the Church in Sicily: Monreale was to be subject only to the pope at Rome; the monks were to elect their own abbot; and the church now oversaw the Greek- and Latin-rite foundations whose jurisdiction had been surrendered to it. Although these need not be discussed here, they included: the abbey of Maniace at Bronte, two churches in Messina, two in the vicinity of Bríndisi, six in Calabria, the town and bishopric of Bitetto in Apulia and the abbey of Saints' Elias and Anastasius at Carbone, whose archimandrite held sway over all the Greek-rite churches in north Calabria and the principality of Salerno.[4]

If the abbey existed only as an ambitious proposal in 1174, then by early 1183 when it was raised to an archbishopric, reference was made to its impressive physical construction, implying that even the extensive internal mosaics were sufficiently complete to have been noteworthy by that point. The church's dimensions were majestic, but not exceptionally so. As far as the time frame of its external construction was concerned, its height was comparable with other Sicilian foundations and within the bounds of medieval building techniques, which did not usually exceed three metres per year without the risk of collapse or bulging walls. The church's original bronze doors are dated to 1186, and it seems safe to conclude that the entire project was complete before William II's death in 1189. The enormous cost of the construction related particularly to its lavish interior decoration of gold-leaf mosaics and the teams of highly skilled artisans required to work on them. The expense could only have been increased by the speed with which it was put together. Indeed, William's reign in general was an expensive one, given that at this same time he was fitting out a large fleet for its unsuccessful overseas adventures. The foundation of Monreale did not bankrupt the crown, but it represented a huge drain on royal resources, not simply in its construction costs, but mainly in the loss of revenue to the crown because the *jizya* and land tax that the largely Muslim population had previously paid to the *dīwān* now went to the abbot instead.

There were hidden political costs and agendas to the project as well, which relate to some of the likely reasons behind Monreale's existence. According to Richard of San Germano, it had been founded so close to Palermo on the advice of Matthew of Salerno.[5] His motives had been entirely self-interested as he hoped to eclipse the power of its archbishop and his rival, Walter, whose cathedral had been undergoing reconstruction from 1172. This then provides a motive for the highly unusual proximity of the two archbishoprics as well as the meteoric rise of Monreale after 1174. The political machinations in Palermo can be seen being played out among the *familiares* in other sources. For example, in 1177, Walter's brother Bartholomew was replaced as a *familiaris* by Richard Palmer but, by 1184, Bartholomew had been reinstated, along with and balanced by the newly created archbishop of Monreale. However, the rivalry continued after William's death, with Walter lending support to the pro-Henry VI faction while the chancellor, Matthew, favoured Tancred. When the foundation and enriching of Monreale is viewed in this light, there seems little doubt that personal political rivalry played an important role in determining its evolution. Further motives may be present within the mosaic cycles themselves where the saintly image of Thomas Becket appears in the apse. Becket, the archbishop of Canterbury, had been in discussion with Richard Palmer and the Sicilians at court over the former's employment and the king's marriage in February 1177 to Joanna, the daughter of Henry II, the English king. However, towards the end of 1170, just before William came of age, Becket was murdered, arguably by Henry's command, over a dispute about the limits of royal and clerical jurisdiction.[6] Within three years, Becket had been canonised by Pope Alexander III, and his martyrdom transformed him into an iconic figure. In Sicily, where family members of his were also attested, the bishop of Catania converted a mosque into the church of Saint Thomas of Canterbury.[7] The prominence given to Becket at Monreale might, therefore, be read in the context of a pious royal statement against the secular tradition in the Latin Church in Sicily by which many high-ranking prelates from non-religious backgrounds had been royally affirmed in their positions.

It remains unclear whether the political wrangling between Matthew and Walter at Palermo was an exacerbated effect of Monreale's existence, rather than a cause of its foundation. Murky as these events were, they do not argue in favour of giving William himself the leading role in Monreale's foundation, in spite of Lynn White's claim that 'we need search for no motive in its erection other than the natural piety of the young King'.[8] If the young William felt the need to live up to his pro-Christian royal titles then the Sicilian attacks against Ṣalāḥ al-Dīn had allowed the crusader posturing at Venice to at least fulfil the required political rhetoric of the day, and had also occurred around the same time that Monreale had been initially conceived. The correlation is thought-provoking, but given that we can detect at least some compound, non-religious, raisons d'être for Monreale, a simple explanation such as piety is insufficiently convincing to stand on its own.

Monreale has often been a vehicle for propaganda, but there is little reason to entertain the nineteenth-century supposition that William's creation was no more than the restoration of a Benedictine chapel originally founded by Gregory the Great in the sixth century. This view was revived by the fiercely pro-Benedictine archbishop, Balsamo, who wrote under the name of Gravina, and sought to confer on his church a sense of unassailable antiquity when the Italian *Risorgimento* movement was gathering pace, at the same time seeking to reconfirm its Benedictine roots which it had yielded to the Cistercians.[9] An anachronistic suggestion for its foundation was offered by Richard of San Germano, who claimed its dedication to the Virgin Mary was due to concern at William and Joanna's failure to produce any offspring.[10] This seems untenable given the youth of both the king and his wife, the fact that they married *after* its foundation, and that, even by the mid-1180s, their lack of an heir was not seen as sufficiently problematic to have affected the engagement of Roger II's daughter, Constance, to the German emperor's son, Henry. The report by Robert of Torigny that, around 1181, William had a son, Bohemond, who had been invested as duke of Apulia at birth, also sounds inherently implausible and bears the hallmarks of invention or misapprehension. Of greater relevance is the notion that the patronage of new foundations had a strong tradition in Norman Sicily, notably Roger II's foundation at Cefalù which had been dogged by problems of legitimacy. Although William I had not founded a major church, he had initiated the building of the Zisa palace which was completed under William II, hence, there was no need for another pleasure palace. Besides which, William had donated relatively little to the Church since his coming of age in 1171. In any event, great foundations served as monuments to their creators: as Cefalù had been intended to house the sarcophagus of its royal founder, so Monreale would also serve as a burial place for Margaret and both kings William. By outdoing his grandfather, William could also create a church for the glory of God, his great European kingdom in the Mediterranean and, therefore, for the prestige of his own dynasty.

The concerns of the Muslim community under William II

It would be marriage alliances, rather than military or diplomatic enterprises which were to have the greatest impact on the long-term direction of the dynasty and the kingdom, with what appeared as two resounding successes at the time. Not only was William married to the young daughter of Henry II of England, but in 1186, after two years of engagement, Constance was married to Frederick Barbarossa's son, Henry. Such arrangements conferred on the kingdom of Sicily a sense of legitimacy in German eyes and confirmed the Hauteville's place among the great dynastic houses of medieval Europe. One wonders what Roger II would have made of this alliance with the feared enemy: John of Salisbury noted how he had favoured personnel from all parts – except from Germany.[11] If William and Joanna's marriage proved to be a childless one, then the kingdom would pass to Constance, and thus, the offspring of her German husband would also have a claim to the throne. By the mid-1170s, it is noticeable how the Muslims had become almost entirely divorced from the key areas of contention determining the direction of the kingdom. Indeed, the concerns of the Muslims form almost a parallel history which ran concurrently to these other debates over which they had little influence, but by which they were ultimately affected.

Since the beginning of the Norman conquest of the island, powerful factions within the Muslim community had always been among the staunchest supporters of the Sicilian rulers: from secular *qā'ids*, notable and accommodating kin groups, compliant *qāḍīs*, to the eunuch officials, commanders of the fleet and loyal 'Saracen' contingents within the army. Yet, by the 1180s, there were clear signs that pressures brought to bear on the Muslim community were causing it to polarise between converts, pseudo-converts and collaborators, on the one hand, and increasingly resistant factions, on the other hand. Indicators of serious malaise were apparent in Ibn Jubayr's eye-witness account of 1184–5 in which the Muslims were said to be in a state of humiliation, oppression and wretchedness under the pact of the *dhimma* – terms and phrases he specifically used to describe their condition. The woes he cited had a defined psychological edge, particularly the feeling of impending doom and profound insecurity brought about by the concern that family units were melting away through apostasy. References were also made to a list of interrelated grievances: oppressive levels of taxation in rural areas; internal and external pressures to convert to Christianity; the financial ruination of their hereditary leader, Abū l-Qāsim; and the institutional suppression of mosques in which the Friday sermon had been prohibited. In addition, certain areas of strategic military importance were off limits to Muslims, and news of an attack on Muslim Majorca had recently arrived. By the end of his Sicilian sojourn, when his initial enthusiasm for the kingdom had worn off, Ibn Jubayr was prepared to believe the worst, convincing himself that the fleet at Trápani was set to attack Alexandria or Ifrīqiya when, in fact, it was destined for Constantinople.

Abū l-Qāsim: the 'leader of the Sicilian Muslims'

In the words of Falcandus, the 'most noble and powerful of the Sicilian Muslims [was] Bulcassim'.[12] Known to us from several independent sources, 'Bulcassim' can be identified safely as Abū l-Qāsim Muḥammad ibn Ḥammūd from the Banū l-Ḥajar. Falcandus was writing about the events of 1167 following the persecution of lapsed Christians when Abū l-Qāsim acted in unison with *qā'id* Richard and the palace eunuchs in order to turn Muslim opinion against the chancellor, Stephen of Perche. The same author, who was writing with hindsight in the knowledge that, by the mid-1180s, Abū l-Qāsim had been financially crippled, drew a contrast between his nobility and the riches of his rival, 'Sedictus'.[13] The latter has been cautiously identified as al-Sadīd al-Ḥuṣrī, whose patronage and acquaintance the Egyptian poet Ibn Qalāqis also enjoyed, and whose house was sufficiently impressive a landmark in Palermo to be mentioned in Falcandus' *Letter to Peter*.[14] Otherwise, Sedictus/al-Sadīd remains largely obscure, but it is clear that he was another whose presence was known around the palaces, perhaps in a capacity which was more political than administrative. The donation to Palermo cathedral of a garden which may once have belonged to him suggests that his property had been broken up by the early thirteenth century.[15] He appears in Falcandus to have been an ally of Stephen of Perche who aggressively favoured a policy of Muslim–Christian separation. This does not necessarily mean that he also shared this outlook, but it is interesting to observe a political dividing line with the faux-Christian eunuchs and Abū l-Qāsim on the one side, and on the other, a Muslim–Christian coalition in which both parties favoured a stricter segregation of the faiths. In any event, a separatist response to the challenge of life under infidel rule contrasts sharply with the integrationalist and/or *taqiyya*-based approach.

In spite of this rivalry, there is no doubt that Abū l-Qāsim was thought at the time to be the most prominent of secular Muslim leaders from the early 1160s until at least 1185 when Ibn Jubayr met him in Trápani. His father was also a Sicilian alumnus, having patronised Ibn Ẓafar's political treatise the *Sulwān al-Muṭā'*, composed in 1159–60, in which he was described as 'the chief of chiefs (*sā'id al-sāda*) and *qā'id* of *qā'ids*'.[16] On his leadership (*ri'āsa*), Ibn Ẓafar pointed to his munificence, but added that he paid no heed to his slanderous critics (*al-wushā*), revealing that not all the Sicilian Muslims accepted his authority without qualification either. When his son, Abū l-Qāsim, met Ibn Jubayr in Trápani, he was described in a not dissimilar manner: 'the leader (*za'īm*) of the people of this island' and 'their master' (*sayyid-hum*). None of these honorific terms was a formal title, nor did they have any specific connotations. *Za'īm*, for instance, conveyed the idea of a notable who might speak on behalf of the community he represented, but nothing more aggrandising than that. From what we know of Abū l-Qāsim, he played precisely this role as the main intermediary between the wider Sicilian Muslim population and the crown. Indeed, he can be inferred to have been a leading director of fiscal affairs in the royal *dīwān*, working alongside *qā'id* Richard, and he was very probably involved with co-ordinating the collection of the *jizya* from the Muslims.[17] He thus spent much of his long political career mixing with men of consequence, respected in the royal palaces and honoured by his own community, especially in western Sicily, Palermo and Trápani where his power bases and known properties were. He is first attested from 1162, when we see him engaged in commercial activities, concluding a loan agreement with overseas merchants, in this case from Genoa.[18] He was thus old enough to have lived through the massacres of Muslims in the early 1160s, and had probably assumed his leadership around that same time. Further biographical details are primarily supplemented by poetic allusions from the pen of Ibn Qalāqis who visited the island for a year from May 1168, during which he was patronised by Abū l-Qāsim.[19]

Leadership and lineage: the Sicilian Ḥammūdids

About his own status, Abū l-Qāsim made two important, interconnected and contentious claims: that his leadership of the Sicilian Muslims was hereditary; and that his family of the Banū l-Ḥajar were descended from the clan of the Banū l-Ḥammūd. Arguments from genealogy were commonplace and reinforced a sense of legitimacy by establishing continuity with the past. This strategy had served the Ḥammūdids in Spain well in the past by giving them an important political edge over their rivals in the fractured statelets of eleventh-century al-Andalus where they ruled over Málaga and Algeçiras (1010–*c.* 1056). Another branch held Ceuta in the western Maghrib between 1010 and 1091. Sometimes described in the context of *ṭā'ifa* Spain as 'Berberised Arabs', they claimed descent from the Banū l-Quraysh, that is, from the tribe of the Prophet Muḥammad himself, via a surviving branch of the Shī'īte Idrīsīds of Fez whose rule had been extinguished by the late tenth century.[20] According to a fourteenth-century source, al-Ṣafadī, when the last of the Málagan Ḥammūdids, Muḥammad II b. Idrīs, was ousted he fled east to Sicily around 1057 where he was welcomed by Roger I, only to fall foul of his ally, Ibn al-Thumna. This forms the basis of a theory which seeks to account for the appearance of Chamutus/Ḥammūd at Castrogiovanni – the former stronghold of Ibn al-Ḥawwās – and could possibly also explain his conversion as an indicator of a political switch for the kin group, although such arguments remain speculative in a particularly difficult period.

In the dim light of the sources, we might be cautious about the claim of the Banū l-Ḥajar to be Ḥammūdids, even more so given that Abū l-Qāsim himself can be shown to have fundamentally changed his mind about his ancestry by the mid-1170s. The first time we hear the explicit claim of Ḥammūdid lineage was when Abū l-Qāsim's panegyricist, Ibn Qalāqis, sang the praises of the Banū l-Ḥajar and stated that he was 'related to the Ḥammūdīd clan'.[21] It might also be noted that Ibn Ẓafar did not include the key term 'Ibn Ḥammūd' or 'al-Ḥammūdī' among the names of Abū l-Qāsim's father, said to have been called Abū 'Abd Allāh ibn Muḥammad ibn Abī l-Qāsim ibn 'Alī ibn al-'Alawī l-Qurashī. Even Ibn Qalāqis gave his father's name only as Abū 'Abd Allāh Ḥammūd ibn Muḥammad ibn 'Alawī ibn al-Ḥajar al-Qurashī. In these cases, emphasis falls on the link with the Quraysh, while 'Ḥammūd' here appears as a personal name (*ism*) rather than a relative adjective (*nisba*), rendering the appellation and affiliation of Abū l-Qāsim ibn Ḥammūd ambiguous.

The evidence for the Ḥammūdids in Norman Sicily is slippery, but it is certainly not to be rejected out of hand as it is clear that this association was widely accepted at the time to confer a sense of legitimacy. Moreover, the famous cartographer, the Sharīf al-Idrīsī, who was patronised by Roger II, included a reference to the Ḥammūdids in the full version of his name.[22] It was claimed that Idrīsī was the son of Muḥammad II b. Idrīs of Málaga, although this connection would require them both to have been extremely long-lived. Idrīsī made no pretence to power or communal leadership in Sicily and, on the contrary, appeared to have been politically inert, in spite of having easy and frequent access to the king's ear.

Identification of various members of the Ḥammūdids, let alone their verification, has proved almost impossible and seriously undermines any interpretations which seek to explain their leadership in terms of genuine kin group identities. Thus, the case for powerful Ḥammūdid influence in Sicily remains controversial, and the Banū l-Ḥajar's claims of affiliation to them even more so. None the less, there is a school of thought that is inseparably wedded to the idea that the Ḥammūdids *had* been a dominant force in Muslim Sicily since the days of the Norman conquest. This is partially supported by the appearance of a certain Christian landholder, 'Roger Hamutus', attested in the Castrogiovanni area between 1179 and 1193 who also acted in the role of a royal justiciar. These suggested links, if true, may well be very significant. However, the argument is too contentious to be made with conviction, especially since the personal name Ḥammūd (as opposed to the tribal version of Ibn Ḥammūd or al-Ḥammūdī) was also among the most popular Arabic names attested on the island.[23]

The collapse of the Fatimids and the Sunnī-Shīʿa dilemma

Abū l-Qāsim had several sons and an unknown number of daughters.[24] Three of the sons were given unambiguously Sunnī names: Abū Bakr, ʿUmar and ʿUthmān, consciously called after the first three orthodox caliphs. This was a curious choice of names since the Ḥammūdids of Málaga were Shīʿites, while Abū l-Qāsim's own brother, Abū ʿAlī Ḥasan, and his other sons bore names which vaguely signal a similar leaning. However, in Norman Sicily of the 1180s, the sermon (*khuṭba*) at the festivals of ʿĪd al-Fiṭr and ʿĪd al-Aḍḥā after Ramaḍān was given in the name of the Abbasid caliph in Baghdad. The implication is that by then, had the Sicilian Muslims wished to restore Muslim rule, they would have looked to do so in the name of mainstream Sunnī orthodoxy, and not as a restoration of the Fatimid Ismāʿīlīs whose dynasty had been snuffed out by Ṣalāḥ al-Dīn by 1171. Indeed, the Fatimids' collapse appears to have provoked a politico-religious rethink among the old guard of Sicilian Muslim leadership. How could the wily, secular leaders of the Banū l-Ḥajar – whose Ḥammūdid credentials came with a touch of Shīʿism that had doubtlessly played well with the Fatimids – throw in their lot with the ascendant heroes of Sunnī orthodoxy, the Almohads and Ṣalāḥ al-Dīn, without the risk of undermining their own claim to hereditary leadership in the process?

Between the surviving sources, some political and diplomatic shuffling can be detected. We know, for example, that when Ibn Qalāqis left the island in April 1169, he was accompanied to Egypt by a Fatimid diplomat. Implicit in a letter the poet later wrote to Abū l-Qāsim is that the latter knew of this emissary, and we can assume that the Fatimids were abreast of developments in the period after Stephen of Perche. But it is also quite likely that this envoy, as with every other Muslim notable who passed through Sicily, had met with Abū l-Qāsim. In any event, he was the last known official of the Fatimids to have had contact with the island before their fall. Thereafter, we can most clearly see how the notion of hereditary leadership was itself conceived as a flexible construct.

A few years later, in 1175, the traveller and author ʿAlī al-Harawī, was passing through Palermo when he was taken ill. He was offered hospitality by Abū l-Qāsim and wrote of the brief time they spent together. In conversation, Abū l-Qāsim had told him that his lineage could be traced back to the Umayyad caliph, ʿUmar ibn ʿAbd al-ʿAzīz (d. 720). This connection was hopelessly inconsistent with his Ḥammūdid-Idrīsid-ʿAlīd claim, but it was one which now emphasised a link to Sunnism via the Orthodox caliph, ʿUmar b. al-Khaṭṭāb (d. 644), the great-grandfather of the Umayyad caliph in question. An additional advantage of having such a distinguished ancestor was that it maintained the prestigious Quraysh connection yet, at the same time, benefited from the common historical memory of a popular and populist Sunnī Muslim ruler, well known for his moves towards reconciliation with the ʿAlids.

However, their meeting had a fascinating diplomatic context. According to Ibn al-Athīr, in the year before, remnants of the Fatimid hierarchy had conspired to overthrow Ṣalāḥ al-Dīn and restore the imām-caliphate with the help of the Normans from Sicily.[25] The plot was uncovered and the named ringleaders were crucified on 6 April 1174. This, however, did not prevent the Normans carrying out combined, but unsuccessful, attacks on Alexandria in August 1174, perhaps with the aim of partially restoring the Fatimids to power and of sharing indirect control over Egypt. The position of Abū l-Qāsim in all this is quite unknown but, irrespective of the Normans' intentions towards Egypt, he was clearly in a difficult situation with regard to Ṣalāḥ al-Dīn. There were inherent dangers in appearing to be too close to the Norman regime but, worse still, he could be considered a source of support (and potential shelter) for elements from the old Fatimid elites.

The adjustments Abū l-Qāsim made to his lineage served his interests only vis-à-vis a Sicilian audience. They would clearly not suffice in terms of serious diplomacy overseas. However, in 1175, as al-Harawī recorded in a remarkable passage, Abū l-Qāsim had given him a letter to take to Ṣalāḥ al-Dīn, inviting him to invade Sicily. The suggestion was vaguely absurd, but its ulterior motive was most probably to clarify Abū l-Qāsim's position as a pro-Sunnī, pro-Ṣalāḥ al-Dīn leader. Indeed, it might have had that effect if al-Harawī's ship had not sunk on leaving the island. In the introduction to his *Kitāb al-Ishārāt*, he recalled how he lost some of his papers at sea, suggesting that the letter never reached its intended destination.[26]

By the time Ibn Jubayr met Abū l-Qāsim in 1185, he gave the impression of being materially and psychologically broken. He had also apparently abandoned the overtures to Egypt and had been successfully accused of making advances to the Almohads, with whom the Sicilians had in place an important truce since 1180.[27] Amari's guess that he was in cahoots with *qā'id* Peter is quite feasible, and it was presumably the peace accord that Abū l-Qāsim had sought to wreck or reverse. Speculation aside, he had certainly fallen out of royal favour: a huge fine had been imposed on him; his inherited urban properties had been confiscated; and his humiliating ruin was completed by his house arrest. It is implicit in the accounts of both Ibn Qalāqis and Ibn Jubayr that a threat of bankruptcy would have significantly undermined his ability to act as a viable leader of the Muslim communities because he would no longer have been in a position to lend financial support to his many dependants, ransom prisoners, save Muslims from the burden of the *jizya* or afford to fund 'good deeds' and acts of munificence for which he had gained a great reputation both within and beyond Sicily. His role as benefactor was instrumental in securing his continued leadership, perhaps all the more so if he had been required to gamble on winning a duplicitous political game over his lineage.

Abū l-Qāsim's hereditary claims were key to his role as a pseudo-tribal patriarch but, by his own arguments, such leadership could not have been long-established on the island since it was a product of the Norman, not the Islamic, period. As pragmatic collaborators, the approval of Christian rulers had always been necessary for their continued success and survival: even if the Muslim leaders were not 'appointed' by the king, they could be ruined by him. For his part, Ibn Jubayr was convinced of Abū l-Qāsim's pious virtues and his tearful wish to be sold as a slave in a Muslim land. However, the Sicilian Muslim leader was again sufficiently flexible to co-operate with the king's bidding to extricate himself from deep crisis. He had been given a chance to redeem himself by undertaking what Ibn Jubayr referred to as 'the execution of important, royal, financial business'.[28] Although unspecified, these tasks had clear fiscal implications and he was said to have carried them out as if he were one of the king's own servants. The successful completion of these tasks had ensured his partial restoration to royal favour.

Ibn Jubayr was vague about when this had occurred, other than that it had happened recently. However, the chronology for his fall from grace, subsequent reaccommodation and execution of royal business must have taken place after the Almohad treaty was concluded in early 1180, but before Ibn Jubayr's arrival in Trápani in early 1185. It is very likely, therefore, that the major task Abū l-Qāsim had carried out between these years was linked to the large-scale and politically sensitive preparations for the transfer of men and crown lands to the jurisdiction of Monreale; his most likely input being to have helped establish the boundaries of estates whose descriptions were described in a confirmation of May 1182 and which mention the involvement of 'the shaykhs of Trápani'. Alternatively, it may have been to draw up a controversial list issued in April 1183, which effectively tied 'free' men to the estates on which they were registered.

The polarisation of the Muslim communities

As Ibn Jubayr explained, the political crisis in the Muslim leadership had a religious cutting edge with much wider implications – a potentially catastrophic, domino conversion effect faced the Muslims were Abū l-Qāsim to convert, since the Christians were convinced that the rest of the Muslim population would follow suit.[29] The presumption of 'top-down' conversion is an important one because an analogous dynamic was likely to have applied wherever there were hierarchical socio-religious and political power structures. These, in effect, existed across the entire island from urban notables to provincial strongmen and local *shaykhs* in the outlying estates.

It is not known whether Abū l-Qāsim ever did succumb to the temptation of apostasy but, by 1200, when the house of 'Gaitus Abulcasim' (that is, *qā'id* Abū l-Qāsim) in Trápani was given to the Genoese by Frederick II, he would have been at least sixty years old or had died. His conversion, therefore, seems unlikely. That said, there is reasonable evidence to suggest that not all his children remained Muslim.[30] Given that all his own sons had carefully chosen Arabic names, it is tempting to suggest from a late thirteenth-century document, that the 'late *qā'id* Philip of Ibn Ḥammūd', whose son John was said to be dead by 1289, were the grandson and great-grandson of Abū l-Qāsim. The *qā'id* Philip of Ibn Ḥammūd has been identified with a royal notary in Palermo in 1240. However, the reference to him as *qā'id* implies that he was either considered a Muslim or an Arab-Christian. And if a change in a name from Arabic to one of either Greek or Frankish usage is to be taken as a sign of religious conversion, then it would seem that either Abū l-Qāsim's sons or his grandsons had converted from Islam and were, therefore, better positioned to maintain their association with the administration of Frederick II. If so, then Abū l-Qāsim's delicate policy of collaboration had ended in his sons' religious switch, but their political survival.

Throughout the Norman period, there is very little direct evidence for religious conversion of Muslims and yet, some leading Muslims under Christian rule had converted. As such, almost every known case might appear to be an exception, noted in the sources precisely because of its unusual nature. However, when taken as a whole, a pattern of carrot and stick pressure on the Muslim elites can be seen to have operated – luring their leaders with rewards if compliant; threatening them with ruin if too reluctant to obey. In some cases, the material benefits of conversion were undoubtedly tempting. For example, Roger II's godson, also called Roger – but known as Aḥmad prior to his conversion – was known to have received estates which he donated to the cathedral of Palermo in 1141.[31]

Ibn Jubayr's suggestion that Muslim families were being split by apostasy is supported by rare evidence in the Monreale grants, in which there is an example of a family which had both Christian and Muslim branches. At Corleone, we find four household heads of the Banū Abī Khubza (literally 'father of the loaf'). This clan, with its distinctive name, is not attested in Sicily outside this area. On the list, the Muslims and Christians of Corleone were registered separately. Only ʿAbd Allāh Ibn Abī Khubza was cited among the Christians; the others (Ibn Abī Khubza, Ḥasan Ibn Abī Khubza and ʿAbd al-Raḥmān Ibn Abī Khubza) were not, and so were presumably Muslim.[32] The desirability of conversion clearly differed according to circumstances and status: rural Sicily was not metropolitan Palermo, villeins were not notables. And yet across the entire socio-economic scale we can infer that coercion or financial incentives to convert were present.

Not all of those among the prestigious circle of Muslims with whom Abū l-Qāsim mixed remained true to their faith. Indeed, it was precisely these groups of community leaders who had been earmarked for conversion from the earliest appearance of the Normans in Sicily. The case of the jurist (*faqīh*), Ibn Zurʿa, has come to us via Ibn Jubayr, and illustrates the processes by which the remaining Muslim leadership was worn down.[33] Ibn Jubayr alleged that his conversion was the result of persuasion which ultimately derived from the king himself. In this instance, conversion also served to fill a professional need: the jurist was required to familiarise himself with the Gospels, canon law and the customs of the *Rūm*. He then gave legal opinions and made pronouncements in both Muslim and Christian courts. Quite why a convert was needed and how this arrangement operated in practice is not obvious. Was the court designed to fulfil the needs of the Arabic-speaking Christian community whose numbers were swollen with converts still familiar with only Islamic law but no longer bound by it? Was a convert required because of a lack of legal and linguistic expertise to be found in the local Arab-Christian communities? Or to deal with legal disputes which arose between different faith communities? An argument in favour of the latter is found in the terms of a purchase agreement from 1190 by which a Palermitan Muslim's house was bought by a royal eunuch (*khadīm*),

Niqūla Ashqar.[34] The transaction was specifically said to have been conducted according to Islamic law, and the sale had been authorised by the *dīwān* itself. Again, while it is impossible to gauge how exceptional such deals were, both this case and that of Ibn Zurʿa highlight the practical difficulties and limitations of the Rogerian 'single state, several systems' concept of government which, on the one hand, encouraged integration of key personnel from Muslim to Christian but, on the other hand, advocated separation of the socio-religious institutional frameworks within which they functioned and from which they derived their expertise, connections and power.

Ibn Zurʿa owned a mosque which he converted into a church. Again, this shows the ways in which a 'trickle-down' model of conversion might have worked in practice. However, quite how far the Norman rulers actively and consistently encouraged conversion is unclear, given that, in other respects, the crown wished to maintain a 'protected' community as a useful and taxable underclass based on faith. Such an arrangement can be seen more clearly in the thirteenth-century colony of Lucera created under Frederick II, and was arguably a mirror of the royal enclave that Muslim western Sicily had become on the eve of its wholesale concession to Monreale. These ideas may have even older precedents stretching back as far as the taxable status of the mainland Jews as a single-faith community, or the 'protected' arrangement for Muslims living in Roger II's Malta, where the local Christians had been fined for attacking them. Significantly, this was a fine that they were required to pay annually as a reminder not to interfere with those under royal protection – itself reminiscent of Count Roger I's ban on conversion in the ranks of his army. All such examples serve to argue against a Norman policy of widespread, 'bottom-up' conversion. Rather, they had created a 'glass ceiling' for Muslims such that, beyond certain points, promotion and progress were difficult to attain without conversion. At the same time, the station of all Muslims close to sources of power was never less than precarious.

In spite of the undoubted successes that there had been in the development of Norman-Sicilian statecraft, there were also indications that the shortcomings of royal justice were keenly felt, particularly among the Muslims. Roger's hybrid and experimental version of a *maẓālim* court with its unprecedented mix of both Muslim *qāḍī* and high-ranking Christian officials in attendance had apparently been discontinued, or, since nothing further was heard of it, we can presume it was a failure. Before 1141, al-Māzarī's response to the issue of obedience to royally appointed *qāḍīs* presupposes that some Muslims had questioned their validity. In 1153, Philip's show trial had divulged the incompatibility of Roger's justice and his palace life. In the 1160s, *qā'id* Martin's court had proved unacceptable to Christians because the religious credentials of the judge were not beyond doubt. In the 1180s, the Muslim and Christian courts over which Ibn Zurʿa presided had raised the eyebrows of the Muslim faithful. His conversion was, in Ibn Jubayr's view, justifiable on the dubious grounds of *taqiyya*. But what legal standing could there have been in the eyes of Muslims to opinions and verdicts delivered by an apostate in an Islamic court? Certain aspects of royal justice were in disarray and satisfactory to few, and evidence for the Muslims' lack of faith in royal justice and protection can be shown by the disposition of Quranic teachers in the 'countless' mosques of Palermo. Ibn Jubayr reported that they actively preferred not to accept the legitimacy of the royal *dhimma*. As a result, they surrendered their rights to 'security' for themselves and their property, women and children – the implication being that this was the price for refusing to pay the *jizya*.[35] Perhaps equally important as an indication of the way in which some of the Sicilian Muslims were alienated from the infidel-run state, but had become polarised within their own community, is that the Quranic teachers were said not to have mixed with their co-religionists, suggesting that the safe havens of the mosques, where they spent their time, were also likely to be the gathering points of greatest resistance to Christian rule. In this respect, Ibn Jubayr also mentioned that the Friday sermon, in which politico-religious sentiments might be articulated to a wider audience, had been prohibited. This, incidentally, suggests that the imāms had not been appointed or approved by the state, but were chosen from within the Muslim community itself.

As Ibn Jubayr related, Muslim disaffection during William's kingship was reflected in the distant recollection of the loss of Crete to the Byzantines in 960–1, after which the Muslim population had been whittled away by gradual, but enforced, conversion. Apart from revealing further evidence that medieval Sicily often kept half an eye on events in Crete, this fearful memory was in no way tempered by agreements in place since the Norman conquest which supposedly guaranteed their religious rights to practise Islam, to remain Muslims and not to be subject to unjust infidel laws. Their reported fears for the future can be understood as clear indications that those who were not mindful of the direction of Christian rule from the outset, were so by the 1180s. The Monreale concessions were further material proof of the king's plans for the Muslims.

The historical context of Sicily in the late 1170s and early 1180s is thus central to understanding the strength of feeling which was building among the Muslim communities, particularly when the long-term effects of Latinisation of both state and society are considered, by which the Muslims at all levels had become marginalised and vulnerable. The early capitulation treaties of the eleventh century had committed Muslims to accept *dhimmī* status and, therefore, later committed them to accepting the principles of indirect rule and royal justice as laid out in the Assizes. However, the permanent devolution of royal powers to the abbot of Monreale to act as justiciar over Muslims in his own lands without recourse to higher authority was an imposed innovation which was to the detriment of the Muslims and hardly likely to have been considered acceptable.

Indicators of religious conversion

As we have seen, the palace eunuchs were given names that were mainly to be found in the Latin West and, at various levels, they had had some exposure to Frankish manners and customs too. But this may not have been a shared experience for all converts. Onomastic studies suggest that where there was socio-religious assimilation of the wider Muslim population, this had tended to occur with their Arabic-speaking neighbours – often indigenous Christians of the Greek rite, who usually bore either Greek, or religiously neutral Arabic names. Abundant evidence for personal names comes from administrative lists of men which survive from the 1090s onwards. Those compiled for the Monreale concession were particularly extensive, providing a snapshot of the population in western Sicily in the late 1170s and 80s.

The difficulty of discerning between Muslims, Muslim converts and Arab-Christians is itself an edifying illustration of the socio-religious, cultural and linguistic mélange in many parts of the island. For example, we might be forgiven for assuming that Muḥammad al-Jannān ('the gardener') and Muḥammad al-Ḥarīrī ('the silk weaver') were Muslims. They were not. Rather, they were listed among the Christians of Corleone, but whether they were converts or whether they were products of fuzzy frontier logic and long-term acculturation in rural areas is impossible to say. At Corleone, deep in western Sicily, the presence of Norman lords who had held land there since the conquest, together with the Latin nunnery of Santa Maria Maddalena, may have served to attract or foster a Christian community which accounted for almost one-fifth of the total population registered on estates in the province. Here, 'Greek' Christians with Arabic, Greek, or Arabicised versions of Greek names, were common. Indeed, they even sported two pig farmers – perhaps the result of an empowered minority using dietary regulation to assert frontier *in*tolerance towards their old, Muslim neighbours while flaunting their own religious identity without fear of retribution.

Scattered in documents throughout the twelfth century are telltale instances of naming changes indicative of social flux. In some rare, important examples, families conceded to lords can be traced across two, or even three generations and show a shift in the use of Arabic first names to Greek first names during the Norman period. This may either be interpreted as a sign of religious conversion (from Muslim to Greek Christian), or as a shift in identity within a single faith community (away from Arab-Christian and toward Greek Christian).[36] It is also noticeable that the route of transmission for some modern Sicilian surnames of Arabic origin was through the medium of Greek. The indicators for socio-religious, cultural and linguistic change thus offer evidence for the tattered margins of the Muslim population and their absorption into the Sicilian 'Greek' community by degrees of assimilation. In this sliding reconfiguration of affiliations, some Muslims reinvented their identity as Arabic-speaking Christians, while Arabic-speaking – or Arabic- and Greek-speaking – Christians reverted more openly towards their Greek origins. Ultimately, this memory and identity would gently fade as the Greek Christians became 'Latinised' in both speech and in their attendance at Latin-rite churches. For the Sicilian Greeks, this was a very protracted process, and the Greek rite survived in Calabria into the sixteenth century, as did Italo-Greek dialects which died out only in the 1960s after 2,500 years of use in the region. These complex transitions varied according to time and place and for which the scant surviving evidence is open to interpretation. Nor were personal name changes always a rectilinear progression, as another family of Christians from Corleone show. In this case, the father of a household was called Nikiphoros (Greek: 'bearer of victory'), the son of a certain Majūna. However, their sons were called by Arabic names: Abū Ghālib (literally, 'father of victory') and Khilfa. Here, the generational naming transition was from Greek to Arabic, not vice-versa. The near-equivalent meanings suggest they were toying with the languages and provide a vital shred of evidence for the survival of Arabic–Greek bilingualism among Christians settled on the predominantly Muslim estates of western Sicily.

In both Falcandus and the marginal note of Romuald, it was claimed that the palace eunuchs outwardly looked like Christians. However, such adoption of identical garb for Muslim and Christian men outside the palaces may have been exceptional. During the anti-Muslim riots of 1161–2, Falcandus commented that some Palermitan Muslims, 'by secretly slipping away in flight, or assuming the guise (*habitum*) of Christians, escaped to the safer Saracen towns in the southern part of Sicily'.[37] Here, the implication is that there was a visual difference between Arab-Muslims and Arab-Christians, but it was one which could be easily masked. The late twelfth- or early thirteenth-century illustrations of Peter of Eboli, which include a depiction of the (male) Muslim population of Palermo, also suggest that Muslims looked different, but the images are so deliberately stylised that they demand a degree of figurative interpretation.[38]

In contrast, the young Palermitan Christian women whom Ibn Jubayr saw entering George of Antioch's church were indistinguishable from Muslim women. He added that

> they are eloquent speakers of Arabic and cover themselves with veils. They go out at this aforesaid festival [at Christmas 1184] clothed in gold silk, covered in shining wraps, colourful veils and with light, gilded sandals. They appear at their churches bearing all the finery of Muslim women in their attire, henna and perfume.[39]

The conundrum here is whether the young women were sartorially indistinct from Muslims because they represented a conservative social force and, as indigenous 'Greek' Christians, they were still thoroughly Arabised (socially and culturally) and Arabicised (linguistically)? Or were they first generation converts who had yet to assimilate into the mores of the 'Latin' Christian community which they found quite alien?

If Ibn Ḥawqal's tenth-century description of rural family structures was correct: namely, that the men were Muslim and the women Christian, then it is possible that family units were unusually susceptible to socio-religious splits along gender lines. In this respect, Ibn Jubayr expressed specific concerns about the dissolution of families through apostasy when disputes arose within them. One wonders how much of the Sicilian Muslim community had dissipated unnoticed as the men (some of whom may have been converts to Islam in the first place) gradually adopted the ways of their mothers, daughters, wives and sisters. However, that there is no solution to unravelling this area of the social and cultural history of the island, is in itself proof of the complexity and ill-defined relationships between Sicilian Arab-Christians, 'Greeks' and local Muslims.

The question of dress code is important since it indicates a degree of separation between culture, fashion and the arts on one level, and political power on another, such that it was possible for Christians to emulate luxurious 'Oriental' styles even though Muslims were obviously marginalised as a politico-religious underclass. As we shall see in the next chapter, similarly fraught relationships between society, religion, the arts and political power are also central to interpretations of Arab elements of Sicilian kingship.

Notes

1 On Monreale, see Lynn White, *Latin Monasticism in Norman Sicily* (Cambridge, MA, 1938), pp. 132–45, and G. A. Loud, *The Latin Church* (Cambridge, 2007), *passim*, but especially pp. 329–39. On Nicodemus, see Malaterra, II.45 p. 53, Amatus, VI.19, p. 282. For the early royal charter materials, see Carlo Alfonso Garufi, *Catalogo illustrato del tabulario di Santa Maria nuova in Monreale* (Palermo, 1902). For the Arabic–Greek and Arabic–Latin confirmations, see Cusa, *Diplomi*, pp. 134–286. A new critical edition of these royal documents is being prepared by myself in collaboration with Jeremy Johns.

2 For William II as a restorer, see Matthew, *Norman Kingdom*, p. 203: 'building on the site of the former archbishop's cathedral ... removes any doubt that the king was already planning to revive a metropolitan see'.

3 Ernst Kitzinger, *The Mosaics of Monreale* (Palermo, 1960).

4 For the background to Monreale and its implications for the church, see White, *Latin Monasticism*, pp. 132–44, and Loud, *Latin Church*, pp. 329–39.

5 Richard of San Germano, p. 6. Trans. G. A. Loud (available online): 'It was in fact on the chancellor's advice that the king had the said church of the Virgin built within the diocese of Palermo and secured an archbishop for it from the Roman church. The archbishop realised that this had been done on the chancellor's prompting, for the two hated each other and, while they appeared friendly in public, they freely criticised each other (through envy) in private.'

6 For an analysis of Anglo-Sicilian connections, see G. A. Loud, 'The kingdom of Sicily and the kingdom of England, 1066–1266', *History* 88 (2003): 540–67.

7 This obscure but important reference is to found in G.-B. De Grossis, *Catana Sacra* (Catania, 1654), pp. 85–6.

8 White, *Latin Monasticism*, p. 132.

9 D. B. Gravina, *Il duomo di Monreale, illustrato con cromolitografie di Richter e Frauenfelder* (Palermo, 1859–65; reprinted, Caltanissetta, 2008). The plates from this were lavishly reproduced in the reprinted version, which omits Gravina's 225–page history and commentary.

10 Richard of San Germano, pp. 4–5.

11 John of Salisbury, *Historia Pontificalis*, Marjorie Chibnall (ed.) (Oxford, 1956; reprinted 1998), p. 66.

12 *Falcandus*, Lat. p. 119; Eng. p. 170.

13 For a tentative identification of 'Sedictus' and an Italian translation of Ibn Qalāqis, see A. De Simone, *Splendori e misteri di Sicilia in un' opera di Ibn Qalāqis* (Messina, 1996), p. 19. For the most recent biography of Abū l-Qāsim, an important discussion and full references, see Johns, *Arabic Administration*, pp. 234–42. In part, these respond to the observations made by Amara and Nef (see note 22 below).

14 Falcandus, *Epistola*, Lat. p. 182; Eng. p. 260. In biographical dictionaries, it is clear that the contemporaries of the young Ibn Qalāqis (who died aged thirty-five) did not take him particularly seriously as a learned poet.

15 Amari-Nallino, *SMS*² III:510.

16 Ibn Ẓafar, *BAS*²Ar. II:836; *BAS*² It. II:622. A rough-and-ready English translation of the *Sulwān al-Muṭāʿ* is available as *The Just Prince: A Manual of Leadership*, trans. Joseph A. Kechichian and R. Hrair Dekmejian (London, 2003). Ibn Ẓafar's work itself is so indebted to literary genre that it has virtually nothing to say about the history of the island. The epithet *sāʾid al-sāda* recalls the honorific title *saʿīd al-sudāʾ* ('fortunate of fortunates') used by poets of their patrons. Ibn Qalāqis, for example, repeatedly eulogised a Fatimid eunuch called ʿAnbar in this way. For these extracts, see P. Smoor, 'Ibn Qalāqis and his poems in praise of ʿAnbar, a Fatimid dignitary', in *Maǧāz: Culture e contatti nell'area del Mediterraneo. Il ruolo dell'Islam*, A. Pellitteri (ed.) (Palermo, 2003), pp. 133–49.

17 Ibn Qalāqis mentions an important reference to the *jizya* and the appeal of the Syracusan Muslims to Abū l-Qāsim to save them from its burden. De Simone, *Splendori e misteri*, p. 107.

18 See the classic work by David Abulafia, *The Two Italies. Economic Relations between the Norman Kingdom of Sicily and the Northern Communes* (Cambridge, 1977), pp. 246–50 for a translation and discussion of Abū l-Qāsim and the Genoese.

19 On leaving Sicily, Ibn Qalāqis composed verses, recorded in Ibn Khallikān's biographical dictionary, concerning the winter winds which had initially driven back his ship, suggesting that he had departed very soon after writing his final poem, datable to 29 April 1169.

20 For genealogical charts, see C. E. Bosworth, *New Islamic Dynasties* (Edinburgh, 1996, reprinted 2004), p. 25 for the Idrīsīds, and p. 16 for the Spanish Ḥammūdids.

21 De Simone, *Splendori e misteri*, p. 37.

22 Allaoua Amara and Annliese Nef, 'Al-Idrīsī et les Ḥammūdides de Sicile: nouvelles données biographiques sur l'auteur du *Livre de Roger*', *Arabica*, 48 (2001): 121–7.

23 In order of popularity, the most commonly attested names among twelfth-century Muslim 'villeins' on the island were: ʿAlī, ʿUmar, Muḥammad, Abū Bakr, ʿUthmān, Ḥasan, ʿAbd Allāh, Maymūn, ʿAbd al-Raḥmān, Yūsuf, Aḥmad, Ibrāhīm, Ḥusayn, Makhlūf, Abū l-Qāsim, Ḥammūd, Abū l-Futūḥ, ʿĪsā, Mūsā and Sulaymān. See Metcalfe, *Muslims and Christians*, p. 245 n. 5.

24 Ibn Qalāqis in De Simone, *Splendori e misteri*, pp. 68–9 for Abū l-Qāsim's sons.

25 For the Sicilian plot to restore the Fatimids in 1174, see Ibn al-Athīr, *Al-Kāmil fī l-ta'rīkh*, C. J. Tornberg (ed.), 13 vols (Leiden, 1851–76; reprinted, Beirut, 1965–7), XI:398–9 and 412–14; Eng. II:218–19 and 229–30 for the subsequent Norman attack on Alexandria. The plotters allegedly included the Yemeni poet, ʿUmāra ibn Abī l-Ḥasan, who had powerful enemies and was crucified along with (only) a small handful old Fatimid elites cautioning against lending *too* much credence to this conspiracy theory. For more of the plot, see Pieter Smoor, 'The Yemeni connection in Cairo: a case of revenge?', in *Authority, Privacy and Public Order in Islam*, Proceedings of the 22nd Congress of the Union Européene des Arabisants et Islamisants, 2004, B. Michalak-Pikulska and A. Pikulska (eds) (Leuven, 2006), pp. 223–38; see also Yaacov Lev, *Saladin in Egypt* (Leiden, 1999), pp. 88–94.

26 For a parallel English–Arabic text of al-Harawī, see *A Lonely Wayfarer's Guide to Pilgrimage*, transl. and intro. J. W. Meri (Princeton, 2004), in particular, pp. 4–5, 82–3, 86–7, 142–5.

27 For the meeting with Abū l-Qāsim in Trápani, see Ibn Jubayr, *BAS*[2] Ar. I:101–3; Eng. trans. Broadhurst, pp. 358–60.

28 *bi-l-nufūdh li-l-muhimm min ashghāli-hi al-sulṭāniyya*. On Abū l-Qāsim's undertaking for the king see, Ibn Jubayr, *BAS*[2] Ar. I:102. Eng. trans. Broadhurst, p. 358.

29 Ibn Jubayr, *BAS*[2] Ar. I:103; Eng. trans. Broadhurst, p. 360.

30 For the alleged sons of Abū l-Qāsim, see L. Sciascia, 'I cammelli e le rose. Gli Abbate di Trapani da Federico II a Martino il vecchio', *Mediterraneo medievale: scritti in onore di Francesco Giunta*, 3 vols (Soveria Mannelli, 1989), III:1173–230. See also Johns, *Arabic Administration*, p. 242.

31 For the donation of lands to the Norman archbishop of Palermo, Roger Fesca, by Roger II's convert godson, Aḥmad, see Cusa, *Diplomi*, pp. 16–19.

32 For the Banū Abī Khubza, see Cusa, *Diplomi*, pp. 139, 140, 145 and 164.

33 For the jurist convert, Ibn Zurʿa, see Ibn Jubayr, *BAS*[2] Ar. I:101; Eng. trans. Broadhurst, pp. 357–8.

34 See Cusa, *Diplomi*, pp. 44–6, for the text, and Johns, *Arabic Administration*, p. 323, for a summary and further references.

35 On Muslims apparently outside the *dhimmī* system, see Ibn Jubayr, *BAS*[2] Ar. I: 93; Eng. trans. Broadhurst, p. 349.

36 For the onomastic evidence concerning the conversion of Muslims, see Jeremy Johns, 'The Greek church and the conversion of Muslims in Norman Sicily', *Byzantinische Forschungen*, 21 (1995): 133–57. See also, the various caveats in Metcalfe, *Muslims and Christians*, pp. 86–8.

37 On the flight of Muslims from Palermo disguised as Christians, see *Falcandus*, Lat. p. 70; Eng. p. 122.

38 For the mixed population of Palermo, see *Peter of Eboli*, p. 47.

39 For the Christian women of Palermo, see Ibn Jubayr, *BAS*[2] Ar. I: 94; Eng. trans. Broadhurst, pp. 349–50.

Figure 6 Roger II's embroidered mantle, made in Palermo in 1133–4.

Figure 7 George of Antioch at the feet of the Virgin Mary (Santa Maria dell'Ammiraglio, Palermo).

Figure 8 'Rogerios Rex' crowned by Christ (Santa Maria dell'Ammiraglio, Palermo).

Figure 9 Fountain spout, waterslide and two musicians (Cappella Palatina ceiling, Palermo).

Figure 10 The 'Grizandus inscription' in Latin, Greek, Hebrew and Arabic characters.

Figure 11 Fountain spout (*salsabīl*) and corrugated waterslide (Zisa palace, Palermo).

Figure 12 Christ Pantokrator depicted on the apse of Santa Maria Nuova at Monreale.

12

The art of leisure

The modern historiography of the kingdom

As an imposing example of Norman Sicilian art, the church of Santa Maria Nuova at Monreale was one of a number of new constructions which reshaped the architectural landscape of the island over the course of the twelfth century. In many areas where Christian settlement had increased substantially, the character of urban environs had also been visually transformed. As at Troina in the 1060s where the early Normans occupied the higher part of the town, so too, a century later, Christians dominated the upper reaches of the bustling north-eastern port of Messina. At Érice, in the far west of the island, Muslims were barred from ascending the lofty stronghold which overlooked Abū l-Qāsim's Trápani. In 1184, when Ibn Jubayr visited the once thriving Muslim town of Cefalù, long dominated by Roger's choice cathedral, he noted that the Norman fort on the huge, steep-sided outcrop rising to almost 300 metres was the most impregnable he had ever seen. He also remarked in a casual way that there were relatively few Muslims left in the town below.[1] What he may not have known is that many of the estates he had seen from a distance on which Muslims lived and worked probably belonged to the church as well. In some areas, crosses even served as boundary markers.

Apart from external, visual statements of Christian dominance, Norman-Sicilian art and architecture were also employed to articulate a sense of royal power and authority in a range of less obvious ways. Indeed, one of the most commonly perceived aspects of the kingship was its tripartite nature which drew on, and sometimes combined, elements found in the Latin West alongside those employed by Byzantine and Arab-Muslim dynasties. Internally, Monreale, like Cefalù, the Cappella Palatina and elsewhere, was richly decorated with an elaborate mosaic cycle and a delicately painted ceiling: gems of Byzantine and Islamic art, respectively. Arab-Islamic elements also found expression in the corresponding use of three royal languages: Latin, Greek and Arabic. The implied accommodation and inclusion of such diverse elements by the kings has informed some of the more openly positive verdicts about the kingdom itself. For Francesco Giunta and Umberto Rizzitano, Norman Sicily was a 'land without crusaders' that had 'found a peaceful solution to the problem of relations between different ethno-religious groups' on an island where 'there was never the type of racial intolerance that happened … in other parts of Italy and Europe'.[2] Even more rose-tinted evaluations of the kingdom than this can be found. The romantic vision of the Palermitan historian and archivist, Isidoro La Lumia (d. 1879) was that:

> among all these various peoples [that is, the Saracens, Jews, Franks, Amalfitans and Pisans], there would reign that peaceful tranquillity which is born of mutual respect … The bells of a new church, the chanting of the monks in a new abbey, would mingle with the cry of the *muezzin* from the minaret, calling the faithful to prayer.[3]

It is notable how the imagined peace and harmony in these versions of the history are happily reconciled with assumptions about royal art, architecture, patronage, learning and religious tolerance, while downplaying the Muslim massacres or, later, their mass deportation. When John Julius Norwich gave his exonerating endorsement of the kingdom to the effect that 'nations should be judged on their achievements rather than on their lapses, and to the very end Norman Sicily stood forth in Europe ... as an example of tolerance and enlightenment', he may have been informed more by the kingdom's art than its settlement patterns or politico-religious dynamics.[4]

A common factor in most overarching analyses of the kingdom is an attempt to synthesise accounts of royal programmes behind the art and architecture, often described as eclectic and syncretic, and link them with the kingdom's peoples, customs, languages and faiths. The enormous challenge of such an undertaking comes with a number of caveats for the unwary, not least because of the extreme complexity and variety of the evidence, much of which is the preserve of specialists. Besides which, it is not clear how best to overcome the sheer inconsistency and vagueness of this same evidence, or whether to assume that the kings and their advisers always knew what they intended at the time, or had envisaged what they might have been capable of achieving in the long run. As we will see, a multifaceted confection such as the Cappella Palatina was not merely a receiver of influence, but was also a source and transmitter of influence itself. The flow of skilled artisans and artistic traditions that swirled around the Mediterranean has been of little help in establishing clear lines of transmission and provenance.

No theory to account for the presentation of the kings' power, royal art, the kingdom and its people and religious groups within it, is ever likely to add up to an entirely coherent whole without yielding to at least some element of supposition. Even the loosest interpretations cannot iron out or overlook the kingdom's many contradictions. None the less, the adoption of Islamic art forms and the use of Arabic were significant and offer important insights into Sicilian kingship and the relationships between the rulers and their subjects.

The Cappella Palatina: shifting forms and functions

Much attention has focused on the Cappella Palatina in the main palace of Roger II in Palermo, the famous painted wooden ceiling of which was completed between *c.* 1140 and *c.* 1147.[5] This medieval jewel, however, is not what it at first appears. In Roger's day, the Cappella Palatina was built to fulfil two main functions.[6] First, it served as a royal reception space. Designed to instil a sense of majesty, power and divinely sanctioned authority while doubtless impressing fear, respect and humility on its audience, it drew on precedents found at court in Fatimid Cairo and Byzantine Constantinople. Secondly, it was a royal chapel in which liturgical services were held, probably with rites in three languages, evidence for which is provided by the text and notes of the exceptional trilingual *Harley Psalter* composed before the end of Roger's reign.[7] The forms and functions of the art and architecture recalled those elsewhere in the Mediterranean in very particular ways: in the case of Byzantine art and ideology, for example, by the internal physical arrangements and symbolism of the chapel's layout, design and decoration which encouraged the audience to draw associations between heaven and earth, Christ and king. Certain protocols such as *proskynesis* or prostrate supplication before the ruler were also practised by the Sicilian kings, perhaps in the Cappella Palatina in its role as an audience chamber. In addition, we might note the use of imperial porphyry, the depiction of Roger in imperial garb on coins and in mosaics and the Greek sermons of Philagathos of Cerami, which were delivered in the royal chapel and picked up similar eulogising themes found in Byzantine hymns and propagandist repertoires of the imperial court.[8] Elsewhere, the mosaic portraits of the kings crowned directly by Christ in George of Antioch's church of Santa Maria dell'Ammiraglio, and later at Monreale, had specific and very old Byzantine precedents that were both visual and conceptual; in this instance, a depiction in ivory of Christ's coronation of Emperor Constantine VII Porphyrogenitos (d. 959).[9]

From the perspective of Islamic art, the masterpiece of the original design of the Cappella Palatina is its wooden ceiling, the earliest example of painted figurative representation of its type, fitted with *muqarnas* or stalactite covings, geometric, stella-like designs and Kufic lettering. It is unfortunate that so little of contemporary Islamic art from Fatimid Egypt or Zirid Ifrīqiya has survived with which comparison might be made. Many questions remain too about the ways in which 'Islamic art' should be described when it refers to royal art in medieval Sicily, particularly when it appears in Christian spaces or draws on designs and themes that were found and developed in Islamic art, but which make only passing reference to Islamic doctrine or ideology. Although there is nothing inherently or exclusively 'Islamic' about a geometric design, Muslim scholarship had a long tradition of forging links wherever possible between concepts of legitimate authority and the ways in which this might be expressed, resulting in a highly developed language of government and accompanying art forms with many subtle connotations and semiotic interpretations – for those sensitive to them. In this respect, the Sicilian kings' adoption of models which picked up direct and indirect references to Islam raises fundamentally important questions: what might the kings have intended by doing this? To what extent were they conscious of the implications such models might carry? And what does this tell us of the relationships between them and their Muslim subjects?

Probably designed to have fitted around a door in Roger's Cappella Palatina are two fragmentary Arabic inscriptions, each of which is almost two metres in length, executed in porphyry letters and set into white marble.[10] Their discovery in the royal palace and the mention of the name 'Rujār', further links them to the king. The abstruse epigraphy has been deciphered as: '… and he will hurry to the kiss and to the greeting. Roger vied with …' and '… kiss its corner after clinging [to it], and contemplate the beauty that it contains, and …' Obscure and disjointed as these references are, there is sufficient in them to recognise an allusion to Fatimid protocols which ultimately related to a ritual performed by Muslim pilgrims to Mecca. Compare, for example, an inscription from the Fatimid palace in Mahdiyya which read 'thus, as the pilgrim kisses the corner [i.e. of the Ka'ba in Mecca], we have kissed the walls of your palace'.[11] This also hints that Fatimid influence may have been introduced in Sicily indirectly via Ifrīqiya, a route for which there is precious little surviving evidence for such an important possibility.

The identification of Islamic elements is particularly intriguing in the light of later refurbishments which modified sections of the Cappella Palatina with significant effects. First, under William I, new mosaics were added to the nave and aisles, conspicuously 'Christianising' a semi-secular space which had originally resembled more of a Fatimid or Byzantine chamber hall than a chapel. Further changes made under William II included the addition of more mosaics, a pulpit, font and candelabrum. Some of the chapel's functions and protocols in Roger's day, which were derived from Byzantine and Fatimid precedents, were also supplanted with more Western Latinate elements. Although the Cappella Palatina served as the chosen place for William I's funeral and William II's marriage and second coronation along with that of his queen bride, there is a clear suggestion that, after Roger's death, it lost its function as a reception space, which instead was displaced to rooms elsewhere within the palace. A greater number of canons and installation of new furnishing accords with the idea of its increased use for religious services.[12]

The apparent de-Islamicising of the Cappella Palatina, the removal of its Arabic inscriptions and its subsequent Christianising raises important questions about the extent to which the emergence of the kingdom coincided with evolving politico-religious agendas since the Norman conquest. Such an argument might be strengthened by the observation that the reference to Muḥammad as God's messenger in the Muslim *shahāda* or testimony of faith had been stripped from the *tarì* coins issued by Roger and his Norman forebears in their comital days.[13] It was under Adelaide that coins were first issued with an overtly religious link made in Arabic between the faith and function of the ruler, asserting her claim to be 'the protector of the Christian faith'.[14] With the creation of the kingdom, the mysterious Greek letter *tau* on *tarìs* in the comital period became more clearly a cross when it was also accompanied by the abbreviated Greek sentence IC XC NIKA ('I[ēsou]s Ch[risto]s conquers'). These sources are reminders that Christian rule over Muslim Sicily did not emerge *ex nihilo*, and some of its principal architects were not the kings, but their advisers and officials. It was they who operated in the intricate matrix of power, administration and diplomacy, and who best understood the construct of south Mediterranean government with all its diverse and arcane expressions.[15]

Royal living spaces: luxury and pleasure

After Roger II's campaigns in the 1130s, the kings had only occasionally been seen at the head of an army. Indeed, there is a striking contrast between the early Normans of the Robert Guiscard generation – rough-hewn, mercenary opportunists from impoverished, but upwardly aspiring, backgrounds – and the luxury-loving line of their royal heirs, who were able to revel in the satisfaction of almost every conceivable material need, fashioned to the highest standards of the day. Arguably, their mentality had not changed wholesale: they had always had a fondness for glitter. As Malaterra said of the early Norman adventurers: 'they delight in fancy clothes and elaborate trappings for their horses and decorations on their other weapons'.[16] These flamboyant predilections in the eleventh century were transformed into conspicuous displays of opulence in the twelfth century with access to far greater riches. Fed by the conquered and taxable wealth of a settled, increasingly well-organised kingdom, central and satellite palaces absorbed unfettered expenditure on material pleasures. Indulgent tastes for the marvellous, the innovative and the eye-catching were in keeping with those of Muslim rulers in whose palaces the greatest available level of sumptuousness could be found and imitated – ideas which were also closely bound to concepts of magnificence. Although the kings' lifestyle aspirations were not unique, they were noticed in specific ways by al-Maqrīzī when speaking of Roger II, and Ibn Jubayr, who claimed of William II that 'no Christian king is more given up to the delights of the realm, or more comfort and luxury-living. He is engrossed in the pleasures of his land ... in a manner which resembles the Muslim kings'.[17]

Besides hunting, royal pastimes are more difficult to infer and only fleeting impressions can be gained from narrative sources alone. It is generally accepted that the seated ruler figure, who appears several times on the Cappella Palatina ceiling, is of a western physiognomy and may, therefore, be that of Roger himself.[18] But whether we might justifiably regard other painted figures there as reliably representing aspects of palace life in a realistic way is doubtful. The female dancers, drinkers and banqueters, chess players, wrestlers, hunters on horseback with falcons and duellers are all so indebted to artistic genre that it is unsound to conclude that these were necessarily accurate portrayals of palace life – even if their actions are perfectly credible in the context. That said, it is equally hard to dismiss the idea that the numerous musicians, for example, seen playing percussion, wind and stringed instruments were merely figments of artistic imagination.[19] If the royal palace ever reverberated to *ʿūḍ*s (lutes), *ṭunbūr*s (long-necked lutes), *rabāb*s (bowed, violin-like instruments), *qānūn*s (psalteria), *zamr*s (flutes), *riqq*s (tambourines) and diverse drums, then Roger indeed knew the sounds and rhythms of the Arab-Islamic world. On the other hand, had the king heard the *Officium Peregrinorum*, originally written in Normandy in the late 1000s, but a version of which is known to have been made in Sicily in Roger's day for the cathedral of Palermo, then he would have also been exposed to a liturgical drama of northern European origins with chanting and lyrics to match.[20] The conflicting contrast of styles and contexts provides much food for thought, if little actual nourishment. We can never hope to derive conclusive judgements from such artistic media, but inquiries into royal pastimes, leisure activities and the use of living spaces can inform our wider understanding of the cultural milieux in which the rulers lived. This included, among Latin and Greek facets, an Arab-Muslim element too. It is again worth emphasising that the following discussions are here confined mainly to the Arab-Islamic aspects of the kingdom.

Providing royal services were Muslim women Ibn Jubayr described as *jawārī* and *ḥaẓāyā* (slave girls and concubines), of whom William II was said to have made great use. The connotations of these almost synonymous terms support the idea that they were women with whom the king slept, although their tasks could have been extremely wide-ranging, depending on their age, education and abilities. The girls attracted the attention of Christian commentators too. Indeed, criticism of perceived sexual licentiousness with Saracen women was also directed at Frederick II in the thirteenth century. In Norman Sicily, royal desire for their company, or a reputation for it, was noted by Benjamin of Tudela on his visit in 1170, who reported that the king used to take trips on the lake of the Favara palace in gold and silver-clad boats 'with his women', in what was presumably a hearsay account, and could just as easily have related to his father who was also attested to have had 'palace girls'. It is highly likely that these references point to the contemporary knowledge that there existed a changing core of royal concubines, referred to in Latin as the *puellae palatii*, whom Falcandus said were raped during the sack of the palace in 1161. Their perceived youth was unwittingly revealed by the same author, claiming their beauty had distracted some of the rebels from the task of pillaging.[21] During the king's capture, Maio's temporary replacement, Henry Aristippus, had taken the daring decision to bring some of them back to his own house for a few days, arousing William's displeasure and suspicion – but nothing more at the time, so Falcandus reported.[22]

According to Ibn Jubayr, all the concubines were Muslim, and they had also persuaded the 'Frankish women' of the palace (it is unclear who these might be) to convert to Islam – a claim which the traveller had heard from John the eunuch embroiderer. This may be an implausible, but pious, fiction given that proselytism was punishable by death according to the royal Assizes. However, the twelfth-century chronicler, Bahā' al-Dīn ibn Shaddād recorded an incident in which two servant girls of Joanna ran away to the Muslims after they had accompanied her to Acre in summer 1191, corroborating other reports that the palace women were also only nominally Christian.[23] Unfortunately, little else can be said of these women or their roles, there being no recorded instances of their purchase, manumission, children, legal status, of any influence they might have had, or of how they were organised. For example, although the term *qahramān* ('major-domo') is attested in Sicily, it is not recorded in the feminine (thereby indicating a harem stewardess), nor in a royal context. On the other hand, the reported conversion of the 'Frankish women' in the palace might be taken to imply the existence of a hierarchical arrangement in which Muslim women were a dominant force. We can only speculate about the relationships between the palace women and the palace eunuchs, but since the harem quarters were off limits to all males except the king, they provided the ideal space for the eunuchs to meet and pray undisturbed and unnoticed.

A world of marvels

The hot-house atmosphere and simmering tensions within the main royal palace created a contested and busy space where privacy befitting a king was limited. Besides, it was a space that had been the object of a sustained violation when it was ransacked in 1161. Thus, several minor, satellite palaces served as retreats from the concerns of the day as well as providing some seasonal respite from the extremes of the climate. The main palace was situated within the walls of the medieval city at the very heart of the kingdom, whereas the other palaces were, in the words of Ibn Jubayr, 'disposed around the higher parts like pearls encircling a woman's full throat'.[24] All, bar one, were known by their Arabic names, and by William II's day, besides Roger's foundations of the Mannānī palace (also known as the L'Uscibene, located towards Baida), the Favara (or Maredolce at Brancaccio) with its twin lakes stocked with fish, and the Parco at Altofonte, were added the Cuba and the Zisa, both a short distance to the west of Palermo in the vicinity of park pavilions built by William II. Finally, there was a royal palace at Messina said to be 'white as a dove and overlooking the shore of the sea'.[25] The surviving remains, most notably in the restored Zisa and Cuba, but also in the unrestored al-Mannānī palace, exhibit a high level of Arab-Islamic influence in their execution, fittings and furnishings, and are consistent with many of the activities which were said to take place within their walls.

As in the palaces of medieval Muslim rulers in particular, the quality of life was enhanced by the technologies of the day. Still extant from the Zisa, initiated by William I and finished by his son between 1165 and 1175, is a type of medieval air-conditioning system by which draughts of air were convected between lower and upper floors. The Mannānī palace was fed with cool water via underground conduits which have survived into the modern period. Another inspiration from the Islamic world was the use of ice chiselled from Mount Etna which was transported across the island, some of which was presumably to be flavoured and used as a sorbet, or as a cooling agent.

In some cases, practical devices served to dazzle and astonish the visitor. Indeed, the celebrated palace cartographer, al-Idrīsī, even went so far as to present Roger himself as having once been both an amateur inventor and scientist, to whom an assortment of creations could be personally attributed, but about which Idrīsī politely decline to comment further.[26] Hyperbole and ambivalence aside, reference to royal Sicilian automata and gadgetry can be found in a royal inscription dated to 1141–2 which hailed, in three languages, the latest contraption to grace the palace at Roger's behest. The Latin simply describes it as a 'clock' (*horologium*), the Arabic, as a 'device to observe the hours'.[27] Only from the Greek do we learn that this, 'new wonder ... regulates the stream of flowing essence, giving out unerring knowledge of the hours of time', prompting the convincing suggestion that this was a clepsydra or water-clock. This may be the same automated clock as that mentioned in al-Qazwīnī's thirteenth-century *Athār al-bilād*, as having been made for the king by a certain Maltese mathematician, in which balls were released into a basin to measure the passing of the hours. In the company of the royal clock was a planisphere made by Idrīsī, using a substantial amount of silver. Its precise form remains a matter of conjecture as it was probably looted or destroyed in the sacking of the palace. While undoubtedly impressive constructions, the clock and planisphere were not merely royal showpieces, but as we shall see, were by-products of serious, applied and integrated scientific activity.

The royal menagerie and gift exchanges

Prized for their size, rarity, novelty value or ferocity, collections of exotic animals kept in enclosed areas followed long and well-established traditions from ancient times. Regionally, 'menageries' were wide-ranging in the medieval period from northern Europe to Muslim Spain, Byzantium and the Islamic lands.[28] Evidence for the existence of a royal menagerie in Norman Sicily comes at the moment of its demise. The German chronicler Otto of Saint Blasien recorded that, on Henry VI's entry to Palermo in 1194, 'he ordered his troops to break into the great royal garden, which was surrounded on all sides by a wall and filled in a charming way with all sorts of beasts – these animals were consumed to supply his army'.[29] In the thirteenth century, Frederick II, like his grandfather in Germany, was also known to have kept a menagerie. The south Italian collection was not exceptional for its inclusion of giraffes, elephants, camels, lions, lynxes, apes, bears, peacocks and ostriches, some of which also featured in military campaigns and imperial processions. Notable were sundry sub-Saharan quadrupeds, although species of big cat were to be found across north Africa that have subsequently disappeared from these areas. By Frederick's day, leopards were bred in the Muslim colony at Lucera on the Italian mainland. If the training of some animals implies an underlying scientific interest in them, then it was of only minimal scope and directed towards practical ends. Most famous in this respect was Frederick's treatise, *The Art of Hunting with Birds*, which drew on an Arabic original.

Apart from the relatively minor purposes of animal husbandry, breeding and the provision of an entertaining spectacle, menageries played an important role in gift exchange between rulers. Given, received and produced in Sicily, ivory caskets with delicately carved reliefs, some depicting exotic fauna, such as giraffes, formed part of prestigious and lucrative long-distance commerce which, in this case, extended into Africa and the sub-Sahara from where the tusks had been initially transported. Material and literary evidence of gift exchange with Muslim rulers from this period shows a high level of sophistication and expense – a far more developed and mutually understood activity than in the days of Bertha of Tuscany. Most notable from Islamic regimes came gifts from the Fatimid rulers, such as a jewel-studded, ceremonial parasol (*miẓalla*) and, most probably, a rock crystal ewer.[30] The use of ceremonial parasols in Sicily was also unambiguously attested in two later Arabic sources, Ibn Ḥammād and al-Maqrīzī.[31] The conspicuous use of gilded saddles in Muslim Sicily is attested by Amatus of Montecassino, and further allusions can be found in both Alexander of Telese and al-Maqrīzī when speaking of Roger II, and in Otto of Saint Blasien when referring to Henry VI in Palermo.[32] However, apparel such as the ceremonial saddle (*ghāshiyya*) is more closely associated with military dynasties such as the Seljuks rather than the Fatimids and may not, in these instances, be specifically related to either. The same might be said of gilded banners used in Roger's processions, as mentioned by Maqrīzī.

In Norman Sicily, as elsewhere, certain animals assumed particular symbolic significance. The motif of the lion, for example, was often linked to the Norman king and appears numerous times in Sicilian art in royal contexts, such as above throne platforms. Roger himself even came to be remembered as having a face like one.[33] On the other hand, camels carried specific associations in the medieval Christian mind as beasts of the Saracens, four of them having been sent by the Normans to Pope Alexander II after the battle of Cerami in 1063. In the thirteenth century, Frederick II was known to have bred camels, a pastime which may have been discontinued as a consequence of this animal's negative association with the 'Saracens'.[34] Among depictions of animals in Sicilian art and sculpture, as in the repertoire of medieval bestiaries in general, there frequently featured the theme of two mismatched animals in combat, usually with one about to emerge as the victor. Noteworthy in this respect, and for the view it offers about the king and his conquered people, is the dramatic imagery of two lions tearing out the throats of two moribund camels, the subject of Roger II's silk-embroidered mantle. One could be forgiven for interpreting this as a gory masterpiece of politico-religious triumphalism.[35] (See fig. 6 on p. 230.)

Recreating paradise on earth

If Roger's mantle to symbolise Christian domination at Muslim expense was ultimately indebted to the traditions of an Islamic institution, the *ṭirāz*, then the royal gardens offer unusual insights into the application of religious ideology from a quite different perspective. The diversions of the pleasure garden, fishing lake and hunting park were widely attested and developed with the multiplication of the palaces. Degrees of separation according to location, purpose, rights of tenure and economic value were made between the kingdom's creatures. However, the all-possessing kings even claimed rights to the fish in the sea, with the concession to 'hunt' them, especially tuna, being a well-attested royal benefice. Romuald reported that Roger II enjoyed a moderate amount of hunting in the extensive royal park outside Palermo which was planted with trees and stocked with animals for the hunt such as fallow and roe deer and wild boar.[36] From Ibn Jubayr, we learn that 'the king [William II] roams through the gardens and courts for amusement and pleasure', and that the food cooked for him came from a trusted Muslim chef.[37] Written evidence by invited Muslim guests to the palaces, who occasionally recalled their sojourns, when added to the surviving archaeology, repeatedly suggests that the gardens were carefully laid out and appointed with very particular fixtures.[38] For instance, at the palace of the Zisa, as well as in the dilapidated al-Mannānī, there can still be seen an ornate combination of fountain spout and corrugated waterslide (*salsabīl* and *shadirwān*). In both cases, although only visible now at the Zisa, this led into a sunken water channel, and out into a garden area via a pool.[39] These types of installation also appear in a small painting on the ceiling of the Cappella Palatina. (See figs 9 and 11 on pp. 232–3.) Clearly, this is an inappropriate place to recall in detail the well-known relationships between garden architecture and descriptions of paradise in the Qur'ān as a garden, or series of gardens, but it is of importance to note that it is for this reason that many decorative garden features carried strong Quranic resonances for Muslims. *Salsabīl*, for instance, was the water fountain that Muslim faithful could expect to see in paradise, and an example of one also appears among the remains of the Qalʿat Banī Ḥammād in eastern Algeria, itself the closest surviving precedent for the Zisa palace.[40]

A common motif in Islamic water gardens was to reproduce the Quranic idea of 'gardens beneath which rivers flow'. The gardens themselves were often divided into four parts, again strongly reminiscent of Quranic descriptions.[41] Contemporary, independent accounts of the palace gardens in Palermo corroborate the idea that these enclosed royal spaces were designed to reflect specific elements of heavenly topography. A poetic, eye-witness description by ʿAbd al-Raḥmān al-Buthīrī (from Butera) of Roger's al-Mannānī palace drew attention to 'its untrodden gardens which have returned the world to bloom,/ the lions of its waterslide (*shadirwān*) which pour forth abundant waters (*miyan kawthariyya*),/its quarters Spring (*al-rabīʿ rubūʿa-hā*) with its beauty has draped with marvellous clothes'.[42] The extant spout of the *salsabīl* presumably led down the *shadirwān*, while other phrases pick up widely understood Quranic references to the river of *al-Kawthar* ('Abundance') in paradise. The royal garden's quadripartite layout is strongly implied by the meaning of the root *r-b-ʿ*, which is tightly bound to the idea of fours or quarters. In addition, an Arabic inscription in the Zisa refers to the area as *Jannat al-Arḍ* ('paradise on earth'), from where the later medieval microtoponym *Genoard* is derived.[43] However, even if the Islamic design idea is not accepted at a literal level, there can be no doubt that this was how it was perceived by Muslim eye-witnesses familiar with the Islamic references. The contrasting perception with Latin descriptions is striking: they are devoid of religious imagery, choosing to interpret the gardens as entirely secular spaces. Thus, Romuald simply remarked that, 'at that time, king William had a lofty and ingeniously designed palace built near Palermo which he called the Zisa (*Sisa*), surrounding it with beautiful fruit trees and delightful pleasure gardens (*viridariis*), furnished with many streams and splendid fish ponds'.[44]

Medieval Sicilian Orientalism?

The ways in which trappings, symbols, protocols – and, indeed, the very mystique of contemporary Arab-Islamic art forms – were borrowed to suit the political ideologies of a fledgling kingship, constituted one of its defining characteristics, and also reflected the outlook and tastes of the realm's authors who created and fashioned it. The adoption and emulation of such models was, in a certain sense, superficial since their coded religious meaning was lost in translation when read by a Christian audience. The effects of the tripartite facets to the kingship were dazzling and disorientating, perhaps not always intentionally so, but their shifting aspects left the kingship as open to interpretation then as it is today.

Muslim observers were particularly impressed by the use of Arabic in the palaces such that each of the kings, as well as George of Antioch and other officials, were attested as knowing Arabic, an observation which was regarded as positive and even marvellous. In the Arab-Islamic world, this type of knowledge distinguished them as more enlightened than barbarous Franks or crusaders.[45] Yet the widespread use of Arabic as a royal language is clear evidence that the kings could not have necessarily or exclusively associated it with Islam. It was precisely this type of disassociation of Islam from wider Arab-Muslim culture which helped allow the Sicilian kings to appropriate art, architecture, language, administration, protocols and so on from 'Islamic' sources without compunction (unless the references were overtly Islamic) for rulers who were otherwise most Christian.

On the other hand, Muslim visitors to the palaces were placed in the company of the palace eunuchs, Arabic-speaking officials, or alternatively, they were admitted as bona fide guests of leading Sicilian Muslim notables. In each case, their guides to the delights of the palaces, their informants and their interpreters of the kingdom were Sicilian Muslims who were, by and large, loyal supporters of the crown, or at least were prepared to work for the best within the framework of Christian rule. Indeed, to this Muslim audience, as to the wider Arab-Muslim world, whose knowledge of the kingdom was supplemented by their reports, evidence suggests that the kingdom's Islamic art and Arabic language transmitted an altogether different set of messages, to the effect that the kings were imagined to be in some sense Islamophile, the art inspired and esoteric, and that the Frankish conquerors had themselves been opened up to the rightly guiding influences of Islam. The rumour recorded by Ibn al-Athīr, which had circulated around Islamic lands, was that Roger himself was a Muslim who listened to a prescient Muslim sage above all others.[46] Idrīsī even said of Roger that, 'in his faith, he was indebted to the religion of justice [i.e. Islam]'.[47]

The kings and their peoples: the *populus trilinguis* and the Muslims

The vexed questions of the projection of royal image and power, and how the Norman kings and their Muslim subjects understood one another, is also central to the interpretation of another characteristic feature of government on the island – that is, the issues surrounding the so-called 'Trinacria' tradition. Ensembles in threes were a common topos in the medieval period, and in the case of Sicily, the island's distinctive shape was well-known to the ancients who used the figurative Greek phrase *treis arkai* to refer to the island's three promontories. A three-pointed design also appeared on Syracusan coinage in the age of the ancient Greek tyrants. Sicily's triangularity was equally well-known to the Muslim cartographers.[48] Certainly by the second half of the twelfth century, one of the survivors of Stephen of Perche's entourage, Peter of Blois, was able to reconnect to the classical tradition and write (albeit disparagingly) of 'Trinacria' on the assumption that it would be understood as a synonym for Sicily. The topography of Palermo itself was described in terms of a three-way division in Falcandus' *Letter to Peter*.[49]

Perhaps most notably, tripartite division was a prominent visual theme in Peter of Eboli's illustrations and his historical poem in which is found his famous line, 'till now a prosperous city [Palermo], its people endowed with three languages', a conscious echo of the Roman-African author, Apuleius, who also spoke of 'the three-tongued Sicilians'.[50] At face value, the *populus trilinguis* appears to refer to two connected ideas: first, that there was a single people; and, secondly, that between them, these people used three languages. However, this ethnic and linguistic description was modified by Peter's illustrations which introduced cultural and implicitly religious distinctions by showing *three* sets of peoples, articulated with all their medieval ambiguities, stereotypically differentiated by appearance and dress and segregated into particular districts of the city. For example, in his figurative sketch of three sets of royal notaries, the rubric describes each as 'Greeks', 'Saracens' and 'Latins'.[51]

The proposition that a single *populus trilinguis* with an overarching identity or binding sense of loyalty which transcended social, ethnic, linguistic and/or religious distinction had been forged, has prompted some historians to argue that this had been a 'Norman policy', the maintenance of which was vital to the integrity of the kingdom.[52] There is much to be said for such an interpretation which links socio-religious with political considerations, but it is a problematic theory, primarily because it is not clear whether the kingdom's peoples could have been coherently understood at that time in such terms.

A medieval audience was unlikely to have been able to elicit unequivocal answers to the question of who spoke which language without a resort to question-begging assumptions. Areas of confusion about what counted as a language included issues of naming and reference between 'tongues' and 'letters', compounded by the not uncommon use of different scripts to represent the same language. Besides which, the island's bilingualism was a widespread phenomenon with some, perhaps many, indigenous Christians speaking both Greek and Arabic. On the other hand, *tri*-lingualism appears to have been very rare, even in the royal administration, and it is quite clear that the kingdom's 'Latins' were the least likely to have known any Arabic or Greek.

The question of language is a revealing one. 'Greeks' were considered to be 'Greek' by a 'Latin' audience irrespective of their actual spoken language(s), and even less by their supposed ethnicity or cultural background. Politically, the kingdom's Greeks had long since ceased to come under Byzantine rule, and had shaken off the perfidious behavioural traits as understood by Latin authors of the eleventh century. Their churches may have recognised the primacy of the pope at Rome, but their congregations were 'Greek' because Greek was the language of their liturgy. The same thinking applied to the kingdom's 'Latin' community, whose cultural, ethnic and linguistic range was far wider than the Greeks, but who could be considered 'Latin' because of their affiliation with the Latin-rite Church. It would thus have been problematic at the time to have used language as an indubitable determinant of religion and a sure-fire indication of ethnicity, especially on an island where such distinctions between Arab-Muslims, Arab-Christians and Greeks were so hazy. Moreover, outside royal circles, it was commonly received wisdom that there was a multitude of variously described 'peoples' to be found in the kingdom: Normans, Lombards, Langobards, Greeks, Genoese, Saracens, Jews and so on. Woolly medieval thought could define these 'peoples' in any number or a combination of ways: by region, race, religion, language, law, culture or custom.

If some common views of a divided population were more muddled than others, the perception of the kingdom's peoples was at its clearest in royal circles. Something of their relative rank may be gleaned from the positions of different languages when they occurred in a royal context. For example, in the main palace, the three layers of epigraphic script which commemorated the water-clock had Latin at the top, Greek next and then Arabic at the bottom. It is tempting to think that this reveals a hierarchical arrangement. When these three languages appeared in vertical columns in the *Harley Psalter*, the preferential position of Latin was at the centre, indicating that the kingdom's peoples were royally perceived as distinct and unequal.

If, instead of a single people, there was a royal divide and rule strategy of engineering a kingdom with diverse peoples, then it was at its most consistent and cogent when understood as a statement about different belief communities, expressed by the characters in which each wrote their holy texts or conducted their rituals. In support of this, multilingualism was not always royally perceived in threes. There were, on occasions, four religious distinctions: Latin-rite Christians, Greek-rite Christians, Muslims and Jews. Hence, the quadriliteral Grizandus inscription could only have had the Jews in mind in order to account for one of its four scripts being in Judeo-Arabic (Hebrew characters and Arabic language), while the others were in Latin, Greek and Arabic.[53] Such an inscription, made in 1149, if understood in the context of Roger's alleged efforts to convert Jews and Muslims makes a thought-provoking interpretation. However, it is notable and empirically obvious, that the Arabic characters again occupy the lowest part of the inscription.

Legally, the Sicilian Saracens acquired and maintained their valid identity as a community under Islamic law only as long as the bilateral agreement held firm which bound them in subordination to the authority of sacral kingship. Once the Muslim revolt broke out, this legal keystone of the Norman state collapsed. Legal interpretations may help to account for the inelegant position of the kingdom's Arabic-speaking Christians, or rather, such a scheme would have left little place for Christians of an Arabic rite since most of them counted themselves as 'Greeks'. Melkites (Orthodox Christians of the Arabic rite), did not fit in easily as one of the peoples of the kingdom since they did not have their own distinct laws in Sicily when the kingdom was created because they had attended Greek-rite churches under the Muslims. Indeed, it is notable that the only credible evidence for the existence of an Arabic rite in Sicily is restricted to the exceptional *Harley Psalter* of the Cappella Palatina. The Arabic rite, performed for a very limited period and not apparently outside a royal context, may thus have been another failed, Rogerian experiment.

Overall, there is sufficient evidence to suggest that the kings *did* see rough degrees of separation between communities, and that these were understood primarily in terms of religious difference. In this respect, even multilingual, multicultural kings could not embody all the essential attributes of people of different faiths over whom they ruled. Instead, the self-reflexive, tripartite, cultural aspects of Sicilian kingship merely drew inspiration from a range of media associated with each of the kingdom's three main religious groups. However, it is significant that such exclusive triplet combinations were not propagated around the kingdom as exempla for others to patronise and emulate. The kaleidoscopic ensembles which comprised the linguistic, cultural, artistic and architectural paradigms of the palaces were so closely associated with the kings that they constituted a royal monopoly. Thus, although the medium of royal art served several purposes, the kings chose not to use it to impress ideals of pluralism, with their inherent sense of toleration, as a form of cultural hegemony onto society. Although some Arab-Muslim leaders had been pushed towards Latin Christianity, the kings' reluctance to promote either cultural diversity or the acceptance of religious diversity among the privileged Latin classes helps to explain why inter-communal dividing lines deepened over time and eventually fractured along them.

Notes

1 For his remarks about Cefalù, see Ibn Jubayr, *BAS*[2] Ar. I:89; Eng. trans. Broadhurst, p. 344.
2 F. Giunta and U. Rizzitano, *Terra senza crociati: popoli e culture nella Sicilia del Medioevo* (Palermo, 1991).
3 I. La Lumia, *Guglielmo II detto il Buono: La Sicilia sotto il suo regno* (Palermo, 1867, reprinted 2000), pp. 32–3. The quotation was translated and cited in full by J. J. Norwich, *The Normans in Sicily. The Magnificent Story of 'The Other Norman Conquest'* (London, 1992), p. 355. Omnibus edition of *The Normans in the South 1016–1130* (London, 1967) and *The Kingdom in the Sun 1130–1194*,(London, 1970).
4 Norwich, *Normans in Sicily*, p. 751.
5 For the tortuous dating argument, see Johns's article in Ernst. J. Grube and Jeremy Johns, *The Painted Ceilings of the Cappella Palatina* (Genova and New York, 2005), pp. 1–12.
6 On the changing form and functions of the royal 'chapel', see William Tronzo, *The Cultures of his Kingdom: Roger II and the Cappella Palatina in Palermo* (Princeton, 1997); Ugo Monneret de Villard, *Le pitture musulmane al soffitto della Cappella Palatina in Palermo* (Rome, 1950).
7 The royal, trilingual psalter is in the British Library (Harley 5786). For a photograph, see Karla Mallette, *The Kingdom of Sicily, 1100–1250: A Literary History* (Philadelphia, 2005), p. 28.
8 Tronzo, *Cultures of his Kingdom*, p. 121. On the use of porphyry, see Francesco Gandalfo, 'Porphyry', in *Nobiles Officinae: perle, filigrane e trame di seta dal Palazzo Reale di Palermo*, Maria Andaloro (ed.), 2 vols (Catania, 2006), II: 417–23. Purple, royal garb was said to have been stolen during the sack of the palace. See *Falcandus*, Lat. p. 56; Eng. p. 109. For the homilies, see Filagato da Cerami, *Omelie per i vangeli domenicali e le feste di tutto l'anno*, Giuseppe Rossi-Taibbi (ed.) (Palermo, 1969).
9 For a comparison, see figures 145–6 in Tronzo, *Cultures of his Kingdom*. On the Martorana, see Ernst Kitzinger, *I mosaici di Santa Maria dell'Ammiraglio a Palermo* (Palermo, 1990).
10 Jeremy Johns, 'The Norman kings of Sicily and the Fatimid caliphate', *Anglo-Norman Studies*, 15 (1993): 148–53, and also Jeremy Johns, 'Three fragments [*sic*] Arabic inscriptions from King Roger's palace in Palermo', *Nobiles Officinae*, I:765–7. For illustrations, see I:498–501. For the block fragments from Messina, see the catalogue entry by Annliese Nef, I:502–9 and 766–70.
11 For additional analysis, see Tronzo, *Cultures of his Kingdom*, pp. 101 and 105.
12 Tronzo, *Cultures of his Kingdom*, pp. 128–9.
13 Jeremy Johns, 'I titoli arabi dei sovrani normanni di Sicilia', *Bollettino di Numismatica*, 6–7 (1986): 11–54 (pp. 14 and 19). The *shahāda* appeared on the first Norman *tarìs* issued by Guiscard from 1072, but was discontinued post-1130. On Sicilian coinage generally, see Lucia Travaini, *La monetazione nell'Italia normanna* (Rome, 1995). A number of well-known examples show that it was not uncommon for fledgling

medieval regimes to adopt non-native models of coinage. Two famous examples included Offa of Mercia's use of the *shahāda* and early Islamic coins which depicted Zoroastrian fire-temples and the face of Khusraw II, the defeated Sassanid Persian emperor. A thirteenth-century example from Byzantium of the treatment of a plate with an Arabic inscription that included the name Muḥammad is discussed in Tronzo, *Cultures of his Kingdom*, p. 138.

14 *nāṣira li-dīn al-Naṣrāniyya*. See Johns, *I titoli arabi*, p. 38.

15 For an authoritative discussion on the Fatimids and titulature, see Johns, *Arabic Administration*, pp. 257–84, especially pp. 268–74.

16 For the early Normans' attraction to fine clothes and accoutrements, see Malaterra I.3, p. 8.

17 Ibn Jubayr, *BAS*[2] Ar. I:86; Eng. trans. Broadhurst, p. 341. For the English translation of Maqrīzī on Roger II, see Johns, *Arabic Administration*, p. 82.

18 On the seated ruler figure, possibly Roger II, see Johns, *Norman Kings of Sicily*, pp. 155–6.

19 David Gramit, 'I dipinti musicali della Cappella Palatina di Palermo', in *Scrinium: quaderni ed estratti di Schede Medievali*, 7 (1986): 5–55. For a selection of illustrations, see Grube and Johns, *Painted Ceilings of the Cappella Palatina*, pp. 46, 48, 52, 54–5, 59–61, 64, 69–72, 84, 91, 128–9 and 146–51.

20 A reproduction of the *Officium Peregrinorum* is available as *Le Jeu des Pèlerins d'Emmaüs: Drame liturgique du XII*[e] *siècle*, dir. Marcel Pérès (Harmonia Mundi compact disc, HMC 901347, 1990). On the differences between Norman and Italian chant, see David Hiley, 'The chant of Norman Sicily: interaction between the Norman and Italian traditions', *Studia Musicologica Academiae Scientiarum Hungaricae*, 30, 1/4 (1988): 379–91.

21 On the sack of the palace, *Falcandus*, Lat. p. 56; Eng. p. 109.

22 For the harem girls' sojourn at the house of Aristippus, see *Falcandus*, Lat. p. 69; Eng. p.120.

23 *The Rare and Excellent History of Saladin*, trans. D. S. Richards (Aldershot, 2002), p. 154.

24 Ibn Jubayr, *BAS*[2] Ar. I:93; Eng. trans. Broadhurst, p. 348.

25 Ibn Jubayr, *BAS*[2] Ar. I:86; Eng. trans. Broadhurst, p. 340.

26 Idrīsī, *BAS*[2] Ar. I:31. *BAS*[2] It. I:35. P. A. Jaubert's *La Géographie d'Edrisi traduite de l'Arabe en Français* (Paris, 1838), reprinted with an introduction by Henri Bresc and Annliese Nef. It should be noted that the complex and, arguably, ambivalent Arabic panegyric of Roger has yet to be satisfactorily rendered into any language.

27 *bi-ʿamal hādhā l-āla li-raṣad al-sāʿāt*. For a recent transcription of the royal trilingual clock inscription in the Cappella Palatina, see Jeremy Johns, 'Trilingual inscription from the clepsydra of King Roger', in *Nobiles Officinae*, I:772–3. On the mechanical timing device of Ibn al-Samanṭī, see al-Qazwīnī, *BAS*[2]Ar. I:157–8; *BAS*[2] It. I:241.

28 A stimulating introduction to medieval Mediterranean menageries is provided by N. P. Ševčenko, 'Wild animals in the Byzantine park', in *Byzantine Garden Culture*, A. Littlewood, H. Maguire, J. Wolschke-Bulmahn (eds) (Washington, DC, 2002), pp. 69–86. For images of animals in Sicilian art and numerous comparisons elsewhere, see Grube and Johns, *The Painted Ceilings of the Cappella Palatina*, pp. 168–243.

29 The Chronicle of Otto of St Blasien, in *MGH SRG*, 47:61–2; translation by Graham Loud available online.

30 On the use of rock crystal and the possible route of transmission for a ewer from Fatimid Egypt to Roger's Palermo to Abbot Suger of Saint-Denis (d. 1151), see Rudolf Distelberger, 'Rock crystal', in *Nobiles Officinae*, II: 414–16.

31 For ʿAbbasid and Fatimid processions, see Paula Saunders in *EI*[2] on *mawākib*, VI:849. See also Sanders, *Ritual, Politics and the City in Fatimid Cairo* (Albany, NY, 1994).

32 For references to gilded saddles in a royal context, see Amatus, V:24, p. 142; Alexander of Telese II:5, p. 26; Otto of St Blasien, *MGH SRG*, 47:63, and al-Maqrīzī, *Kitāb al-Muqaffā*, M. al-Yaʿlawī (ed.), 8 vols (Beirut, 1991), III:19–20. For English translations of the relevant passages in al-Maqrīzī and Ibn Ḥammād, see Johns, *Arabic Administration*, pp. 81–2 and p. 265.

33 For the retrospective description of Roger II as having a 'lion-like face', see *Romuald*, Lat. p. 237; Eng. p. 221 For the common depiction of lions in Norman-Sicilian art, see the illustrations in Grube and Johns, *Painted Ceilings of the Cappella Palatina*, pp. 192–223.

34 Julie Taylor, *The Muslims in Medieval Italy: The Colony at Lucera* (Lanham, MD, 2003), p. 102.

35 For more on lions and what the royal mantle might symbolise, see William Tronzo, 'King Roger's mantle, part and whole', in *Nobiles Officinae*, II:443–6.

36 *Romuald*, Lat. p. 232; Eng. p. 219. For an erudite survey of the kingdom's human–animal relations, see Salvatore Tramontana, *Il regno di Sicilia: uomo e natura dall'XI al XIII secolo*, (Torino, 1999).

37 Ibn Jubayr, *BAS*[2] Ar. I:86; Eng. trans. Broadhurst, p. 340. Some culinary customs have endured, most distinctively the Sicilian cassata. The professional name *al-Qassāṭī* is first attested in 1178 in the province of Corleone.

38 Among many articles on medieval Sicilian gardens, see Henri Bresc, 'Les jardins de Palerme (1290–1460), *Mélanges de L'École Française de Rome. Moyen Âge-Temps Modernes*', 84/1 (1972): 55–127, reprinted in *Politique et société en Sicile XII*[e]*–XV*[e] *siècles* (Aldershot, 1990); also, Paola Caselli, 'La Conca d'oro e il giadino della Zisa a Palermo', in *Il Giardino islamico: architettura, natura, paesaggio*, A. Petruccioli (ed.) (Milan, 1994), pp. 185–200. It is not impossible that the royal palace gardens inspired the construction of the water garden of Everswell, first attested in 1165, for Henry II's Woodstock palace. See, *The History of the King's Works*, H. M. Colvin *et al.* (eds), 6 vols (London, 1963), II:1014–17. Outside royal contexts, the beauty of Palermitan gardens was mentioned by Arab-Muslim and Latin authors in references spanning both the Islamic and the Norman periods, notably by Ibn Ḥawqal, al-Idrīsī and Falcandus, *Letter to Peter.* For a brief, poetic description of the Favara palace gardens, including a marble fountain, see Ibn Qalāqis in De Simone, *Spendori e misteri*, pp. 63–7.

39 G. Marçais, 'Salsabīl et Šādirwān', in *Études d'Orientalisme dédiées à la mémoire de Lévi-Provençal*, 2 vols (Paris, 1962), II:639–48.

40 On architectural forms and precedents, see U. Scerrato, 'L'architettura', in *Gli arabi in Italia*, F. Gabrieli and U. Scerrato (eds) (Milan, 1979), pp. 307–42.

41 In the Qur'ān, the phrase, 'gardens beneath which rivers flow', describing heaven, occurs twenty-one times. On the notion of a quadripartite garden in paradise ('two gardens on the right hand and the left'), see Qur'ān:34.15. For the only mention of *Salsabīl* in the Qur'ān, see Qur'ān:76.17–18, 'There are they [i.e., the faithful] watered with a cup whereof the mixture is of Zanjabil / (The water of) a spring

therein, named Salsabil'. Trans. M. M. Pickthall.

42 Cited in Imād al-Dīn al-Iṣfahānī, *BAS*² Ar. II:706–7; *BAS*² It. II:436–7.

43 For reference to William II (*al-musta'izz*), and paradise on earth (*jannat al-arḍ*) as part of the luxury and splendour which befits the king, see Amari, *Epigrafi*, p. 81.

44 *Romuald*, Lat. pp. 252–3; Eng. p. 237 (with minor adjustments).

45 On the question of communication around the palaces, see Metcalfe, *Muslims and Christians*, pp. 99–113.

46 For the predicted fall of Edessa in 1144 by a prescient Muslim scholar (*min al-'ulamā' al-Muslimīn*) acting as counsellor to Roger II, see Ibn al-Athīr, *BAS*² Ar. I:328–9, *BAS*² It. I:463–4.

47 For Idrīsī on Roger's faith and Islam (*wa-dāna fī millati-hi bi-dīni l-'adl*), see *BAS*² Ar. I.30; *BAS*² It. I:33.

48 On the classical Trinacria, see Virgil, *Aeneid*, iii.429, 440, 582 and Ovid, *Metamorphoses*, v.476, xiii.724–7.

49 Peter of Blois, Epistle 43, in *Patrologia Latina*, J. P. Migne (ed.) (Paris, 1844–64, col. 134. *Falcandus*, Lat. pp. 180–1; Eng. pp. 260–1.

50 *hactenus urbs felix populo dotata trilingui*. See *Peter of Eboli*, line 56, pp. 44 and 45, cf. Apuleius, *Metamorphoses*, 11.5.2.

51 For Greek, 'Saracens' and Latin notaries, and the three peoples of Palermo, see the sketches in *Peter of Eboli*, pp. 59 and 47, respectively.

52 Johns, *Arabic Administration*, pp. 284–6. For longer-term developments, see the important article by Henri Bresc, 'La formazione del populo siciliano', in *Politique et société en Sicile, XIIe–XVe siècles* (Aldershot, 1990), reprinted from *Tre millenni di storia linguistica della Sicilia, Atti del Convegno della Società italiana di Glottologia, Palermo*, 1983 (Pisa, 1985); see also Jeremy Johns, 'The Arabic inscriptions of the Norman kings of Sicily: a reinterpretation', in *Nobiles Officinae*, II:324–37.

53 For a translation of the inscription, see Jeremy Johns, 'Three funerary memorials to Anna and Drogo, parents of the royal priest Grizandus', in *Nobiles Officinae*, I:775–8.

13

The science of power

The Sicilian translation movement and transfer of knowledge

Between the eighth and tenth centuries, many works of ancient Greek and Hellenistic thinkers reached new and appreciative audiences via their eventual translation into Arabic in Abbasid Iraq. During the twelfth and thirteenth centuries, the kingdom of Sicily was second only to centres in the Iberian peninsula, particularly Toledo, as a site for a return wave of translations when Latin versions of Greek and Arabic literary and scientific texts came to be made and diffused in Europe. Sicily did not rival Spain in the quantity of its outputs, but it had an important advantage with its pool of educated, bilingual Arabic–Greek and Greek–Latin translators, as well as a greater access to texts in Greek and/or classical Greek authors whose works existed in Arabic. Patronage in Norman Sicily also provided a forum for scholarship which played an important role in the 'twelfth-century Renaissance' prefiguring the promotion of science and the arts in the later medieval and early modern periods.[1] Indeed, the key ingredients allowing knowledge transfer were present in Spain and Sicily in ways in which they were not in other Mediterranean frontier regions, such as the crusader states. Active participation was encouraged at the highest levels while patronage and a secular environment of the royal palace in Palermo stimulated scholarly co-operation that, in turn, enabled the recovery, transmission, development and application of intellectual ideas which were neither based in theology nor reliant on monastic scholarship for their execution. Works composed in Arabic, or translated from Arabic, featured prominently among the intellectual achievements of the Norman kingdom and, indeed, they are linked to issues of socio-religious toleration, cultural mélange and kingship.

The first half of the twelfth century had witnessed the resurgence of Byzantine monasticism, the patronage of art from Byzantine models, the commissioning of new homilies and histories in Greek and the participation of Greek administrators in power. The period thereafter saw the translation of classical Greek works into Latin. However, the two sets of activities should not be mistaken as being closely interrelated. The Byzantine revival in Sicily was a politico-religious one, of which Norman sponsorship was limited to the Rogerian periods. The recovery of ancient Greek learning occurred under William I and II; it was devoid of overtly political aims, and came in a period of political decline for Greek influence in ruling circles.

One of the central figures of the Sicilian translation movement was Henry Aristippus, whose political career and scholarly interests are known towards the end of his life, mainly in his role as Maio's stop-gap replacement in 1160 and his brief spell as royal familiar until his arrest and death in prison around 1162. During these latter years of his life, he made the first Latin translations of Plato's dialogues, the *Meno* and *Phaedo*. He also produced a Latin version of the fourth book of Aristotle's *Meteorology*, which was widely circulated. In addition, he had involvement with, or knowledge of, several other works of classical Greek mathematics, science, history and philosophy as well as the early Christian theologian, Gregory of Nazianzus (d. 389), whose work William I had personally encouraged him to translate. Further biographical details concerning Aristippus are elusive. The church of Sant'Agata at Catania, of which he was attested archdeacon from summer 1156, maintained until the late 1160s close historic links with the Norman monks of Robert Guiscard's foundation of Sant'Eufemia in Calabria, prompting the conjecture that he was either a Norman or a Greek. If he was a first- or second-generation Norman who had been exposed to a smattering of Greek learning, then he may be considered to be a product of the Rogerian half of the twelfth century, alongside an important handful of personnel in royal circles with similar backgrounds. If Henry Aristippus was a culturally Hellenophile Norman, perhaps like Roger II himself, or the royal priest Grizandus (from the Greek name, 'Chrysanthos'), the son of Drogo (a Frankish name), then he was among the last of his kind in Sicily. He was said by Falcandus to be as well-read in Latin as in Greek, and he appears to have had a genuine interest in scientific inquiry – or at least, he was keen to present himself in this light.

'Aristippus' was an ancient Greek name, not a Byzantine Greek one. It is likely that Henry had adopted it for himself as a pseudonym and, on one occasion, he used it self-referentially. The most obvious place for him to have learned of the original Aristippus, that is, the classical Greek philosopher from north Africa and companion of Socrates, was in Diogenes Laertius' *Lives and Opinions of Eminent Philosophers* – a work which he was preparing for translation. Indeed, as Haskins conjectured, his adoption of this name may have informed his decision to translate Plato's *Meno* and *Phaedo*, the only two Socratic dialogues in which the character Aristippus appears.[2] What is perplexing about this choice is that the original, pagan Aristippus espoused sensual pleasure as the highest good, and his sullied reputation for unfettered hedonism, sexual licentiousness, excessive luxury, effeminacy and idiotic short-term thinking was preserved by Diogenes in his anecdotal biography. Although Henry's choice might be explicable in this light, it is perhaps more plausible that he perceived Aristippus simply as a Socratic companion, exposing only a superficial level of engagement with the texts, their characters and their philosophical content. Similarly, whether motivated by a personal interest in the texts or to acquire the kudos which a pretence to classical learning bestowed, Aristippus' flowery description of William I's court as an academy, and the king himself as a philosopher whose every utterance was an aphorism, rings hollow. Although the 'court' at Palermo was the focus of translation activity, both commissioned and translated works were closely associated with the eulogising of a sponsor. Patronage, along with the curious mix of individuals who found themselves in the same place at the same time, rather than the systematic structure of a 'school', might provide a more convincing explanation for the haphazard production of texts in Sicily. Aristippus' own involvement with translation work was relatively short-lived, taking place between c. 1154 and c. 1160, as was that of some of those who had encouraged him, including Maio and Archbishop Hugh of Palermo. All three died between 1160 and 1162. The scholarly movement in Palermo was thus not only highly sensitive to changes in personnel, but also required the continual input of patronage to sustain it.

Patronage, science, the stars and medicine

Prior to the translation movement, which is most clearly seen from the mid-1150s, Roger's reign had been marked by the commissioning of new works, such as Alexander of Telese's Latin biography and a lost biography (presumably in Arabic) by a scribe known as al-Ḥanash.[3] To these can be added a Greek treatise by Neilos Doxapatres concerning the hierarchy of the patriarchal sees of the Eastern Church, in which it was argued that the papacy at Rome had lost its primacy with the transfer to Constantinople.[4] If the translation of religious works was limited, Roger II's patronage of Doxapatres for politico-religious purposes serves as an important example because the treatise was composed in 1142–3 for motives which may have concerned relations between Rome and Palermo, and the possibility of a papal–German alliance.

In Norman Sicily, the range of translated academic subject-matter from the past was of limited scope. The *amīr* Eugenios had translated from Arabic, but his chosen topics were literary and scientific rather than political. Unlike contemporary translators in al-Andalus, whose disingenuous interest in Islam had resulted in a Latin translation of the Qur'ān, there is no evidence from the Norman period of any interest in producing discourses on the tenets of Islam or the ways in which Islamic thought might have a bearing on shared problems in Christian theology, even if some churches and monasteries had copies of Islamic texts. For example, a fragment of the Qur'ān was preserved in the Cappella Palatina archive, and the fourteenth-century abbey of San Martino delle Scale had somehow acquired a biography of Muḥammad, but there is no indication that anyone had ever read them. Indeed, in terms of available resources which were not apparently consulted, Henry Aristippus mentioned in the preface to the *Phaedo*, dedicated to an English colleague, the wealth of material in the library at Syracuse which had presumably survived from the Byzantine period. It is notable that under Muslim rule, Greek texts were not the focus of sustained, co-operative study by Arabic–Greek bilinguals on the island either.

A small, paper fragment found in the Cappella Palatina listing in Sicilian Arabic a draft inventory of books suggests that the royal palace had a library collection of some sort by at least the mid-1150s. The books cited are mainly secular but also include some Christian works, probably all of which were written in Latin. A century later, Frederick II was attested to have had a large library with a collection acquired from both within and beyond the kingdom.

The intersection of diplomatic activity, gift exchange and the transmission of learning were neatly combined in 1158 when, as an envoy to Constantinople, Aristippus returned with a copy of Ptolemy's *Megistē Syntaxis*, more commonly known by its Arabicised name, the *Almagest*. This was a work of widespread importance which, since classical Greek times, had exerted a huge technical and conceptual impact on questions of astronomy and cosmology. Medieval Muslim geographers had been able to read it in Arabic since the mid-ninth century and, although it assumed a geocentric arrangement of the universe, its influence was carried forward into late medieval and early modern Europe. Sicily's contribution to this end was that the *Almagest* was first (anonymously) translated from Greek in Palermo around 1160. Later, in 1175, a more widely used translation from Arabic was made by Gerard of Cremona in Toledo.

Under William II, the seminal work of the celebrated scholar and astronomer ʿAbd al-Raḥmān al-Ṣūfī (d. 986), the *Kitāb ṣuwar al-kawākib*, was translated into Latin as the *Liber de locis stellarum fixarum*. Building on the *Almagest*, al-Ṣūfī synthesised and integrated the names of stars and their constellations as understood by Greek and Muslim traditions with those of the early Arab system of the *anwā'*, or rough reckoning of calendar measurements by astronomical observation which was linked to the prediction of forthcoming weather patterns. For Western science, this Latin translation was instrumentally important for the transmission of Arabic star names into European astronomy, although it was superseded by a thirteenth-century Spanish translation made for Alfonso X of León-Castile (d. 1284). A silver planisphere which al-Ṣūfī made in Iraq for his patron, the great Būyid *amīr* ʿAḍūd al-Dawla (d. 983), was later said to have been kept in the Fatimid library in Cairo.

Miniature book illustrations, as found in the chronicles of John Skylitzes and Peter of Eboli, show familiarity with, and influence from, Muslim artistic traditions. While there were, of course, long traditions of manuscript illustration at Bari, Salerno and Naples, it is also notable how many of the translated Arabic texts in Sicily – al-Ṣūfī, Dioscurides, *Kalīla wa-Dimna*, Manfred's additions to *The Art of Hunting with Birds* – contained miniature pictures, not as gratuitous embellishments, but as a visual clarification of the text, stylistically indebted to illustrated Arabic books of the tenth century, and forming key links between artistic and scientific depiction.[5]

The south Italian mainland had its own scholarly tradition which was partly connected to Arabic science and perhaps best epitomised by Constantine 'the African', a Christian translator of Latin texts into Arabic. Constantine hailed from Carthage and was associated with both the early medical school at Salerno and the abbey at Montecassino, where he died as a monk in 1085. Among the many works attributed to him was the medical compendium, the *Liber Pantegni*, which transmitted knowledge of Arab-Muslim and Greek medical science into Europe. The work was continued and later extended by his bilingual pupils until a new translation was made by Stephen of Pisa with trilingual reference terms in Latin, Greek and Arabic. By Stephen's day in the 1120s, it is possible to see how the political and commercial development of the southern Mediterranean had created academic matrices across which scholars might work and travel. In so doing, they were well-positioned to construct the essential academic apparatus for further study to take place. Stephen, for example, claimed that Arabic- and Greek-speaking scholars could be consulted with ease in Sicily and Salerno, but was himself working mainly in George of Antioch's native city which had developed as an academic centre, had a thriving Pisan quarter and whose prince, Bohemond II, was Robert Guiscard's grandson.

Composed with a similar, and by no means, unusual methodology, was Idrīsī's multilingual compendium on 'simple' drugs in which synonyms were recorded across several languages. It is not known for certain that it was composed in Sicily, but it was influential in its day and was frequently cited by the famous botanist Ibn al-Bayṭār (d. 1248) of Andalusi origin, who had produced, *inter alia*, a commentary on Dioscurides, which itself included multilingual vocabularies – in his case, with equivalent terms in Arabic, Berber and Latin.[6] Indeed, the widespread scientific plurilingualism of the south Mediterranean offers a number of thought-provoking contexts for the development of the lingua franca of governance, diplomacy and politics of the 1100s. It is not coincidental that this same period witnessed increased rigour and regulation of medical practitioners via systems of approbation, validation and registration, fostering a sense of 'professionalism', arguably one of the earliest of its type in Europe.

The convergence of shared intellectual interests in two main centres within the kingdom, which enhanced the development of both through a long period of academic study and exchange, is shown by the links between the medical school at Salerno and the movement of scholars to and from Palermo. Significant from the twelfth century was the anonymous translator of the *Almagest*, who hailed from the so-called *Schola Medica Salernitana* and who had travelled south to Palermo to carry out his translation in the company of Aristippus and Eugenios. He had also worked on Euclid and Proclus in order to train himself up for the task. The widely travelled Adelard of Bath (d. *c.* 1122), known for his work on the astrolabe, al-Khwārizmī's astronomical tables and a translation of Euclid's *Elements*, was attested as having visited Salerno and probably Sicily too. Overseas regimes also drew on Sicilian expertise: in the early 1100s, an expensive and ill-starred plan of the Fatimid *wazīr* al-Afḍal, to build an observatory (*raṣad*) in Cairo involved the Sicilian instrument-maker and geometer, Abū Muḥammad ʿAbd al-Karīm. The idea was not simply to gaze at the stars, but was driven by economic and fiscal motives to produce accurate dating tables for planting and reaping crops.[7]

Sicily thus experienced the ebb and flow of visiting scholarship, but the pull of the kingdom as an academic centre was certainly not irresistible: some eminent translators, for example Gerard of Cremona (d. 1187), preferred to head west for the Iberian peninsula, rather than south to Sicily. Nor were the south Italian physicians, who included Romuald of Salerno and perhaps Peter of Eboli too, alone in their influence as royal doctors since Peter's own illustration of the dying William II shows him being attended by an unknown, but presumably Muslim, physician called either Aḥmad or Ḥakīm.[8]

The parameters of academic and intellectual inquiry

There was a level of intellectual exchange in Sicily which was exceptional for Latin Europe outside the Iberian peninsula. However, the exchanges were narrow in their type and direction. The palace may have become famous for its perceived plurilingualism and multiculturalism, but translations were not multidirectional. Rather, they were made from Arabic and Greek into Latin, or from Arabic into Greek and then, later, into Latin. The flow was overwhelmingly towards the prestige target language. Although there were administrative translations between both Arabic and Greek, and a copy of the Assizes was made in Greek, no text, either administrative, scholarly or legal is known to have been translated from Latin into Arabic. Nor were the royally commissioned and original works of Doxapatres and Idrīsī translated at the time. An important, but incomplete, Latin version of Idrīsī was made only in the early seventeenth century.

The learning of classical antiquity, whether or not through the medium of Arabic, was not without its parameters either, and concentrated mainly on the fields of the natural sciences, philosophy and astrology. The *amīr* Eugenios had once translated from Greek into Latin the prophecy of the Erithryean Sibyl – itself translated from Aramaic into Greek by Neilos Doxapatres – but otherwise there was barely any awareness of, let alone inquisitive interest in, the classical authors themselves who were once associated with the island, such as Plato or Cicero.

For its part, medieval Muslim knowledge of pagan Sicily was derived more from folklore than scholarship: Ibn Ḥawqal's (mistaken) observation that Aristotle could be found suspended in a beam of the main mosque at Palermo, and al-Harawī's (mistaken) belief that Galen was buried at Misilmeri were fascinating, but exceptional, instances. Nor did the revival of classical scholarship inspire any interest in the ancient remains which were in evidence all around the island and on the mainland too. It was sufficient for Roger II to have believed that there had once existed kings on whose palaces he had built his own, but there was no desire to return to, or to romanticise, a bygone age any further than hearing about the deeds of ancient rulers as his father had done. Nor was there any sense that careful analysis of the historical past might yield useful guidance for the present or future. On the contrary, Arab-Muslim or Greek Byzantine views of the past might even be considered worthy of political suppression, not sponsorship. The commissioning of historical works thus tended toward biographies primarily intended to magnify and justify the deeds of the patron.

Evidence for the transmission of ideas rarely leaves a paper trail. Some works were commissioned but never translated, others were translated but not consulted. The movement changed direction with its patrons and translators; for instance, with the unexpected rise of Hebrew as a target language in the 1300s led by Arabic-speaking Jewish translators. Some seeds of useful knowledge germinated, others were transplanted unpredictably over long distances, and would only take root centuries later. However, the translation movement was to be continued under the Staufen rulers who patronised celebrated translators, such as Michael Scot, Bartholomew of Messina, Moses of Palermo and Faraj Ben Salim among others. Under Frederick II and his son Manfred, the site of academic activity was dislocated northward from the island and onto the mainland, but the diffusion into Europe of scientific and literary works translated from Arabic continued, some of which later came to be printed in the 1500s. Thus, while the overall impacts of these movements are not always immediately tangible and sometimes best observed from a distance, Sicily and south Italy played key roles in laying the foundations on which later academic advances would be built and which stimulated the flourishing of science, literature and the arts in Renaissance and early modern Europe.

Integrated science: clocks, maps, lands and administration

The task of accurately reckoning the days and their subdivisions was a medieval preoccupation. This sophisticated and technologically advanced art had become a particular specialism of Muslim science and scholarship, justified and initially driven by the need to determine festival dates and to punctuate prayers into a daily routine. Such derivative sciences were intimately related to questions of direction finding and location description in order to enable, among other things, the duty of pilgrimage to Mecca to be fulfilled. Hence, the refining of ways to record measurements of distance and the speed of passing time had long been considered a religiously sanctioned activity in the Islamic world.

This knowledge had valuable practical applications, not least because it was vital for understanding mobility and viability within a realm, the location of natural resources and populated centres, the effective organisation of provinces and issues of logistics, communications and deployment of the army. Thus, in the same way that the act of writing God's word, the art of calligraphy and the science of grammar and logic were firmly connected in the minds of scribes trained in Arab-Islamic chanceries – and, therefore, that these disciplines went hand in hand with the art of diplomatics and well-formed expressions of governance – so too, other derivative 'Islamic' sciences, such as mathematics, geometry, time-keeping, astronomy and cartography, were inextricably linked to the administrative and military faculties of government. To the Sicilian kings, the scientific potential which the known world's most advanced sources could offer, whatever their provenance, proved irresistible to the foundling kingdom and could be disregarded only at the potential cost to its own security. Royal appropriation of Arab-Islamic art and learning during Roger's reign thus came as part of a much wider package: it not only coincided with the rise of the royal *dīwān*, but also with an increasingly varied and sophisticated palace life including the patronage of science and scholarship as well as the practical application of these valuable skills.

As far as lands in Sicily were concerned, there was a general and tacit assumption from the early Norman period, that their confines matched older, pre-existing boundaries.[9] But when Roger I had come to divide up conquered areas in the 1090s, what had emerged were not definitions of the land written in Arabic. Rather, Arabic lists of men had been issued, which were based on data from the Islamic period. Thus, although the old Muslim administration possessed these as well as some form of land registers, probably only with the names of estates, landholders and the taxes due from them, there is no evidence that detailed, written definitions of the actual boundaries were used. Instead, they relied on the trusted testimony of the *shaykhs* who lived on the lands and, therefore, knew where their boundaries were. This system was heavily dependent on the expertise of a settled population.

When written descriptions of the boundaries first began to appear on the island during the 1100s, they were composed in a highly stylised manner. In this respect, the Arabic appears to have absorbed influences from Greek. This is evident from the characteristic and common use of noun duplication to express a measure of extent or distance. For example, we find in Greek, τὴν ὁδόν ὁδόν; in Arabic, *al-ṭarīq al-ṭarīq*; or later, in Latin, *per viam viam*, meaning 'right along the road'.[10] This distinctive trait is neither Arabic nor Latin in origin. However, it is very commonly found in Greek boundary descriptions (*perioismoi*) in Sicily and was sometimes attested in areas of former Byzantine control on the mainland. It appears that this figure of speech from south Italian Greek was adopted by the Arabic scribes and by Latin scribes too. It is probably not by chance that this usage coincides with the rise of influence of Greek administrators from the early Norman period. An alternative explanation, that the Greek influence on Arabic was a long-surviving continuity from the old Byzantine *theme* of Sicily, seems unlikely given the length of time involved and the fundamental changes to the base of the population and settlement patterns since the sixth century.

Thus, it is possible to discern the different inputs which made up Norman Sicilian boundary descriptions: they were written down for the first time during the 1100s in one of three languages following a Greek style, but the data they contained was drawn from older, verbally transmitted information dating back to the Islamic period. With the development of the royal *dīwān*, whose offices kept their records in Arabic and whose outputs borrowed from diplomatic and chancery models found in contemporary Egypt, the ways in which boundaries were written and presented became institutionalised as the in-house standard. The information in their record books was then used as the basis for later translations. So influential and pervasive was noun duplication, that it came to form part of a bureaucratic lingua franca of interchangeable terms and expressions. Indeed, it endured in Sicilian usage until the early modern period.

The most ambitious academic work to be commissioned in the Norman period was al-Idrīsī's Arabic description of the world. This was accompanied by a map series and was commonly known as the *Book of Roger*. Recently, the discovery of the *Book of Curiosities*, which pre-dates Idrīsī by almost a century, has undermined the originality value of his world maps since they can now be shown to have been copied from previous material.[11] None the less, Idrīsī's work and his presence in Palermo was highly significant in several respects. His preface to the work in praise of his patron dates from January 1154, only a matter of weeks before Roger's death, and reveals something of the king's personal interest in science and of both his and Idrīsī's working methods – even when treated with the caution such eulogy of his patron deserves. It is also noteworthy that Idrīsī's introduction phrased Roger's interests, achievements and conduct of affairs as all having happened in the past, almost as if he were composing not merely a eulogy, but also an epitaph. Or, indeed, in the context of a dying royal recluse, it might suggest that Roger no longer did the things that he used to. In at least a stylistic contrast, Aristippus' praise of William I was couched entirely in terms of an ongoing engagement with the present.

Roger's scientific interest was said by Idrīsī to have spanned some fifteen years, that is to say from 1139 to 1154. The dates accord perfectly with the high-points of Roger's reign, following the kingdom's consolidation and pacification, and coinciding with its phases of internal reorganisation and overseas expansion. Idrīsī explained that consultation of existing sources had proved inadequate, resulting in Roger's invitation to scholars in the region to explain and improve upon these. As the answers were still unsatisfactory, Roger had cast his net further afield to entice scholars to the palace whom he questioned via an intermediary (*wāsiṭa*), presumably a technical interpreter. What was said to have particularly interested Roger was the possibility of establishing some agreement over the relative size of different regions, and of harmonising map data with consistent accounts from oral and written sources. A major outcome of the work was Idrīsī's huge silver planisphere, which comprised key features of physical and human geography and was engraved with seven *climes* according to the Ptolemaic configuration. To accompany it, the *Book of Roger* described each territory, its natural resources and ethno-geographic data relating to its population. In addition, it provided detailed sections on the Sicilian kingdom itself.

Some elements of Roger's character which Idrīsī recalled are echoed elsewhere. The king's meticulous attention to detail, for example, was noted in a variety of contemporary sources, not all of whom were panegyricists. Falco of Benevento recorded how in 1140, after the capitulation of Naples, Roger had its city walls measured to a pace. Alexander of Telese claimed that Roger had personally calculated the revenues of the kingdom and knew them better than the scribes. Later, Idrīsī reported that he was an expert in both mathematics and science, although such interests were not the exclusive preserve of medieval Mediterranean rulers, nor was it uncommon to find such acclamations in praise of a patron.

Of obvious importance is that Idrīsī was writing his descriptive geography of the world and the kingdom at the same time and in the same place as Arab scribes in the royal *dīwān* were defining the provinces with their outer boundaries and internal estates. The rich coincidence of shared scholarly interests and disciplines is all the more striking given the presence of the mechanical timepiece and Idrīsī's planisphere in the palace. It can also be inferred from boundary descriptions made by the scribes of the fiscal administration that they had worked from maps of the provinces and estates. Indeed, it is inconceivable that there could have been no meaningful intellectual exchange between the Arab scribes and one of the world's most famous cartographers in whose endeavours Roger had taken a personal interest. On his sources of information, Idrīsī mentioned those which have been established by translators, transcribed and compiled in record books (*daftars*).[12] The sense here seems to refer to general methods of information gathering, but for the kingdom of Sicily itself, it probably refers to records held by the royal *dīwān*. On the other hand, Idrīsī appears to have been relatively closed to non-Arabic sources of information, such as Latin works on the topography of Europe, which would have proved especially useful. Numerous people from beyond the Alps were on hand, or could be interrogated, but Idrīsī made no great effort to consult them or to draw on the oral testimony of those who had been there. None the less, his sources are themselves revealing: the description of Normandy, for example, is effectively a tour of the great ecclesiastical centres and reflects little that would have been of interest to the lay aristocracy.

Overall, what Idrīsī had provided for the kingdom was a systematically constructed framework within which Roger could conceptualise his kingdom and its constituent parts relative to lands overseas. This filled a gap in the knowledge of the kingdom's geography with respect to the internal arrangement of its provinces, towns and estates which complemented the administration's fiscal data the *dīwān* had collected about crown lands and the families that lived on them.

The administrative lingua franca: lost in translation

Translations from Greek and Arabic occurred frequently in the royal *dīwān* and elsewhere in the palace, but only occasionally can connections be made between the translators of contemporary administrative documents and ancient academic texts. By and large, the two activities seem to have been considered as separate. Following the discovery after the sack of the palace that the administrative record books were missing, Henry Aristippus – then a *familiaris regis* – was said to be among those who did not have the requisite knowledge of Sicilian land tenure to reconstruct them. A good knowledge of written Arabic would have also been essential, and Matthew of Salerno was brought out of prison to undertake the work. However, most translation work undertaken in the *dīwān* was the task of relatively low-level scribes and notaries who remain unknown to us as personalities and do not seem to have crossed into the field of academic translations. An important exception to this was Eugenios the *amīr* (d. 1202), who was reported to have been unusually competent in Greek, Arabic and Latin, presumably in that order. He was frequently attested in sources from

1174 to 1190 as one of the masters of the *duana baronum*, and during his lifetime he produced a Greek translation of the popular, literary fables called in Arabic *Kalīla wa-Dimna*, and a Latin version of the Arabic text of Ptolemy's *Optics*.[13]

The largest single piece of administrative translation work accompanied the largest of the royal grants relating to the boundaries of fifty estates in western Sicily that had been conceded to Monreale. These were rendered into Latin from Arabic by William II's chief Latin notary, Alexander, probably between June 1180 and May 1182, and almost certainly with the aid of an Arabic-speaking assistant. The end product, written in Arabic and Latin, was of impressive length, filling seven sheets of parchment each measuring between sixty to seventy centimetres in width. Its total length exceeded five metres. However, the Latin was of limited practical use. Many of the Arabic place names had been translated, rather than transliterated, making them unrecognisable to the local population and to later generations who came to rely on the Latin version of the text instead of the original Arabic. So, among dozens of examples, one of the hills south of Palermo, *Jabal al-Maʿaz* (literally, 'Mountain of the Goats') – which to this day is called Gibilmesi – was translated as *Mons Caprarum*, a place that presumably no one had ever heard of.[14] The privileging of Latin in this important royal document, where Latin accompanied Arabic for the first time in this way, can also be seen by its physical position occupying the opening sheets of the parchment on which it was composed. The more original Arabic description was relegated to the lower sections. Perhaps analogous to this is the observation that Christian *shaykhs* were named before Muslims at boundary inquests, implying that their testimony carried more weight.

Once established and authenticated, the defective Latin then formed the basis for subsequent consultation and copies, thereby adding to the confusion over land tenure and claims to 'ancient' rights and privileges often made in later times. This situation was irrevocably muddled by the demographic collapse of western Sicily with the mass deportations of the Muslims in the thirteenth century. With the population went the ancestral memory of the land as preserved by the oral testimony of the Arabic-speaking Muslim *shaykhs* of the towns and villages upon whose trusted knowledge the *dīwān* had always relied to establish and confirm their limits. Worse still, the land was not repopulated prior to the depredations of the Sicilian Vespers or the Black Death.

Much later, when islanders turned their minds to questions of historical change and continuity, they could often produce some 'ancient tradition' to account for the present in terms of the past. Derived for the most part from previously unattested anecdotes, often blended with a dash of history, these subtle and firmly held beliefs contributed to the development of popular regional histories. Not all the ancient traditions, however, were particularly ancient, and they certainly did not refer back to classical antiquity either, which rarely featured in Sicilians' recollections of events considered as relevant. Indeed, eras prior to the advent of Latin-Christianity were of a time immemorial, and claims to lawful precedents and rights over lands harked back to Norman times in search of their earliest feasible origins. The problem was that many Latin charters were believed to point back to the existence of some older source on which they were based. However, the lack of toponymic continuity and garbled renditions of Arabic place names made verification of estates and their boundaries a matter of even greater conjecture than would otherwise have been the case. To this day, much archival and archaeological research remains to be done in this important field on an island where rights to lands and water are still matters of life and death. But such has been the ignorance of the medieval Arabic charters in particular, that it was possible for a Maltese priest, Giuseppe Vella, to pass off as authentic, a multi-volume history dealing with the late Islamic period.[15] Published between 1789 and 1792, this work of fiction, composed in a species of faux-Arabic, even related the personal correspondence of the Fatimid caliphs to their Sicilian *amīrs* and the early Normans to a credulous readership. If only it were true, the translation of the first four volumes (of six) into German might have been more justifiable. Remarkably, many of the genuine Arabic charters are yet to appear in the form of modern scholarly editions.

The administration of Muslims in western Sicily

From the 1140s, the royal *dīwān* was increasingly capable of making practical and conceptual links between different kingdoms of the world, royal lands in Sicily and Calabria, their location, arrangement and subdivision into constituent parts, as well as their status relative to the crown and landholders. At the same time, the royal administration had developed a range of relatively sophisticated methods and media for surveying, recording and evaluating the lands and men of royal estates. In practice, it was still a system that was only fully comprehensible to the cognoscenti who had helped to construct, manage and monopolise it.

Crown lands were subdivided into provinces (Arabic, *iqlīm*; Greek, *diakratēsis*). In Latin, they were the *magnae divisae* or 'great boundaries'. Idrīsī mentioned 130 strongholds on the island, although it is not known whether these should be identified as administrative centres or, indeed, what their relationship is, if any, to the old Fatimid provinces. The same might be said of their relationship to the island's diocese boundaries. In the sections of Idrīsī's description of the kingdom and island of Sicily within the world's seven regions or *climes*, the walled strongholds at the centre of each *iqlīm* were described in terms of their location, their distance from the next major settlement, their defences and natural resources. Thus, for example, we learn of the important Muslim provincial centre of Jāṭū (modern San Giuseppe Iato):

> the stronghold of Jāṭū is in a high location. Adding to its strength is a wide expanse of planted fields bordering on it. There is an underground prison where those with whom the king is displeased are incarcerated. In this stronghold, there is no flowing water, nor streams nearby around it. From Jāṭū to [Qalʿat al-]Ṭrazī there is a distance of nine miles.[16]

At least some of the data Idrīsī provided about the island can be shown to have been up to date information from the Norman period. Another example is the locality recorded in Arabic as Ḥajar Sarlū ('Serlo's Rock'), which was named after the Norman commander and nephew of Roger I whose last stand on this outcrop was recorded by Malaterra.[17] Indeed, Idrīsī may have spent some considerable time compiling and checking such information, almost certainly in co-operation with trained assistants.

In theory, the administration of each provincial centre on the ground was the task of a royal official (*ʿāmil*, *strategotus*, or *stratēgos*), who co-ordinated the collection of taxes to be sent to the *dīwān* in Palermo as well as organising the conduct of boundary inquests and cadastral surveys. In the case of Iato, in the time of Roger II, rare details of these *ʿāmils* suggest that they had been Arabic-speaking 'Greek' Christians. Thus, in 1114, the *ʿāmil* of Iato had been George of Antioch, and attested in 1149 was a certain Stephen, the son of *shaykh* Abū l-Ṭayyib. Such officials were likely to have been withdrawn from the area when the lands were turned over to Monreale, whose affairs were overseen by Benedictine monks from Cava brought from the Italian mainland.

In spite of great progress, the records held by the royal *dīwān* were, even after the renewals of the 1140s, sketchy, and the lands and men conceded to Monreale comprise the most coherent corpus of surviving data. Of the main provinces, Corleone and Jāṭū are particularly complete examples, but we are missing the boundaries of some internal estates of Corleone, and (curiously) any record of the named population living within the walls of Iato itself. None the less, information concerning the lands of Iato appears to have been well organised and composed according to a particular *modus operandi*. First, the 'great boundary' (*magna divisa* or *al-ḥadd al-kabīr*) which encircled and closed the outer limits of the *iqlīm* was described. In the case of Iato, the direction taken was clockwise. Such definitions lacked cardinal points and appear to have been conceived as theoretically circular. Roads, rivers, ditches and hill crests served as the principal points of reference, and stones were set up to act as border markers. Secondly, unwalled estates (*casalia*, *raḥāʾil* or *chōría*; singular *casale*, *raḥl* or *chōríon*) whose boundaries were contiguous with the outer limit of the *iqlīm* were defined. The direction taken was also clockwise, although not always systematically so. Often appended to these definitions was information concerning land usage, especially measures of pasturage, plough-lands, sowing yields, disputed land or that which was otherwise uncultivated. Thirdly, the boundaries of the internal, unwalled, estates were defined, which appear not to have had any contact with the external limits of the province. These estates in particular were conceived of as quadrilateral, with each side described as north, south, east and west. The most common order in which the borders were presented was east, south, west and north, while the order in which each estate successively appeared in the text of the concession was, in the case of Jāṭū, anti-clockwise for the most part. Again, data relating to land use was sometimes included, with sowing yields and plough-lands calculated in measurements of volume (*mudd* or *salme*), occasionally expressed in terms of area (*zawj*).

Like the information regarding lands, that relating to the people on the lands was patchy and, at worst, non-existent. It many areas it was, and remained, incomplete. As we have seen, it is likely that only limited records from the late Islamic period had survived, and those which had may have been hopelessly outdated, or uselessly updated during the great renewals of the mid-1140s. Practical concerns over the perennial problem of a displaced local population and with it a memory of the land boundaries probably accounts for the twelfth-century drift towards the increased inclusion of written land boundaries accompaning grants of men in concessions as a less fickle way of marking territory. Cadastral and fiscal records had in any case been interrupted by the sack of the palace in 1161 with the disappearance and subsequent reconstruction of some of the in-house record books. Thus, the imperial *dīwān*'s pretence in 1229 that there existed a full set of fully furnished boundary registers (*quaternos*) in which one could read 'the limits of every city, stronghold, village and estate of Sicily' followed the twelfth-century bureaucratic precedent in proclaiming to know more than it could ever have.[18]

The Monreale Muslims: 'men of the registers' and 'smooth men'

Documentary material, mainly in Greek and Arabic, gathered from charters and in-house records compiled mainly between the 1090s and the 1180s has produced a large corpus of data relating to the terms and conditions of the population who lived in the towns and estates of the countryside.[19] Over a dozen different terms were employed across three languages to refer to them. However, many of these were used synonymously and those in Arabic and Greek can be resolved into two basic categories: families who were 'registered' and those who were 'unregistered'. In Arabic, those who were registered were called either *rijāl al-jarā'id* ('men of the registers'), *ahl al-jarā'id* ('people of the registers'), or *ḥursh* ('rough men'). In Greek, they were known as the *enapógraphoi* (the 'registered'). As the terms imply, the names of these people were recorded on lists as being attached to certain towns and estates. Their sons and newly-weds were also recorded on the lists, indicating that their condition was hereditary, and that they had formed new taxable household units. All Muslims who lived on crown lands, or had been conceded to Monreale, paid both the *jizya* and a land tax (the *qānūn*).

In contradistinction, all those who were not registered on the lands where they lived and worked were considered as 'unregistered'. In Greek, these were called the *exógraphoi* (the 'unregistered'). In Arabic, they were known as *muls* ('smooth men'). Within this broad category there were important subdivisions. For instance, an immigrant family who had settled in Sicily from overseas or from another part of the island would be initially assigned 'unregistered' status. In support of this, we find within certain groups of 'smooth men', a high proportion of non-Sicilian names. For example, with one exception, fifteen families of 'smooth men' on a list issued to the church at Triocolà in 1141 (when the term *muls* is first attested) had names which suggested a direct association with north Africa.[20] Later, in 1183, found among the twenty-six families of 'smooth men' at Corleone were ten with African place names, including Djerba, Fez, Mahdiyya, Sfax, Būna and Tripoli.[21] Similarly, we sometimes see *ghurbā'* ('aliens') or, in Greek, *xénoi* ('outsiders') subsumed within this category because they were entirely new to the system or because they had not been picked up by any previous administrative census. When they came to be surveyed again, they would cease to be 'unregistered' and become listed as 'men of the registers'. Given that large numbers of Muslims had been forced to flee into areas of western Sicily from Palermo and from towns and estates further east, it is very likely that many of them were completely unknown to the authorities. And presumably, they paid no taxes to them either.

We should not assume that wealth was evenly distributed among these communities, or that there was any sense of material equality. In a Latin list of 'villeins' (*villani*) in the 'Rollus Rubeus' chartulary of Cefalù, probably dating from between 1145 and 1154, we find eighty-three household heads with Arab-Muslim names.[22] Exceptionally, the amount each was due to pay was also given. Unfortunately, their status was recorded ambiguously, but they appear to be 'smooth men' (*de villanis exteris*). All were required to give twenty-four days a year in labour (*angariis*) and services (*collecta*). Almost a quarter of those listed had names which imply a profession, and up to a dozen different jobs are represented, including a baker, blacksmith, builder, carpenter, cotton farmer, donkey driver, farmer, salt collector, soldier and tanner. One person was Maltese; another may have been a fugitive.[23] The amounts of tax paid varied, reflecting wealth disparity among the community. In the Latin, *rays Omor* or, in (reconstructed) Arabic, 'Umar the *ra'īs* ('chief') paid twelve *tarì*, two of his sons paid half that, the third son paid eight. One person rendered a substantial sum of forty *tarì*, yet almost all the rest paid less than eight each, the average being seven and a half; the median and mode was six. Increments were generally of two *tarì*, and nearly everyone paid an even number with younger families contributing slightly less. The garbled Latin text makes the total amount they rendered relative to other villeins impossible to calculate with any certainty, but one interpretation is that they paid half.[24]

It should not be assumed that all 'smooth men' were first generation immigrants to Sicily because many, probably most, were those who had left their home towns and villages (voluntarily or not) in order to form new communities, or to bolster the population of existing ones. They, too, were therefore newcomers to an area by virtue of which they were also considered as 'unregistered'. It is likely that they were given generous terms and conditions of tenure in order to ease their introduction, probably with a period of grace or a lighter burden of taxes; hence, perhaps, the source of their alternative description implying 'smoothness'. It is not clear for how long this status continued or whether it was renewable, but this category of men was not able to reproduce itself. That is to say, terms and condition of tenure were not hereditary and could not be passed on automatically to their sons.

It may be significant that, while settlers from overseas made their way to the towns such as Corleone, most other 'smooth men' lived on open, unwalled estates or *casalia*. Although they were 'new' to the area, it is striking in the Monreale lists how this minority contained a disproportionately high number of prestige or high-status individuals among them. For example, there was a significantly higher proportion of *shaykhs*. And we find, amongst others, a *muqaddam* ('headman'); a certain 'Alī, the *mutaqabbil al-sūq* – that is to say, someone entrusted with the collection of local market taxes. Another illustrative example is Aḥmad 'the *wakīl*' referring to a local administrative agent or deputy whose name again implies a fiscal connotation. There is even a very explicit reference to 'Aḥmad, the chief of the village' (*shaykh al-qarya*), a 'smooth man' from Abū Kināna, an estate with 117 families – perhaps 500 people in total. In other words, he had been commended into an established community, but he was specifically said to be its leader. Thus, the 'smooth men' category, found predominantly in the unwalled villages, contained a privileged minority of individuals who were the local elites of *boni homines*, *gerontoi* and *shaykhs*.

On the Monreale estates, the 'men of the registers' account for about 60 per cent of the population; the 'smooth men' represent about 30 per cent. The remaining 10 per cent were the *rijāl al-maḥallāt* or 'men of the settlements' or perhaps 'camps', a little-understood category that may have represented the vestiges of those originally found on the land, since occasionally they were called the *entópoi* ('locals') in Greek in place of the usual, transliterated term of *machallét*. Alternatively, they may have had this status in view of the way in which they had arranged to pay their taxes. Another possibility is that, since some the hamlets known as the *maḥallāt* were tiny satellite fractions, the term may be more closely linked to categories of settlement or estates which had changed their status in the past.

Significantly, the proliferation of Greek and Arabic synonyms with their delicate distinctions were not shared by Latin scribes for whom all the above categories used to describe the local population were often resolved to a single term: *villani*.[25] The term in Sicily should not be confused with villeins in a northern European sense. Although later assizes recognised the hereditary distinction between those *villani* whose status was defined in virtue of the land they held (*inscriptitii*), on the one hand, and in terms of their persons (*adscriptitii*), on the other hand, the Monreale concession may have introduced a change which affected the status of the 'smooth men'. The argument is that since their names now appeared on a list just like those of the 'men of the registers', they too were, in effect, tied to the particular estates on which they were registered in hereditary service, thereby collapsing one of the key distinctions of their accustomed condition of tenure.[26] However, this interpretation is problematic, not least because the continuity of their status was specifically assured in the terms of the grant. Besides which, the names of 'smooth men' had elsewhere been written down and issued on lists since the 1140s. In addition, as if to acknowledge that a subtle distinction between different types of register still existed, the 1183 list of 'smooth men' was referred to in Arabic as an *iblāṭiyya* [*al-muls*] (from the Greek *plateia*), as opposed to the 1178 list which was a *jarīdat al-rijāl*.

However, there is also evidence that the *dīwān* had recently taken the opportunity to redistribute villeins onto open estates. Some of these estates had been conceded to Latin lords in the post-conquest period, but they had subsequently been abandoned. Thus, in the Monreale boundary description 1183, we read of 'the ruins that used to be an estate belonging to Bāyān D.gh.r.j', referring to Paganis de Gorgis, a Norman lord.[27] A royal order in 1183 refers to a transfer (*intiqāl*) of men – it is not clear whether this means an legal conveyance or a relocation. The root of the word, and the context of the grant, implies a physical movement.[28] Clearer indications are found in the lists themselves: above all, the existence of a distinct set of seventy villeins who had not been assigned to any particular village.[29] Several of their names unmistakably identify them with families from different estates in the area indicating that they were a composite group. In some cases, they appear to have included those from a younger generation. The *dīwān*'s most obvious motive for a relocation was to stimulate the rural economy by moving families away from the urban centres and further into the countryside. The local reaction is unknown, but given that villeins later moved *away* from open estates whenever the opportunity arose, it is fair to conclude that not all the 'smooth men' were willingly commended into these small rural villages.

Examination of the lists suggests that information the *dīwān* had on its own books was incomplete and, in some cases, disorderly. The surveys, by reviewing and revising this data, are likely to have detected Muslim refugees from the cities who had fled to safety. Some were presumably enrolled for taxation in new areas for the first time; others may have found themselves resettled as aliens. But for all concerned, the very presence of royal officials in the towns and estates of western Sicily, busily gathering information for the benefit of the church, may itself have been an unsettling experience. Indeed, by the 1180s, it is possible to identify long- and short-term disaffection in both city and countryside, and at all social and political levels within Muslim communities that had been worn down to an insecure underclass by the forces of a privileged minority to whom they had yielded power little over a century before.

Notes

1 For a well-informed introduction, see Walter Berschin, *Greek Letters and the Latin Middle Ages. From Jerome to Nicholas of Cusa*, trans. J. C. Frakes (Washington, 1988).

2 C. H. Haskins and D. P. Lockwood, 'The Sicilian translators of the twelfth century and the first Latin version of Ptolemy's Almagest', *Harvard Studies in Classical Philology*, 21 (1910): 75–102.

3 See Johns, *Arabic Administration*, p. 82, for the translation of the relevant passages in al-Maqrīzī. The unusually named author may have been associated with the Banū Ḥanash, who were prominent in the Cefalù area.

4 *Patrologia graeca*, J.-P. Migne (ed.) (Paris, 1864), 132, cols. 1079–1115.

5 E. Hoffman, 'The beginnings of the Arabic illustrated book: an intersection between art and scholarship', *Muqarnas*, 17 (2000): 37–52.

6 On Ibn al-Bayṭār, see J. Vernet, *EI*[2] III:737; on al-Idrīsī, see G. Oman, *EI*[2] III:1032. For Idrīsī's botanical work, M. Meyerhof, 'Über die Pharmakologie und Botanik des arabischen Geographen Edrisi', in *Archiv für Geschichte des Mathematik, der Naturwissenschaften und der Technik*, 12 (1930): 45–53, 225–36.

7 For a brief, but incisive, introduction to the Fatimids' observatory, see Heinz Halm, *The Fatimids and their Traditions of Learning* (London, 1997), pp. 87–90.

8 For 'Achím medic[us]' attending the dying King William II, see *Peter of Eboli*, p. 43. In the same image, an (unnamed) astrologer consulting an astrolabe also appears to be a Muslim.

9 *secundum antiquas divisiones Sarracenorum*. The document is not edited, but discussed in Johns, *Arabic Administration*, pp. 39–42.

10 On noun duplication in Greek, Arabic and Latin, see Metcalfe, *Muslims and Christians*, pp. 118–26. For moves towards a trilingual lingua franca in the *dīwān*, see pp. 135–40.

11 For the *Kitāb Gharā'ib al-funūn*, see *The Book of Curiosities: A critical edition*, World-Wide-Web publication, E. Savage-Smith and Y. Rapoport (eds) at: www.bodley.ox.ac.uk/bookofcuriosities (accessed March 2007).

12 Idrīsī, *BAS*[2] Ar. I:31; *BAS*[2] It. I:36.

13 Albert Lejeune, *L'Optique de Claude Ptolémée dans la version latine d'après l'arabe de l'émir Eugène de Sicile* (Louvain, 1956).

14 On discrepancies between the Arabic and Latin, and of a translation scheme, see Alex Metcalfe, 'Trusting the text as far as we can throw the scribe: further notes on reading a bilingual *jarīdat al-ḥudūd* from the royal *dīwān* of Norman Sicily', in *From Al-Andalus to Khurasan: Documents from the Medieval Muslim World*, P. M. Sijpesteijn *et al.* (eds) (Leiden, 2007), pp. 78–98; and Alex Metcalfe, '*De Saracenico in Latinum transferri*: causes and effects of translation in the fiscal administration of Norman Sicily', *Al-Masāq*, 13 (2001): 43–86.

15 On the Vella conspiracy, see Richard Gottheil, 'Two forged antiques', *Journal of the American Oriental Society*, 33 (1913): 306–12; also Adelaide Baviera Albanese, *L'arabica impostura* (Palermo, 1978). Colombia University Library holds a rare (unique?) copy of Vella's manuscript.

16 Idrīsī, *BAS*[2] Ar. I:53; *BAS*[2] It. I:86.

17 'Serlo's Rock', or at least the site that tradition holds to be the spot of Serlo's death, is near Nissoria, about 16 km north-east of Enna. It was known locally as the 'Rocca di Sarro' or 'di Sarno', but has been extensively excavated as a commercial quarry and no longer exists.

18 Johns, *Arabic Administration*, pp. 172–3, n. 9.

19 For an overview of the wider period, see Henri Bresc, 'Féodalité coloniale en terre d'Islam. La Sicile (1070)', in *MEFR*, 44 (Rome, 1980): 631–47, reprinted in *Politique e société en Sicile XII*[e]*–XV*[e] *siècles* (Aldershot, 1990). For a detailed but dated introduction to questions of Sicilian villeinage, see I. Peri, *Uomini, città e campagne in Sicilia dall'XI al XIII secolo*, (Rome–Bari, 1978). The most recent and updated account is found in Johns, *Arabic Administration*, pp. 170–92.

20 The *jarīda* written for San Giorgio di Triocalà was published by M. Eugenia Gálvez, 'Noticia sobre los documentos árabes de Sicilia del Archivio Ducal de Medinaceli', in *Del nuovo sulla Sicilia musulmana (Rome, 3 maggio 1993)*, Accademia Nazionale dei Lincei: Fondazione Leone caetani, Giornata di Studio, no. 26, Rome, B. Scarcia Amoretti (ed.) (Rome, 1995), pp. 167–82 (173–6). However, this is clearly not a definitive version. On its defects, and for the *muls* of Triocalà, see Johns, *Arabic Administration*, pp. 107 and 147.

21 For the 'smooth men' of Corleone, see Cusa, *Diplomi*, pp. 263–4.

22 *Rollus Rubeus: privilegia ecclesie Cephaleditane*, C. Mirto (ed.) (Palermo, 1972), pp. 39–41. See also the discussion of their status in Johns, *Arabic Administration*, p. 62.

23 Othime[n] maltí ('Uthmān al-Mālṭī) and Abtella Far ('Abd Allāh al-Fārr).

24 Only a handful of charters record the amounts due from villeins. However, the differing arrangements agreed between different villeins and their lords makes calculations of equivalence an almost impossible task. The most explicit contemporary example, from *c.* 1177, recorded that three Muslim 'men of the registers' paid thirty *tarì* in *jizya* and a land tax of twenty measures [*mudd*] of corn and ten of barley. For editions of the charter, see Cusa, *Diplomi*, pp. 111–12 and, more accurately, Jeremy Johns, 'The boys from Mezzoiuso. Muslim *jizya*-payers in Christian Sicily', in *Islamic Reflections, Arabic Musings: Studies in Honour of Professor Alan Jones*, R. Hoyland and P. Kennedy (eds) (Cambridge, 2004), pp. 243–55. By any reckoning, these were significant amounts indicating the extent of some villeins' wealth derived from the land.

25 For thought-provoking views on the term 'villanus' in the context of Sicily, and a full bibliography, see Adalgisa de Simone, 'Ancora sui «villani» di Sicilia: alcune

osservazioni lessicali', in *MEFRM*, 116/1 (Rome, 2004): 471–500.

26 On issues of servitude and the relationship of villeins to the land, see also Annliese Nef, 'Conquêtes et reconquêtes médiévales: la Sicile normande est-elle une terre de réduction en servitude généralisée?', in *MEFRM*, 112 (Rome, 2000): 579–607.

27 Cusa, *Diplomi*, p. 242.

28 The royal order in 1183 was 'to return all men to the *Dīwān al-Maʿmūr*, whether they are [men] of the registers, of the *maḥallāt* or 'smooth men' (*muls*), who are living on the lands of holy churches and barons of all Sicily … and transfer (*intiqāl*) them from there to the lands of the *Dīwān al-Maʿmūr*', Cusa, *Diplomi*, p. 245. The implication is that all villeins were recalled to their original location within the boundaries of the royal demesne prior to being formally handed over to Monreale.

29 Their names can be found in Cusa, *Diplomi*, pp. 162–4.

14

The Muslim revolts and the colony at Lucera

The death of William II and the 'Sicilian Tragedy'

William II unexpectedly died on 18 November 1189 aged thirty-six, with no child as heir to the throne, and the kingdom was plunged into a succession crisis. If the crown were to pass to Roger II's middle-aged daughter, Constance and her husband Henry VI of Germany, then the two kingdoms faced a likely union – that is, the encirclement so often feared by the papacy and by some factions within Sicily, particularly among the remaining *familiares* in Palermo. An alternative solution was offered by the potential elevation to the throne of the illegitimate grandson of Roger II, Tancred. He had been one of the ringleaders of the anti-Muslim riots in 1161 and was subsequently exiled for his part in the rebellion. He had, however, been reaccommodated as count of Lecce from 1169, and as the Great Constable and Master Justiciar of Apulia and Terra di Lavoro. Having largely defeated his mainland rivals, led by Roger, count of Andria, and following an unprecedented assembly of barons, Tancred was elected king and crowned in January 1190. Such were the complex, trans-European machinations of the fraught years of 1190–1 – with Henry VI beset by baronial revolt in Germany; the death of his father, Frederick I Barbarossa, in June 1190 en route to Jerusalem; the arrival of Richard I of England at Messina in October with a crusader army demanding inheritance for his sister, William II's widow, Joanna; the southward advance of Henry's army deep into the Italian peninsula; and Tancred's subsequent reconsolidation of rebellious areas on the mainland – that when a major Muslim revolt broke out in western Sicily on William's death it attracted little attention in the primary sources.[1] The *Annales Casinenses* recorded briefly that, 'trouble arose at Palermo between Christians and Saracens. After many of their men had been massacred, the Saracens fled and went to live in the mountains'.[2] These remarks were echoed by Roger of Howden, who added that substantial numbers of Muslims were involved.[3]

The sense of impending disaster facing the kingdom in the spring of 1190 was recorded by Falcandus in his *Letter to Peter Concerning the Sicilian Tragedy*, voicing a vain hope that both Muslims and Christian leaders might offer a united political front against German invasion. With the wisdom of hindsight he observed that in the tinderbox that Sicily had become:

> it would be difficult for the Christian population not to oppress the Muslims in a crisis as great as this, with the fear of the king removed, worn down by many injuries at the hands of the Christians they would ... occupy forts along the coast or strongholds in the mountains, so that it would be necessary both to fight the Germans... and also to deal with attacks from the Muslims ... who will do whatever they can in their wretched situation to surrender to the foreigners.[4]

The timing of the Muslim revolt on the death of the king lent it the appearance of having purely opportunist motives. However, this would ignore the long-term malaise and brewing discontent in the Muslim community which, with the breaking of the royal *dhimma*, now resulted in open dissent to the authority of Monreale while the attention of most other parties was distracted. It also overlooks the attacks that again had been directed against the Muslims when central authority had broken down, exposing their vulnerability to another generation, some of whom would still have been able to recall the massacres of the 1160s. The renewed troubles sparked further, poorly attested, displacements of Muslims, the wealthier of whom realised their assets and presumably went overseas. It is perhaps no coincidence that in surviving Arabic deeds of sale from the late 1180s and 1190s, the vendors are Muslim and the purchasers Christian.[5] For those who had fled to the hills, the troubles brought together the distressed from the cities with the disaffected from the countryside in the uplands and mountain strongholds of western Sicily.

The revolt was the first time in over a century that the Sicilian Muslims had offered sustained resistance to a Christian ruler, and it was unlike any other in the kingdom in that it was not a baronial rebellion, nor was it sparked, encouraged or assisted (at this stage) by forces from outside the kingdom. Nor did it aim at outright control of the kingdom. Rather, since the protagonists were mainly Muslims who had been corralled onto the Monreale estates, the events quickly assumed religious overtones. However, the revolt was not continuous, nor did the Muslims always act in isolation. The pragmatic and informed approach of their leaders was shown by the initial cessation of the revolt via negotiation and local, personal diplomacy of those who had led the evacuation to the mountains. Their five leaders, described as 'Muslim mini-kings' (*reguli Sarracenorum*) by the chronicler Richard of San Germano, were said to have returned reluctantly to Palermo where Tancred was able to diffuse the revolt by resorting to his favoured policy of paying off those who threatened him.[6] The Muslims had thus not reverted to the *status quo ante* of paying the *jizya* either to the state or to Monreale, in fact, they were now in receipt of royal funds in what must have been celebrated as a triumph at the time. Elsewhere, the new king's tenuous control of the kingdom had also been menaced by the demands of Richard I at Messina, who was pacified by a vast payment of gold, the equivalent of a million *tarìs*. But with an accord reached between Tancred and Richard, the Muslims' stance was weakened as more attention could now be turned to them. Indeed, their perilous position depended on events which were being played out beyond their control as they were increasingly caught up as minor players in the thirteenth-century struggle for dominance of the kingdom between the major powers of medieval Europe.

Constance, Markward, Frederick and the Muslim rebels

When Tancred died on 20 February 1194, the crown passed to his ill-fated infant son, William III, whose mother, Sibyl, acted as regent. Henry VI, meanwhile, had been able to raise a German invasion force with strong Pisan and Genoese support, funded, in part, by the windfall revenue gained from the huge ransom payment for Richard I following his sequestration by Leopold V of Austria at the end of 1192. By September 1194, Henry had reached Sicily, entered Palermo the following month, and on Christmas Day was crowned. The following day, in Jesi near Ancona, his son, Frederick, the future German emperor and king of Sicily was born.

The *Annali genovesi*, an important source for the events of thirteenth-century campaigns, reported that Muslim soldiers had served in William III's army suggesting that they (and indeed the Muslim contingents who would fight in later Sicilian armies) had not rejected irreversibly and absolutely either Christian authority or that of the Sicilian kings. Moreover, it implies that in the midst of the invasion crisis there were significant differences of opinion within the Muslim communities which are otherwise unattested. In the period prior to the death of Henry in September 1197, however, little is heard of the Sicilian Muslims and there appears to have been relative calm in western Sicily.

In spite of her marriage, Constance had sought to reject German claims to Sicily and distance herself from the imperial seneschal, Markward of Anweiler, the powerful diplomatic and administrative representative in the Italian peninsula, putting her infant son under the protection of Pope Innocent III prior to her own death in November 1198.[7] Thus, Sicily was made a papal fief and Markward's initial support turned to opposition. In October 1199, Markward returned to Sicily from the mainland, re-entering from Trápani and, having successfully negotiated with the Sicilian Muslims, gained control of western parts of the island by the end of the year.

Innocent III's call for a crusade placed new fiscal pressures on the Church in Sicily to raise funds for the campaigns, and papal letters to prelates on the island during 1199 reveal the problems that the churches there were having in organising this.[8] Thus, when Innocent castigated Sicilian converts whom he claimed had lapsed and returned to Islam, he did so in the specific context of urging Sicilian clerics to condemn them and raise money for the crusade. For a major foundation like Monreale, the most obvious source of income for such an undertaking would have come from the lands and men in its possession – predominantly Muslims over whom they had little effective control, even prior to the pope's demand to raise revenue for the crusades.

Impatient to proceed, Innocent denounced Markward's entente with the Muslims and famously branded him as 'another Saladin'.[9] Such an unholy alignment of interests and a distraction from the call of crusade allowed the pope to direct the rhetoric of holy war against Markward in defence of papal rights as well as for a war against the Muslims. The same indulgences offered to those fighting the Muslims on crusade were now offered to those fighting against Markward. By the same token, the Sicilian Muslims had manoeuvred themselves into a potentially disastrous position vis-à-vis the papacy in its new fief or any future ruler's interests in the kingdom. Innocent's condemnation of Markward's coalition with the Muslims set a precedent which had much wider relevance in the evolution of politico-religious ideology as more defined and hostile attitudes came to focus on questions of heresy and heretical alliances in the years prior to the Albigensian crusade against the Cathars of Languedoc from 1209, the call for another crusade to the east in 1213, the Fourth Lateran Council of 1215 with its anti-Jewish legislation and the eventual launch of the 'papal' Fifth Crusade in 1217.[10]

The victory of the pope's coalition forces over Markward and the Muslims at the battle of Monreale in July 1200 did not leave the papacy in control of the island, but it did serve to weaken the makeshift alliance, which in any event was terminated by Markward's death in 1202. The situation locally was further complicated by the problems the abbey was experiencing, both internally between the monks and their archbishop, and in the towns and estates where they had been granted legal and fiscal rights, but over which they had little means of exercising their power. In 1203, Innocent accused the monks of Monreale of rebelling against their abbot and of having made an alliance with Markward's successor in Palermo, William Capparone, a Norman knight. The accusations were combined with an attack on the perceived moral laxity of the monks, their plundering of the church's treasury and their debauched life of luxury in Iato and Calatrasi where they had taken up residency[11] – two important Muslim strongholds which had been granted to Monreale and where Christian settlement seems otherwise to have been minimal.

In a papal letter of September 1206, addressed to the *archadius* (here, referring to the *qāḍī*) and all the *gaeti* (*qā'ids*) of the island, who by now enjoyed high levels of independence in strongholds specified as Iato, Entella, Celso and Platani, Innocent requested that they maintain their factional support of the church and for Frederick's kingship.[12] The letter's appeal for fealty confirms the *de facto* independence which the Muslims had already carved out for themselves. In retrospect, Innocent's offer was a generous, and an apparently genuine, one of partial rapprochement – charitable in the context of the crusader rhetoric which had preceded it and which it modified. Ironically, a negotiated agreement with Innocent may have represented the Muslims' best option, since their chances of long-term autonomy in western Sicily looked slim if they were not to become marginalised on politico-religious grounds as long as they posed a threat to the security of Monreale, and also to Palermo itself. Indeed, the Muslims had already made expansive gains with the fall in 1208 of the provincial centre, Corleone, securing most of the blocks of land formerly conceded to Monreale for themselves. Otherwise, the Muslims' chances rested with their ability to maintain unity and avoid supporting a losing faction or, in the event of greater consolidation of Christian forces, to negotiate from the standpoint of political compliancy. However, given that the Muslim leadership in western Sicily was isolated from discussions taking place in Rome and Germany, they received their information about the unfolding diplomacy indirectly, and presumably, in piecemeal form. As peace broke out among the Christians – at Palermo between archbishop Walter and William Capparone, and at Monreale between the monks and their abbot – the Muslims' options were again restricted by factors beyond their control.

The temporary smoothing of papal–German relations with Innocent's coronation of Otto IV of Brunswick as emperor in 1209 proved to be short-lived when Otto was excommunicated the following year. Again, the Sicilian Muslims came to play a peripheral, but risky, role, offering their support to Otto in 1211 as he attempted to extend imperial power on the island. Had the political gains Otto made in Germany not faltered, and had he not been calamitously defeated by French forces at Bouvines in the famous encounter of summer 1214, the Muslims might have been better placed to secure an enhanced negotiating position. But having consolidated support from the nobility in Germany, the young Frederick was prompted to restore rights in western Sicily by granting Monreale powers to rein in 'all rebels and dissidents … against the jurisdiction of the church', and by confirming to the church of Palermo previous grants of lands and men elsewhere in western Sicily.[13] Whether, in practice, the church would have been able to exercise its rights in these areas is questionable, but Frederick's attempts to strengthen such powers is early evidence of his disposition towards the Muslims and issues of their submission and obedience to established authority.[14] Indeed, Monreale's inability to act in its own interests in tandem with the distractions in Germany had doubtless contributed to lulling the Muslims into a false sense of security, even if they had proved themselves capable of inflicting military successes as shown by their assault on Palermo in

1216, and in the south with the kidnapping at Agrigento of its bishop, Urso, who was held hostage for over a year, during which the town and its church were plundered.[15] The relatively modest ransom of 5,000 *tarì* which was paid for his release may also indicate an element of cash-strapped brigandage within the Muslim factions.

In economic terms, the main centres of resistance appear to have been cut off from the traditional markets which much of their produce and crafts supplied. Attaining a basic, sustainable level of self-sufficiency would have been a relatively achievable goal, but the once-thriving towns and countryside of western Sicily could not flourish as before under such isolated conditions. Archaeological surveys show a population displacement trend away from the open estates on the plains and toward the more defensible centres, a movement which was likely to have accelerated during the campaigns of the early 1220s. As the only participants in the continuing resistance to Frederick's authority in Sicily, the Muslims had shifted from their dependency on fragile alliances to become an easily identifiable and, perhaps most dangerously, a defeatable target.

After his coronation as emperor in Rome in 1220 by Honorius III, Frederick spent most of his reign in south Italy, apart from time on crusade (1228–9) and a brief return to Germany (1236–7). Unlike the Norman monarchs, whose multicultural court he attempted to emulate, and whose centralised systems of governance and legislation he sought to recreate and build upon, Frederick was based largely on the mainland rather than the island. He also lacked the focal centre of a fixed capital and pleasure palaces of Palermitan proportions where cultural life was more easily integrated with the artistic richness of its surroundings.

Frederick's relations with the Muslims were multifaceted and ambivalent, and remain open to interpretation. Indeed, many of the same ambiguities and paradoxes, which can be seen in the Norman kings, are also applicable to Frederick. He was attested as knowing Arabic; he drew directly on works of Arab science and learning; he patronised Muslim and Jewish scholars and translations from Arabic; he employed Muslims in his armies; he maintained an exotic menagerie whose leopard-breeders were Muslims, and even dispatched philosophical questions in Arabic (*al-masā'il al-Ṣiqilliyya*) to Muslim thinkers in the hope of enlightenment from beyond the realm. In spite of such an implicitly positive (or non-hostile) disposition towards Arab-Muslim scholarship and culture, his attempts to reawaken Rogerian greatness were limited and the Staufen court amounted to little more than a pale imitation of its predecessors, lacking the numbers of itinerant scholars, artisans and a local, supporting cast of similarly minded notables and patrons whose presence was an essential ingredient for an authentic multicultural court life. Besides which, apart from the relative absence of Greek elements and personnel, there was no Arabic *dīwān* such as that which had existed during the Norman period, there were no prominent Muslims in the higher echelons of government and there was no reliance on professional, crypto-Muslim eunuchs. Instead, a handful of Arab-Christians, such as Oberto Fallamonaca (whose ancestry may once have been Muslim), were among the last authors of Arabic diplomata to be issued by an administration in Italy. Royally sponsored Arab-Norman art may have been a function of political propaganda, but it was also a reflection of the kingdom's peoples in a way in which Frederick II's court was not.

Politically and diplomatically, Frederick's contacts with the Islamic world were also complex, not least his well-known reluctance to go on crusade, culminating in the negotiated handover of Jerusalem and his own controversial coronation as its king. More locally, it was Frederick who was to defeat the rebels of western Sicily and transport Muslims from around the kingdom to a single, isolated colony on the mainland. Two major phases of campaigns in western Sicily were undertaken between 1222–4 and 1243–6, during which there appear to have been numerous attacks and incursions – in effect, a type of guerrilla warfare. In July 1220, Frederick had again ordered that all lands and men originally conceded to Monreale should be returned to the church, a point he reiterated in March 1221 in response to a specific appeal from the archbishop of Monreale, revealing that the church was still unsuccessful in its efforts to bring the Muslims to heel.[16] By the spring of 1221, Frederick had entered the island with an army to reassert and consolidate his authority, taking Trápani and Agrigento by the autumn before turning his attention to the mountain strongholds.

The restoration of the Muslim amirate under Ibn ʿAbbād

For the events surrounding the great Muslim revolt, reliance is not entirely placed on Latin narrative sources, imperial documents and papal correspondence. Two brief accounts in Arabic dealing with the leaders of the Sicilian Muslims and their demise are offered by al-Ḥimyarī (d. 1329) and al-Ḥamawī (fl. mid-1200s).[17] There are, however, a number of inconsistencies across these sketchy reports which prevent establishing even some of the basic narrative with certainty. The fullest account is given by al-Ḥamawī, who noted that the Muslim leader, Muḥammad Ibn ʿAbbād, was not native to the island. Rather, he was an Ifrīqiyan from Mahdiyya who had migrated to Sicily in his youth where he had married the daughter of a local notable called Ibn Fākhir. Described as *qā'id*, judge (*hākim*) and ruler (*sulṭān*) of the Muslims, Ibn ʿAbbād was sufficiently old to be counted among at least the second generation of Muslim chiefs after the five *reguli* of the Tancred era, in what appears to have been a consolidation of the leadership in western Sicily itself. The extent of that leadership – which was secular and not necessarily inherited through the male line – is qualified by al-Ḥamawī's point that outside the mountains and elsewhere, he held sway over (only) 'some of the plains'. However, corroborative evidence is provided by coins referring to him by the Almohad title of *amīr al-Muslimīn bi-Ṣiqilliyya* or 'commander of the Muslims in Sicily'.[18] Legally speaking, in Sicily the private issuing of coinage was considered as a species of forgery: contravention of the Rogerian Assize which prohibited it was a capital offence. Ibn 'Abbād's action may be seen as one of defiance as well as one which proclaimed his authority as rightful Muslim leader while providing a source of financial liquidity.

The Arabic sources indicate that Ibn 'Abbād's base was the stronghold of Entella. However, when Frederick's army besieged Iato in 1222, Latin sources claimed that this was part of a campaign against Ibn 'Abbād, supporting the idea that his leadership was recognised in key areas across western Sicily and known beyond it. Indeed, Frederick's attack on Djerba in the following year may be linked with the Sicilian rebellion to cut off a source of supply or to fire a broadside to Almohad-Ḥafsid Ifrīqiya whose moral support for their co-religionists, if nothing else, could be counted on.

In summer 1222, Frederick besieged Iato and, in September, the stronghold of Calatrasi. However, it was only in the following summer, the third of consecutive campaigning, that Ibn 'Abbād was killed, Iato fell and the first deportations of Muslims from the island began. The extant accounts of Ibn 'Abbād's death offer few details, some of which are contradictory: al-Ḥamawī recorded that at the height of the siege, a powerful group among the Muslims, led by the son of the *qāḍī*, had persuaded the unwilling Ibn 'Abbād to sue for peace. In the supposed safety of Frederick's own tent, he was assaulted and later killed. For their part, the Latin *Annales Siculi* recorded only his execution by hanging at Palermo.[19] After his death, the leadership passed to a certain *qā'id* Marzūq, who reportedly tricked and killed 115 of Frederick's men having offered to surrender to them. Mentioned in passing in the chronicle of Alberic of Three Fountains was Ibn 'Abbād's alliance with the Sicilian-Genoese admiral, William Porcus, and a notable from Marseilles, Hugo Fer, who was also close to the Genoese, hinting at the existence of a Genoese–Muslim alliance against Frederick, perhaps in an attempt to restore mercantile trading concessions and privileges.[20]

The brief account of al-Ḥimyārī blends a modicum of serious history with metaphor and literary topos focusing on the alleged leadership of Ibn 'Abbād's (unnamed) daughter. In part, the episodes serve to act as a somewhat trite vehicle, echoing themes in the Qur'ān, but here complete with direct speech, to demonstrate the power of female cunning which was more than a match for the guile of a Christian emperor and his agents, who had betrayed and killed her father after he had negotiated safe passage to Ifrīqiya following a truce concluded in 1219–20.[21] The themes of betrayal and counter-betrayal also feature in the version of a close contemporary source, Ibn Sa'īd al-Maghribī, whose account was written by *c.* 1243. Most of the key ingredients of the tale are present: Frederick's duplicity; Ibn 'Abbād's death; his anonymous daughter's subsequent leadership at Entella; and her ruse which led to the death of 300 Frankish knights who had been tricked into thinking that the town had surrendered. To these are added the telling observations that not one Muslim ruler had offered to help and that she had eventually used poison to kill herself. Described in modern secondary literature as a 'heroine of the resistance', the daughter's tale lends itself to a bleaker figurative interpretation to explain the final days of the Muslims in Sicily, reduced to resorting to a female commander who could do little but use her innate power to deceive. When this failed, she lost the will to continue and ended her life in an un-Islamic manner through an act of self-murder.[22]

Early deportations and the mission to al-Malik al-Kāmil

Prior to the military campaigns, Frederick had repeatedly attempted to persuade the Muslims to recognise the authority of the archbishop of Monreale, to return to the estates on which they were registered, and to adhere to the terms of the original concessions made by William II. The evidence suggests that, had the Muslims complied and avoided seeking alliances with forces from outside the island, this would have been sufficient from the perspectives of both king and pope to prevent further campaigns against them. As such, the driving forces behind Frederick's strategies can be explained in political and socio-economic terms. However, this same explanation, with its strong elements of continuity and a desire to return to the pre-1189 conditions of tenure, cannot satisfactorily explain Frederick's decision to uproot the community and transplant the rebels from the island to Lucera on the mainland.[23]

On the eve of the campaigns against the Muslims, Frederick had issued new legislation, including assizes, informed by the spirit of the Fourth Lateran Council. For example, the outsider status of prostitutes was confirmed in theory by their isolation outside the city walls, while Jews were theoretically required to adopt distinctive dress and beards. The Luceran Muslims, like Jews in Staufen Sicily and Germany, had the status of being *servi nostre camere*. That is to say, although they were not slaves and had inheritance rights, they were considered to be as the protected, personal property of the royal chamber.[24] Given that religious rights were guaranteed and that conversion of the Muslims, while sometimes advocated and partially successful, was neither the sole nor the primary aim of the Luceran colony, then precedents might be seen in the imperial disposition towards the Jews. Alternatively, the Muslims' status might be interpreted as an extension of the fiscal-religious arrangement under the Norman kings – a hybrid, European counterpart of the *dhimmī* system. In either case, the relationship between royal authority and non-Christian faith communities was expressed in terms of the perceived political and moral superiority of the ruling party over the other, who, as imperial property, enjoyed a limited degree of rights and responsibilities. The move, however, cannot be understood as entirely conservative since Frederick's treatment of the Muslims had brought them into *his* possession rather than being restored to the (now rundown) church of Monreale to which they had been initially granted in perpetuity by William II. Thus, the grand largesse of the last Norman king to the Latin Church came to benefit Staufen revenues because an estimated colony population of 20,000 paid the *jizya* and land tax into imperial coffers.[25]

Frederick had been slow to act on his coronation commitment to go on crusade. He had been excommunicated twice before finally arriving in Syria–Palestine where, in February 1229, he reached agreement with the Ayyubid sultan, al-Malik al-Kāmil (d. 1238) by which the emperor gained control of Jerusalem. At some point between autumn 1229 and May 1230, a certain Aḥmad ibn Abī l-Qāsim al-Rummānī, one of the *shaykhs* from the village of Gh.l.w (Ghulūw? Gallo?) in the mountains of Sicily, arrived in Ḥarrān, now in modern Turkey.[26] There, he was able to brief the sultan on events. Al-Rummānī, who may have belonged to the Banū l-Rummānī from the estate of al-Quriyānī in western Sicily, was described as a pilgrim, implying that he was returning from Mecca.[27] Whether he had fled from the island for good is debatable, as is whether this departure should be interpreted as evidence for the further emigration of Sicilian Muslims. However, the immigrant status of Ibn ʿAbbād perhaps serves as a caveat against the assumption that, even in times of crisis, migratory movements were unidirectional. Al-Rummānī told al-Kāmil that 170,000 people had been turned out of their homelands, stripped of their wealth and transported to the Italian mainland. In addition, half that number had been killed, the mountains were empty, Cinisi, Iato and Entella were the main surviving strongholds and his own village was a ruin. The report of the man from Ghulūw was clearly an exaggeration, and it was not taken seriously enough to merit the sultan's intervention. None the less, he had been made aware of the Sicilian Muslims' plight but, given their peripheral importance, his own problems locally and the ten-year truce in place with Frederick, the sultan chose not to act.

The mention of neglected estates, however, is telling. In the Monreale description of boundaries from 1182, this wider area of western Sicily was said to be littered with derelict buildings (*khirāb*). There is a chance that these were damaged by the earthquake of 1169; if so, they had not been put to rights after thirteen years, and it was still several years before the rebellions had even begun. Given this tale of decline in the 1180s, how much worse must the condition of western Sicily have been by the time it had become isolated, warlord territory at the end of the 1220s?

In October 1239, groups of Muslims agreed to be transferred from western Sicily to Palermo, a move which appears to have been a precursor to a more distant deportation to the mainland, since reference was made the following month to 'all the Muslims whom *a short while ago* we instructed to come [to Lucera] from areas around Sicily'.[28] Systematic elements of the logistics and transportation are confirmed by the relative absence of archaeological finds around Iato relating to objects of daily life, which suggests that the evacuation had been organised, orderly and with a degree of mutual consent as the population took their belongings with them. Life for Muslims in an exclusively Muslim colony where the vestigial Christian community, including its bishop, were minor players would not necessarily have been perceived negatively, given the circumstances of their defeat. In medieval terms, it may have seemed an honourable solution by comparison with the prospect of sale into slavery. Anyway, the Muslims' historic agreement to adhere to the concept of indirect rule had accepted some degree of isolation within the parameters set by the royal *dhimma* prior to the revolt. Besides which, there were any number of precedents for relocation of political opponents in the medieval Mediterranean in general, although fewer are to be found specifically within Sicily itself. As we have seen, the dislocation principle was used as early as the Norman conquest of the island. That it was also a policy of Roger II's is perhaps shown by his segregation of political prisoners in the jail in the Muslim stronghold at Iato. For his part, Frederick himself had recently dispersed the rebellious (Christian) population of the town of Celano in Abruzzo in 1223.

The end of Muslim Malta and final deportations to Lucera

It is likely that the Celano rebels were eventually resettled in Malta, contributing to the increased Latinisation and Christianisation of the island which had begun slowly with the creation of a somewhat inactive bishopric in 1156. By the time of its initial capture by the Normans and later reconsolidation under Count Roger II in the late 1120s, the island still had a majority Muslim population. Indeed, there is no strong evidence to suggest that it was any more than lightly Christianised until toward the end of the twelfth century. Malta had been briefly conceded from the royal demesne by Tancred but was restored by Constance, who pledged that 'the faithful subjects of Malta and Gozo' would remain for ever within the property of the crown. At the same time, the annual fine imposed on the Maltese Christian community by Roger II for the killing of a Muslim was repealed, thereby easing the burden of the Christians and sending a symbolic message to the Muslims that their protection had now been downgraded. The processes towards Latin Christianity thus accelerated under Constance and continued under Frederick with the first deportations of the island's Muslims to Lucera in 1224, in spite of their impeccable loyalty to their overlords.

Whether later deportations occurred remains controversial. Evidence comes from a chronologically confused passage in Ibn Khaldūn suggesting that further removals had taken place from 1245.[29] If the readings of another contentious report, composed around 1241, are to be trusted, then the relative proportion of Christians to Muslims said to be living on Malta and Gozo was approximately 3:2.[30] Moreover, the tax burden of the Maltese Muslims under Frederick was higher than that of their Christian neighbours since they were liable to pay both the *jizya* and a tax on produce. Even so, the processes of Christianisation were clearly not complete by this stage. Thus, Malta poses another historical and linguistic conundrum: the known history of the Maltese Muslims appears to run broadly parallel to that of Muslim Sicily. However, in the case of Malta, the most widely accepted explanation for its Christianisation, in spite of the lack of specific evidence, is that conversion must have happened under Frederick II in order to avoid the burden of discriminatory taxes. Accompanying this explanation is the inference that the long-term Arabicisation of Malta's indigenous and converted Christian population had given rise to a level of Arabicisation that was sufficiently strong for them to reproduce themselves as a largely monolingual, Arabic-speaking community long after the Muslims had begun to convert or to be expelled – quite unlike the situation in Sicily where Arabic became extinct as the island continued its linguistic re-Latinisation. If such hypotheses are accepted, then the socio-religious and linguistic dynamics of the Muslims and Arabic-speaking Christians of medieval Sicily and Malta were far from analogous. Rather, immigration and Sicilian bilingualism gave the Christians living there alternative languages, which the indigenous Maltese lacked, irrespective of religion. Hence, although the islands were both strongly Christianised, the Sicilians came to speak Italo-Romance dialects whereas modern Maltese is rooted in a dialect of Maghribi Arabic with Romance superstrata, but devoid of any significant Greek substratum.

Mention at this juncture should also be made of Pantelleria situated 107 kilometres from Mazara in Sicily but only seventy-one kilometres from the Cap Bon peninsula of modern Tunisia. The island was sufficiently remote to have retained a Muslim community until the 1300s in addition to Arabic-speakers beyond that date. Now part of modern Italy, the historical influence of Arabic is marked by its distinctive toponymy and dialect of Pantesco.

According to the *Annales Siculi*, during July 1243, 'all the Saracens of Sicily, as if rebels, went up into the mountains and took Iato and Entella'.[31] The renewed revolt could not have happened at a worse time for Frederick, whose priorities throughout his reign had concentrated on relations with the papacy, Guelf and Ghibelline factions, the German nobility, Lombard towns, the Italian mainland communes and the dilemma of when (or if) to take the cross. The flare-up of the Muslim revolt was particularly problematic since it followed on the heels of Innocent IV's election to the papacy and his denunciation of the emperor at the Council in Lyons in 1245, which criticised his well-known penchant for Arab-Islamic arts and 'Oriental' aspects to his lifestyle that left him exposed to pejorative, guilt by association accusations and added to the question of his having usurped papal rights and Church lands. Moreover, the revolt and failed siege of Viterbo to the north of Rome had ushered in a period of particularly intense exchanges between pope and emperor. So, compared with Frederick's primary concerns, the Muslim rebels in western Sicily were a sideshow, and only sporadic references to the events of the clashes can be gleaned from the Latin sources. The claim made in 1245 by the count of Caserta that all the Muslims had by then been transported to Lucera was exaggerated, yet it is clear that after three years of engagements with the imperial army, the rebels had, by summer 1246, largely surrendered and were being deported to Lucera. By November, the last had been transferred. There is relatively little archaeological evidence to support much settlement on Monte Iato after this period.

As we have already seen, in the 'Rollus Rubeus' chartulary from Cefalù, composed *c.* 1329, a list of Muslim 'villeins' once said to have been granted by Roger II was written out for the benefit of posterity.[32] The reason for this was that the church had lost all trace of its possessions due to the confusion within its own administration, compounded by 'the unlawful violation of the barons, or the change of rulers, in addition to the crises of wars'. Matching the description of the 1189–1246 chaos, the text goes on to explain that some 'villeins' became monks of the church, whereas others took up arms and fled, with the result that Cefalù's knowledge of their whereabouts was either non-existent or otherwise very sparse. Significantly for the rebellions, the register of men provides evidence for the conversion of Muslim villeins to Latin-rite Christianity, as well as implying that the Muslim revolts had extended much further than simply the mountains of western Sicily, since the 'villeins' of Cefalù's estates were mainly in the north-central areas. A cryptic endnote to the text added that some on the list had been replaced by Jews, a point of detail which can be corroborated only generally since Frederick had encouraged Jews from north Africa to settle in Sicily to compensate for the serious shortfall in agricultural skills which the deportation of the Muslims had created.

The development of Lucera as a Muslim colony

In 1239–40, Frederick offered a thousand head of cattle to the Luceran Muslims in order to tie them to the land, 'as was the case in the time of King William', strengthening the idea that Lucera was intended as a type of imperial tax farm.[33]

Frederick had repeatedly tried to restrict the movement of Muslims to the lands on which they were registered, an issue that had perhaps been a sensitive one since the time that concessions were first made to Monreale. But Frederick had also been eager to stimulate the rural economy – and in this respect Lucera certainly prospered. Indeed, the occupations of the Luceran Muslims were almost as wide-ranging as they had been in western Sicily. Many names indicating an involvement in a 'profession', which are found among the population of Monreale in the 1170s and 1180s, are also attested (in much less rich sources) at Lucera. In addition to the various tasks which existed in any south Italian medieval town surrounded by countryside, specifically attested in *both* Monreale and Lucera were: those involved with stock breeding and animal husbandry (including rearers and keepers of pigs, goats, sheep, horses, donkeys and bees), shepherds, butchers, tanners, saddlers, falconers and huntsmen, millers, bakers, potters, stonemasons, cotton growers, vintners and fruit growers, tailors, tent-makers, carpenters, soldiers, guards, castellans and stewards, in addition to a range of smiths and metal-workers, buglers, musicians, bath-house keepers, notaries, minor officials and *qā'ids* – who in the case of Lucera were clearly associated with the military.[34]

As a consolidated urban centre, Lucera was much larger and more impressive than any single settlement in rural western Sicily, yet it is possible to observe a high degree of continuity between the two locations in terms of occupations and activities, even if some of the institutional structures and organisation of Lucera were different from those of western Sicily. There are also some notable absences and in part such a comparison is blighted by the extent of the available evidence. For example, western Sicily had been an important site for silk production and possibly its manufacture – a point of supply which would have been severed from the demand of its markets during the rebellion – but this does not seem to have been quite such a prominent activity among the Luceran Muslims. On the other hand, no silversmiths were attested in documents relating to western Sicily, nor can any trace of camels or leopard breeders be found there, yet all were known in Lucera.

Lucera's location and its rich and mixed material resources easily enhanced its potential for generating substantial – and taxable – economic wealth. Not only were levels of taxation very high, but some of the wealthier Lucerans were considered to be a convenient source for raising capital, and were required to provide loans, for example to alleviate cash-flow crises under the Angevin king of Naples, Charles II (r. 1285–1309). But, while farming and agriculture were fundamentally important to the Luceran economy, the population also played vital military roles both as a resource for soldiers (especially light cavalry and archers) and as manufacturers of specialist weaponry such as bows, arrows and shields. Over this formidable arsenal, the Muslims acted as reliable guardians within the walls of the city. The distinct possibility that western Sicily had served as a recruiting ground for the Norman army cannot be discounted, especially since many 'villeins' recorded on the Monreale registers had names which clearly suggest they had (or had once had) roles in the military. However, it is unlikely to have rivalled Lucera as a source of such specific manpower. The castle at Lucera, built by the 1240s and probably begun shortly after the earliest Muslim settlement, served not only as a well-appointed palace which Frederick himself had often visited, but also as an armoury, illustrating the considerable extent of mutual trust and understanding that existed between Frederick and the Muslims – a political relationship continued by his son, Manfred, who took refuge in the town in 1254 when fleeing papal forces. Such was the importance of arms-manufacturing at Lucera that at the start of the Wars of the Sicilian Vespers in 1282, some 60,000 arrows were commissioned from there. The established tradition of military service was the principal mechanism open to the Muslims for socio-economic improvement, and families known to have been associated with the army were also attested as landholders. Indeed, given the colony's strategic military role as a fortress and armoury, the Luceran military – subject to Christian command – constituted a prestigious, responsible and privileged group within the community.

As had been the case in Sicily, the Muslims in Lucera possessed their own slaves and were regulated by the legal expertise of jurists and *qāḍīs*, some of whom may have made the pilgrimage to Mecca. Lucera, like rural western Sicily, was never an intellectual centre for Islam, but the record of a Muslim 'gymnasium' suggests that some form of institutional education kept up minimum standards of legal competence and religious learning in a functioning Muslim community. However, there were many indicators of the long-term and irreversible decline of Italo-Islamic culture: the key features of Sunnī Islamic lands elsewhere in the late twelfth and thirteenth centuries were simply not apparent in late Muslim Sicily or Lucera. While the triumph, imposition and popularisation of orthodox forms of Islam in the 1200s saw the development of the *madrasa* system and the institutionalisation of the Sufi movement, these developments passed by the island and the continent. There was barely any scholarship in the Islamic sciences to speak of at all, and little in the arts, architecture or high material culture of any kind. The loss of the requisite skills has left little trace of epigraphy either. The sharp decline in Arab-Islamic intellectual activity in the twelfth century thus collapsed completely in the thirteenth century.

At Lucera, the preservation of Arabic language, manners, customs and religion, serves as a clear indicator of a strong identity and perhaps a stubborn resistance to rapid assimilation. 'Frontier tolerance' continued, as it did elsewhere, at the margins of the Islamic world, in that dietary restrictions on wine and swine, for example, were relaxed in ways that were not inconsistent with life as it had been on insular Sicily. Sustaining Islamic cultural norms was always possible in an isolated environment so long as there was a sufficiently strong will to do so – which there clearly was. Where assimilation into the background culture was attested, it was in the direction of Latinisation – or, rather, south Italianisation. Thus, the limited onomastic evidence available reveals a number of Muslims who had adopted (alternative?) names chosen from Frankish, New Testament or saintly repertoires such as Richard, Roger, Jordan, Matthew, John, Peter, Anthony and Paschal. This broke with the tradition of the previous century on insular Sicily where the tendency had been to merge with the local Arabic-speaking Christians, most of whom bore Greek or Arabic personal names. However, there too, the indications are that any remaining Muslims were absorbed by conversion, and that assimilation increasingly gravitated towards Latinate models for both Muslim converts and Arabic-speaking Christians. In Sicily, Arabic was likely to have fallen from use with some rapidity from 1250. Thus, one of the last known Arabic signatures was that of a former judge and captain of Messina, Baldwin Mussonus, in 1282.[35]

The language in both its spoken and written forms was, however, preserved by the largely bilingual Jewish communities of the island. None the less, the relative absence of Arabic terms in later Sicilian dialects after over 400 years of use is testament to the ways in which it had come to be almost entirely supplanted by mainland dialects, including many from the north of the peninsula. Two features which distinguish modern Sicilian dialects from most others of south Italy, and which have resulted from historical settlement and conquest patterns, are the presence of grammar and vocabulary associated with 'north' Italian usages alongside the use of (a tiny number) Arabic terms. At Lucera, linguistic evidence, too, suggests that while the Muslims continued to speak Arabic, they were said to have at least understood the local language(s) of the surrounding Christian population: that is, various forms of Italianate dialects.

Archaeology and the socio-economic collapse of western Sicily

The former homelands of the Luceran Muslims in the countryside of western Sicily saw the transformation of an agricultural system which, for over 300 years, had developed into complex, diversified, intensive and extensive systems of production that could nourish large surrounding populations and market towns as well as export excess yields. However, successful production and operation was predicated on a platform of political stability sufficient to maintain and regulate such features as irrigation systems. This socio-economic equilibrium was sensitive to a range of factors which could disrupt it – in particular, political upheaval, the severance of demand from supply, excessive taxation, the threat of usurpation and, above all, radical changes to the population base. The deportation of the Muslims thus set the population and economy of western Sicily on a steeply slanted, downward spiral such that the rich diversity of crops once grown by a thriving population was given over to a monoculture of cereal crops harvested by a considerably smaller number of tenant farmers.[36]

Although much archaeological work remains to be undertaken in western Sicily, findings from surveys and excavations suggest that fundamental changes to the material culture of the region correlate with its precipitous socio-economic decline in the thirteenth century and the demographic collapse following the expulsion of the Muslims by 1246, the damage caused by the Wars of the Sicilian Vespers between 1282 and 1302, and the devastation of the Black Death which reached Messina in October 1347. The impact of these consecutive catastrophes was so enormous that the island's population, henceforth under colonial rule, would not recover in number until the late 1800s.

The changing socio-economic and cultural orientation of the island across the Islamic, Norman and Staufen periods can be shown by the shifting distribution patterns of archaeological finds, such that, during the later Islamic period of the eleventh century, exports of Sicilian ceramic ware to Cyrenaica in northern Libya were common.[37] By the first half of the twelfth century, the direction of export had moved northwards to the Tyrrhenian coastal towns, but by the latter half of the twelfth century, there is little evidence of the export of Sicilian pottery at all, indicating a significant weakening of Sicily as a centre of production. Furthermore, this same period of decline coincides with a stylistic change from Ifrīqiyan ceramics, with which there had previously been close similarities, indicating that there were no longer high levels of exchange between products, ideas and the artisans themselves which the two regions had traditionally enjoyed. In the first half of the thirteenth century, clear-cut differences in both form and function of ceramic ware are observable and a contrast can be drawn between the conservative production of western Sicily and the innovative areas of 'Latinised' south-eastern Sicily, which had introduced Ligurian styles associated with north Italy. Finally, no evidence from the 1300s has been recovered that can be linked to the traditions of the Muslim potters, implying the extinction of these particular forms by this period, which neatly accords with the rapid collapse of Arab-Islamic cultural traditions on the island in the wake of the deportations to Lucera. Overall, the archaeological findings to date represent an index of decline, disjuncture and displacement.

Archaeological work carried out between 1989 and 1995 around the site of Segesta in the north-west of the island, outside the areas conceded to Monreale but only thirty kilometres from both Iato and Calatrasi, has revealed the progressive expansion of a settlement followed by its abrupt abandonment.[38] Based on the relative quantities of datable materials, such as coins, pot sherds and glassware, in tandem with the extant remains of buildings, the evidence points to the creation of a simple, rural settlement in the early 1100s. That the population was Muslim appears to be confirmed by the discovery of a rectangular ground plan with a *miḥrāb* or prayer niche in the south-facing wall, suggesting to the excavators that this village included a mosque – indeed, one of the very few even to be tentatively identified in Sicily. The presence of a local (Latin) lord by the mid-thirteenth century was signalled by the construction and extension of a castle keep or *donjon* in the centre of the estate. A hypothesis deriving from the building of a small church and the demolition of the mosque is that there had been an attempt to concentrate the villagers in the estate and convert them to Christianity – a strategy which can be shown to have failed by the dispersal of the community by the second half of the thirteenth century. Alternatively, the Muslim villagers had either become caught up in the rebellion and/or deported with their co-religionists from the hills to the east. In spite of the inherent conjectures and assumptions in the reconstruction of this history, the conclusions present thought-provoking data and scenarios which are by no means implausible. Indeed, the legacies of post-rebellion abandonment are amply confirmed by several archaeological surveys as are their longer-term effects.

From *Lucera Sarracenorum* to *Lucera Christianorum* under the Angevins

Following the death of Frederick II, the second half of the thirteenth century ushered in a period of political upheaval in both south Italy and insular Sicily. At Lucera, Frederick's son, Manfred, had been quick to rally the support of its population against papal forces, once again involving the Muslims in a wider and perilous political game. The unholy coalition of Manfred and the Muslims was condemned in a crusader bull issued by Alexander IV in 1255 and, later in that year, the pope offered the crown of Sicily to Edmund, the young son of the English king, Henry III. However, by 1258, the English had withdrawn from their expensive Mediterranean ambitions and Manfred was crowned as king of Sicily. The new pope, Urban IV, sought the support of Charles I of Anjou with sustained and widespread preaching in France and northern Italy in the early 1260s against Manfred and the Muslims, with indulgences offered to those who would fight against them as if the campaign were a crusade. At the pivotal battle of Benevento in February 1266, Charles defeated Manfred and his Muslim forces, and in the confused aftermath, during which Lucera surrendered, some of its inhabitants fled north to the hills of Abruzzo.

Conradin, the son of Manfred's half-brother, Conrad IV, and thus with a legitimate claim as heir to rule Sicily, arrived in the Italian peninsula to take the crown. Against a background of serious food shortages and uprisings against the Angevins in 1268, Lucera, now under the control of Charles, also rebelled.

Again, the alliance between the Staufens and the Muslims, compounded by what may have been a genuine fear of a wider Muslim alliance with the Mamlūk forces of Baybars, served as the pretext for crusader preaching against them. The Luceran Muslims did not capitulate even following the defeat and death of Conradin in August 1268, leading to a major siege of the city and blockade of the surrounding area during the next year. The siege was ultimately successful and Charles sought to recoup part of the expenses incurred from taxes levied on the Muslims whose *status quo ante* was restored in return for their fealty to the Angevins. Perhaps here was the clearest example of the triumph of economic expediency over more abstract religious concerns that Charles may have had, since the revolt would have provided him with the excuse to disband the colony in the perceived interests of Christianity and the papacy. However, Luceran life, its heavy tax burden and its strategic role as a military stronghold continued much as it had before. Within a decade of the revolt, the numbers of Christian castellans and military officers who had been put in place to oversee and ensure control of the castle were substantially reduced, suggesting that further Muslim revolts were not anticipated.[39] In addition, Christian settlers, mainly from Provence, were introduced into the colony and lived in a fortified precinct within the walls. However, they clearly had an uncomfortable and prickly relationship with their Muslim neighbours and found it difficult to thrive in the unfamiliar environment. Even as late as 1296, the bishop at Lucera was said be living in poor conditions.

Under the Angevins, a fortress with moat, walls and cisterns to withstand sieges was constructed, in part with finances and labour from the colony itself, showing the continued importance it had as a military base and storehouse of weaponry. It again reveals how, for a generation under the Angevins, political pragmatism had overcome the religious rhetoric previously aimed at Frederick II and his successors.

There is no single, satisfactory explanation for the eventual disbanding of Lucera in 1300 by Charles II. Rather, standard accounts comprise overlapping strands of religious, political or economic motives for action, prioritised to varying extents.[40] A further consideration is the degree to which immediate and pressing matters of the day outweighed the longer-term benefits of maintaining the colony, converting its population or selling them into slavery. Economically, for instance, Lucera had provided high yields of tax and produce and it, therefore, made little sense to jettison such a profitable source of revenue. Besides which, its destruction had foreseeable and negative consequences for the surrounding areas into which its strong economy fed. Economic motives may have been informed by the need to find a direct and convenient way to finance the severe, short-term cash crisis that had been caused by the expenses of funding the Sicilian Vespers. Viewed in this light, the carefully documented sale of the

Luceran Muslims provided a windfall of instant revenue towards the very end of the wars marked by the Treaty of Caltabellotta in 1302, ratified in the following year. Moreover, the actions could be presented as a political victory against the infidel, consistent with the treatment of non-Christian minorities elsewhere and scored by a king who had not taken up the cross.

Religion was inevitably a significant factor in dealings with Lucera, and thus qualifies any attempt to explain the end of Lucera entirely in political or economic terms. Under the Angevins, who had encouraged greater Christian presence within the colony, religion had not always proved to be a decisive factor, even against an historical background of Charles II's expulsion of Jews from Anjou and Maine in France, territorial losses in the Latin East with the fall of Acre in 1291 and vigorous Church preaching and inquisitorial action led by the Dominicans particularly against heretics and Jews. Two months prior to the dissolution of the colony, Charles had offered tax exemptions to its Christians suggesting that a plan had already been hatched to dispose of the Muslims, but that a final chance for their conversion and salvation was being offered. The details of the destruction process under the auspices of the count of Altamura, who had been appointed to oversee its execution, recall how the Muslims were sold into slavery and how even conversion at this late stage did not help their plight since manumission was not offered to converts. Nor were the Muslims permitted to sell their possessions, although some converts among the Luceran elites were grudgingly allowed back goods that had been confiscated. In one attested case, this came far too late to have been of any material use for the offspring whose inheritance it was, as they had all died before the restitution could be made. Thus, in effect, even the sons of converts were disinherited. This again points to the crown's desire to benefit materially at the expense of the Muslims, indicating economic motives over religiously inspired reasons for action. Attacks attested on remaining Muslims and those who had been moved to holding centres prior to their sale also implies a degree of local hostility towards them, while orders issued to recapture fugitives signals how some had managed to escape. Indeed, small bands of Muslims were reported in towns around south Italy until they too fled or were absorbed by the pressure to convert and assimilate. Finally, in an attempt to rebrand Lucera as a Christian entity disassociated from its Muslim past, the city was renamed with the conspicuously Christian description of 'Civitas Sanctae Mariae' and was sometimes referred to as 'Lucera Christianorum' where, shortly after the final expulsions, the cathedral – also dedicated to the Virgin Mary – came to be built on top of the last functioning mosque in medieval Italy.

Notes

1 Amari-Nallino's coverage of events in found in *SMS*² III: 578–600. The archaeology of the period and area is covered in numerous conference proceedings. Of particular note are: Hans Isler, 'Gli arabi a monte Iato', in *Dagli scavi di Montevago e di Rocca d'Entella: un contributo di conoscenze per la Storia dei Musulmani della Valle del Belice dal X al XIII secolo*, Atti del Convegno Nazionale (Montevago, 27–8 October 1990), G. Castellana (ed.) (Agrigento, 1992), pp. 105–25; *Entella I*, Giuseppe Nenci (ed.) (Pisa, 1995); and the published findings of the *Monreale Survey* led by Jeremy Johns. For events and analysis of the Muslim revolt from both archaeological and documentary perspectives, see Ferdinando Maurici, *L'emirato sulle montagne. Note per una storia della resistenza musulmana in Sicilia nell'età di Federico II di Svevia* (Palermo, 1987); by the same author, see also 'Uno stato musulmano nell'Europa christiana del XIII secolo: l'emirato siciliano di Mohammed Ibn Abbad', *Acta historica et archaeologica medievalia*, 18 (1997): 257–80.

2 *Annales Casinenses*, in *MGH*, *SS*, xix.314. A translation by G. A. Loud of the *Annales Casinenses* covering the period 1189–95 is available online.

3 Roger of Howden, *Gesta Rogeris Ricardi*, in *Gesta Regis Henrici Secundi*, W. Stubbs (ed.) (London, Rolls Series, 2 vols, 1867), II:141; *Chronica*, W. Stubbs (ed.) (London, Rolls Series, 4 vols, 1870), III:69.

4 Falcandus, *Letter to Peter*, Lat. p. 173; Eng. pp. 252–63 (p. 255).

5 For convenience of reference, see the summaries in Johns, *Arabic Administration*, pp. 322–4.

6 Richard of San Germano, p. 9.

7 For monograph studies, the modern historiography begins with the dated work of T. C. Van Cleve, *Markward of Anweiler and the Sicilian Regency* (Princeton, 1937).

8 *Patrologia Latina*, J. P. Migne (ed.), 221 vols (Paris, 1844–64), Letters of Innocent III, ccxiv, no. 302, cols. 263–5; no. 508, cols. 470–1, and no. 509, cols. 471–2. For the modern edition, see *Die Register Innocenz III. 1 Pontifikatsjahr 1198/1199*, Othmar Hageneder and Anton Haidacher (eds) (Graz and Cologne, 1964).

9 On the crusade against Markward, see Elizabeth M. Kennan, 'Innocent III and the first political Crusade: a comment on the limitations of papal power', *Traditio*, 27 (1971): 231–49.

10 A wider study lies beyond the scope of this work. Notable, however, alongside crusader history, are contemporary events in the western Mediterranean where the defeat of the Almohads at Las Navas de Tolosa in 1212 allowed Ferdinand III of Castile's capture of Baeza (1227), Úbeda (1238), Córdoba (1236), Valencia (1238), Múrcia (1243), Jaén (1246) and Seville (1248), accelerating Christian dominance in the south of the peninsula.

11 *Historia Diplomatica Friderici Secundi, sive constitutiones, privilegia, mandata, instrumenta quae supersunt istius imperatoris et filiorum eius*, Jean-Louis Alphonse Huillard-Bréholles (ed.), 6 vols, 11 parts (Paris, 1852–61, reprinted Turin, 1963). I/1:100–2. Henceforth, *HDFS*.

12 *HDFS*, I/1:118–20.

13 E. Winkelmann, *Acta imperii inedita saeculi XIII* (Innsbruck, 1880), I:93.

14 *HDFS*, I/1:191–5.

15 *Le più antiche carte dell'Archivio capitolare di Agrigento (1092–1282)*, Paolo Collura

(ed.), *Documenti per servire alla storia di Sicilia*, 1st series, vol. 25 (Palermo, 1961): 155–71, no. 78.

16 *HDFS*, II/1:149–52.

17 *Al-Rawḍ al-Miʿṭār* of al-Ḥimyarī; *Kitāb al-Mughrib* of Ibn Saʿīd al-Maghribī, and the *Taʾrīkh al-Manṣūrī* of al-Ḥamawī, *BAS²* Ar. I:360–74; *BAS²* It. appendix, pp. 42–65; also B. Moritz, 'Ibn Sa'id Beschreibung von Sicilien', in *Centenario della nascita di Michele Amari*, 2 vols (Palermo, 1910), I:293–305. Arabic, French and Italian versions of the relevant passages in al-Ḥimyarī can be found in *Entella: Ultima Luna*, ed. and trans. F. Gabrieli and E. Lévi-Provençal (Palermo: Centro di documentazione e ricerca per la Sicilia antica "Paolo Orsi", n.d.). The short volume also contains an unusual example of oral testimony and its transmission by Maria Carcasio, 'La leggenda della "Regina" di Entella nella tradizione popolare di Contessa Entellina'. The tale narrates a version of events from the late Islamic period, but derives from the modern period and comes from an area resettled by Albanians in the sixteenth century. Arguably, it serves less as evidence for some continuity of settlement, than to highlight the fascinating uselessness of folk history and oral testimony.

18 Franco D'Angelo, 'La monetazione di Muhammad ibn Abbad emiro ribelle a Federico II di Sicilia', *Studi magrebini*, 7 (1975): 149–53. Photographs are also reproduced in Maurici, *L'emirato sulle montagne*, p. 10. Other than a resemblance in the name, there is nothing to support the idea that Ibn ʿAbbād was related to *Benavert*, the Muslim rebel of the 1070 and 1080s. For a contrary opinion, see F. Gabrieli, 'Benevert', in *EI²* I:1166.

19 On the execution of 'Beneveth [Ibn ʿAbbād?] cum filiis suis', see *Annales Siculi* (appended to *Malaterra*, *RIS*, 1928), p. 117.

20 *Chronica Alberici Monachi Trium Fontanium*, in *MGH SS*, 23:893–4.

21 On the relative strength of female stratagems compared with those of Satan, see Qur'ān 12:28 (Lo! the guile (*kayd*) of you [women] is very great'), and Qur'ān 4:76 (Lo! the devil's strategy (*kayd*) is ever weak). Trans. M. M. Pickthall.

22 E. Lévi-Provençal, 'Un héroïne de la résistance musulmane en Sicile au début du XIIIe siècle', *Oriente moderno*, 34 (1954): 283–8.

23 For the Muslim colony at Lucera, see Julie Taylor, *The Muslims in Medieval Italy: The Colony at Lucera* (Lanham, MD, 2003). Taylor provides an extensive bibliography and builds on the pioneering work of Pietro Egidi, 'La colonia saracena di Lucera a la sua distruzione', *Archivio storico per le provincie napoletane*, 36 (1911): 597–694; 37 (1912): 71–89; 38 (1913): 681–707; 39 (1914): 697–766. See also Jean-Marie Martin, 'La colonie sarrasine de Lucera et son environment: quelques réflexions', in *Mediterraneo medievale: scritti in onore di Francesco Giunta*, 3 vols (Soveria Mannelli, 1989), II: 795–811. For a good overview with an emphasis on the 1200s, Frederick II, the Jews and Malta, see David Abulafia, 'The end of Muslim Sicily', in *Muslims under Latin Rule*, James M. Powell (ed.) (Princeton, 1990), pp. 103–33. In the same volume, see James M. Powell, 'The papacy and the Muslim frontier', in *Muslims under Latin rule*, J. M. Powell (ed.) (Princeton, 1990), pp. 175–203, for the Dominicans' influence at Lucera with the papacy. On Frederick II, the papacy, the Genoese and Mediterranean economy, late Islamic Sicily and the crusades of the 1200s, a useful collection of seventeen articles to can be found in James M. Powell, *The Crusades, the Kingdom of Sicily and the Mediterranean* (Aldershot, 2007), in addition to the sections of David Abulafia's *Frederick II: A Medieval Emperor* (Oxford, 1988), relating to Italy.

24 David Abulafia, 'Ethnic variety and its implications: Frederick II's relations with Jews and Muslims', in *Intellectual Life at the Court of Frederick II Hohenstaufen*, William Tronzo (ed.) (Hanover and London, 1994), pp. 213–24.

25 Reference to 'more than 15,000 wretched Muslims' driven by famine to come down from the mountains in 1224 is found in the *Chronica S. Mariae de Ferraria*, p. 38.

26 Al-Ḥamawī, *BAS*[2] Ar. I:373–4.

27 A certain Ibn al-Rummānī is attested as a 'smooth man' (*muls*) from al-Quriyānī in 1183 (Cusa, *Diplomi*, p. 280). The name literally means 'son of the pomegranate seller', but probably refers here to a kin group, the Banū l-Rummān(ī). The estate of Quriyānī (< Greek, Kur Ioannis?) has not been identified, but in the Monreale register of boundaries from 1182 it was mentioned on three occasions (Cusa, *Diplomi*, pp. 204, 211 and 241). It appears to have occupied an elevated position and its identification with Pizzo/Monte Galiello seems sound. See G. Nania, *Toponomastica e topografia storica nelle valli del Belice e dello Jato* (Palermo, 1995), p. 65, n. 1. This is corroborated, *inter alia*, by the order of estates given in the Monreale register of men from 1183, in which those from Quriyānī were listed between those from Malbit and Ghār Shuʿayb (Cusa, *Diplomi*, p. 280). The locations of these latter estates are more safely identifiable. Significantly, they lie close to either side of Monte Galiello. *Ghulūw* (< Arabic, 'exaggeration'?) is more problematic as no such estate is attested in the Monreale lists. Maurici (*L'emirato*, pp. 67–8) cautiously identifies it with the locality of Pizzo di Gallo, an upland area of western Sicily close to the localities of Cautalí (Qalʿat ʿAlī) Grande and Piccolo, about 16 km to the south-west of Galiello. His suggestion that Gallo might be Cautalí is clearly problematic on linguistic grounds. That Quriyānī/Galiello somehow became Ghulūw at court in Ḥarrān is only marginally more credible in the context of al-Rummānī's report and its transmission.

28 Maurici, *L'emirato*, pp. 47–8. *HDFS*, V/1, p. 626. For the gentle encouragement around this same period of Muslims to repopulate the Seralcadi area of Palermo, which was now dilapidated, see *HDFS*, V/1, p. 427. The suggestion by Maurici that this was a cynical ploy to shepherd the Muslims into places where they could more easily be controlled or to use the suburb as a holding centre for the planned deportations, seems feasible in the context.

29 Ibn Khaldūn, *BAS*[2] Ar. II:543; *BAS*[2] It. II:213.

30 See the review by Jeremy Johns of Luttrell's *Making of Christian Malta*, in *Journal of Islamic Studies*, 15/1 (2004): 84–9.

31 The phrase *et ceperunt Jatum et Alicatam* is clearly problematic, since it suggests the seizure of Licata, rather than Entella as the historical context and Latin sources demand. See *Annales Siculi*, p. 118, and Amari-Nallino, *SMS* II/3, p. 630.

32 For the most recent defective edition, see *Rollus Rubeus: privilegia ecclesie Cephaleditane*, C. Mirto (ed.) (Palermo, 1972), pp. 39–41.

33 Harking back to the *status quo ante* as in the time of William II, the archbishop of Monreale was empowered to retake possession over previously granted concessions to the church, cf. *HDFS*, II/1:149–52.

34 On the Luceran Muslims' occupations, see Taylor, *Lucera*, pp. 99–125. For a socio-economic sketch of Monreale's lands, see H. Bercher, A. Courteaux, J.-M. Mouton, 'Une abbaye latine dans la société musulmane: Monreale au XIIe siècle', in *Annales: économies, sociétés, civilisations*, 34 (1979): 525–47.

35 For context and discussion, see Henri Bresc, '1282: classes sociales et révolution

nationale', in *Politique et société en Sicile, XIIe–XVe siècles* (Aldershot, 1990), a reprinted article from *XI Congresso di storia della corona d'Aragona: la società mediterranea all'epoca del Vespro*, (Palermo, 1982), II:241–58.

36 For the post-Muslim economy and economic effects of demographic collapse, see Henri Bresc, *Un monde méditerranéen: économie et société en Sicile 1300–1450*, 2 vols (Palermo and Rome, 1986).

37 For an illustrated overview, see Umberto Scerrato, 'Arte islamica in Italia', in *Gli Arabi in Italia*, pp. 275–570, especially pp. 399–445 on ceramics. There are several articles on ceramics by Alessandra Molinari, Ghislaine Noyé and Franco D'Angelo; for a recent survey with wider bibliographical references, see Franco D'Angelo, 'La ceramica islamica in Sicilia', *MEFRM*, 116 (Rome, 2004): 129–45. A large storage jar, currently located in the Zisa palace, Palermo, has a handle with a crude inscription which reads Bū Sha'īr (*not* Bū Sa'īd), indicating that it was used for the storage of barley and does not refer to the name of the Arab potter.

38 Alessandra Molinari, *Segesta II. Il castello e la moschea (scavi 1989–1995)* (Palermo, 1997).

39 On the Luceran castellans, see Taylor, *Lucera*, pp. 151–3.

40 For the colony under the Angevins until its fall, see Taylor, *Lucera*, pp. 139–210.

Index